Multidisciplinary Handbook of Social Exclusion Research

Multidisciplinary Handbook of Social Exclusion Research

Edited by

Dominic Abrams
University of Kent, United Kingdom

Julie Christian
University of Birmingham, United Kingdom

and

David Gordon
University of Bristol, United Kingdom

John Wiley & Sons, Ltd

Other Wiley Editorial Offices

John Wiley & Sons Inc., 111 River Street, Hoboken, NJ 07030, USA

Jossey-Bass, 989 Market Street, San Francisco, CA 94103-1741, USA

Wiley-VCH Verlag GmbH, Boschstr. 12, D-69469 Weinheim, Germany

John Wiley & Sons Australia Ltd, 42 McDougall Street, Milton, Queensland 4064, Australia

John Wiley & Sons (Asia) Pte Ltd, 2 Clementi Loop #02-01, Jin Xing Distripark, Singapore 129809

John Wily & Sons Canada Ltd, 6045 Freemont Blvd, Mississauga, ONT, L5R 4J3, Canada

Wiley also publishes its books in a variety of electronic formats. Some content that appears in print may not
be available in electronic books.

Anniversary Logo Design: Richard J. Pacifico

Library of Congress Cataloging-in-Publication Data

Multidisciplinary handbook of social exclusion research / edited by Dominic Abrams, Julie Christian, and
David Gordon.
    p.   cm.
    Includes bibliographical references and index.
    ISBN 978-0-470-09513-3 (cloth : alk. paper)
  1. Social isolation.   I. Abrams, Dominic, 1958-   II. Christian, Julie.   III. Gordon, David, 1959-
    HM1131.M85 2007
    302.5'45—dc22   2007039321

British Library Cataloguing in Publication Data

A catalogue record for this book is available from the British Library

ISBN   978-0-470-09513-3

Typeset in 10/12pt Times by SNP Best-set Typesetter Ltd., Hong Kong
Printed and bound in Great Britain by Antony Rowe, Chippenham, Wiltshire
This book is printed on acid-free paper responsibly manufactured from sustainable forestry
in which at least two trees are planted for each one used for paper production.

Contents

About the Editors

Dominic Abrams obtained his MSc from the London School of Economics and Political Science, and his PhD from the University of Kent. He lectured at Bristol and Dundee Universities for 5 years before returning to Kent in 1989. He is a Professor of Social Psychology and the Director of the Centre for the Study of Group Processes. He is chief editor (with Michael A. Hogg) of the journal *Group Processes and Intergroup Relations* (Sage). He has been on the Council of the Academy of Social Sciences, the Secretary of the European Association of Experimental Social Psychology, and the Chair of the Research Board of the British Psychological Society. He is currently the Chair of the Joint Committee for Psychology in Higher Education, representing the BPS, the Experimental Psychology Society and the Association of Heads of Psychology Departments. He has published several books on social identity and intergroup relations and published widely on the social inclusion and exclusion. With Diane M. Houston, he co-authored a report to the Equalities Review on *Equality, Diversity and Prejudice in Britain* (2006). He is currently developing a module in the next European Social Survey on Expressions and Experiences of Ageism.

Julie Christian gained a PhD degree from the University of Wales in 1998. She completed a postdoctoral fellowship at the London School of Economics and further postdoctoral appointments at Cardiff University (City and Regional Planning and Psychology) before being appointed at the University of Birmingham in 2001. Since then she has an established track record in researching social attitudes, social identity and housing tenure (private and social housing), publishing over 30 scientific papers and government reports. As a direct extension of this work, she holds advisory board positions with several UK companies and charities.

David Gordon is the Director of the Townsend Centre for International Poverty Research. Professor Gordon combined his background in biology and geology with anti-poverty policy, while helping to find safe public water supplies in the South Pacific. He has researched and published in the field of the scientific measurement of poverty, crime and poverty, childhood disability, area-based anti-poverty measures, the causal effects of poverty on ill health, housing policy and rural poverty. The Townsend Centre for International Poverty Research is dedicated to multidisciplinary research on poverty in both the industrialised and developing world. The Centre has been established by the University of Bristol in response to the United Nations First International Decade for the Eradication of Poverty (1997–2006) and in recognition of the work of Prof. Peter Townsend. The University sector can support the goal of eradicating poverty by providing high quality interdisciplinary research into effective anti-poverty policies.

Contributors

David Clapham is Professor of Housing at the School of City and Regional Planning at Cardiff University in Wales. Before this he was at the Department of Urban Studies at Glasgow University. He has undertaken research on a wide variety of housing issues including housing management, tenant participation, housing co-operatives, and housing and community care as well as homelessness. He is joint editor with Susan Hutson of the book *Homelessness: Public Policies and Private Troubles* published in 1999 by Cassel. He has a long-standing interest in the links between housing and social policy and was one of the authors of a book (with Peter Kemp and Susan Smith) entitled *Housing and Social Policy* published by Routledge in 1990. He also has interests in the application of social theory to housing. He is the author of *The Meaning of Housing: A Pathways Approach* published in 2005 by Policy Press and is the editor of the journal *Housing, Theory and Society.*

Marian FitzGerald is a visiting professor of criminology at Kent Crime and Justice Centre, University of Kent. At the Home Office, between 1988 and 1999, she authored and supervised a number of studies concerned with crime, the criminal justice system and minority ethnic groups. On leaving the Home Office, she undertook a major study of stop and search for the MPS (1999), followed by "Policing for London" (with Mike Hough, 2002)—an independent study of police–community relations in the capital. She then did a study for the Youth Justice Board of young people's involvement in street crime with Dr Jan Stockdale at LSE and Prof. Chris Hale at the University of Kent (2003). This was followed by research on the role of police officers in schools and an international study of juvenile violence which she undertook for the EU with colleagues at Kent. At the time of writing, she is engaged on a study of young people, gangs and weapons for the Youth Justice Board, and an evaluation of knife crime initiatives in London for the Metropolitan Police.

Chris Hale is the Head of the School of Social Policy, Sociology & Social Research, Director of the Kent Crime and Justice Centre and a professor of criminology at the University of Kent. His research interests include the quantitative analysis of crime data, both official statistics and crime surveys, examining the relationships between crime and fear of crime with wider economic and social changes, large-scale evaluations of new interventions and crime reduction strategies. He has undertaken many Home Office-funded studies including "Ethnic Minorities: Victimisation and Racial Harassment", "Evaluation of Restorative Justice Schemes" and "The Introduction of Referral Orders into the Youth Justice System". His recent research projects include a "Review of the current knowledge on the statistical development, core risk and protective factors and measures to reduce juvenile violence in the EU member states" for the European Union Crime Prevention Network, and a "Referral Order Re-conviction Study", for the Youth Justice Board.

Peter Hick is Senior Lecturer in the Centre for Inclusive Education and SEN in the Institute of Education at Manchester Metropolitan University. His previous appointments as a lecturer were at the University of Birmingham, the University of Manchester, the Open University, the University of Bolton and Bolton Community College. Before his university lecturing, he trained as an educational psychologist and was employed by the local authority in Oldham. His research interests currently focus on race and disproportionality in the identification of special educational needs; and on sociocultural understandings of inclusive learning mediated with ICT. He recently edited a book proposing significant new perspectives for reframing psychology as positively contributing theoretical and practical resources to support the development of more inclusive practices in education (Hick, Kershner & Farrell, 2007, *Psychology for Inclusive Education: New Directions in Theory and Practice*, London: Routledge).

Diane M. Houston is a professor and the Head of Department of Psychology at the University of Kent in the UK. Her research interests are within applied social psychology and its interface with sociology and social policy. She was Research and Strategy Advisor to the Women and Equality Unit from 2003 to 2006 and was academic advisor to the Women and Work Commission which reported to the Prime Minister in 2006. She has also acted as an advisor to work conducted by the Chartered Institute of Personnel Development, Equal Opportunities Commission and the Equalities Review in the Cabinet Office. Her research focuses on women's work participation, work–family balance, the career consequences of flexible working and how different policy contexts shape gender equality and gender stereotyping. Her recent publications include *Work Life Balance in the Twenty-First Century* (2005) (Palgrave Macmillan) and *Equality, Diversity and Prejudice in Britain* (2006) (Cabinet Office).

Paul Hutchison is a Senior Lecturer in Social Psychology at London Metropolitan University. He obtained his MSc and PhD degrees from the University of Kent. Following this he spent three years as a research fellow in the School of Psychology at the University of Exeter and one year at the Institute of Psychological Sciences, University of Leads. His research is concerned mainly with the contribution of group membership and social identity to processes such as social inclusion and exclusion, conformity and deviance, stereotyping, and collective action.

Sonia Jackson, OBE is Professor and Research Director at the Thomas Coram Research Unit, Institute of Education, University of London, an Academician of the Academy of Social Sciences and Honorary Fellow of the Joint University Council. She was previously Head of Social Policy and Applied Social Studies at the University of Wales, Swansea, where she initiated and directed the first comparative study of the health of children looked after by local authorities. Her earlier research, at Bristol University, was on childminding and young children in day care, and her book with Elinor Goldschmied, *People Under Three*, now in its second edition, has been translated into five languages. Originally a clinical psychologist, her interests have always been interdisciplinary, in particular crossing the education/care divide. She first drew attention to the neglected education of children in care in the early 1980s and since then has published extensively on the subject and acted as consultant to government departments, the Cabinet Office, NGOs and numerous local authorities. She has also carried out research and published on many other aspects of social care, such as placement instablility, adoption, private foster care and teenage pregnancy. She directed the "By Degrees" project, the only study to date of university students with a background in care, *Going to University from Care* (Institute of Education, 2005), and in January 2008 will begin a new study comparing participation in post-compulsory education in five European countries. She was awarded the OBE in 2003 for services to children in care.

Natasha MacNab

Natasha MacNab is a Research Fellow at the School of Education at the University of Birmingham. She is currently working on two projects, an evaluation of the European Working Time Directive for Junior Doctors and the Independent Learning Habits of Undergraduates in the School of Education. Her EdD focuses on provision for 14–16 year olds with social, emotional and behavioural difficulties. She has worked at the School of Education since 2001 on projects including the "National Evaluation of the Children's Fund", "Learning in and for Inter-school Work to Promote Creativity", "Provision for Emotionally Vulnerable Young People" and a seminar series funded by the ESRC Teaching and Learning Research Programme entitled "Quality in Educational Research" with Prof. Gary Thomas. Elsewhere in the school, she contributes to postgraduate teaching courses.

Tom Mason, PhD, BSc (Hons), RMN, RNMH, RGN has been in nursing for 30 years. He has been in clinical practice for 17 years and the remainder in research posts. He has worked in forensic psychiatric establishments, predominantly but not exclusively in high security hospitals and has published 10 books and over 70 journal articles. Tom was honoured with the International Association of Forensic Nurses Achievement Award in 1999 and was granted a Senior Robert Baxter Fellowship in the same year. His main professional interests are in the management of violence and aggression, psychiatric service delivery and the professional role of the forensic nurse. He is currently Professor of Mental Health and Learning Disability, University of Chester. Tom is also a keen sailor and avid reader.

Elizabeth Mason-Whitehead, PhD, BA (Hons), PGDE, RGN, RM, RHV, ONC has been in nursing, midwifery and health visiting for 30 years. She has been in clinical practice for 20 years and the later 10 years have been in research and teaching in higher education. Elizabeth is currently a Reader in the Faculty of Health and Social Care at the University of Chester. Her areas of research and publishing interest include teenage pregnancy, social exclusion, and education and community health. She has published five books and a number of research papers.

Jane Millar, OBE is Professor of Social Policy and the Director of the Centre for the Analysis of Social Policy at the University of Bath, UK. Her research interests include income maintenance (social security and tax) policy; labour market policies, especially for lone parents; poverty, inequality and social exclusion; family policy and the policy implications of family change; gender and social policy; and comparative social policy. Recent publications include *Understanding Social Security* (Millar, ed., 2003, Bristol: The Policy Press), *Lone Parents, Employment and Social Policy: Cross-national Comparisons* (Millar & Rowlingson, eds, 2001, Bristol: The Policy Press), *The Dynamics of Social Exclusion in Europe* (Apospori & Millar, eds, 2003, London: Edward Elgar Publications) and *Poverty and Social Exclusion in Europe* (Barnes, Heady, Middleton, Millar, Papadopoulos & Tsakloglou, 2002, London: Edward Elgar Publications).

Ken Peattie is Professor of Marketing and Strategy and the Director of the ESRC-funded BRASS Research Centre based at Cardiff University. The Centre specialises in research into business sustainability and social responsibility. He joined Cardiff Business School in 1986 after industrial experience in marketing and strategic planning in the paper and electronics industries. He has published widely on themes relating to corporate social responsibility, and the impact of environmental and social concerns on marketing and corporate strategies.

Greville Percival worked for AC Nielsen Marketing Research from 1984 to 1991, and was responsible for statistical controls and ad hoc research efforts. In 1991, he joined the Commission for Racial Equality becoming head of research. In this role, Greville also provided research consultancy on behalf of the CRE to the Electoral Commission, CABE, the Environment Agency and The Guardian. He was appointed to the Advisory Group set up by the University of Manchester for its new Centre for Research on Social and Cultural change (CRESC). Since 2005, Greville has headed up a private consultancy firm working with clients to implement, manage and evaluate a wide range of projects associated with the Government's agenda on social inclusion and cohesion.

John Visser is Associate Professor at the University of Birmingham where he is Programme Tutor for professional development courses in the area of social, emotional and behavioural difficulties. He has acted as a consultant to schools, services and LEA's nationally and internationally in the area of special education and school improvement. He is widely known for his professionally relevant staff development work on classroom management; pupils with emotional, behavioural and social difficulties; teaching and learning, particularly differentiation and special educational needs. His research work with colleagues at the School of Education has been widely reported and applied by educators. He has an extensive list of publications, the most recent cover issues of classroom behaviour, the effects of permanent exclusion and teaching and learning in relation to pupils with social, emotional and behavioural difficulties.

Preface and Overview

Julie Christian and Dominic Abrams

The term social exclusion has different definitions and meanings for different academic and policy constituencies, a point that is readily illustrated by the different chapters in this book. Emphasis on different aspects of exclusion reflects different purposes and contexts. Consequently, achieving a single overarching definition may not be desirable. But at the same time, given the convergence in concerns over the effects of social exclusion, there is a need to work towards a more widely shared framework and language for understanding what it is. In particular, development of a broader perspective is useful for thinking about where, when and how interventions might be most effective. For example, it is important to be aware that interventions that might tackle social exclusion in one context could have contradictory effects in others. This book explores exclusion in the contexts of education, health, housing, business and community integration. It also looks at social exclusion policy at the national and European levels, as well as historically. It considers how exclusion affects major social categories, particularly gender, but also age and ethnicity. And it considers the mechanisms and processes that surround social exclusion on an individual level.

Beyond questions of definition and evaluation, there is a more fundamental issue facing social exclusion researchers and policy makers today. The existence of social exclusion often reflects a conflict between different sets of values in society. On the one hand, people strongly value individual choice, freedom, rewards for effort and ability, and so on. These values mean that society will always be differentiated and meritocratic. Some people will be left far behind others. On the other hand, people value equality, fairness and justice (see Schwartz, 2007; Schwartz & Bardi, 2001). Yet, if these principles are imposed too strongly (e.g. as affirmative action), people are liable to object because individual effort, merit and freedom to be different are not adequately recognised. This, of course, leads to questions about researching social exclusion.

Our own interest began with a seminar series funded by the Economic and Social Research Council in 2002 (Abrams & Hewstone, 2004). The series was aimed at social psychologists working on social exclusion and at forging closer links with policy makers. A large number of researchers, including many distinguished international scholars, contributed to the meeting, which in turn, opened a fruitful dialogue with policy makers and civil servants (see also, Abrams, Hogg & Marques, 2005). It was through these meetings and exchanges that we saw, first hand, how fruitful it could be to encourage researchers and policy makers to engage actively with one another's worlds.

The present volume represents a further step in this process. As well as working across the research and policy domains, we wanted to draw together different perspectives in social science. Thus, the contributors were invited to address central themes we believed to be essential elements for developing the conceptualisation of exclusion. As such, the contributors were recruited to provide a balanced range of the issues most salient to understanding exclusion in the 21st century.

One of the main, frequently noted, challenges for researchers is to link theory and outputs to specific practical recommendations for intervention. As illustrated by many of the chapters in this book, policy initiatives that highlight particular interventions aimed at redressing social exclusion are often stimulated by political agendas that do not always reflect implications of the evidence. Equally, however, those who have to devise and specify policy are likely to find that theory-based research is difficult to interpret and that they cannot be confident about its policy implications. An aim of this book is to bring together experts who have devoted considerable time to understanding different aspects of social exclusion to provide an integrated view of the terrain. Inevitably, the book does not span every conceivable aspect of social exclusion. For example, the important philosophical, genetic, evolutionary and economic aspects of exclusion are not covered by separate chapters. Nonetheless, we believe these aspects are embraced in various ways, and can be accommodated in our framing of the overall domain of social exclusion processes (Chapter 12). More generally, a message from the book is that it is necessary to view social exclusion from multiple perspectives if we are to establish defensible and effective policies.

SOCIAL EXCLUSION IN CONTEXT—THE CHAPTERS IN THIS BOOK

The contributors to this volume represent several different domains because, as we have highlighted above, the issues central to exclusion are rooted and have been developed in many literatures. However, our journey through this is guided by a core theme which runs throughout the chapters in this book, namely, the need to understand that exclusion is likely to take many forms that are often quite specific in both time and context. Viewing social exclusion more as a state than a trait, regards it as potentially dynamic. This encourages us to explore social exclusion less as a chronic and inescapable outcome that is necessarily permanently disabling and more as a condition that arises from a particular set of relationships and circumstances. It also reminds us that the extent to which certain individuals and groups are more or less excluded in society may be as much a matter of political priority as it is a consequence of economic, demographic or other structural forces.

In Chapter 1, Jane Millar explores the ways that social exclusion has been defined and operationalised in the context of the European Union. She concludes that exclusion is relational, dynamic and involves agency. Moreover, the evidence is quite clear that while exclusion is a multidimensional phenomenon, most instances of exclusion arise on only a limited subset of these dimensions, and generally are not perpetual. Material poverty is not always synonymous with social exclusion. Exclusion can involve absence of resources in the form of goods, opportunities and standards of living, but it can also be defined, as by Burchardt, Le Grand and Piachaud (2002) as being blocked from participating in key activities of a society. Yet, Millar argues, there is a gap between the different levels of analysis, measurement and operationalisation of social exclusion. The quality of measurement of social exclusion needs improvement, and in particular there is a need to connect policy initiatives with people's actual experiences of exclusion. One the one hand, some of the evidence suggests that most people will pull themselves out of their exclusion, on the other, policies to reduce social exclusion may need to use multiple methods of detection and multiple approaches to tackling exclusion in order to respond to the diverse forms it can take.

In Chapter 2, Diane Houston reviews the way the dominant approaches to social exclusion, such as the framework offered by Burchardt *et al.* (2002), neglect the single most excluded category in society—women. Women's overwhelming lack of representation in the higher echelons of business, law, education and politics is, Houston argues, a considerably larger problem than any other. That is, both in terms of the number of excluded people and as a proportion of their category, the absence of women in these roles involves a level of segregation and inequality that would be deemed unacceptable if it occurred on any other social axis. Yet, focus on this inequality is almost completely absent from the social exclusion policy context. Houston argues that this is in part because people tacitly understand that there is little more that women themselves can do, or that can be legislated for on their behalf. While changes in women's attitudes and aspirations mean that they are in an increasingly strong position to gain equality, it will also require a change in men's attitudes, behaviour and roles (e.g. becoming actively engaged as parents and carers) for women's situation to improve substantially.

In Chapter 3, Paul Hutchison, Dominic Abrams and Julie Christian describe social psychological evidence on social exclusion. Rather than focusing on a particular domain (e.g. crime) or treating social exclusion as an endpoint of social structural effects, this work focuses on the processes occurring when people are excluded and when they exclude others. This research shows powerfully that exclusion has very harmful (and immediate) effects on people's well-being, motivation and behaviour. The research also shows why this happens. People's needs for belongingness, their needs for control and for meaning are all compromised when they are excluded. On the other hand, social exclusion is often a part of a competitive social dynamic between groups, and it is often an inherent feature of the way groups sustain themselves, such as by highlighting and controlling dissenters, or by disavowing associations with people that bring them into disrepute. Thus, illustrating and explaining the point in Millar's chapter, the processes and mechanics of social exclusion are fundamentally relational. Evidence that has considered psychological variables alongside demographic variables as predictors of social participation and inclusion seems to show that the psychological variables carry far more variance. It seems that these are affected by people's particular sets of social relationships, suggesting that policy interventions need to focus on building relationships and not just providing services.

In Chapter 4, Elizabeth Mason-Whitehead and Tom Mason focus on the nature of stigma and exclusion in healthcare settings. While policy on exclusion in health tends to focus on access to treatment or on treatment outcomes, Mason-Whitehead and Mason highlight that the consequences of social exclusion lie in the difficulties faced by someone reintegrating into society after a stigmatising illness or injury. They highlight that these psychosocial processes are profoundly important in people's lives and the way others interact with them. Stigmatisation comes to the fore in healthcare settings and yet there is a lack of coherent policy to deal with either the presence or consequences of stigmatisation. Policy interventions need to raise awareness of these processes and to adopt a multi-agency approach to tackling them.

In Chapter 5, David Clapham analyses the way research and policy on homelessness map on to the research and policy on social exclusion. He argues that the two frameworks have much in common. Both involve causal discourses that focus on large structural causes but also on individual responsibility and agency, with concomitant distinctions between the deserving and undeserving. Yet, both lack an integrative analysis and a real focus on the individuals' experience and understanding of their own situation, which Clapham regards as a key aspect of exclusion. He sees a viable way out of the agency/structure dichotomy by focusing instead in "pathways" through homelessness, poverty and social exclusion more generally. In this approach, homelessness is an episode or episodes in a person's housing pathway rather than a fixed state. This more dynamic and holistic approach, Clapham argues, requires ethnographic, or biographic methods in addition to analysis of the structures. But much of the research on homelessness tends to be focused on particular variables rather than the whole picture, and to be positivist rather than ana-lysing the meanings and time dimension of being homeless. Understanding the processes at work is at least as important as measuring homelessness as an outcome. In particular, Clapham regards enhancement of individuals' control over their circumstances as a key objective for policy. Indeed, he concludes, the key is to empower individuals through increasing self-esteem and capacity to influence their own circumstances.

In Chapter 6, Peter Hick, John Visser and Natasha MacNab examine how the themes of inclusion and exclusion pervade different approaches to education. While on the one hand there is an inclusion agenda that incorporates mainstreaming and widening participa-tion, on the other there are exclusion agendas focusing on maintenance of "standards", with the use of discipline, control and targeted interventions as well as unofficial exclu-sions. Moreover, these are disproportionately likely to involve people from already mar-ginalised situations. Hick and colleagues examine several forms of exclusion via the institutional structures of schools; streaming, setting, and learning support units that affect groups of learners, specifically, black and minority ethnic communities, children with special educational needs, children with mental health difficulties and "looked after" children. They conclude that despite policy initiatives in support of an inclusion agenda, there is little evidence so far of positive impact on social inequality.

In Chapter 7, Sonia Jackson shows how social exclusion has persisted and is perpetuated for one particular set of people in UK society: children who are raised in various forms of "public care". Jackson pinpoints the fundamental barrier to these children as the fact that insufficient priority is placed on ensuring they are effectively and well educated. So much attention is devoted to physical and emotional well-being that these children's educa-tion is partial, disjointed and often ignored. Consequently they leave care equipped with few of the basic requirements for employment or self-sustenance. They achieve substan-tially below their potential, and often spiral into deprived and socially harmful situations and relationships. Jackson describes the detailed *By Degrees* study of 129 care leavers who succeeded in achieving a university education to reveal how it is that some children leaving care escape the educational fate of most of their peers (Jackson, Ajayi & Quigley, 2003). This work demonstrates clear evidence that specific policy interventions could have a substantial impact to reduce chronic social exclusion of these highly vulnerable children.

In Chapter 8, Chris Hale and Marian Fitzgerald consider social exclusion in the criminal justice system. They argue forcefully that the Burchardt *et al.* (2002) definition of social exclusion adopted by the UK government fails to address the processes underlying social exclusion and the multidimensionality of these processes. In particular, they show how economic marginalisation does not explain criminality. Ironically, as employment rates increase, often due to greater participation by women, so do rates of crime, perhaps due to weakening of informal social ties and mutual monitoring within communities. In addition, even if absolute poverty is declining, young people's aspirations as consumers are accelerating despite their high dependency on parental income. They argue that the very policies that are implemented in the name of building community cohesion (e.g. the use of antisocial behaviour orders) can actually create additional and potentially more damaging forms of exclusion. The crux of the problem is that government policies to tackle social exclusion tend to blame the victim by focusing only at the individual level. This approach has led to disproportionate incarceration and exclusion of people from groups that are already excluded for other social structural reasons. Hale and FitzGerald propose solutions that make great sense to most social researchers but that politicians and policy makers may find harder to promote. These include recognising the limited role of the criminal justice system in deterring crime, regarding criminalisation as a problem rather than an indicator of "success", and that output measures should assess the combined effect of all stages of the criminal justice process on social cohesion.

In Chapter 9, Greville Percival provides a critical analysis of the UK Government's use of social inclusion as an agenda to frame policy in a wide set of domains, but particularly race and ethnicity. Percival argues, in concordance with Hale and FitzGerald, that the performance-related target approach has been used too uncritically. In this chapter, Percival comments on the transition from a redistribution approach (old Labour) to a wealth creation approach (new Labour) for tackling poverty and disadvantage. Thus, a rhetoric of empowerment and opportunity developed that increasingly assumed that if public service provision was sufficiently open and available, it would simply be a matter of getting people to make use of it. Yet this model runs into difficulties because it also implies a completely integrationist approach to ethnic and cultural differences. Percival suggests that social exclusion is often rooted not in economic disadvantage per se but in cultural and religious differences, and that the assumption that reducing exclusion will increase cohesion is not necessarily a sound one. The current individual-focused policies for tackling social exclusion run the risk of producing new social fault lines by increasing the relative advantages of some communities but not others.

In Chapter 10, Ken Peattie, noting that at present there is only a limited body of knowledge, introduces a comprehensive account of the role of business in social inclusion and exclusion. Although capitalism generally can be cited as a significant source of social exclusion, Peattie highlights the constructive role that businesses can play as "corporate citizens" that take corporate social responsibility. Peattie highlights that business is involved in all of Burchardt et al.'s (2002) list of normal activities (consumption, production, saving, political, social). First, businesses are legally obligated to attend to the inclusion of people from different social categories. Second, businesses can constructively engage with volunteering and charitable activities to reduce social exclusion. Peattie reviews the contribution of business in each of the five areas and concludes that business plays and can play an increasing role in promoting social inclusion. Within the social domain, Peattie illustrates this point with reference to house building and housing, transport, media, information technology, care and healthcare. He advocates the development of new and innovative business models that include "social enterprises which operate with primarily social rather than financial goals".

In Chapter 11, David Gordon provides a further analysis of the way "social exclusion" has been framed and turned into a policy orientation internationally. He first describes how the notion of social exclusion developed from the French concept of solidarity and argues that it does not fit well in the UK's class-based society. Thus he contrasts the social integration orientation that is more pervasive in Germany and France with the poverty alleviation orientation in the UK (a distinction also noted by Hale and Fitzgerald). Gordon then reviews European Union social exclusion initiatives, in particular the problematic definition of poverty and the move to the more relativistic notion of exclusion. Yet, despite a quite broad set of goals for eliminating social exclusion, the indicators used to monitor social exclusion focus largely on poverty, income and labour market position. A similar story is true for the UNESCO initiative on social cohesion. Gordon somewhat pessimistically observes that despite a large volume of research, the policy outcomes have been limited and that there still remains no coherent analysis of what social exclusion is. There is a strong tendency to default to economic indicators. However, we should not underestimate the value of observation that the use of the social inclusion umbrella. It has enabled the EU to sustain an anti-poverty programme despite the varying political flavours of the member countries.

Finally, in Chapter 12, Abrams and Christian consider the limitations of previous approaches to social exclusion, and draw on the converging themes from the preceding chapters to propose a relational framework for a social science analysis of the dynamics of social exclusion. Using examples from the first UK national survey of ageism and the 2005 National Survey of Prejudice, Abrams and Christian propose that analysis of social exclusion needs to take into account four components, corresponding to the questions of who, where, how and why exclusion is happening. They propose that designing interventions and policies can be greatly improved by greater precision using such a framework. Thus, to decide upon policy it is necessary to specify explicitly the actors in the exclusion relationship, the relationship context (ranging from transnational to intrapersonal), the modes of exclusion (ranging from ideological to specific acts or communications), and the dynamics at work (including motivations, time frame, resource inequalities and so on).

CONCLUSION

Social exclusion remains one of the key problems both nationally and globally. We hope that this book highlights both the richness and the complexity of the problem, thereby stimulating further developments in research and policy. We particularly hope that by bringing together multiple perspectives in one volume, this book promotes understanding, dialogue and collaboration amongst researchers and practitioners who are motivated to understand and address social exclusion.

REFERENCES

Abrams, D. & Hewstone, M. (2004). *ESRC Seminar Series on Social Inclusion and Exclusion: Informing Policy through Social Psychology: Conclusion Report* (No. R451265070). See also www.social-inclusion.org.uk

Abrams, D., Hogg, M.A. & Marques, J.M. (2005). *The Social Psychology of Inclusion and Exclusion*. New York and Hove: Psychology Press.

Burchardt, T., Le Grand, J. & Piachaud, D. (2002). Degrees of exclusion: developing a multidimensional, dynamic measure. In J. Hills, J. Le Grand & D. Piachaud (eds), *Understanding Social Exclusion* (pp. 30–43). New York: Oxford University Press.

Jackson, S., Ajayi, S. & Quigley, M. (2003). *By Degrees—The First Year: From Care to University.* London: National Children's Bureau.

Schwartz, S.H. (2007). Value orientations: measurement, antecedents and consequences. In R. Jowell, C. Roberts, R. Fitzgerald & G. Eva (eds), *Measuring Attitudes Cross-nationally: Lessons from the European Social Survey* (pp. 169–204). London: Sage Publications.

Schwartz, S.H. & Bardi, A. (2001). Value hierarchies across cultures: taking a similarities perspective. *Journal of Cross-Cultural Psychology, 32,* 268–290.

Acknowledgements

While editing this book, we received considerable support and inspiration from our colleagues, friends and university departments. In particular, we would like to express our gratitude to Emma Haycraft from the University of Birmingham who has greatly helped in coordinating efforts and ensuring that this book was completed in good time. Additionally, we owe special thanks to Ruth Graham, Nicole Burnett, Sarah Tilley and Gillian Leslie, our colleagues at Wiley Blackwell, who responded to various changes and updates with considerable patience. We were encouraged and sustained in the editing of this book by our conversations with numerous civil servants and policy experts from several government departments as well as the Commission for Equality and Human Rights, the British Institute of Human Rights and Age Concern England. Last but not least, we thank our families for their unwavering support and continuous encouragement.

CHAPTER 1

Social Exclusion and Social Policy Research: Defining Exclusion

Jane Millar

University of Bath, United Kingdom

ABSTRACT

This chapter examines recent social policy research on social exclusion, exploring the way in which the term has been conceptualized and defined. It discusses research on the multidimensional measurement of social exclusion, on the process of social exclusion, and on the use of social indicators to monitor trends in social exclusion across countries over time. The empirical research that has captured and measured multidimensional disadvantage has identified various dimensions, including material and situational circumstances, with the aim of exploring the extent of social exclusion. The research indicates that there is a degree of consensus in the social policy literature and that material poverty is not the same as social exclusion. Overall, the results from these studies tend to suggest that, although some people and groups experience relatively high rates of social exclusion as measured by these indicators, there is not a large degree of overlap across the various dimensions.

INTRODUCTION

Social exclusion is a concept that has increasingly entered the policy discourse in recent years. For example, the UK Government is committed to reducing social exclusion and has established a new department, the Social Exclusion Unit, to develop innovative policy proposals (also see Hale & FitzGerald, Chapter 8 and Gordon, Chapter 11). The European Union has agreed to tackle the issue of social exclusion through the development of national plans of action, and has identified a set of statistical indicators for measuring social inclusion. Also, there has been a substantial investment in research, examining social exclusion and the relationship between social exclusion, poverty and citizenship. This chapter focuses on recent research in social exclusion within the field of social policy. It has four main sections. The first considers how the concept of social exclusion has been

Multidisciplinary Handbook of Social Exclusion Research. Edited by D. Abrams, J. Christian and D. Gordon.

defined in social policy research and outlines some of the various definitions of social exclusion that have been developed in the UK and elsewhere. These definitions stress the importance of taking a multidimensional approach to social exclusion and the need to understand the dynamics of social exclusion over time. The second section discusses the way in which the multidimensional nature of social exclusion has been operationalised in practice for research purposes, drawing on various UK and European research studies. The third section focuses on research which explores social exclusion as a process, examining the ways in which people come to be at risk of social exclusion and the resources they can draw on to protect and sustain themselves. The fourth section turns attention to the way in which the UK Government and the European Union have sought to develop indicators of social exclusion, in order to monitor progress on the goal of tackling social exclusion.

DEFINING SOCIAL EXCLUSION

Whilst there is widespread, if by no means unanimous, agreement about the definition of poverty as a lack of material resources to meet needs, the definition of social exclusion remains a contested term defined in different ways by different authors (see Atkinson, 1998; Room, 1995; Tsakloglou & Papadopoulos, 2002). However, the various definitions have in common an understanding that social exclusion is not only about material poverty and lack of material resources, but also about the processes by which some individuals and groups become marginalised in society. They are excluded not only from the goods and standards of living available to the majority but also from their opportunities, choices and life chances.

There are many definitions of social exclusion to be found in the social policy literature. Room (1995), in one of the first studies to specifically focus on social exclusion, argued that social exclusion implies a major discontinuity in relationships with the rest of society and points to five key factors which he suggests are central to the definition of social exclusion:

- Multidimensional: social exclusion cannot be measured by income alone but should include a wide range of indicators of living standards.
- Dynamic: analysing social exclusion means understanding processes and identifying the factors which can trigger entry or exit.
- Collective: social exclusion is not just about individual living standards, but also about the collective resources (or lack of these) in the neighbourhood or community. This means insufficient or unsatisfactory community facilities, such as run-down schools, remotely sited shops, poor public transport networks and so on.
- Relational: the notion of poverty is primarily focused upon distributional issues, the lack of resources at the disposal of an individual or a household. In contrast, social exclusion focuses more on relational issues. In other words, it refers to inadequate social participation, lack of social integration and lack of power.
- Catastrophic: a catastrophic separation from society, as a consequence of long-standing and multiple deprivation across all the above.

Another definition is offered by Atkinson (1998) who proposes that social exclusion has three main elements:

- Relativity: it implies exclusion from a particular society at a particular time and place.
- Agency: it implies an act or acts, by an agent or agents, people are excluded by the actions of others.
- Dynamics: people are excluded not just because of their current situation, but also because they have little prospect for the future.

Similarly, Tsakloglou and Papadopoulos (2002) suggest that there is a consensus around five key attributes of the concept of social exclusion:

- Multidimensional: across a wide range of indicators of living standards, including neighbourhood or community resources.
- Dynamic: it relates not just to the current situation but also to prospects for the future.
- Relative: it implies exclusion in a particular society at a particular time.
- Agency: it lies beyond the narrow responsibility of the individual.
- Relational: meaning a major discontinuity with the rest of society.

These definitions are all relating social exclusion to the inability of people to participate in the society in which they live, and arguing that this applies across several dimensions, including the material but also the social and political. Thus, Burchardt, Le Grand and Piachaud (1999, 2002) from the Centre for the Analysis of Social Exclusion (CASE) at the London School of Economics, provide a succinct definition which focuses on participation: "An individual is socially excluded if he or she does not participate in the key activities of the society in which he or she lives" (Burchardt, Le Grand & Piachaud, 2002, p. 30).

This implies that the opposite of social exclusion is not integration or inclusion, but rather that it is *participation*. This point is argued strongly by Steinert and Pilgram (2003, p. 6), who point out that the concept of inclusion implies that individuals must conform "to all social norms and demands . . . even having to prove such conformity under penalty of being excluded". In multicultural and multi-ethnic societies, in which there is a variety of values, attitudes and beliefs, there is not necessarily a consensus about what people should have, about how people should live, or about what people should do. Their definition of social exclusion thus focuses on participation, both as an individual and a social goal:

> Social exclusion can thus be understood as the continuous and gradual exclusion from full participation in the social, including material and symbolic, resources produced, supplied and exploited in a society for making a living, organising a life and taking part in the development of a (hopefully better) future. (Steinert & Pilgram, 2003, p. 5)

The conceptualization of social exclusion, therefore, points towards empirical approaches that encompass various different elements of the extent to which people can participate in the society in which they live. The key elements are that research should be *relational*—not simply treating people as separate individuals but locating them within the contexts of family, household, community and nation. It should include the range of *resources* available to people—not just income, but also access to goods and services, community facilities, political engagement, leisure and social activity. It should be *dynamic*—not just about current circumstances, but also about future opportunities and capabilities to take advantage of these. And it should recognise *agency*—that people are excluded by the actions of other individuals and institutions but also that individuals have different ways of coping with the risk or actuality of social exclusion. These coping opportunities and strategies can be enhanced, or diminished, by government activity in respect of social policy.

The next two sections of the chapter discuss examples of research which have set out to explore the extent and experience of social exclusion. It is not an exhaustive or systematic review of the literature, but rather it is focused on a number of recent UK and EU research studies which have been selected to illustrate two main approaches to researching social exclusion. First, we look at examples of research studies which seek to identify those who are socially excluded by establishing multidimensional indicators of social exclusion, and identifying those who are excluded according to these measures. These studies are concerned with the state, or the condition, of social exclusion: with *being socially excluded*. Second, we look at examples of research studies which explore the ways in which people experience social exclusion, the risks they face, the sorts of responses and coping strategies that they have, and the support offered by the institutions of the welfare state. These studies are concerned with the processes of social exclusion: with *becoming socially excluded*.

BEING SOCIALLY EXCLUDED: MULTIDIMENSIONAL INDICATORS

As discussed above, there is a general consensus in the social policy literature that social exclusion is a multidimensional phenomenon that cannot be captured by measures of income only, or even material resources more broadly, but must include a wider range of other factors. These other factors have been defined in various ways, and this section provides some examples of the ways in which these dimensions of social exclusion have been defined. There are two parts to this process of defining and measuring social exclusion: first establishing the key dimensions and second deciding on the measurement of the indicators to apply to each. Burchardt, Le Grand and Piachaud (2002) included four main dimensions, each measured by particular indicators:

- Consumption: measured by the capacity to buy goods and services and by savings.
- Production: measured by participation in economically or socially valued activities.
- Political engagement: measured by involvement in local or national decision making.
- Social: measured by regularity and frequency of meeting with family, friends and neighbours.

The *UK Poverty and Social Exclusion* (PSE) Survey carried out in 1999, Gordon *et al.* (2000); see also Pantazis, Gordon and Levitas (2006), also included four dimensions:

- Impoverishment: measured by lack of material resources.
- Labour market exclusion: measured by lack of work, poor conditions or quality of work.
- Service exclusion: measured by lack of access to public and private services.
- Exclusion from social relationships: covering five key areas, including non-participation in common activities, the extent and quality of social networks, the support people can call upon routinely and in crisis, disengagement from political and civic activity, and confinement resulting from fear of crime, disability of other factors.

In an EU-funded study of social exclusion in six European countries (Austria, Germany, Greece, Norway, Portugal and the UK), using the European Community Household Panel, we compared across the domains of income poverty, household deprivation (lacking amenities, lacking necessary durables), subjective feelings of well-being, and social isolation (Apospori & Millar, 2003; Barnes *et al.*, 2002). Tsakloglou and Papadopoulos (2002) extended this approach to 12 European countries (the EU-12 countries), and more formally grouped the indicators into four groups:

- Income poverty: measured by incomes below 60% of median equivalised income *per capita*.
- Living conditions: measured by scoring below 80% of the median, using a weighted scale based on 22 household items (e.g. lack of space, environment problems, consumer durables).
- Necessities of life: measured by scoring below 60% of the median, using a weighted scale of activities (e.g. being able to afford heating, holidays).
- Social relations: measured by meeting friends, talking to neighbours, membership of clubs or groups including political parties.

There is clearly some, although not complete, agreement on the dimensions or domains of social exclusion. The studies cited above all include some measure of material deprivation (low income, lack of material resources, low expenditure, etc.) and some measure of social relations (contact with family and friends, membership of clubs, etc.). The latter is most comprehensively developed in the PSE study, which also includes political and civic engagement as part of social relations, while others make this a separate dimension. Barnes (2005) explored the relationship between different dimensions using factor analysis. He identified "three distinct and integral elements of social exclusion", which were "household economic deprivation" (income poverty, material deprivation, housing), "personal civic exclusion" (neighbourhood perception, social relations) and "personal health exclusion" (physical and mental health). The inclusion of physical and mental health indicators provides a link to research into quality of life. Layard (2005), for example, stresses the central importance of mental health as a key factor affecting happiness among individuals and societies. There is also some attempt in these studies to include measures at different levels—individual, household and neighbourhood—although the latter are often based on subjective perceptions of neighbourhood facilities rather than being separately observed.

In practice, the choice of the actual indicators used in each of the identified domains is often dependent on the nature of the data that are available to the researchers. As Levitas (2006) notes, much of the research into the multidimensional nature of social exclusion relies on the analysis of existing large-scale, and often multi-purpose, data sets, rather than involving the (expensive) collection of new data. This means that, rather than "moving, as social research ideally should, from definition to operationalisation to measurement, the process is reversed" (Levitas, 2006, p. 127). The choice of indicators may be driven more by the data available than by conceptual imperative. Thus, there is sometimes a gap between the factors that the researchers would ideally like to measure and the data that are available to them. For example, social isolation may be measured by the amount of contact with neighbourhoods, with little regard for the nature and quality of that contact; political participation may be measured simply by voting or membership of political parties, and so on. These sorts of measures can be particularly difficult to interpret cross-nationally because the way we engage with our neighbours, or with political institutions, will reflect cultural norms, as well as national, regional and ethnic identities. Thus, for example, Tsakloglou and Papadopoulos (2002, p. 215) find that social isolation tends to be very low in the southern countries of the EU, and rather higher in richer countries like Germany. The meaning of social isolation, as well as the relationship to social exclusion, is likely to be rather different in these different contexts.

Having identified the dimensions, or domains, of social exclusion, these studies examine the levels of social exclusion, the risk of social exclusion according to socio-economic and demographic factors, whether and how material exclusion is related to other forms of exclusion, and (where longitudinal data are available) the persistence of social exclusion over time. The results show a complex picture of social exclusion varying across countries and according to social divisions of age, social class, gender and ethnicity. Three results in particular are noteworthy. First, there is a relationship between poverty and social exclusion such that people with low incomes tend to be at greater risk of social exclusion than people with high incomes. However, the extent of this varies with the different measures of poverty and social exclusion used, and social relations tend to be less likely to be associated with poverty in this way than do measures of material deprivation. Second, there is not a substantial degree of overlap between the different dimensions and it is a relatively small minority of people who are excluded across a number of these dimensions. Third, although there are more people who have some experience of social exclusion over time than at a single point in time, persistent exclusion for the same people continuously over a period of years is very rare.

For example, Burchardt, Le Grand and Piachaud (2002), using data from the 1998 British Household Panel Survey (BHPS), find that about 58 % of people of working age were not excluded across any of the four dimensions of consumption, production, political engagement and social interaction. About 30 % were excluded across one dimension, about 10 % across two, just over 2 % across three and only 0.1 % were excluded across all four. There was a clear relationship between income levels and other dimensions of exclusion. This was strongest for production, with just 6 % of the top quintile were excluded on this dimension (measured by employment status), compared with 46 % of the bottom quintile. For social interaction, 16 % of the top quintile were excluded compared with 28 % of the bottom quintile. Looking at social exclusion over time, they found that only a very small proportion of individuals remained permanently excluded over time, especially when multiple dimensions are considered. Thus, after 4 years of observations, the very small group (1.5 % in the first year) of people excluded on all of the possible dimensions had ceased to exist.

The results were very similar to those in the study by Barnes (2005) who examined both UK and European data. For the UK in 1996, looking at seven dimensions (income poverty, access to material possessions, housing circumstances, perceptions of neighbourhood conditions, social relations, physical health and mental health), he found 49 % with no social exclusion, 30 % excluded on one dimension, 14 % on two, 5 % on three and 3 % excluded on four or more. Over time, defining permanent exclusion as being deprived on at least one of these measures in seven out of nine possible observations, he estimates that just 2 % of individuals experience long-term persistent exclusion. Thus, there does not appear to be any strong evidence for any "underclass" of people, excluded across all dimensions and for long periods of time, or for Room's (1995) "catastrophic" and irreversible separation from society.

However, this is not to suggest that there is no substantial problem of social exclusion. As Burchardt, Le Grand and Piachaud (2002, p. 31) point out in their discussion of the dimensions of social exclusion, each of these is important in its own right, so that "participation in every dimension is regarded as necessary for social inclusion; conversely lack of participation in any one dimension is sufficient for social exclusion". The relatively small proportions of people excluded across several dimensions over a period of time are drawn from a much larger pool of people who may move in and out of disadvantaged and difficult circumstances, but who may not be able to move very far and who continue to face a high risk of social exclusion. It is the lack of opportunity to escape the risk of social exclusion which presents an important challenge for policy: "People are excluded not just because they are currently without a job or income, but because they have little prospect for the future or for their children's future" (Atkinson et al., 2005, p. 18). On this point, Byrne (1999, p. 128) argues that social exclusion is inevitable in modern post-industrial capitalist societies, with flexible labour markets and very weak collective power of working people. The existence of social exclusion is "necessary and inherent" under such conditions and many people are thus at risk of social exclusion, because their range of mobility is restricted between unemployment and low-paid work.

BECOMING SOCIALLY EXCLUDED: RISKS AND RESOURCES

Understanding the processes that put people at risk of being socially excluded, or which protect them from it, is an important part of the research agenda for policy purposes. This section considers instances of research that focus on the processes of social exclusion. As discussed above, many definitions of social exclusion stress the issue of agency, arguing that social exclusion happens as a consequence of actions, or indeed non-actions, by individuals, groups and institutions. Agency also refers to the active way in which people themselves respond to their situations, and in particular, their responses to risk events, or contingencies, and the resources that they are able to call upon. This section discusses some examples of research studies which aim to explore how people cope and manage when faced with risk events—such as losing a job, or disability, or migration—and the nature and effectiveness of the institutional support they receive. The approach to these questions often involves qualitative methods—case-studies, in-depth interviews, ethnographic studies—in order to try and capture the nature and experience of these processes.

The research reported in the edited collection by Steinert and Pilgram (2003) is an example of this sort of approach. The research was based in eight cities in seven countries (Austria, Denmark, Germany, Italy, Spain, Sweden and the UK), and carried out by a cross-national research team which placed a strong emphasis on the importance of recognising the agency of people at risk of, or experiencing, social exclusion. The aim of this research was to explore the ways in which people "develop their own strategies for managing the routines of life . . . their own remedial strategies to re-gain control and routine after a problematic episode" (Steinert & Pilgram, 2003, p. 6) and how this relates to the mix of individual and family resources that people can call upon to sustain their living standards or protect themselves from adversity. Such resources might include incomes from earnings, resources in cash and kind from the people they live with and from wider family and friends, and resources from the state in the form of benefits and services. This approach examines the nature and processes of social exclusion by exploring how people respond to particular events, such as losing their jobs, or having a child, or divorce, or becoming a single parent. What mix of resources can people call upon in such circumstances? Do those resources enable them to cope with the particular event or contingency? What role do state services and provisions play in this?

In their project, the research team operationalise this empirically by means of community case studies in various different countries, focusing on events or episodes (as they call them) as the unit of analysis, rather than upon individuals or households. Thus, for example, there are chapters that compare across the cities the experience of social assistance recipients, of migrant workers and their families, of people on the margins of the labour market, and those on the margins of the labour market. There are also chapters that examine the role of local agencies, family and community in providing resources to enable people to cope with, or avoid, poverty and social exclusion. These analyses draw on data from in-depth interviews with people living in different cities, and with different experiences of employment, family and national and local state services. In the concluding chapter, the authors note that, "Situations in which no change seems possible and in which there is a vicious circle with a downward dynamic, are the extreme, not the average case" (Steinert & Pilgram, 2003, p. 255). They also set out a typology of resources, derived from their empirical work, which identifies four main types of resources potentially available to people facing adverse situations or risks: *welfare state resources* (benefits and services), *access resources* (getting information, advice and support), *resources of mutual help* and *reciprocity* (in the family, neighbourhood and other networks) and *"getting together" resources* (grass-roots and self-help organisations). Each of these can provide positive support, but not to everyone and not in all circumstances. Thus, for example, family may be a precarious and short-term resource, and access to state resources is restricted by various forms of conditionality. State rules that make it difficult for people to call on a range of resources—to combine wages, family and welfare—make it more difficult for people to cope.

In another cross-national European study, Chamberlayne, Rustin and Wengraf (2002) use what they describe as "socio-biographical methods" to explore how people deal with risk events. Their data are drawn from "life journey" interviews, that are "narratives related by individuals, which were focused on life journeys such as those brought about by enforced redundancy or early retirement, by difficulty entering the labour market after formal education, or by exile and migration" (p. 3). These very detailed and in-depth personal biographies from seven countries (Britain, France, Germany, Greece, Italy, Spain and Sweden) provide a way into analysing the complex ways in which individual attitudes and motivations, personal and family circumstances, and institutional agencies interact when people face particular events and circumstances. Again, the research starts with a stress on the importance of understanding people as active agents in constructing their responses to situations and circumstances:

> Even though damaging life contingencies often imposed themselves with unexpected suddenness and force, we found that many of our subjects had actively negotiated threats to their well-being, and were rarely passive in the face of them. Others transitions, such as migration depended on substantial individual and family commitments . . . Individuals make life choices in multi dimensional ways. They choose courses of action for emotional and moral reasons, as well as for material ones. Our

> biographical subjects were concerned, in different instances, with questions of dignity
> and recognition (especially when they were denied respect by the treatment they
> received); with meaning and satisfaction (for example in their work); and with sustain-
> ing relationships. (Chamberlayne, Rustin & Wengraf, 2002, p. 4)

In their discussion, Chamberlayne and her colleagues distinguish between "tactical" and "strategic" approaches to coping with risk events. Some people are in such situations that they can only "live life one day at a time", responding to circumstances rather than being able to control these, they can only be tactical, they cannot be strategic. This resonates with UK research that highlights the problem of the "hardship trap", a term that has been used to refer to people trapped out of work by the fact that their poverty and hardship is so time-consuming and so demoralising that they are unable to think about employment, let alone take steps to find a job (Marsh *et al.*, 2001). The same sort of division can be seen in studies of how people cope financially on low incomes. Kempson (1996), for example, suggests that there are two main strategies that poor people adopt. On the one hand they place a very tight control over all aspects of their expenditure, and on the other hand they adopt a more contingent approach of paying whatever is the most pressing need or debt. She shows that people move between these two approaches. As Kempson concludes, it is not that there are different types of people who do different things, but that there are different strategies that people use at different times. Of course, ultimately, if there is not enough income it does not matter which strategy you use, you cannot make ends meet.

These two EU cross-national studies include very rich data from the individual accounts, and the qualitative approach provides a valuable focus on the relationship between every-day experiences and societal institutions. But, it is also possible to explore risk situations and circumstances and social exclusion using large-scale quantitative data. For example, in our EU study of social exclusion, we examined the situations of four "transitions" or "risk" groups, in order to consider the extent to which being in one of these groups was associated with social exclusion (Apospori & Millar, 2003; Barnes *et al.*, 2002). Two of these transitions—the transition from childhood to becoming a young adult, and the transition from work to retirement—are life events that we all face and were chosen as important points of transition between being in and out of the labour market. The other two—becoming a single parent, and becoming long-term sick or disabled—are events that happen to some (and to an increasing proportion in many countries) but not to everyone, which makes them particularly interesting for cross-national comparison. Focusing upon these times of transition was thus intended to allow an exploration of the extent to which life course changes can make people particularly vulnerable to poverty and social exclusion, and to compare different national outcomes. The results showed that lone parents and sick and disabled people face a substantially higher risk of income poverty, of non-monetary material disadvantage and multidimensional disadvantage than the average for their country. The same is true for retired people in the southern countries and in the UK, although not in Austria, Germany or Norway. By contrast, young people did not face higher than average risks of social exclusion in Austria, Norway, Greece or Portugal, but did in Germany and the UK. Looked at over time, it was the young people who were most likely to be able to exit from poverty and deprivation, but otherwise there was quite a mixed picture in terms of changes over time. Thus, as the authors conclude:

> Different people have different histories of income and purchases, and so experience
> a different effect of current poverty on current deprivation . . . deprivation is a dynamic
> experience and can only be understood as the result of a history of experiences.
> (Barnes *et al.*, 2002, p. 150)

In summary, these three cross-national comparative studies used different methods to explore risk events and to consider how people respond to these events, and to explore the resources—both public and private—on which they can draw. As with the studies discussed in the previous section, these authors agree that there is no "socially excluded" underclass group, and conclude that the events and contingencies that potentially create social exclusion are both identifiable and amenable to policy intervention. This focuses attention in the role of the state in prevention and the protection of people from social exclusion, as well as alleviation of the problem. Room (2000) has argued that research which provides an analysis of the relationship between state, private and voluntary institutions and individual, family and household action is needed in order to understand the trajectories of social exclusion over time, and to assess whether welfare institutions provide "buffers" against risk events and/or "passports" to take advantage of opportunities (Room, 2000).

MONITORING SOCIAL EXCLUSION: SOCIAL INDICATORS

This final section on social policy research into social exclusion looks at the development and use of social indicators for the purposes of monitoring progress on policies aimed at tackling social exclusion.

Monitoring Policy in the UK

The Social Exclusion Unit (SEU), established in 1997 and located in the Office of the Deputy Prime Minister, acts as a cross-departmental centre for both specific projects (for example on issues such as rough sleeping, teenage pregnancy, school truancy) and more general assessments of policy trends and future issues.[1] Two reports, *Tackling Social Exclusion* and *Breaking the Cycle*, provide an overview of Government policy since 1997 and discuss policy priorities for the future (SEU, 2004a, 2004b). These reports provide data on some key indicators, such as levels of child and pensioner poverty, unemployment and worklessness, educational attainment, homelessness, crime levels and teenage pregnancy rates. The five main priorities for future action are identified by the SEU (2004b) as low educational attainment, economic inactivity and concentrations of unemployed, health inequalities, concentrations of crime and poor quality environments, and homelessness.

The Department for Work and Pensions (formerly the Department of Social Security) takes the responsibility for regular statistical monitoring of government progress through the annual report, *Opportunity for All*. This report also provides a set of quantitative social indicators intended to monitor progress in tackling poverty and inequality. The baseline for reporting is 1997 (the year that the Labour Party was elected to government) and the

---

[1] Now the Social Exclusion Taskforce (www.cabinetoffice.gov.uk/social_exclusion/)

indicators are divided into four headings including three population groups—children and young people, people of working age, older people—with the final set focused on communities. Within each heading, policy priorities are identified and specific indicators attached to these. For example, under the heading of working-age people, one of the goals identified is "supporting vulnerable groups and those most at risk of discrimination and disadvantage". Additionally, concerning the latter, there are four specific indicators to do this: (a) a reduction in the number of people sleeping rough, (b) a reduction in cocaine and heroin use by young people, (c) a reduction in adult smoking rates, and (d) a reduction in deaths rates from suicide and undetermined injury. The goal of "improving opportunities for older people" also has four indicators: (a) a reduction in the proportion of older people affected by fear of crime, (b) an increase in healthy life expectancy at age 65, (c) a reduction in poor housing among household with someone aged over 75, and (d) an increase in the proportion of older people living independently.

The published annual report, *Opportunity for All* (see Department of Social Security, 1999 and Department for Work and Pensions for subsequent years), summarises the policy activity in each of the five key areas, including information on expenditure on new and ongoing initiatives, and summarises the trends for the key indicators. In general the trend data show an improvement over time. The seventh annual report, for 2005, concluded that the trends for 41 key indicators were "moving in the right direction"; seven key indicators were "broadly constant"; and seven key indicators were "going in the wrong direction" (Department for Work and Pensions, 2005). The latter included educational outcomes for children "in care", infant mortality rates, obesity for children aged 2 to 10, families in temporary accommodation, employment of disadvantaged groups (lowest qualified), the number of people contributing to a non-state pension, and life expectancy at birth (see also Jackson, Chapter 7 and Clapham, Chapter 5).

These audits provide a valuable snapshot of the situation each year and the direction of change. The reports are, however, a compilation of indicators of different types from various data sources, covering different geographical areas and different time periods. The main sources are administrative data and social surveys. Barnes (2005) and Levitas (2000) discuss some of the limitations of this sort of audit list approach. First, the indicators seem rather arbitrary and are certainly not theoretically justified. Second, some of the indicators—for example, smoking rates, drug use—do not seem to be directly related to poverty and social exclusion. Third, the indicators mix measures of risk factors (for example, lack of education and skills, teenage pregnancy) and output indicators (for example, health, poverty rates) without distinguishing between these. Also, the impact of government policy cannot be assessed from these figures—if trends are going in the right direction, it may be in spite of, not because of, the policy measures adopted (although if they are going in the wrong direction, that could be a valuable signal for a reassessment of current policy measures). Levitas (2000) also argues that these indicators are largely based in one particular model of the "causes of social exclusion", in which social exclusion is seen as primarily a problem of exclusion from employment, and so there is a strong focus on indicators relating to labour market position and skills.

Other approaches have been adopted to overcome such problems. The Joseph Rowntree Foundation has also published a series of annual audits, *Monitoring Poverty and Social Exclusion*, based on the work of the New Policy Institute (NPI), with seven reports for Great Britain (1998–2004) and two for Scotland (2002 and 2004). The first report (Howarth *et al.*, 1998) sets out the baseline and the indicators, using official statistics, cover many of the same areas as the government reports (the main headings are income, children, young adults, adults 25 to retirement, older people and communities), but with some different indicators. This, therefore, provides an additional measure of change across a range of policy areas. In 2004, looking back over 5 to 6 years, they judged 18 indicators to be improved, 17 to be steady, one to be mixed and eight to have worsened. In the report for Great Britain, Palmer, Carr and Kenway (2004a) conclude that there are four key issues to be tackled: the situation of working-age people without dependent children, the situation of the economically inactive people who would like to work, the poor quality of jobs at the lower end of the labour market and the situation of young adults with low, or no, educational qualifications. For Scotland, Palmer, Carr and Kenway (2004b) also add Scotland's relatively high levels of poor health. These are consistent with indicators highlighted by the European Council in 2000.

Social Inclusion and the European Union (EU)

Social indicators are a crucial element in the "Open Method of Coordination", a process for co-ordinated policy development in EU member states, which was agreed by the European Council in 2000. The aim of the Open Method of Coordination is to promote policy learning across the EU by providing a means for countries to benchmark their progress against others, while still maintaining the capacity to develop specific policies that meet national circumstances and priorities.[2] It has five key stages: the agreement of common policy objectives, the establishment of common indicators to monitor progress and compare practice, the development of National Action Plans, the publication of reports on these plans, and the establishment of a Community Action programme to facilitate exchange and learning (Employment and Social Affairs Unit, European Commission).[3] The process has been applied to the issue of social exclusion, with the indicators of social exclusion developed by leading experts in the field (Atkinson et al., 2002).

Nolan (2003) summarises the key methodological factors that were applied in choosing these indicators, including for example, that they should address outputs rather than inputs, be robust, be responsive to policy interventions, be comparable across countries, and that the portfolio of indicators should be balanced across different dimensions. Three tiers of indicators were developed. The first tier of primary indicators includes various measures of low income and the distribution of income, of employment and unemployment, of early school-leavers not in education or training, of life expectancy at birth and of self-defined health status. The secondary indicators cover the same areas but with more specific measures. The third tier consists of specific national measures, reflecting local circumstances and priorities.

Three joint reports have been published (European Commission, 2002, 2004, 2005), with the latter being a report specifically focused on the 10 new member states and social exclusion. These can be read alongside a review by Atkinson et al. (2005), which provides a comprehensive discussion of the key issues and progress since 2000. In the latter report,

---

[2] For a more general discussion of European and EU policy initiatives, see Mayes, Berghman and Salais (2001) and Begg and Berghman (2002).
[3] See the website at www.europa.eu.int/comm/employment_social/social_inclusion/index_en.htm.

the researchers make various recommendations for modifying the measures of exclusion (dropping some, adding or revising others). The revised list of primary indicators includes the existing indicators (at-risk-of-poverty rate, at-risk-of-poverty threshold, income quintile ratio, children living in jobless households, adults living in jobless households, long-term unemployment rate and early school leavers not in education or training) and five new indicators (premature mortality or life expectancy, aggregate index of four housing problems, homelessness, aggregate index of nine deprivation items and children-focused non-income-based indicator) (Atkinson *et al.*, 2005; table 5.2a). The report also calls for the more systematic use of these, and other data, in policy analysis, and for a "children mainstreaming" to ensure that the circumstances and needs of children are visible and central to the social inclusion goals.

CONCLUSION

This review, although not comprehensive, has indicated that there is a degree of consensus about the meaning of social exclusion. It is multidimensional (including social and political, as well as material, dimensions), it is dynamic (including future options and opportunities, as well as current circumstances), and it is relational (located in specific social and economic contexts). The process of social exclusion implies agency. On the one hand, social exclusion is created in society, with people excluded by the actions of others. On the other hand, people respond to social exclusion, or to the risk of social exclusion, in active ways. They seek ways to manage and to cope, and if possible to improve their situations and, where they can, they call on a range of resources including state support to do this.

People move in and out of disadvantage over time, although they may not move very far, nor escape the risk of facing social exclusion in the future. Research focusing on the process of social exclusion, and on how people cope with risks, highlights the importance of the range of resources available to people. As with the quantitative analyses, these qualitative studies do not find much evidence for extreme and long-term social exclusion, although the resources that people can draw upon when they face difficult situations may vary significantly for different social groups and in different national and local contexts.

While social exclusion has certainly become an important concept in policy discourses and debates, and the research base is expanding rapidly, there are a number of challenges for future research. First, there is a need for the continuous improvement of the data available, with more robust indicators, better longitudinal data and a wider range of analytical techniques to explore causal relationships. Second, there is a gap in research that links "information about institutional strategies, administrative processes, policy context and household-level experience" (Heady & Room, 2003, p. 177). Such research could provide a stronger link between the processes that lead to social exclusion and the outcomes for individuals over time. Finally, social inclusion, understood in terms of participation, also implies a more democratic approach to research and policy. The most effective way to understand the resources and opportunities available to people, the barriers to making use of these, and their advantages and disadvantages, is from people themselves. This implies putting the experiences of people, and their attitudes and behaviour, at the centre and starting the policy analysis from that perspective.

REFERENCES

Apospori, E. & Millar, J. (eds) (2003). *The Dynamics of Social Exclusion in Europe*. London: Edward Elgar Publications.

Atkinson, A.B. (1998). Social exclusion, poverty and unemployment. In A.B. Atkinson & J. Hills (eds), *Exclusion, Employment and Opportunity*. CASE Paper number 4, London: Centre for Analysis of Social Exclusion.

Atkinson, A.B., Cantillon, B., Marlier, E. & Nolan, B. (2002). *Social Indicators: The EU and Social Exclusion*. Oxford: Oxford University Press.

Atkinson, A.B., Cantillon, B., Marlier, E. & Nolan, B. (2005). *Taking Forward the EU Social Inclusion Process*. Luxembourg: Luxembourg Ministry for Family and Integration. www.fm. etat.lu

Barnes, M. (2005). *Social Exclusion in Great Britain: An Empirical Investigation and Comparison with the EU*. Aldershot: Ashgate Publishing Limited.

Barnes, M., Heady, C., Middleton, S., *et al.* (2002). *Poverty and Social Exclusion in Europe*. London: Edward Elgar Publications.

Begg, I. & Berghman, J. (eds) (2002). Special issue: social exclusion and reforming the European social model. *Journal of European Social Policy*, *12*(3), 179–239.

Burchardt, T., Le Grand, J. & Piachaud, D. (1999). Social exclusion in Britain 1991–1995. *Social Policy and Administration*, *33*(3), 227–244.

Burchardt, T., Le Grand, J. & Piachaud, D. (2002). *Understanding Social Exclusion*. Oxford: Oxford University Press.

Byrne, D. (1999). *Social Exclusion*. Buckingham: Open University Press.

Chamberlayne, P., Rustin, M. & Wengraf, T. (2002). *Biography and Social Exclusion in Europe*. Bristol: Policy Press.

Department of Social Security. (1999). *Opportunity for All: Tackling Poverty and Social Exclusion, First Annual Report*. Cm 4445. London: The Stationery Office.

Department for Work and Pensions. (2005). *Opportunity for All: Seventh Annual Report*. Cm 6673. London: The Stationery Office.

European Commission. (2002). *Joint Report on Social Inclusion*. Luxembourg: Office for Official Publications of the European Communities.

European Commission. (2004). *Joint Report on Social Inclusion 2004*. Luxembourg: Office for Official Publications of the European Communities.

European Commission. (2005). *Report on Social Inclusion in the Ten New Member States 2005*. Luxembourg: Office for Official Publications of the European Communities.

Gordon, D., Adelman, L., Ashworth, K., *et al.* (2000). *Poverty and Social Exclusion in Britain*. York: The Joseph Rowntree Foundation.

Heady, C. & Room, G. (2003). Tackling poverty and social exclusion. In E. Apospori & J. Millar (eds), *The Dynamics of Social Exclusion in Europe* (pp. 164–177). London: Edward Elgar Publications.

Howarth, C., Kenway, P., Palmer, G. & Street, C. (1998). *Monitoring Poverty and Social Exclusion: Labour's Inheritance*. York: The Joseph Rowntree Foundation.

Kempson, E. (1996). *Life on a Low Income*. York: York Publishing Services Ltd.

Layard, R. (2005). *Happiness: Lessons from a New Science*. London: Allen Lane.

Levitas, R. (2000). What is social exclusion? In D. Gordon & P. Townsend (eds), *Breadline Europe: the Measurement of Poverty* (pp. 357–384). Bristol: Policy Press.

Levitas, R. (2006). The concept and measurement of social exclusion. In C. Pantazis, D. Gordon & R. Levitas (eds), *Poverty and Social Exclusion in Britain* (pp. 123–162). Bristol: Policy Press.

Marsh, A., McKay, S., Smith, A. & Stephenson, A. (2001). *Low-Income Families in Britain: Work, Welfare and Social Security in 1999*. Department of Social Security Research Report No 138 Leeds: Corporate Document Services.

Mayes, D.G., Berghman, J. & Salais, R. (2001). *Social Exclusion and European Policy*. Cheltenham: Edward Elgar Publishing.

Nolan, B. (2003). Indicators for social inclusion in the European Union. In P. Krause, G. Bäcker & W. Hanesh (eds), *Combating Poverty in Europe: The German Welfare Regime in Practice* (pp. 75–92). Aldershot: Ashgate Publishing Limited.

Palmer, G., Carr, J. & Kenway, P. (2004a). *Monitoring Poverty and Social Exclusion*. London: The New Policy Institute and York: the Joseph Rowntree Foundation. Retrieved from http://www. poverty.org.uk/reports/mpse2004.pdf

Palmer, G., Carr, J., & Kenway, P. (2004b). *Monitoring Poverty and Social Exclusion in Scotland 2004*. York: The Joseph Rowntree Foundation.

Pantazis, C., Gordon, D. & Levitas, R. (2006). *Poverty and Social Exclusion in Britain*. Bristol: Policy Press.

Room, G. (ed.) (1995). *Beyond the Threshold: the Measurement and Analysis of Social Exclusion*. Bristol: The Policy Press.

Room, G. (2000). Trajectories of social exclusion: the wider context for the third and first worlds. In D. Gordon & P. Townsend (eds), *Breadline Europe: the Measurement of Poverty* (pp. 407–440). Bristol: Policy Press.

Social Exclusion Unit (SEU). (2004a). *Tackling Social Exclusion: Taking Stock and Looking to the Future*. London: Social Exclusion Unit.

Social Exclusion Unit (SEU). (2004b). *Breaking the Cycle: Taking Stock of Progress*. London: Social Exclusion Unit.

Steinert, H. & Pilgram, A. (2003). *Welfare from Below: Struggles Against Social Exclusion in Europe*. Aldershot: Ashgate Publishing Limited.

Tsakloglou, P. & Papadopoulos, F. (2002). Aggregate level and determining factors of social exclusion in twelve European countries. *Journal of European Social Policy, 12*(3), 211–226.

CHAPTER 2

Women's Social Exclusion

Diane M. Houston
University of Kent, United Kingdom

ABSTRACT

In this chapter, the social exclusion of women as a group within UK society is demonstrated by examination of data from a number of national surveys. The Burchardt, Le
Grand and Piachaud (2002) framework is employed to demonstrate that women, as a
group, are socially excluded in terms of their participation in consumption, production,
political engagement and social interaction. In this context, aspects of the Burchardt *et al.*
framework are challenged in terms of the power of some of the behaviours specified to
adequately represent inclusion.

INTRODUCTION

Burchardt, Le Grand and Piachaud (1999) proposed a working definition of social exclusion, designed to provide a means of operationalising the concept in such a way that social
exclusion in the UK could be quantified. The definition proposed was that:

> An individual is socially excluded if (a) he or she is geographically resident in a society
> and (b) he or she does not participate in the normal activities of citizens of the society.
> (Burchardt, Le Grand & Piachaud, 1999)

In 2002, this definition was refined as:

> An individual is socially excluded if he or she does not participate in the key activities
> of the society in which he or she lives. (Burchardt, Le Grand & Piachaud, 2002)

In both the 1999 and 2002 papers, Burchardt *et al.* clarify the relative nature of social
exclusion—that it is defined in the context of a particular time and place. In this context,
they identify four dimensions for Britain in the 1990s: consumption, production, political
engagement and social interaction.

Burchardt, Le Grand and Piachaud (1999, 2002) used data from the British Household
Panel Survey (BHPS) to examine the proportions of people who could be categorized as
socially excluded according to the four dimensions. Consumption is defined as the capacity

to purchase goods and services; this is quantified using BHPS data in terms of household net income being under half the mean income in the UK. Production is participation in paid or socially valued activities, measured through BHPS as not being engaged in employment, self-employment, education/training or looking after a family. Political engagement defined in terms of participation in local or national decision making, quantified as voting in the last general election or membership of campaigning organizations (political, trade union, parents/residents associations, etc.). Social interaction is defined as integration with family, friends and community; this is quantified by BHPS questions which ask if the respondent has someone who can listen when they need to talk, help in crisis, be them self with, really appreciate them and comfort them. From these criteria, the 1997 data from the BHPS generate proportions of social exclusion in UK society as 16%, 12%, 21% and 9%, respectively.

In this chapter, the social exclusion of women as a group within UK society is demonstrated by examination of data from a number of national surveys. The Burchardt, Le Grand and Piachaud (2002) framework is employed to demonstrate that women, as a group, are socially excluded in terms of their participation in consumption, production, political engagement and social interaction. In this context, aspects of the Burchardt *et al.* framework are challenged in terms of the power of some of the behaviours specified to adequately represent inclusion.

Burchardt, Le Grand and Piachaud (2002) used household level data to measure social exclusion. In the present analysis, national survey data which measure at the individual level are examined. This allows for the assessment of differences between men and women, as individuals, whether or not they live as part of a couple, or in wider extended family. There could be debate as to whether this is appropriate given that many families divide their activities in a non-symmetrical way, such that a woman within a household may appear to be socially excluded, when the household is not. There has also been debate around the extent to which this is an active choice for women within households (cf. Crompton & Harris, 1998; Hakim, 1991; Houston & Marks, 2005). In a more general manner, Burchardt *et al.* also discuss ways in which social exclusion may be voluntary or of no consequence to the individual. They argue that it is possible that some individuals, or groups, may exclude themselves voluntarily from wider society, in such a way that this does not have any negative impact on the individual concerned. Similarly, they propose that some individuals may be involuntarily excluded, but without any consequent negative impact on that individual. In these cases, the issue is whether society as a whole is negatively impacted by such social exclusion. In the case of women as a group, it would be hard to argue that their exclusion did not impact upon society, as they represent half of society.

Using data from the Labour Force Survey (2007), Department for Work and Pensions (DWP) Family Resources Survey (2003/4), the Annual Survey of Hours and Earning (2006), The Time Use Survey (2005) and a variety of national statistics on representation, this chapter compares women's position to that of men on the set of criteria used by Burchardt, Le Grand and Piachaud (2002).

Consumption

The DWP Family Resources Survey provides data on the weekly individual income of women and men by type of family, source of income, age, marital status, region and employment status. The gender disaggregation of this data, in the report Individual

Incomes (Women and Equality Unit, 2006), provides a means of comparing the income accruing to women with that accruing to men. Income in this context includes earnings, tax credits, investments, pensions and benefits. Thus, it provides a different perspective from pay statistics, which only provide information about earned income. Individual Incomes (WEU, 2006) reports that the weekly median total individual income for all women in 2004/05 was £173—55% of that for all men at £315. This is just 5% over the "under half mean income" criterion used by Burchardt *et al.* and demonstrates a clear difference between men and women in terms of their capacity of purchasing goods and services in their own right.

Women's individual incomes are lower than men's across the lifespan, but proportionately the difference is greatest between 30 and 50 years of age, illustrating the impact of family responsibilities on women's individual incomes (WEU, 2006).

Production

Thirty percent of women in the UK do no paid work, and half of all women who work do so part-time (ONS, 2007). For the majority of women, family responsibilities are the major reason for not working or working part-time, 79% of women who work part-time state that they do not want a full-time job, and of these, 74% say that children or domestic responsibilities are their reason for working part-time. Similarly, forty-five percent of all women who are not in work state that family responsibilities are their reason for not working (ONS, 2007).

Burchardt, Le Grand and Piachaud (1999, 2002) define production in terms of it being "socially valued activity" and include looking after a home and family as one such activity. However, the actual value placed on these activities in 21st century Britain is low. In the UK, there is no taxation benefit explicitly offered to families in which one partner undertakes an unpaid caring role. Indeed the benefits system is designed to promote paid work *rather than* care. Piachaud and Sutherland (2002) cite a DSS statement in 1999 which explicitly includes carers as one group—along with those with long-term illness and lone parents—for whom the focus must move from positive assistance to find work, rather than just benefit payment. Piachaud and Sutherland argue that one of the aims of working families' tax credit is to "make work pay". In 2006, the Department for Work and Pensions set a target of employment rates of 70% for lone parents by 2010. Current employment rates for lone parents are 55.5%, rather lower than that of partnered mothers (71.4%, ONS, 2007). Thus, it would appear that current government policy dictates that if value is to be attached to looking after a family rather than work, it is only "valuable" if those doing so are in an economic unit with someone who is engaged in more formal means of production.

While the social value attached to caring work may be low, the market value given to care and domestic work is amongst the lowest for any paid job. The Annual Survey of Hours and Earnings reports that the mean hourly pay of all employees is £13.07 per hour (ASHE, 2006). The mean hourly pay for cleaners is £6.39, care assistants £7.60 and nursery nurses £7.26. Thus the kind of work women do at home has an average market value of £7.08, and this is 54% of the average hourly pay, only 4% more than the "half mean income" used by Burchardt *et al.* in terms of exclusion in relation to production.

Not only is women's role in looking after home and family not valued by society, women are excluded from high status, highly paid work as a consequence of their roles as mothers, carers and housekeepers. On initial inspection, women's labour force participation in the UK looks close to that of men, 70% of working-age women and 79% of working-age men are in work (ONS, 2007). While women's participation in the workplace has increased steadily since the 1950s, almost all this can be accounted for by an increase in part-time work. Hakim (2004) used census and Labour Force Survey data to demonstrate that women's full-time employment rate increased by only 6% from 1951 to 2003 (from 30.3% of women to 36%). Hakim argues that women's full-time employment rates have been virtually stable since the 1850s, and that increases in both jobs and female labour market participation can be accounted for by the increase in part-time work of partnered women.

Working part-time carries a significant wage penalty; women working part-time earn 40% less per hour than men who work full-time (ASHE, 2006). In addition, part-time work carries a career penalty: Francesconi and Gosling (2005) found that women who spend just 1 year in part-time work, and then work full-time again, can expect to earn 10% less after 15 years than those who did not work part-time. In general, women moving from full- to part-time work tend to make a downward occupational move (Houston & Marks, 2003; Manning & Petrongolo, 2004). Green (2005) found that half of all working women with children under 5 are over-educated for the work they do.

Those women who work full-time also experience a substantial pay gap (17%; ASHE, 2006), a proportion of which can be explained by occupational segregation. Nearly two thirds of women are employed in 12 occupation groups: the five "c"s—caring, cashiering, catering, cleaning and clerical occupations—plus teaching, health associate professionals (including nurses), and "functional" managers, such as financial managers, marketing and sales managers, and personnel managers. By contrast, men are employed in a wider range of jobs. Two thirds of men are employed in 26 occupation groups including more professional, management and technical roles than women, for example, functional and production managers, transport drivers, engineers, and information and communication technology professionals (ASHE, 2006).

The gender segregation of occupations did decline to a larger extent during the 1990s than in previous decades. This is attributed to the increased concentration of both men and women in service-related occupations (ASHE, 2005). In addition, medicine, pharmacy, law and accountancy have become much less segregated by gender. Three quarters of all pharmacists, a third of medical practitioners, nearly half of all lawyers and nearly 40% of all accountants are female. The proportion of managers and senior officials who are women has increased from less than 10% in the early 1990s to a third in 2005 (ASHE, 2006). Despite the reduction in the gender segregation of these occupations, gender pay gaps remain. For example, full-time, female medical practitioners earn 23% less, female legal professionals earn 21% less, and female accountants earn 15% less than the median hourly earnings of their male counterparts. In other occupations, progress on reducing segregation has been negligible or has actually reversed. For example, only 14% of science and technology professionals are women and the numbers of female ICT professionals are actually falling (ASHE, 2006).

Political Engagement

Burchardt *et al.* defined political engagement in terms of participation in local or national decision making, quantified as voting in the last general election or membership of campaigning organizations. Women are slightly, but not significantly, more likely to vote in local or national elections than men. The European Social Survey (2002) reports that 68 % of women and 66 % of men in the UK reported voting in the last national election.

Women are also slightly more likely than men to sign a petition or buy a production for a political reason. However, men are much more likely than women to work for or be a member of a political party. While participation rates are low for both genders, only 2 % of women are members of, or work for, a political party in comparison to 4 % of men (The Electoral Commission, 2004). This "activism gap" is the most likely cause of an even greater gap in actual representation in local and national decision making. In the UK, women currently make up only 29 % of local councillors and just 19.8 % of members of parliament. Thus, while women may be as likely to vote as men, the decision-making bodies that represent them are not representative of their gender.

A key issue here is if social exclusion goes beyond voting behaviour. It can be argued that, in political terms, inclusion should be defined as representation. Being able to vote offers a level of political engagement, but not necessarily a representation of the issues and experiences that any one group in society might consider important. Women do vote, but they are not adequately represented in local or national decision-making bodies. The same is true of minority ethnic groups; 8.3 % of the population define themselves as belonging to a group which is not "white" (Social Trends, 2006), yet only 0.023 % of parliament (15 MPs) is made up of members from minority ethnic groups (www. parliament.uk). There are clearly complex issues to be resolved in terms of representation, some of which relate to the ethnic mix in different constituencies. However, what remains astonishing about women's political representation is that all constituencies are approximately 50 % female.

Women's exclusion from political engagement may reflect particularities of the political world as well as the processes of election and representation. Alternatively, it may also reflect one aspect of the "glass ceiling". Indeed, there are proportionately more women in parliament than in many other senior posts. Women represent just 15 % of university professors and 10 % of FTSE 100 board members. Only 8.4 % of University Vice Chancellors, 7 % of High Court Judges and 3.4 % of Executive Director posts are women (Aston, Clegg, Diplock, Ritchie & Willison, 2004).

Social Interaction

Burchardt, Le Grand and Piachaud (2002) define social interaction as integration with family, friends and community. The BHPS question they used to measure exclusion in terms of social interaction asks if the respondent has someone who "can listen when they need to talk, help in crisis, be them self with, really appreciate them and comfort them". While this may measure some aspects of social interaction, it is really a measure of intimacy, rather than integration with friends, family and the community. It is quite possible to be in a relationship with one individual, or a small number of people within a home or family, who provide the kind of support measured by the BHPS question, yet still be completely isolated from a wider group of family, friends and community. A more appropriate measure could be time spent on activities which demonstrate integration with friends, family and the community.

Lader, Short and Gershuny (2006) report findings from the 2005 Time Use Survey which was designed to measure the amount of time spent by the UK population on various activities, through pre-coded time use diaries. The Time Use survey shows that, on average, women spend less time each day on recreational and social activities such as viewing TV/DVD or listening to music, using computers, taking part in hobbies, sport and outdoor activities. They spend the same amount of time as men on voluntary work and educational activities, but much less time on paid work. Women were more likely to report, and spend time on, being with family and friends at home (38 % of women sampled, an average of 57 minutes; 27 % of men sampled, an average of 42 minutes). Men are more likely to report "going out" with friends and family (16 % of men sampled, an average of 28 minutes; 12 % of women sampled, an average of 21 minutes). Women were more likely than men to report having contact with friends and family whilst at home (e.g. on the telephone) and to spend time reading. Thus the activities which women spend longer time on than do men are those which involve home-based socialising and recreation, rather than activities outside the home—activity which could be defined as providing social integration. The Office for National Statistics (ONS, 2006) presents Time Use statistics combining all activities within the leisure category and estimates that men spend 5.25 hours per day and women 4.53; thus women spend 14 % less time on social integration in its broadest sense.

Women also experience factors which may make them less likely to feel that they have freedom to choose how and where their social interaction takes place. Women are between two and three times more likely than men to be very worried about being mugged or physically attacked, and five times more likely than men to be very worried about being sexually assaulted (Aston *et al.*, 2004). In addition to being more fearful about their personal safety, women are less likely than men to have access to personal transport. Sixty-one per cent of women have a full driving licence compared to 81 % of men; men are significantly more likely to report that a car is their main form of transport and women are less likely to be the driver and more likely to be the passenger (Aston *et al.*, 2004).

Women's roles in domestic and caring work are also likely to limit the time available for social integration. Overall, women spend on average 178 minutes each day on housework, compared to 100 minutes for men. Women who work full-time are more likely to do housework and to spend much longer time on such activities than men who work full-time. Forty-two per cent of women full-time workers report doing housework compared to only 17 % of male full-time workers (Lader, Short & Gershuny 2006).

SUMMARY

Using Burchardt *et al.*'s definitions of social exclusion, a variety of different measures and statistics has been examined. These present a detailed perspective on women's inclusion in society. In order to attempt to provide one key figure to represent an estimate of women's social exclusion, the most robust and/or salient to Burchardt *et al.*'s original definition has been used and can be summarized as follows:

Consumption	45 %	The difference between men and women in individual incomes, that is, their capacity to purchase goods and services in their own right.
Production	40 %	The gender pay gap, represented by the pattern of work which is most representative of each gender, women part-time, men full-time.

Political Representation   80%   Women's representation in the UK parliament, which is currently 20%.

Social Integration   14%   Integration with family, friends and community, the figure being the percentage difference between men and women in their reported number of minutes daily leisure activity.

These are dramatic figures, but they are taken from well-established national statistics. These four figures represent robust differences between men and women in 21st century Britain.

DISCUSSION

Given that women appear to be socially excluded in 21st century Britain, why is this not reflected in theory or policy? The UK Government's social exclusion unit (www.socialexclusionunit.gov.uk) does not identify women as a group who experience exclusion. The volume from the ESRC Research Centre for Analysis of Social Exclusion (Hills, Le Grand & Piachaud, 2002) does not address the issue of gender beyond mentioning that women tend to be amongst the low paid and that lone parents experience social exclusion. Within the European policy agenda, the concepts of social exclusion and gender equality have had greater linkage, though until 2003 the focus tended to be on employment alone (Rubery et al., 2003). In March 2006, the European Commission issued its roadmap for equality between men and women, laying down Commission's activities in this field for 2006–2010. This roadmap describes six fields of priority action for the EU in terms of gender equality: equal economic independence for men and women, reconciliation between professional life and private life, equal representation in decision making, ending all forms of violence and trafficking in human beings based on gender, removal of gender stereotypes within society and the promotion of equality between the sexes outside the EU.

One reason why women as a group are not commonly regarded as socially excluded is that most policy making at a national level within the EU focuses on exclusion at the level of the household. Thus women are not viewed as suffering from social exclusion, yet single parents are. There are 2.3 million lone parents in the UK, 90% of whom are women. The evidence presented in this chapter shows that women as a group are socially excluded, but as individuals their exclusion is determined at a household level—through their relationship with a male partner. Using the Burchardt et al. operationalisation of social exclusion, a woman could be doing only domestic work, with no independent income and no social interaction beyond family members, yet not defined as socially excluded. However, the present chapter demonstrates that the Burchardt, Le Grand and Piachaud (2002) framework can also be used to demonstrate that women, as a group within society, experience social exclusion in far greater proportions than the proportions of households identified by their original analyses.

In their original conceptualization, Burchardt, Le Grand and Piachaud (1999) focused on the amount of social exclusion (what they termed "total social exclusion") and left open the extent to which this level of social exclusion is problematic. In their subsequent work, Burchardt, Le Grand and Piachaud (2002) stated that the volitional nature of exclusion proved too difficult to operationalise and argued that "voluntary non participation is unlikely where the thresholds for participation are set very low". Barry (2002) suggests that any apparently voluntary social exclusion should be viewed sceptically, that any withdrawal from participation may reflect the limitation of options available and thus may simply be an alternative to discrimination or other negative experiences. Further, Barry (2002) suggests that "individuals or groups are socially excluded if they are denied the opportunity of participation, whether they actually desire to participate or not".

Women's role in society as mothers, carers and homemakers is a key factor in their more limited participation in public life, and in the activities which may determine social inclusion. A key question is whether women choose to be socially excluded? And does it matter?

Women's Work Orientation

The concept of women's choices has been extensively debated within sociology, economics and social policy in relation to women's employment, and in debates surrounding the reconciliation of work and family life (e.g. Crompton & Harris, 1998; Fagan & Rubery, 1996; Hakim, 1991, 2000, 2005; Houston & Marks, 2005). Crompton and Harris (1998) have argued that the work patterns of women are a product of their particular circumstances, their opportunities and constraints, and the decisions that they make in response to these. They suggested that work and home orientations might fluctuate according to occupation, life cycle and national context. By contrast, Preference Theory (Hakim, 2000) states that women in affluent societies can make a real choice between family work and market work. Hakim argues that women can be classified as home-centred (20 %), adaptive (60 %), or work-centred (20 %). She states:

> A minority of women have no interest in employment, careers, or economic independence and do not plan to work long term unless things go seriously wrong for them. Their aim is to marry as well as they can and give up paid employment to become full-time homemakers and mothers. . . . In contrast, other women actively reject the sexual division of labour in the home, expect to work full-time and continuously throughout life. . . . The third group is numerically dominant: women who are determined to combine employment and family work, so become secondary earners. They may work full-time early in life, but later switch to part-time jobs on a semi-permanent basis, and/or to intermittent employment. (Hakim, 2000, p. 189)

Hakim (2000) argues that adaptive women do not want to make a choice between work and family—they want both and "if they give priority to family or to paid work, it is a temporary emphasis rather than a lifetime commitment". Only adaptive women are influenced by life-cycle changes; as a consequence, they are less likely to make significant achievements in the world of work because they prefer a balanced life. By contrast, work and home-centred women remain committed to these domains across the lifespan. Hakim (2000) suggests that even childless women may be home-centred, prioritizing the domestic sphere, and that women who are work-centred may choose to be childless or will have children "in the same ways as among men, as an expression of normality and a weekend hobby". Hakim's primary argument is that women can now make choices about the balance between work and home, and these choices underpin different behavioural outcomes.

McRae (2003) conducted analyses of longitudinal data from the UK's maternity rights surveys which include items on women's work histories and attitudes. She concluded that her findings provided support for Hakim's argument that employment careers are centrally important for only a minority of women, but that there was little evidence to support the assertion that it is preferences that determine work behaviour. McRae's analysis demonstrated that only 10 % of first-time mothers in the UK had maintained full-time employment by the time their first child was 11 years old. McRae (2003) suggests that women with similar preferences, but different capacities for overcoming constraints, may have very different work patterns.

Work and Family Life

Houston and Marks (2003, 2005) report findings from a longitudinal study of over 400 women which examined the determinants of first-time mother's intentions about work and childcare, and their experiences during the 3 years after the birth of their child. This work has also resulted in analysis of women's preferences and the extent to which they are able to work in accordance with the preferences they express before their first child is born. Houston and Marks (2005) found that around 20 % of first-time mothers made an active decision not to return to work, this had increased to 35 % by the time the first child was 3 years old and a second child had been born. Around half of women with pre-school children in the UK do not work (ONS, 2005). In the Houston and Marks study, the women who gave up paid work in order to care for their child held a very strong belief that this is the best thing for their child and the "right" thing to do. Qualitative data showed a strong element of making a decision based on morality, and sometimes sacrifice. The capacity of male partners to provide support—both moral and practical—was a key determinant of women's intentions to remain in the labour market (Houston & Marks, 2003).

Houston and Marks (2003) found that the majority of women were able to return to work after the birth of their first child, in a manner consistent with their preferences. However, 24 % of women who expressed an intention to work after their maternity leave either did not work or worked less than they had intended to. This study also demonstrated that the amount of planning women had done prior to their maternity leave and the support provided by their workplace were causal factors in determining whether women were able to carry out their intentions to return to work. While these findings can be interpreted as consistent with Preference Theory (Hakim, 2000), they also support the argument that personal and structural constraints determine whether women are able to fulfil their ambitions for work, if they also choose to have children.

When their children were 3 years old, the mothers in their study were asked by Houston and Marks (2005) what they would do about work and childcare if all options were available to them, and the income of the household were unaffected. Half of those who were not working said their preference would be to do some work outside the home. However, virtually none of the women, whatever their working pattern, said they would choose to have both partners working full-time (only 1.3 % wanted this option). There was strong support for the sharing of work and family roles between parents and frustration that current norms and working patterns made this difficult (Houston & Marks, 2005). Houston and Waumsley (2003) also demonstrated strong support amongst both men and women for working flexibly and sharing childcare and work in the home. However, this study also demonstrated concern about the impact of flexible working on job security and career success.

Universal childcare was part of the feminist manifesto in the 1960s and 1970s and state-funded childcare for all was a key Equal Opportunities Commission campaign in the late 1980s. The Labour Government in the UK initially focused on day care as a means of increasing women's participation in the labour market and in increasing opportunities for lone parents and children living in poverty. However, women's work patterns (ONS, 2007) and preferences (Houston & Marks, 2005; Houston & Waumsley, 2003) would appear to be for more flexible part-time work and family-based childcare before the age of 2 or 3. These preferences are in line with evidence that day care may have negative effects on some aspects of social and emotional development in children under 2 (Melhuish *et al.*, 1999).

Women still tend to take the largest share of childcare, mothers doing three quarters of childcare during the week and two thirds at weekends (The Time Use Survey, 2005). Women are also most likely to care for elderly or disabled relatives and friends, and are most likely to be carers in all age groups under 75 years (Carers UK, 2005). Crompton, Brockman and Lyonette (2005) show that whilst gender role attitudes became less traditional in the UK between 1994 and 2002, there has been little change in the gendered allocation of household tasks, suggesting a stabilizing of men's involvement in domestic work. They suggest that intensification of work may be making increased participation in domestic work by men more difficult.

CONCLUSION

From the evidence available, it is perhaps possible to conclude that women do seem to choose to take more responsibility for domestic and caring roles than do men and that the consequence of this "private" engagement may be less time and/or inclination to engage in "public" activities which determine social inclusion. However, following Barry (2002), it can be argued that women's choices in relation to activities which determine inclusion may simply reflect the limitation of options available to them. Legislation in Western Europe over the last 40 years has ensured that women and men have legal equality. However, the present analysis has demonstrated that they do not have equal participation in the key activities of their society—consumption, production, political engagement and social interaction.

Women's social exclusion is problematic. Nationally, public life remains male-dominated and is thus not representative of half the population. This inevitably determines the cultures and customs of public life, which in turn perpetuate women's social exclusion.

ACKNOWLEDGEMENT

Part of this work was supported by a grant 'Paid and Unpaid Work in Early Parenthood' number 212 25 2607 from the ESRC.

I would like to thank Helen Grimshaw, Economic Advisor to the Women and Work Commission, for comments and material for this chapter. The views expressed are however the author's own.

REFERENCES

Annual Survey of Hours and Earnings (ASHE). (2006). Office for National Statistics.

Aston, J., Clegg, M., Diplock, E., Ritchie, H. & Willison, R. (2004). Interim Update of Key Indicators of Women's Position in Britain, WEU/DTI, London.

Barry, B. (2002). Social exclusion, social isolation, and the distribution of income. In J. Hills, J. Le Grand & D. Piachaud (eds), *Understanding Social Exclusion*. Oxford: Oxford University Press.

Burchardt, T., Le Grand, J. & Piachaud, D. (1999). Social exclusion in Britain 1991–1995. *Social Policy and Administration*, *13*(3), 227–244.

Burchardt, T., Le Grand, J. & Piachaud, D. (2002). Degrees of exclusion: developing a dynamic multidimensional measure. In J. Hills, J. Le Grand & D. Piachaud (eds), *Understanding Social Exclusion*. Oxford: Oxford University Press.

Carers UK. (2005). *We Care, Do You?* Sheffield Hallam University, ACE National Action for Carers and Employment.

Crompton, R. & Harris, F. (1998). Explaining women's employment patterns: orientations to work revisited. *British Journal of Sociology*, *30*, 427–425.

Crompton, R., Brockman, M. & Lyonette, C. (2005). Attitudes, women's employment and the domestic division of labour: a cross national analysis in two halves. *Work, Employment and Society*, *19*(2), 213–233.

European Social Survey. (2002). www.eruopeansocialsurvey.org

Fagan, C. & Rubery, J. (1996). The salience of the part-time divide in the European Union. *European Sociological Review*, *12*, 227–250.

Family Resources Survey. (2003/4). Retrieved from www.dwp.gov.uk/asd/frs

Francesconi, M. & Gosling, A. (2005). Career paths of part-time workers. Equal Opportunities Commission, Working Paper Series No. 19. University of Essex.

Green, F. (2005). *Trends in the Proportions of Overeducated and Under Educated Workers—Analysis of Skills Survey Data*. Women and Work Commission.

Hakim, C. (1991). Grateful slaves and self-made women: fact and fantasy in women's work orientations. *European Sociological Review*, *7*, 101–121.

Hakim, C. (2000). *Work-Lifestyle Choices in the 21st Century: Preference Theory*. Oxford: Oxford University Press.

Hakim, C. (2004). *Key Issues in Women's Work: Female Heterogeneity and the Polarisation of Women's Employment*. London: Athlone Press.

Hakim, C. (2005). Sex differences in work-life balance goals. In D.M. Houston (ed.), *Work Life Balance in the Twenty First Century*. London: Palgrave.

Hills, J. Le Grand, J. & Piachaud, D. (eds) (2002). *Understanding Social Exclusion*. Oxford: Oxford University Press.

Houston, D.M. & Marks, G. (2003). The role of planning and workplace support in returning to work after maternity leave. British Journal of Industrial Relations, *41*, 197–214.

Houston, D.M. & Marks, G. (2005). Working, caring and sharing: work-life dilemmas in early motherhood. In D.M. Houston (ed.), Work Life Balance in the Twenty-First Century. London: Palgrave Macmillan.

Houston, D.M. & Marks, G. (2007). Predicting the work intentions and behaviour of first-time mothers using the theory of planned behaviour. (Paper under editorial consideration)

Houston, D.M. & Waumsley, J.A. (2003). Attitudes to Work and Family Life. Bristol: JRF Policy Press.

Lader, D., Short, S. & Gershuny, J. (2006). *The Time Use Survey, 2005: How We Spend our Time*. London: ONS.

Manning, A. & Petrongolo, B. (2004). *The Part-time Pay Penalty*. Women and Equality Unit, DTI.

McRae, S. (2003). Constraints and choices in mothers' employment careers: a consideration of Hakim's Preference Theory. *British Journal of Sociology, 54*, 317–338.

Melhuish, E.C., Sylva, K., Sammons, P., *et al.* (1999). *The Effective Provision of Pre-school Education (EPPE) Project: Technical Paper 4—Parent, Family and Child Characteristics in Relation to Type of Pre-school and Socio-economic Differences.* London: DfEE / Institute of Education, University of London.

Office for National Statistics (ONS). (2005). Labour Force Survey. www.statistics.gov.uk

Office for National Statistics (ONS). (2007). Labour Market Statistics: First Release. www.statistics.gov.uk

Piachaud, D. & Sutherland, H. (2002). Child poverty. In J. Hills, J. Le Grand & D. Piachaud (eds), *Understanding Social Exclusion.* Oxford: Oxford University Press.

Rubery, J., Grimshaw, D., Fagan, C., *et al.* (2003). Gender equality still on the European agenda: but for how long? *Industrial Relations Journal, 34*, 477–497.

Social Trends. (2006). Office for National Statistics, London.

The Electoral Commission. (2004). *Gender and Political Participation.* London: The Electoral Commission.

The Time Use Survey. (2005). Office for National Statistics.

Women and Equality Unit (WEU). (2006). Individual Incomes of Men and Women, London, DTI.

CHAPTER 3

The Social Psychology of Exclusion

Paul Hutchison

London Metropolitan University, United Kingdom

Dominic Abrams

University of Kent, United Kingdom

and

Julie Christian

University of Birmingham, United Kingdom

ABSTRACT

This chapter reviews research on the consequences of being excluded from desired social relationships or groups, as well as the social psychological processes through which this occurs. Exclusion challenges people's fundamental need to belong to a social unit. It causes a number of dysfunctional reactions including lowered self-esteem, greater anger, inability to reason well, depression and anxiety, and self-defeating perceptions and behaviours. Being excluded also evokes antisocial and aggressive responses, most likely because of the threat it poses to people's need for control. Other responses are more passive and include withdrawal or self-harm, whereas more constructive responses include trying harder to engage with the majority or conforming more strongly to relevant norms. Social categories and groups can serve both as the target of and a haven from social exclusion. Under certain conditions, people may develop a strong political commitment to a devalued or excluded in-group. Additionally, groups may use exclusion as a means of controlling both the behaviour of individual members and the subjective validity of the group's values or norms. When these values are threatened, it is more likely that groups will display intolerance and attempt to increase their internal cohesiveness. Strategies that promote intergroup contact on the one hand, and a shared sense of identity on the other, might go some way towards promoting inclusionary responses by both the excluders and excluded, respectively.

Multidisciplinary Handbook of Social Exclusion Research. Edited by D. Abrams, J. Christian and D. Gordon.
© 2007 John Wiley & Sons, Ltd.

THE SOCIAL PSYCHOLOGY OF EXCLUSION

Social exclusion is a complex concept that encompasses a variety of interconnected processes and problems. It has far-reaching consequences for individuals and groups and has been linked to a host of negative outcomes, including poor health and well-being, academic underachievement, antisocial and criminal behaviour, and reduced access to housing, employment and social justice (see Abrams, Hogg & Marques, 2005). Recent years have witnessed a dramatic increase in social psychological research on both the causes and consequences of social exclusion. Researchers have often attempted to delineate meaningful distinctions between various different types of exclusion experiences (e.g. Leary, 2005), but it remains unclear whether these result in different types of outcomes for the individuals and groups involved. In this chapter we use the term social exclusion to refer to the consequences of being excluded, rejected, or marginalized from desired relationships or groups as well as the social psychological processes through which this occurs. The chapter is organized into four sections. The first section reviews research on the psychological and behavioural correlates and consequences of social exclusion for targeted individuals and groups. The second section reviews research on how people react to and cope with group-based exclusion and discrimination. The third section focuses on the intra- and intergroup dynamics that predict when groups will choose to include or exclude others. The final section focuses on some ongoing lines of research that might usefully inform policy development.

CONSEQUENCES OF SOCIAL EXCLUSION FOR TARGETED INDIVIDUALS AND GROUPS

Most people, at some point in their lives, have had the experience of feeling excluded or being rejected by significant others. Almost without exception, the consequences of social exclusion for targeted individuals and groups are negative. This may be related to a basic human need to belong. It has been suggested that after basic survival needs such as the need for nourishment and the need for shelter, the need to belong is one of the strongest human motivations (Baumeister & Leary, 1995; see also Brewer, 1991). Similarly, developmental theorists have argued that people have a basic need to form attachments with others in order to feel secure (Bowlby, 1973). These needs may have an evolutionary basis in that people who formed and maintained strong bonds with others may have been better equipped to survive and reproduce than those living alone (Leary, 2001). Perhaps as a consequence, people will devote often considerable time and energy to forming and maintaining social attachments and are negatively affected when they are absent or break down (Baumeister & Leary, 1995; Leary, 1990; Williams, 2001).

Psychological and Emotional Responses to Social Exclusion

Many studies have examined people's reactions to social exclusion on various self-report measures of psychological adjustment, well-being and affect. Several studies have shown that people who are excluded from desired relationships or groups feel a range of negative emotions, including sadness, disappointment, jealousy, anger and shame (e.g. Baumeister & Tice, 1990; Leary, 1990; Marcus & Askari, 1999; Williams, Cheung & Choi, 2000). Being excluded also makes people more anxious (Barden *et al.*, 1985; Baumeister & Tice, 1990; Hoyle & Crawford, 1994) and reduces their life satisfaction, sense of meaningful existence and hope (Gonsalkorale & Williams, 2007; Smith & Williams, 2004; Social Exclusion Unit, 2001; Williams, Cheung & Choi, 2000; Zadro, Williams & Richardson, 2004). These effects emerge regardless of the source of exclusion. For example, Gonsalko-rale and Williams (2007) found that people who were rejected by despised out-group members found this equally aversive as people who were rejected by an in-group or a rival out-group. Moreover, when people are excluded from a group, they lose all the psychological and material benefits associated with membership—e.g. social networks, social and informational support, access to resources, and so on. It is therefore not surprising that people often feel a reduction in self-efficacy following social exclusion (McLaughlin-Volpe *et al.*, 2005). Reduced self-efficacy can in turn undermine perceptions of control, which itself has been shown to correlate with a range of negative emotions, including anxiety, frustration and anger (Abramson, Seligman & Teasdale, 1978; Deci & Ryan, 1991; Dweck & Leggett, 1988; McLaughlin-Volpe *et al.*, 2005; Skinner, 1992).

Other research suggests that people's sense of belonging may be reduced following social exclusion (Gonsalkorale & Williams, 2007; Smith & Williams, 2004; Williams, Cheung & Choi, 2000; Zadro, Williams & Richardson, 2004). People with a lowered sense of belonging are also more likely to experience a range of ill effects, including depression (e.g. Cuijpers & van Lammeren, 1999; Hagerty *et al.*, 1996; Hoyle & Crawford, 1994; McLaren *et al.*, 2001), negative affect (e.g. Barden *et al.*, 1985; Baumeister & Tice, 1990; Black & Hutchison, 2007), and low self-esteem and psychological well-being (e.g. Baumeister & Leary, 1995; Black & Hutchison, 2007; Coyne & Downey, 1991; Ganster & Victor, 1988). Similarly, individuals who report more cultural estrangement or who perceive themselves as misfits (Cozzarelli & Karafa, 1998) score higher on self-report measures of depression and anxiety (Bernard, Gebauer & Maio, 2006). Additionally, a considerable amount of research has reported reductions in self-esteem following social exclusion or rejection experiences (Leary, 1990; Leary *et al.*, 1995; Sommer *et al.*, 2001; Spanier & Casto, 1979; Williams, Cheung & Choi, 2000; Zadro, Williams & Richardson, 2004).

The feeling of being excluded is also akin to physical pain (MacDonald & Leary, 2005). Williams and Fitness (2004, cited in Williams, 2007) found that when people were asked to recall physically or socially painful events, currently experienced pain was greater for recalled social pain experiences, especially those that involved rejection or ostracism. Moreover, Eisenberger, Lieberman and Williams (2003) used functional magnetic resonance imaging (*f*MRI) to examine the neural correlates of social exclusion and found that the same region of the brain that is activated during the experience of physical pain is also activated during social exclusion.

When feelings of exclusion persist over extended periods of time, chronic expectations of exclusion may result (Mendoza-Denton *et al.*, 2002). People who develop such expectations are more likely to feel depressed, have low self-esteem and experience more negative affect than those who expect to be accepted (Ayduk, Downey & Kim, 2001; Downey & Feldman, 1996; Mendoza-Denton *et al.*, 2002). Such individuals may lack the confidence and motivation to seek out new social relationships and may attribute their marginal status to their own perceived deficiencies (Crocker & Major, 1989; Crocker, Major & Steele,

1998; Hortulanus, Machielse & Meeuwesen, 2006). Consequently, exclusion becomes a self-perpetuating process.

Social Exclusion and Health

Increasingly, researchers have been giving attention to the effects of social exclusion on the physical health and well-being of members of socially excluded or marginalized groups. The majority of this work has focused on health disparities across racial and ethnic groups. Such disparities have been repeatedly documented in both the United Kingdom (e.g. Bhopal, 2007; Erens, Primatesta & Prior, 2001; Harding & Maxwell, 1997; Marmot *et al.*, 1984; Nazroo, 2003; Parliamentary Office of Science and Technology, 2007; Rudat, 1994; Social Exclusion Unit, 2001) and the United States (e.g. Geronimus *et al.*, 1996; Heckler, 1985; McCord & Freeman, 1990; MMWR, 2005; Williams, 1995; Williams & Jackson, 2005). In the United Kingdom, ethnic minorities report some of the poorest levels of health. Surveys continually show that Black and ethnic minority groups as a whole are more likely to report ill-health, and that ill-health in members of such groups starts at a younger age than in White British people. For example, Black and ethnic minority groups tend to have higher rates of cardiovascular disease than White British people and are more likely to die of a stroke. Such groups also face significantly higher levels of stress and mental health problems (Parliamentary Office of Science and Technology, 2007; Social Exclusion Unit, 2001). Likewise, in the United States, compared to all other major racial groups, Black Americans have the highest rates of morbidity and mortality for almost all diseases. Black Americans also have higher infant mortality rates, higher disability rates and shorter life expectancies (Allison, 1998; Feagin & McKinney, 2003; Geronimus *et al.*, 1996; Kochanek *et al.*, 2004; Levine *et al.*, 2001; Major & O'Brien, 2005; MMWR, 2005; Smith *et al.*, 1998; Williams, 1995; Williams & Jackson, 2005).

Health disparities that affect ethnic and racial groups no doubt arise from many different factors, such as cultural differences in lifestyle, material wealth, educational attainment, job security, housing conditions and access to healthcare services (Mays, Cochran & Barnes, 2007; Parliamentary Office of Science and Technology, 2007; Williams, Spencer & Jackson, 1999). Controversially, some researchers have argued that these disparities may be biologically determined (Rushton, 1995). However, there is growing consensus that it is scientifically untenable to view racial categories as representing biological distinctiveness (e.g. Braun, 2002; Cooper & David, 1986; Gould, 1977; Lewontin, 1972; Williams, 1997). More compelling accounts suggest that such disparities are shaped by social and economic inequalities that are reflected in discrepancies in access to health-related services and resources (e.g. Marmot, 2005; Percival, Chapter 9; Williams & Jackson, 2005). Indeed, many of the groups identified as having the poorest health in most countries are also those that experience significantly poorer access to employment, education and healthcare services (Boardman, 2004; Link & Phelan, 2001; Roberts, 1997, 1999). Such groups are also more likely to have lower incomes and live in high-crime areas in unpopular and overcrowded housing (Social Exclusion Unit, 2001). However, social and economic inequalities alone cannot explain all of the reported health disparities across racial and ethnic groups: even when socio-economic variables are controlled for, significant disparities remain (e.g. Franks *et al.*, 2006).

Another social process that may account for health disparities across racial and ethnic groups is pervasive discrimination. Some researchers have suggested that race-based prejudice or discrimination, whether experienced or perceived, may be as important as objective life circumstances in predicting health-related outcomes among socially excluded and marginalized groups (Allison, 1998; Branscombe, Schmitt & Harvey, 1999; Clark, 2003; Clark, Anderson & Williams, 1999; Cochran & Mays, 1994; Cooper, 1993; Everson-Rose & Lewis, 2005; Finch, Kolody & Vega, 2000; Harrell, Merritt & Kalu, 1998; Krieger et al., 1993; Nazroo, 2003; Williams, Spencer & Jackson, 1999). Discrimination may be viewed as a type of social exclusion to the extent that it confirms to the targets that they are not valued as potential in-group members (Crocker, Major & Steele, 1998). Consistent with this, emotional responses to discrimination have been shown to be similar to those reported in studies on the effects of social exclusion or rejection (Armstead et al., 1989; Branscombe, Schmitt & Harvey, 1999; Essed, 1991; Feagin, 1991; Swim et al., 2001). Moreover, experiences of racial discrimination have been shown to correlate with self-reported poor health, depressive symptoms, diagnosed depression and lower levels of life satisfaction among Black Americans (Jackson, Williams & Torres, 1995, cited in Williams, Spencer & Jackson, 1999) and with depressive symptoms in a sample of immigrant youths in the USA (Rumbaut, 1994). Additionally, backlash aimed at Iraqi refugees has been related to poor physical and mental health, as well as post-traumatic stress disorder (Kira et al., 2006). There is also evidence of a dose–response relationship between people's experiences of racial discrimination and their psychological distress. Sander Thompson (1996) found that psychological distress symptoms (e.g. nightmares, intrusive thoughts and images) were more pronounced when the level of racism experienced was moderate or severe than when it was mild.

Similar trends have emerged in research on perceptions of discrimination. People's perceptions of discrimination have been shown to correlate with increasing anger, anxiety, hopelessness, worthlessness, resentment and fear (e.g. Armstead et al., 1989; Branscombe, Schmitt & Harvey, 1999; Essed, 1991; Feagin, 1991; Swim et al., 2001). Moreover, perceptions of racial discrimination were shown to correlate with resting blood pressure levels among Black Americans (James et al., 1984; Krieger, 1990; Krieger & Sidney, 1996) and were associated with increasing alcohol consumption (Taylor & Jackson, 1990) and smoking (Landrine & Klonoff, 2000) among Black American adults.

It is not only among racial and ethnic groups that the negative effects of discrimination on health and well-being have been observed. Schmitt et al. (2002) found that perceived prejudice against women was inversely related to self-reported psychological well-being (depression, anxiety, self-esteem and life satisfaction). Along similar lines, Greenhill and Hutchison (2007) found that women who experienced gender-based discrimination at work reported increased levels of work-related stress. Similarly, Adler et al. (2000) found that subjective social status among a sample of women was related to psychological and physiological health, even having controlled for objective indicators of social status (see also Ostrove et al., 2000).

Behavioural Responses to Social Exclusion

The preceding evidence suggests that the effects of social exclusion on the health and well-being of targeted individuals and groups are uniformly negative. In contrast, behavioural responses are typically more varied. Some studies suggest that a link exists between social exclusion and antisocial, aggressive, and self-defeating behaviours, whereas other research has provided evidence of prosocial and conciliatory responses to exclusion and rejection experiences.

Antisocial and aggressive responses to social exclusion

People who are socially excluded may seek revenge, criticize the group from which they are excluded and potentially even harm it (Lewin, 1948; Schuetz, 1944; Twenge et al., 2001). In a series of laboratory experiments, Twenge and colleagues found that, relative to included individuals, those who were excluded were more aggressive towards other people (Twenge et al., 2001), were less willing to assist or cooperate with others (Twenge et al., 2007), and were more likely engage in risky, unhealthy and self-defeating behaviours (Twenge, Catanese & Baumeister, 2002). Along similar lines, Dion and Earn (1975) found that Jewish participants displayed significantly higher levels of aggression in a manipulated "discrimination" condition than did those in a "no discrimination" condition.

Similar trends appear in wider society. For example, children who are rejected by their peers engage in less prosocial and more antisocial behaviours than those who are accepted (Asher & Coie, 1990; Mize & Ladd, 1988). In addition, longitudinal research has shown that early peer rejection reliably predicts aggressive adolescent behaviours (Dodge et al., 2003). There is also evidence that perpetrators of antisocial and violent behaviour are predominantly young males who do not have close relationships with their family or age-mates (Garbarino, 1999; Social Exclusion Unit, 2001; Walsh, Beyer & Petee, 1987). Furthermore, a study of diary recordings of individuals involved in school shootings in the USA revealed that the majority of perpetrators had been somehow excluded or rejected in the period leading up to the shooting (Leary et al., 2003). Similarly, a study of men who killed their wives found that a husband's rejection by his spouse was the most common precipitant of the fatal incident (Barnard et al., 1982).

This tendency of excluded people to be aggressive may be a result of threats to their basic needs for control (Williams, 2001). Several studies suggest that the more that exclusion diminishes an individual's sense of control, the more likely that person will respond with aggression (Leary, Twenge & Quinlivan, 2006; Warburton, Williams & Cairns, 2006). This was illustrated in a laboratory experiment by Warburton, Williams and Cairns, (2006), in which participants were either included or excluded in an initial group task and then exposed to aversive stimuli, the onset of which they either could or could not control. Initially excluded individuals without control were more aggressive than others to strangers on a subsequent task, whereas excluded participants with control were no more aggressive than those who were initially included. This suggests that acts of aggression may provide a sense of control for those who feel a lack of control due to their excluded or marginalized status.

Passive and self-defeating responses to social exclusion

Other people react more passively to social exclusion. Some people respond by distancing themselves from the group from which they have been excluded. Others withdraw completely from situations and relationships where the potential for exclusion exists. For example, children who feel excluded at school or who feel that they are treated differently because they belong to a stigmatized group may drop out of school (Buhs, Ladd & Herald, 2006; Steele, 1997). Individuals with disabilities may avoid places where they feel that a lack of appropriate facilities will prevent them from full participation (Morris, 2001). Homosexuals may avoid institutions with a history of anti-gay prejudice such as the church or the military (Wells-Petry, 1993). Women may avoid pursuing careers in organizations where they feel they will be denied the privileges and opportunities afforded to similarly qualified men (Houston, Chapter 2). Although withdrawal of this type can often provide a temporary reprieve from the immediately aversive consequences of being rejected or ostracized, the longer term prospects for those involved are far from positive. Several studies have found that people who respond passively to discrimination are up to four times more likely to experience health problems than those who respond actively (Krieger, 1990; Krieger & Sidney, 1996). Moreover, withdrawal can be especially harmful if participation is important to long-term success, such as performance at school or work (Buhs, Ladd & Herald, 2006). Another consequence is that other people may use an individual's withdrawal as a rationale for further exclusion (Major & Eccleston, 2005).

Social exclusion has also been found to correlate with instances of suicide and suicide ideation. Durkheim (1951) argued that a lack of social integration was related to suicide rates in different societies. Among the people Durkheim identified as being most at risk are those that are extremely individuated, have limited linkages to family and community, are perceived as misfits, are alienated, and/or suffer from thwarted opportunities. Recent research corroborates these findings: a feeling of not belonging or of being disconnected from others, a sense of isolation, alienation, abandonment, rejection and lack of support networks have all been shown to correlate with suicide rates in different societies (e.g. Baker, 1990; Bateman, 2001; Blum et al., 2000; Boardman et al., 1999; Gibbs, 1997; Joiner, 2005; Lewinsohn, Rohde & Seeley, 1993; Shneidman, 1993; Towl, Snow & McHugh, 2002). Similar trends emerge in research on self-harm (e.g. Crighton & Towl, 2002; Gratz, 2003). In contrast, strong family ties (Compton, Thompson & Kaslow, 2005), religious affiliations (Dervic et al., 2004) and engagement in collective leisure activities (Bailey & McLaren, 2005) are all associated with a sense of belonging or connectedness, which can buffer negative thought processes and self-defeating behaviours.

Prosocial and conciliatory reactions to social exclusion

The preceding evidence suggests that a feeling of being excluded or of not belonging may lead those involved to behave in ways that will increase their excluded status, whether intentionally or not. In contrast, several studies have shown that people often try to change or alleviate their exclusion by behaving in prosocial or conciliatory ways. This might involve working harder for the group or conforming to the opinions of others. Along these lines, Williams and Sommer (1997) found that individuals who had been excluded from a task worked harder on a subsequent task in which the contributions of individual group members were combined to form a group total than on a task in which individual contributions were not combined. Additionally, Williams, Cheung and Choi (2000) found that targets of exclusion were more likely than their included counterparts to conform to the unanimous but incorrect opinions of others. Other studies suggest that excluded individuals often behave in ways that will endear themselves to others. Perhaps as a consequence, such people are more likely to be influenced by authoritative figures and extremist groups (Williams, 2001).

Other research suggests that group members may respond to the threat of exclusion by emphasizing their prototypicality—their representativeness and fit to the group's core values and norms (Turner *et al.*, 1987). Several studies have shown that prototypical in-group members are generally more popular and have more influence in the group than non-prototypical members (Hogg, 1992; Marques & Paez, 1994; Turner, 1991). Consequently, individuals may feel threatened by events, interactions or outcomes that suggest that they have a peripheral or marginal status within the group. Such people may respond by emphasizing their credentials for inclusion. This might involve aligning themselves closer to the group prototype, rejecting other people who are not a good match to the prototype or discriminating against out-group members. For example, Pickett, Bonner and Coleman (2002) found that honours students who were told that they were not typical of honours students self-stereotyped in terms of honours students more than those who believed that they were typical group members. Schmitt and Branscombe (2001) found that males who were told that they were not typical of their gender group were more negative towards other atypical males than were those who believed that they were typical males (see also Maass *et al.*, 2003). Along similar lines, Jetten *et al.* (2003) found that under threat of exclusion, highly identified university students perceived greater homogeneity among fellow university students, which could be interpreted as an attempt to feel more included (see also Pickett & Brewer, 2001).

Some evidence shows that individuals whose in-group inclusion is threatened derogate out-groups more strongly. For example, Peres (1971) showed that low status Israeli Jews displayed more intense hostility and prejudice towards Arabs than did their higher status Jewish counterparts. Along similar lines, Noel, Wann and Branscombe (1995) manipulated membership status in a desirable in-group using bogus feedback that placed participants either at the core or periphery of an attractive, socially skilled personality category. Results indicated that peripheral group members were more likely than core members to describe members of a different personality category more negatively and to endorse coercive out-group strategies, but only when their responses were to be made public. Noel *et al.* suggested that publicly derogating an out-group category may allow individuals whose inclusion is threatened to demonstrate that they are "true" group members, thereby increasing their prospects for inclusion. Together, these studies suggest that people whose membership in a group is more tenuous will advertise their commitment to in-group norms in an attempt to enhance their prospects for inclusion (see also Abrams, 1992; Abrams & Emler, 1992; Breakwell, 1979; Gonsalkorale & Williams, 2007).

COPING WITH GROUP-BASED EXCLUSION AND DISCRIMINATION

It is clear from the studies reviewed above that many instances of social exclusion are based on the shared values, beliefs or motivations of one social group vis-à-vis another. Certain people are systematically devalued and excluded from particular domains simply because they are members of a specific social category or group. Increasingly, researchers have examined the strategies that members of such groups use to cope with their devalued, marginalized or excluded status.

Social Exclusion and Group Identification

Even though membership in a devalued group can be psychologically and physically harmful, as the preceding evidence suggests, members of such groups often respond by emphasizing their loyalty and commitment to the group. This has been observed on a range of measures, including political commitment, self-stereotyping, perceived in-group homogeneity and group identification. Abrams and Emler (1992) found that young people's political affiliations in Scotland were more likely to be nationalistic the more deprived they believed Scotland to be. Foster and Matheson (1999) found that making women aware of their stigmatized status led them to self-stereotype more in terms of their gender identity (see also Abrams, Thomas & Hogg, 1990; Hogg & Turner, 1987). Along similar lines, Spears, Doosje and Ellemers (1997), across a range of social groups, found that highly identified members self-stereotyped more than low identifiers following threats to their group's status or distinctiveness, whereas this difference was absent when there was no threat to the in-group. More recently, Hutchison *et al.* (2006) found that highly committed university students defined students at their own university as a whole in more normative terms when its identity was threatened by its relatively low status than when there was no threat to the value of their university's identity.

Another way that members might display loyalty and commitment to the group is by emphasizing in-group homogeneity or cohesion. Several studies have found a relationship between threats to the in-group and perceived in-group homogeneity. Rothgerber (1997) found that university students who believed that their group had been judged unfairly by students from a rival university perceived more in-group homogeneity than did those who believed that they had been judged fairly. Along similar lines, Lee and Ottati (1995) found that Chinese students at an American university who were confronted with traits that were stereotype consistent and threatening perceived more in-group homogeneity than those confronted with non-stereotypic traits. In contrast, Chinese students confronted with traits that were stereotype consistent but non-threatening perceived more in-group heterogeneity than those who were confronted with non-stereotypic traits. Finally, Doosje, Ellemers and Spears (1995) manipulated identity threat by informing psychology students that their group was either more or less intelligent than a comparison out-group (business students) and found that, relative to low identifiers, highly identified psychology students judged their group to be more homogeneous when its status was threatened, whereas this difference was absent when there was no threat to the in-group.

It has been suggested that members of devalued or minority groups may feel threatened in terms of their self-esteem (e.g. Simon & Brown, 1987). Perceiving the in-group as homogeneous may allow individuals to feel included in a distinctive and entitative group (Campbell, 1958). It may also help in the mobilization of group members and prepare the way for collective action designed to resist and overcome the group's exclusionary status (Reicher, 1996; Simon & Klandermans, 2001; Stott, Hutchison & Drury, 2001; Tajfel & Turner, 1986; Wright, 2001). A possible implication is that although such group-based strategies may protect members from personal exclusion, the group as a whole may become more excluded from wider society.

Other research has examined directly the relationship between threats to the in-group and group identification. Branscombe, Schmitt and Harvey (1999) found that self-reported racial prejudice was associated with increasing minority group identification in a sample of African Americans (see also Gurin et al., 1969). Along similar lines, Greenhill and Hutchison (2007) found that experiences of gender discrimination in the workplace were associated with increasing gender group identification among a sample of women (see also Gurin & Townsend, 1986). Similar associations have been reported in studies conducted with groups of lesbians (Crosby et al., 1989), Jews (Rollins, 1973), people with body piercings (Jetten et al., 2001) and members of college subcultures (Cozzarelli & Karafa, 1998). Together, these studies suggest that perceiving discrimination against an important in-group may lead members to see themselves more in group-defining terms and to feel greater attachment and commitment to the group (Branscombe, Schmitt & Harvey, 1999).

Group Identification and Psychological Well-being

A related line of research suggests that there may be a link between group identification and psychological well-being. Group identification has been found to correlate positively with various measures of psychological well-being and affect. This effect has been demonstrated in studies conducted with various different groups, including African Americans (e.g. Branscombe, Schmitt & Harvey, 1999; Rowley et al., 1998), deaf people (Bat-Chava, 1994; Jambor & Eliot, 2005), older adults (Garstka et al., 2004), women (e.g. Eccleston & Major, 2004, cited in Major & O'Brien, 2005; Schmitt et al., 2002) and international students (Black & Hutchison, 2007; Schmitt, Spears & Branscombe, 2003). It has been suggested that identification with a devalued group might go some way towards alleviating some of the negative effects of discrimination or exclusion on psychological well-being (e.g. Schmitt & Branscombe, 2002). Consistent with this, Branscombe, Schmitt and Harvey (1999) found that perceived discrimination against African Americans was negatively associated with various indicators of psychological well-being (personal self-esteem, collective self-esteem and negative emotions) and positively associated with minority group identification. Moreover, minority group identification was found to attenuate the ill effects of recognizing the disadvantaged status of African Americans. Similar results were reported by Schmitt et al. (2002), who found that the more women perceived discrimination based on their gender group membership, the lower psychological well-being they reported (personal self-esteem, depression, anxiety and general life satisfaction) and the more strongly they identified with other women. Moreover, as in the Branscombe, Schmitt and Harvey (1999) study, gender identification suppressed the negative effects of perceived discrimination on well-being.

Although these studies suggest that group identification may have an important role in protecting individuals from the negative consequences of group-based exclusion or discrimination, it is not entirely clear why increased identification with a devalued group should have such a positive buffering effect (Schmitt & Branscombe, 2002). Indeed, it may appear counter-intuitive that increasing identification with a devalued group should increase rather than decrease an individual's self-esteem or well-being (cf. Abrams &

Hogg, 1988). One possibility is that affiliation with similarly devalued others provides an opportunity to receive and benefit from social support, which itself can buffer the ill effects of perceived discrimination on well-being (Schmitt & Branscombe, 2002). Consistent with this, a number of studies have reported positive relationships between social support, group identification, and various indicators of psychological health and well-being (e.g. Haslam *et al.*, 2005). For example, Haslam *et al.* (2005) examined relationships between these variables in groups exposed to extreme levels of stress and found that group identification was positively associated with perceived social support and life satisfaction, and negatively related to stress. Moreover, perceived social support mediated the relationship between group identification and life satisfaction, and group identification and stress. In other words, the more people identified with other people experiencing similar types of stress, the more social support they perceived, and the greater was their well-being. This suggests that group membership and social identification may play an important role in protecting individuals from adverse reactions to potentially harmful situations, including experiences of discrimination, marginalization and exclusion (Schmitt & Branscombe, 2002).

GROUP PROCESSES, INTERGROUP RELATIONS AND SOCIAL EXCLUSION

It is clear from the preceding evidence that groups provide a collective sense of identity for their members. They can also provide shelter, support, and a sense of belonging or connectedness. This in turn can have positive effects on psychological health and well-being, and buffer negative thought processes and self-defeating behaviours. However, it is also clear that groups have the potential to cause considerable harm to their members: members are often exiled to the margins of the group, excluded from the group altogether, and in some situations treated worse than out-group members. An increasing amount of research has examined the conditions under which this potential for harm may be realized.

Group Processes and Social Exclusion

A common finding in small group research is that when a member of a group expresses an opinion that deviates from the opinion of other members, those others will exert pressure on the deviant to conform and will reject the deviant if he or she fails to conform. Festinger (1950) argued that pressures towards uniformity within groups arise for at least two reasons. One reason is that people need to validate their opinions by having others agree with them. Another reason is that groups often require consensus to reach important goals. When there is non-uniformity in the group, people will direct most of their communications towards deviants in an attempt to persuade them to conform. Those who resist this persuasive pressure will ultimately be rejected from the group. This often takes the form of derogatory attitudes and judgments, and in some cases can result in outright exclusion from the group (e.g. Cota *et al.*, 1995; Festinger, Schachter & Back, 1950; Jones & DeCharms, 1957; Schachter, 1951).

Perhaps the most well-known study in this domain is that of Schachter (1951), who assigned students to discussion groups. One confederate in each group was instructed to agree with the majority of the group (the mode). Another two confederates were told to either consistently disagree with the group (the deviant) or to initially disagree and then increasingly agree (the slider). Among other things, it was observed that throughout the discussion, participants directed more communications towards the deviant than towards other members. However, as it became evident that the deviant would not conform (unlike the slider), communication decreased and eventually ceased altogether. Following the discussion, group members assigned one another to various tasks for future discussions and nominated one member who should be excluded from those discussions. Results showed that the most unimportant and boring tasks were assigned to the deviant, who was also excluded from future discussions more than other members.

Along similar lines, Jones and DeCharms (1957) assigned participants to groups in which a "deviant" confederate was instructed to show a lack of interest in the task and its attainment. Participants were either informed that they would be rewarded for their work on the basis of their own performance or on the basis of the group's collective performance. The deviant group member was rejected more extremely in the collective reward condition than in the individual reward condition. Similar results were reported in a study by Berkowitz and Howard (1959), in which discussion groups were asked to appraise an organizational conflict. Again, participants were told that they would be rewarded either for their own performance or the group's performance. During the course of the discussion the group learned that one member disagreed with the majority. Results showed that the disagreeing member was rejected more strongly as a prospective co-worker in the group reward condition than in the individual reward condition. Together, these studies clearly show that groups will seek to exclude members who resist pressures towards uniformity on relevant matters of opinion or who fail to contribute towards attainment of important group goals (see also Levine, 1989; Marques et al., 2001).

Social Identity and Social Exclusion

Research informed by the social identity perspective (Hogg & Abrams, 1988; Tajfel & Turner, 1979; Turner et al., 1987) has provided further insight into the role of group membership and group identification in the treatment of deviant, undesirable or non-prototypical members. According to social identity theory (Tajfel & Turner, 1979), people attain an important part of their self-concept from their memberships in different social categories or groups. When a group provides a psychologically meaningful basis for self-definition, members are motivated to establish and maintain a positive distinction between that group and other relevant out-groups. Through this process, the evaluative features of the group are assimilated and contribute to the valance of collective self-esteem (Abrams & Hogg, 1988; Luhtanen & Crocker, 1990). Excluding deviant or otherwise undesirable members from the in-group thus serves the important function of maintaining a positive and distinctive social identity (Abrams et al. 2004; Hutchison & Abrams, 2003; Marques & Paez, 1994; Marques & Yzerbyt, 1988; Yzerbyt et al., 2000).

Support for these ideas comes from numerous studies conducted with various social categories and groups showing that desirable in-group members are judged more positively than identical out-group members, whereas undesirable in-group members are judged more negatively than identical out-group members—the *black sheep effect* (e.g. Marques & Yzerbyt, 1988). It has been suggested that extreme reactions towards undesirable in-group members may reflect a motivation to exclude from the in-group those members who negatively contribute to social identity (Hutchison & Abrams, 2003; Marques & Paez, 1994). Consistent with this, Eidelman, Silvia and Biernat (2006) found that Republicans who supported the Iraq war (as did most Republicans at the time of the study) evaluated an anti-war Republican more negatively than an anti-war Democrat (most democrats opposed the war), but only when target evaluation was the participants' first response option. Given an initial opportunity to redefine the groups' boundaries so as to exclude the targets from their respective groups, liking for anti-war Republicans increased whereas liking for anti-war Democrats decreased. These findings suggest that devaluation may indeed be an attempt to exclude undesirable members from the in-group. This converges with the above-described findings reported by Schachter (1951), who observed that communication directed towards deviant group members ceased once exclusion had occurred.

Further support comes from a series of studies showing that groups are more likely to reject undesirable members when their identity is threatened externally (Branscombe *et al.*, 1993; Hutchison & Abrams, 2007; Marques, Abrams & Serôdio, 2001). Hutchison and Abrams (2007) manipulated identity threat among university students through false feedback concerning how their university compared with a rival university and found that highly identified students derogated undesirable students from their own university more extremely than similar students from the rival university, but only when they felt that their own university's identity was threatened. When there was no threat to their identity, in-group members were evaluated no differently to their out-group counterparts. Similar results were reported by Marques, Abrams, and Serôdio (2001) who, across a range of different social groups, found that rejection of in-group deviants relative to similar out-group members was reinforced when the status of the in-group was insecure rather than secure. These studies suggest that groups may selectively exclude members as a means of establishing or maintaining a positive and distinctive social identity.

Other research has assessed directly the relationship between group identification, judgements of individual group members and identity maintenance (Abrams, Rutland & Cameron, 2003; Abrams *et al.*, 2007; Hutchison & Abrams, 2003; Hutchison *et al.*, 2007; Marques *et al.*, 1998). Hutchison *et al.* (2007) asked psychology students with varying degrees of identification with the group "psychologists" to rate psychologists as a whole on various positive and negative stereotypical dimensions both before and after they read about and evaluated a desirable (competent, ethical) or an undesirable (incompetent, unethical) psychologist. Results confirmed that the more the psychology students identified with psychologists as a group, the more harshly they evaluated the undesirable psychologist and the more positively they evaluated psychologists as a whole. A second experiment focused on rival universities and required students to judge either their own university or a rival university following an encounter with a deviant and clearly undesirable student from one of the universities. Those who identified more strongly with their university judged their own university more positively after they viewed information about an undesirable in-group member, but judged the rival university more negatively after they viewed an undesirable student from that university. Together, these studies suggest that reactions to undesirable ingroup and outgroup members may reflect a strategy to protect the ingroups identity (see also Yzerbyt *et al.*, 2000).

Evidence that Inclusion of Deviants Can Benefit the Group

The research reviewed above suggests that many groups view diversity as an unwanted evil (see also Turner *et al.*, 1987). Groups either try to persuade deviants to conform or, should this fail, condemn and vilify them or exclude them from the group altogether. While it may be easy to think of examples of people who are treated in this way, perhaps justifiably so, it is also clear that deviance can serve a number of important functions for groups. Times, situations, and the needs of the group may change, and so norms and conventions must change to be adaptive in new conditions. Without deviance, however, social change would be difficult to envisage (Moscovici, 1976). According to Moscovici (1976), the power of deviants in initiating social change lies in their ability to create conflict between themselves and the majority. Confronted with a different point of view, the majority must make a decision either to stick to their existing position or accept the minority's alternative. Consistent with this reasoning, a considerable amount of research suggests that a consistent counter-normative minority can produce lasting change in the majority position (see Wood *et al.*, 1994).

There is also evidence that dissent created by in-group members can be beneficial for the group (e.g. Nemeth, Rogers & Brown, 2001; Nemeth & Staw, 1989). Several studies suggest that groups that encourage diversity of opinions function better than those that seek to maintain consensus at all costs (e.g. Janis, 1982; Postmes, Spears & Cihangir, 2001; Stasser, Stewart & Wittenbaum, 1995). Additionally, internal criticism of a group's norms or values can help to invigorate the group and set in motion positive social change (Hornsey & Imani, 2004).

Thus, although groups may seek to exchide deviant or non-prototypical group members, as much of the preceding evidence suggests, their inclusion in the group can often lead to enhanced group performance. However, for such members to be welcomed and accepted rather than condemned or excluded from the group, the group may need to have diversity as a central component of its identity. This is often the case, for example, in multicultural or individualistic societies (Hutchison *et al.*, 2006; Jetten, Postmes & McAuliffe, 2002). While some groups may feel that it is their commonalities that make them a distinctive and entitative group (Campbell, 1958), other groups may believe that it is the diversity among its members that defines the in-group and distinguishes it from other groups (Jetten, Postmes & McAuliffe, 2002; van Knippenberg & Haslam, 2003). Consistent with this, recent research suggests that reactions to non-prototypical or dissenting group members may vary as a function of group composition perceptions.

Hutchison, Jetten and Gutierrez (2007) manipulated group composition perceptions (homogenous in-group vs. heterogeneous in-group) among members of a university's halls of residence and asked participants to judge individual residents who either agreed with the majority of residents or who disagreed. Dissenting residents were judged more harshly in the homogeneous in-group condition than in the heterogeneous in-group condition. In a second study, which focused on university students in general, relative to low identifiers, highly identified students were more negative towards dissenting students in the homogeneous in-group condition, but were more positive towards dissenters in the heterogeneous in-group condition. Along similar lines, Hornsey *et al.* (2006) manipulated group norms of "individualism" or "collectivism" and asked participants to evaluate a group member who expressed an attitude either dissenting from or concordant with the in-group position. Group members with concordant attitudes were evaluated more positively than those with dissenting attitudes in the collectivist norm condition. However, for high identifiers, the preference for concordant over dissenting members was attenuated when group norms prescribed individualism. Together, these studies suggest that exclusion is not just driven by groups' desire for uniformity, but by their desire to ensure that its central values (even diversity values) are upheld (see also Abrams *et al.*, 2005).

Group Norms and Social Exclusion

Abrams, Marques and colleagues (Abrams, 2000; Abrams *et al.*, 2004, 2005; Marques *et al.*, 2001) proposed a model of *subjective group dynamics* to account for the processes through which groups selectively and strategically include or exclude members. The model follows the social identity theory-derived prediction that people generally strive to main-tain a positive and distinctive social identity via favourable intergroup comparisons (Hogg & Abrams, 1988; Tajfel & Turner, 1979). It also proposes that people are motivated to ensure that the sense of superiority that ensues from favourable intergroup comparisons is justified or valid—that it reflects an objective reality and not personal biases. This sense of validity is strengthened if in-group members are seen as sharing a common set of norms or values (Abrams, 1990, 1992; Abrams & Hogg, 1988; Marques & Paez, 1994). To this extent, groups will welcome evidence that bolsters in-group norms and will resist evidence that undermines their norms. Thus, in an intergroup context in which dissenters imply support for an opposing group's norms, normative in-group members should be preferred over deviant in-group members, whereas dissenting members of an out-group should be preferred over normative out-group members. Marques *et al.* (1998) demonstrated this effect in a series of minimal group studies in which dissenting members endorsed posi-tions in line with an out-group's norms. Abrams *et al.* (2000, 2002) found similar effects in studies with naturalistic groups, including teenagers, university students and bank employees.

The above studies suggest that reactions to deviant or dissenting group members may not always be based on the extremity of deviance or the actual behaviour of those members: groups may tolerate many kinds of diversity and idiosyncrasies among their members as long as these do not challenge norms that are "prescriptive"—those that are central to the group's identity. Further support for this idea comes from research on reac-tions to "pro-norm" deviance (Abrams *et al.*, 2000, 2002). Abrams *et al.* (2000) defined pro-norm deviance as behaviour that diverges from a group's normative position but in a direction that is nevertheless consistent with the prevailing ethos of the group—i.e. as a form of extremism (see also Ewald & Jiobu, 1985; Hughes & Coakley, 1991). Several studies suggest that groups are particularly sensitive to the direction in which members deviate. Abrams *et al.* (2000, 2002) found, across a range of social categories and groups, that pro-norm deviants were consistently treated more favourably than anti-norm deviants, and often as favourably as normative group members. This suggests that not all forms of deviance invite exclusion, but exclusionary reactions are predictable on the basis of the extent to which deviance threatens the group's core norms or values.

APPLICATIONS OF SOCIAL PSYCHOLOGICAL RESEARCH TO PROBLEMS OF SOCIAL EXCLUSION

While a considerable amount of research has focused on the psychological and behavioural consequences of being excluded from desired social groups and the dynamics surrounding social exclusion, relatively few attempts have been made to systematically apply insights from such research to the reduction of social exclusion or the promotion of inclusion. The final section of this chapter reviews findings from some ongoing lines of research that might usefully inform policy development.

Intergroup Contact Research

The contact hypothesis (Allport, 1954; Williams, 1947) proposes that bringing together members from opposing groups can reduce prejudice and improve intergroup relations. Allport (1954) suggested that positive effects of contact were more likely if various pre-requisite conditions were in place: equal status between the groups, cooperative intergroup interaction, opportunities for personal acquaintance between group members, and supportive norms legitimized through institutional support. Several other conditions were later added, including voluntary participation and intimate contact (e.g. Amir, 1976; Stephan, 1987; see Brown & Hewstone, 2005). However, in a meta-analysis, Pettigrew and Tropp (2006) found that it is not always necessary for all of these conditions be present for more positive intergroup relations to develop. Contact alone can often produce improved attitudes that generalize beyond the interacting individuals to the entire out-group.

Tests of the contact hypothesis have traditionally been conducted with the aim of improving attitudes towards racial and ethnic minority groups (e.g. Brown & Hewstone, 2005; Eller & Abrams, 2003, 2004; Hewstone & Brown, 1986; Riordan & Ruggiero, 1980). Increasingly, however, researchers have reported positive effects of contact on attitudes towards a range of socially excluded or marginalized groups, including homosexuals (Herek & Capitanio, 1996), the elderly (Abrams, Eller & Bryant, 2006; Caspi, 1984), the mentally ill (Desforges et al., 1991; Link & Cullen, 1986), people with disabilities (Makas, 1993; Yuker, 1988), people with AIDS (Werth & Lord, 1992) and homeless people (Lee, Farrell & Link, 2004).

Various extensions of the basic contact hypothesis have also been proposed. The extended contact hypothesis (Wright et al., 1997) proposes that knowledge that an in-group member has a close relationship with an out-group member can lead to more positive intergroup attitudes. In a series of studies, Wright et al. (1997) showed that respondents who perceived an in-group member to have a friend in a particular out-group or who observed an apparent cross-group friendship expressed less prejudice towards the out-group. Other research suggests that mere exposure to members of a stigmatized out-group can have beneficial effects on intergroup attitudes. For example, Lee, Farrell and Link (2004) examined attitudes towards homelessness as a function of various types of exposure: third-party information, observation in public places, interaction with homeless people, and having been or knowing someone who is or has been homeless. Results showed that all forms of exposure resulted in more positive attitudes towards homeless people. There is also evidence that simply asking people to imagine intergroup contact can improve their attitudes towards out-groups (Turner, Crisp & Lambert, 2007). When groups have a history of segregation or mutual distrust and when potential encounters might evoke anxiety, it is unlikely that people from opposing groups will view one another positively. Yet it is precisely these types of situation where interventions to prevent exclusion are needed the most. Extended contact and imagined contact effects therefore have promising implications for positive and lasting social change, in part because they can circumvent the barriers that can occur in many direct contact situations.

Considerable research has shown that greater intergroup contact promotes more positive intergroup attitudes and relations, but there is nevertheless plenty of opportunity for contact to backfire. It is therefore important to attend carefully to the circumstances and nature of contact experiences. For example, research consistently shows that the relationships between contact and prejudice tend to be weaker among members of minority groups than among members of majority groups (see Tropp & Pettigrew, 2005). These differences suggest that the same contact situation may be perceived quite differently by different groups and individuals. Thus, while encouraging interactions across group boundaries can under certain conditions improve intergroup relationships and attitudes, researchers may need to invest more effort in establishing additional types of contact experience that may augment or even exceed these benefits.

Factors that Predict Uptake of Services Aimed at Increasing Inclusion

A second line of research has examined factors that predict individuals' participation in services and programmes aimed at reducing social exclusion. Christian and colleagues (Christian & Abrams, 2003, 2004; Christian, Armitage & Abrams, 2004) conducted a series of field studies to examine issues related to homelessness and service user behaviour. Homeless people are not necessarily a homogeneous social group. Each homeless person may consider their situation to be unique and, initially at least, may feel that they have little or nothing in common with other homeless people other than a lack of a home (Christian & Abrams, 2004). Nevertheless, service providers often treat homeless people as a uniform category and they are often depicted as similar in terms of socio-economic status and other socio-demographic variables. Christian and colleague's work shows that such variables play little role in whether homeless people engage in behaviour that reduces their social exclusion.

Across seven studies (some comparative and others longitudinal), results consistently showed that social psychological variables (e.g. attitudes towards services and service uptake, intentions to participate in welfare programmes, and perceived self-control) accounted for more of the variance in behaviours likely to lead to greater inclusion than did socio-economic and demographic variables. Another potentially important finding from this research is that different psychological variables predicted service uptake over time (Christian, Armitage & Abrams, 2004). Specifically, homeless people's initial service participation was predictable from their own personal attitudes, perceptions and norms. One year later, however, these variables no longer predicted service use. Instead, service use was reliably predicted by identification with the specific service and with service case workers and other users of the service. This suggests that while individuals' initial evaluation of a service may be influential in helping introducing those people to procedures designed to increase their inclusionary status, social relationships and group identifications formed around the service are more likely to influence sustained service use (Christian & Abrams, 2004). In other words, those homeless people who over time become more psychologically engaged with a service and its providers are more likely to continue to make use of the service, and thus are more likely to find a sustainable route out of social exclusion. This suggests that psychological variables may help to offset some of the more structural determinants of social exclusion to the extent that there is scope for change. This is not to underestimate the debilitating consequences of poverty, disadvantage and group-based discrimination, but it highlights that these are only a part of the picture. More significantly, we would emphasize that whereas changes in structural factors are probably difficult and slow to achieve, relevant social psychological processes are likely to be more malleable and dynamically responsive to interventions designed to promote greater inclusion.

CONCLUSIONS

In this chapter, we have tried to convey the breadth and depth of social psychological research on social exclusion. An important point is that, to some extent, exclusion is liable to be a natural product of sustaining coherent social units. Thus, it is not always useful to pathologize either the excluders or the excluded, but rather to focus on the social psychological processes at work. We believe that analysis of these processes is important to the extent that it focuses on the actual experiences of exclusion for the individuals and groups involved and, in turn, opens potential avenues for strategic intervention aimed at promoting inclusion. This is not to say that exclusion can be dealt with only at a social psychological level, but on the other hand, the social science and social policy literature has barely considered the actual mechanisms at work or how interventions at the levels of individuals and groups might be implemented. Thus, we hope that the present contribution fills a gap in the narrative and provides a useful resource for researchers and practitioners seeking to understand and tackle problems associated with social exclusion.

REFERENCES

Abrams, D. (1990). How do group members regulate their behaviour? An integration of social identity and self-awareness theories. In D. Abrams & M.A. Hogg (eds), *Social identity theory: Constructive and Critical Advances* (pp. 89–112). London: Harvester Wheatsheaf.

Abrams, D. (1992). Processes of social identification. In G. Breakwell (ed.), *Social Psychology of Identity and the Self-concept* (pp. 57–99). San Diego: Academic Press.

Abrams, D., Eller, A. & Bryant, J. (2006). An age apart: the effects of intergenerational contact and stereotype threat on performance and intergroup bias. *Psychology and Aging, 21,* 691–702.

Abrams, D. & Emler, N.P. (1992). Self-denial as a paradox of political and regional social identity: findings from the ESRC's "16–19 Initiative". *European Journal of Social Psychology, 22,* 279–295.

Abrams, D. & Hogg, M.A. (1988). Comments on the motivational status of self-esteem in social identity and intergroup discrimination. *European Journal of Social Psychology, 18,* 317–334.

Abrams, D., Hogg, M.A. & Marques, J.M. (eds) (2005). The Social Psychology of Inclusion and Exclusion. New York: Psychology Press.

Abrams, D., Marques, J.M., Bown, N.J. & Dougill, M. (2002). Anti-norm and pro-norm deviance in the bank and on the campus: two experiments on subjective group dynamics. *Group Processes and Intergroup Relations, 5*, 163–182.

Abrams, D., Marques, J.M., Bown, N.J. & Henson, M. (2000). Pro-norm and anti-norm deviance within in-groups and out-groups. *Journal of Personality and Social Psychology, 78*, 906–912.

Abrams, D., Marques, J.M., Randsley de Moura, G., *et al.* (2004). The maintenance of entitativity: a subjective group dynamics approach. In V.Y. Yzerbyt, C.M. Judd & O. Corneille (eds), *The Psychology of Group Perception: Contributions to the Study of Homogeneity, Entitativity, and Essentialism* (pp. 361–380). Philadelphia, PA: Psychology Press.

Abrams, D., Randsley de Moura, G., Hutchison, P. & Viki, G.T. (2005). When bad becomes good (and vice versa): why social exclusion is not based on difference. In D. Abrams, M.A. Hogg & J.M. Marques (eds), *The Social Psychology of Inclusion and Exclusion* (pp. 161–190). Philadelphia, PA: Psychology Press.

Abrams, D., Rutland, A. & Cameron, L. (2003). The development of subjective group dynamics: children's judgments of normative and deviant in-group and out-group individuals. *Child Development, 74*, 1840–1856.

Abrams, D., Rutland, A., Cameron, L. & Ferrell, J. (2007). Older but wilier: in-group accountability and the development of judgments of groups and their members. *Developmental Psychology, 43*, 134–148.

Abrams, D., Thomas J. & Hogg, M.A. (1990). Numerical distinctiveness, social identity and gender salience. *British Journal of Social Psychology, 29*, 87–92.

Abramson, L.Y., Seligman, M.E.P. & Teasdale, J.D. (1978). Learned helplessness in humans: critique and reformulation. *Journal of Abnormal Psychology, 87*, 49–74.

Adler, N.E., Epel, E.S., Castallazzo, G. & Ickovics, J.R. (2000). Relationship of subjective and objective social status with psychological and physiological functioning: preliminary data in healthy white women. *Health Psychology, 19*, 586–592.

Allison, K.W. (1998). Stress and oppressed category membership. In J.K. Swim & C. Stangor (eds), *Prejudice: The Target's Perspective* (pp. 145–170). San Diego, CA: Academic Press.

Allport, G. (1954). *The Nature of Prejudice.* Reading, MA: Addison-Wesley.

Amir, Y. (1976). The role of intergroup contact in change of prejudice and ethnic relations. In P.A. Katz (ed.), *Towards the Elimination of Racism* (pp. 245–308). Elmsford, NY: Pergamon Press.

Armstead, C.A., Lawler, K.A., Gorden, G., *et al.* (1989). Relationship of racial stressors to blood pressure responses and anger expression in black college students. Special issue: race, reactivity, and blood pressure regulation. *Health Psychology, 8*, 541–556.

Asher, S.R. & Coie, J.D. (eds) (1990). *Peer Rejection in Childhood.* New York: Cambridge University Press.

Ayduk, O., Downey, G. & Kim, M. (2001). Rejection sensitivity and depression in women. *Personality and Social Psychology Bulletin, 27*, 868–877.

Bailey, M. & McLaren, S. (2005). Physical activity alone and with others as predictors of sense of belonging and mental health in retirees. *Aging & Mental Health, 9*, 82–90.

Baker, F.M. (1990). Black youth suicide: literature review with a focus on prevention. *Journal of the National Medical Association, 82*, 495–507.

Barden, R.C., Garber, J., Leiman, B., *et al.* (1985). Factors governing the effective remediation of negative affect and its cognitive and behavioral consequences. *Journal of Personality and Social Psychology, 49*, 1040–1053.

Barnard, G.W., Vera, H., Vera, M.I. & Newman, G. (1982). Till death do us part: a study of spouse murder. *Bulletin of the American Association of Psychiatry and Law, 10*, 271–280.

Bat-Chava, Y. (1994). Group identification and self-esteem of deaf adults. *Personality and Social Psychology Bulletin, 20*, 494–502.

Bateman, C. (2001).Young, black, female and miserable. *South African Medical Journal, 91*, 716–717.

Baumeister, R.F. & Leary, M.R. (1995). The need to belong: desire for interpersonal attachments as a fundamental human motivation. *Psychological Bulletin, 117*, 497–529.

Baumeister, R.F. & Tice, D.M. (1990). Anxiety and social exclusion. *Journal of Social and Clinical Psychology, 9*, 165–195.

Berkowitz, L. & Howard, R. (1959). Reaction to opinion deviates as affected by affiliation need and group member interdependence. *Sociometry*, *22*, 81–91.

Bernard, M.M., Gebauer, J.E. & Maio, G.R. (2006). Cultural estrangement: the role of personal and societal value discrepancies. *Personality and Social Psychology Bulletin*, *32*, 78–92.

Bhopal, R.S. (2007). *Ethnicity, Race, and Health in Multicultural Societies: Foundations for Better Epidemiology, Public Health, and Health Care*. Oxford: Oxford University Press.

Black, E. & Hutchison, P. (2007). *Third Culture Kids: Why Is Coming 'Home' for University So Difficult*. Unpublished dissertation. University of Leeds.

Blum, R.W., Beuhring, T., Shew, M.L., *et al.* (2000). The effects of race/ethnicity, income, and family structure on adolescent risk behaviors. *American Journal Public Health*, *90*, 1879–1884.

Boardman, A.P., Grimbaldeston, A.H., Handley, C., *et al.* (1999). The North Staffordshire Suicide Study: a case-control study of suicide in one health district. *Psychological Medicine*, *29*, 27–33.

Boardman, J.D. (2004). Stress and physical health: the role of neighborhoods as mediating and moderating mechanisms. *Social Science and Medicine*, *58*, 2473–2483.

Bowlby, J. (1973). *Attachment and Loss: Vol. 2. Separation: Anxiety and Anger*. New York: Basic Books.

Branscombe, N.R., Schmitt, M.T. & Harvey, R.D. (1999). Perceiving discrimination among African Americans: implications for group identification and well-being. *Journal of Personality and Social Psychology*, *77*, 135–149.

Branscombe, N. & Wann, D.L., Noel, J.G. & Coleman, J. (1993). In-group or out-group extremity: importance of threatened social identity. *Personality and Social Psychology Bulletin*, *17*, 381–388.

Braun, L. (2002). Race, ethnicity, and health: can genetics explain disparities? *Perspectives in Biology and Medicine*, *45*, 159–174.

Breakwell, G.M. (1979). Illegitimate group membership and inter-group differentiation. *British Journal of Social Psychology*, *18*, 141–149.

Brewer, M. (1991). The social self: on being the same and different at the same time. *Personality and Social Psychology Bulletin*, *17*, 475–482.

Brown, R.J. & Hewstone, M. (2005) An integrative theory of intergroup contact. *Advances in Experimental Social Psychology*, *37*, 255–343.

Buhs, E., Ladd, G. & Herald, S. (2006). Peer exclusion and victimization: processes that mediate the relation between peer group rejection and children's classroom engagement and achievement. *Journal of Educational Psychology*, *98*, 1–13.

Campbell, D.T. (1958). Common fate, similarity, and other indices of the status of aggregates of persons as social entities. *Behavioural Science*, *3*, 14–25.

Caspi, A. (1984). Contact hypothesis and inter-age attitudes: a field study of cross-age contact. *Social Psychology Quarterly*, *47*, 74–80.

Christian, J.N. & Abrams, D. (2003). The effects of social identification, norms and attitudes on use of outreach services by homeless people. *Journal of Community and Applied Social Psychology*, *13*, 138–157.

Christian, J.N. & Abrams, D. (2004). A tale of two cities: predicting homeless people's uptake of outreach programs in London and New York. *Basic and Applied Social Psychology*, *26*, 169–182.

Christian, J., Armitage, C.J. & Abrams, D. (2004). Predicting uptake of housing services: the role of self-categorization in the theory of planned behaviour. *Current Psychology*, *22*, 206–217.

Clark, R. (2003). Self-reported racism and social support predict blood pressure reactivity in blacks. *Annals of Behavioral Medicine*, *25*, 127–136.

Clark, R., Anderson, N.B. & Williams, D.R. (1999). Racism as a stressor for African Americans: a biopsychological model. *American Psychologist*, *54*, 805–816.

Cochran, S.D. & Mays, V.M. (1994). Depressive distress among homosexually active African American men and women. *American Journal of Psychiatry*, *151*, 524–529.

Compton, M.T., Thompson, N.J. & Kaslow, N.J. (2005). Social environment factors associated with suicide attempt among low-income African Americans: the protective role of family relationships and social support. *Social Psychiatry and Psychiatric Epidemiology*, *40*, 175–185.

Cooper, R.S. (1993). Health and the social status of blacks in the United States. *Annals of Epidemiology, 3,* 137–144.

Cooper, R.S. & David, R. (1986). The biological concept of race and its application to public health and epidemiology. *Journal of Health and Politics, Policy and Law, 11,* 97–116.

Cota, A.A., Evans, C.R., Dion, K.L., *et al.* (1995). The structure of group cohesion. *Personality and Social Psychology Bulletin, 21,* 572–580.

Coyne, J.C. & Downey, G. (1991). Social factors and psychopathology: stress, social support, and coping processes. *Annual Review of Psychology, 42,* 401–425.

Cozzarelli, C. & Karafa, J.A. (1998). Cultural estrangement and terror management theory. *Personality and Social Psychology Bulletin, 24,* 253–267.

Crighton, D. & Towl, G. (2002). Intentional self-injury. In G. Towl, L. Snow & M. McHugh (eds), *Suicide in Prisons* (pp. 48–56). Leicester: British Psychological Society.

Crocker, J. & Major, B. (1989). Social stigma and self-esteem: the self-protective properties of stigma. *Psychological Review, 26,* 608–630.

Crocker, J., Major, B. & Steele, C. (1998). Social stigma. In S. Fiske, D. Gilbert & G. Lindzey (eds), *Handbook of Social Psychology* (Vol. 2; pp. 504–553). Boston, MA: McGraw Hill.

Crosby, F.J., Pufall, A., Snyder, R.C., *et al.* (1989). The denial of personal disadvantage among you, me, and all the other ostriches. In M. Crawford & M. Gentry (eds), *Gender and Thought* (pp. 79–99). New York: Springer-Verlag.

Cuijpers, P. & van Lammeren, P. (1999). Depressive symptoms in chronically ill elderly people in residential homes. *Aging and Mental Health, 3,* 221–226.

Deci, E.L. & Ryan, R.M. (1991). A motivational approach to self: integration in personality. In R. Dienstbier (ed.), *Nebraska Symposium on Motivation* (pp. 237–288). Lincoln, NE: University of Nebraska Press.

Dervic, K., Oquendo, M.A., Grunebaum, M.F., *et al.* (2004). Religious affiliation and suicide attempt. *American Journal of Psychiatry, 161,* 2303–2308.

Desforges, D.M., Lord, C.G., Ramsey, S.L., *et al.* (1991). Effects of structured cooperative contact on changing negative attitudes toward stigmatized social groups. *Journal of Personality and Social Psychology, 60,* 531–544.

Dion, K. & Earn, B.M. (1975). The phenomenology of being a target of prejudice. *Journal of Personality and Social Psychology, 32,* 944–950.

Dodge, K.A., Lansford, J.E., Salzer Burks, V., *et al.* (2003). Peer rejection and social information-processing factors in the development of aggressive behavior problems in children. *Child Development, 74,* 374–393.

Doosje, B., Ellemers, N. & Spears, R. (1995). Perceived intragroup variability as a function of group status and identification. *Journal of Experimental Social Psychology, 31,* 410–436.

Downey, G. & Feldman, S.I. (1996). Implications of rejection sensitivity for intimate relationships. *Journal of Personality and Social Psychology, 70,* 1327–1343.

Durkheim, E. (1951). *Suicide: A Study in Sociology* (translated by J.A. Spaulding & G. Simpson). Glencoe, IL: Free Press.

Dweck, C.S. & Leggett, E. (1988). A social-cognitive approach to motivation and personality. *Psychological Review, 95,* 256–273.

Eidelman, S., Silvia, P.J. & Biernat, M. (2006). Responding to deviance: target exclusion and differential devaluation. *Personality and Social Psychology Bulletin, 32,* 1153–1164.

Eisenberger, N.I., Lieberman, M.D. & Williams, K.D. (2003). Does rejection hurt? An fMRI study of social exclusion. *Science, 302,* 290–292.

Eller, A. & Abrams, D. (2003). "Gringos" in Mexico: longitudinal effects of language school-promoted contact on intergroup bias. Special issue on the contact hypothesis. *Group Processes and Intergroup Relations, 6,* 55–75.

Eller, A. & Abrams, D. (2004). Come together: longitudinal comparisons of Pettigrew's Reformulated Intergroup Contact Model and the Common In-group Identity Model in Anglo-French and Mexican-American contexts. *European Journal of Social Psychology, 34,* 229–256.

Erens, B., Primatesta, P. & Prior, G. (2001). *Health Survey for England 1999: The Health of Ethnic Minority Groups.* London: The Stationery Office.

Essed, P. (1991). *Understanding Everyday Racism*. Knobbier Park, CA: Sage.

Everson-Rose, S.A. & Lewis, T.T. (2005). Psychosocial factors and cardiovascular disease. *Annual Review of Public Health, 26*, 469–500.

Ewald, K. & Jiobu, R.M. (1985). Explaining positive deviance: Becker's model and the case of runners and bodybuilders. *Sociology of Sport Journal, 2*, 144–156.

Feagin, J.R. (1991). The continuing significance of race: antiblack discrimination in public places. *American Sociological Review, 56*, 101–116.

Feagin, J.R. & McKinney, K.D. (2003). *The Many Costs of White Racism*. Lanham, MD: Rowman & Littlefield.

Festinger, L. (1950). Informal social communication. *Psychological Review, 57*, 271–282.

Festinger, L., Schachter, S. & Back, K. (1950). *Social Pressures in Informal Groups*. New York: Harper and Row.

Finch, B.K., Kolody, B. & Vega, W.A. (2000). Perceived discrimination and depression among Mexican-origin adults in California. *Journal of Health and Social Behavior, 41*, 295–313.

Foster, M.D. & Matheson, K. (1999). Perceiving and responding to the personal/group discrimination discrepancy. *Personality and Social Psychology Bulletin, 25*, 1319–1329.

Franks, P., Muenning, P., Lubetkin, E. & Jia, H. (2006). The burden of disease associated with being African-American in the United States and the contribution of socio-economic status. *Social Science and Medicine, 62*, 2469–2478.

Ganster, D.C. & Victor, B. (1988). The impact of social support on mental and physical health. *British Journal of Medical Psychology, 61*, 17–36.

Garbarino, J. (1999). *Lost Boys*. Old Tappan, NJ: Simon & Schuster.

Garstka, T.A., Schmitt, M.T., Branscombe, N.R. & Hummert, M.L. (2004). How young and older adults differ in their responses to perceived age discrimination. *Psychology and Aging, 19*, 326–335.

Geronimus, A.T., Bound, J., Wadimann, T.A., *et al.* (1996). Excess mortality among blacks and whites in the United States. *New England Journal of Medicine, 35*, 1552–1558.

Gibbs, J.T. (1997). African-American suicide: a cultural paradox. *Suicide and Life Threatening Behavior, 27*, 68–79.

Gonsalkorale, K. & Williams, K.D. (2007). The KKK won't let me play: ostracism even by a despised out-group hurts. *European Journal of Social Psychology*. DOI:10.1002ejsp.392

Gould, S.J. (1977). Why we should not name human races. A biological view. In S.J. Gould (ed.), *Ever Since Darwin* (pp. 231–236). New York: Norton.

Gratz, K.L. (2003). Risk factors for and functions of deliberate self-harm: an empirical and conceptual review. *Clinical Psychology: Science and Practice, 10*, 192–205.

Greenhill, M. & Hutchison, P. (2007). *Coping with Gender-based Discrimination in the Workplace: The Role of Gender Identification and Social Support*. Unpublished manuscript. University of Leeds.

Gurin, P., Gurin, G., Lao, R.C. & Beattie, M. (1969). Internal-external control and motivational dynamic of Negro youth. *Journal of Social Issues, 25*, 29–53.

Gurin, P. & Townsend, A. (1986). Properties of gender identity and their implications for gender consciousness. *British Journal of Social Psychology, 25*, 139–148.

Hagerty, B.M.K., Williams, R.A., Coyne, J.C. & Early, M.R. (1996). Sense of belonging and indicators of social and psychological functioning. *Archives of Psychiatric Nursing, 10*, 235–244.

Harding, S. & Maxwell, R. (1997). Differences in mortality of migrants. In F. Drever & M. Whitehead (eds), *Health Inequalities: Decennial Supplement No. 15*. London: The Stationary Office.

Harrell, J.P., Merritt, M. & Kalu, J. (1998). Racism, stress, and disease. In R. Jones (ed.), *African American Mental Health: Theory, Research and Intervention* (pp. 247–280). Hampton, VA: Cobb & Henry.

Haslam, S.A., O'Brien, A., Jetten, J., *et al.* (2005). Taking the strain: social identity, social support and the experience of stress. *British Journal of Social Psychology, 44*, 355–370.

Heckler, M.M. (1985). *U.S. Task Force on Black and Minority Health*. Report of the secretary's task force on black and minority health. Washington, DC: U.S. Department of Health and Human Services.

Herek, G.M. & Capitanio, J.P. (1996). "Some of my best friends": intergroup contact, concealable stigma, and heterosexuals' attitudes toward gay men and lesbians. *Personality and Social Psychology Bulletin*, 22, 412–424.

Hewstone, M. & Brown, R.J. (1986). *Contact and Conflict in Intergroup Encounters*. Oxford: Blackwell.

Hogg, M.A. (1992). *The Social Psychology of Group Cohesiveness: From Attraction to Social Identity*. Hemel Hempstead: Harvester Wheatsheaf.

Hogg, M.A. & Abrams, D. (1988). *Social Identifications: A Social Psychology of Intergroup Relations and Group Processes*. London: Routledge.

Hogg, M.A. & Turner, J.C. (1987). Intergroup behaviour, self-stereotyping and the salience of social categories. *British Journal of Social Psychology*, 26, 325–340.

Hornsey, M.J. & Imani, A. (2004). Criticizing groups from the inside and the outside: an identity perspective on the intergroup sensitivity effect. *Personality and Social Psychology Bulletin*, 30, 365–383.

Hornsey, M.J., Jetten, J., McAuliffe, B. & Hogg, M.A. (2006). The impact of individualist and collectivist group norms on evaluations of dissenting group members. *Journal of Experimental Social Psychology*, 42, 57–68.

Hortulanus, R., Machielse, A. & Meeuwesen, L. (2006). *Social Isolation in Modern Society*. Oxford: Routledge.

Hoyle, R.H. & Crawford, A.M. (1994). Use of individual-level data to investigate group phenomena issues and strategies. *Small Group Research*, 25, 464–485.

Hughes, R. & Coakley, J. (1991). Positive deviance among athletes: the implications of over-conformity to the sport ethic. *Sociology of Sport Journal*, 8, 307–325.

Hutchison, P. & Abrams, D. (2003). In-group identification moderates stereotype change in reaction to in-group deviance. *European Journal of Social Psychology*, 33, 497–506.

Hutchison, P. & Abrams, D. (2007). *Deviance and Sanctioning in Low and High Status Groups*. Unpublished manuscript. University of Leeds.

Hutchison, P., Abrams, D., Gutierrez, R. & Viki, G.T. (2007). Getting rid of the bad ones: the relationship between group identification, deviant derogation, and identity maintenance. *Journal of Experimental Social Psychology*. DOI:1016/j.jesp.2007.09.001

Hutchison, P., Jetten, J., Christian, J. & Haycraft, E. (2006). Protecting threatened identity: sticking with the group by emphasizing in-group heterogeneity. *Personality and Social Psychology Bulletin*, 32, 1620–1633.

Hutchison, P., Jetten, J. & Gutierrez, R. (2007). Fitting in by being different: Reactions to deviance in homogenous and heterogeneous groups. Manuscript submitted for publication. London Metropolitan University.

Jambor, E. & Eliot, M. (2005). Self-esteem and coping strategies among deaf students. *The Journal of Deaf Studies and Deaf Education*, 10, 63–81.

James, S.A., LaCroix, A.Z., Kleinbaum, D.G. & Strogatz, D.S. (1984). John Henryism and blood pressure differences among black men, II: the role of occupational stressors. *Journal of Behavioral Medicine*, 7, 259–275.

Janis, I.L. (1982). *Groupthink: Psychological Studies of Policy Decisions and Fiascoes* (2nd edn). Boston, MA: Houghton Mifflin.

Jetten, J., Branscombe, N.R., Schmitt, M.T. & Spears, R. (2001). Rebels with a cause: group identification as a response to perceived discrimination from the mainstream. *Personality and Social Psychology Bulletin*, 27, 1204–1213.

Jetten, J., Branscombe, N.R., Spears, R. & McKimmie, B. (2003). Predicting the paths of peripherals: the interaction of identification and future possibilities. *Personality and Social Psychology Bulletin*, 29, 130–140.

Jetten, J., Postmes, T. & McAuliffe, B.J. (2002). "We're all individuals": group norms of individualism and collectivism, levels of identification, and identity threat. *European Journal of Social Psychology*, 32, 189–207.

Joiner, T. (2005). *Why People Die by Suicide*. Cambridge, MA: Harvard University Press.

Jones, E.E. & DeCharms, R. (1957). Changes in social perception as a function of the personal relevance of behavior. *Sociometry, 20,* 175–185.

Kira, I.A., Lewandowski, L., Templin, T., *et al.* (2006). The mental health effects of retributive justice: the case of Iraqi refugees. *Journal of Muslim Mental Health, 1,* 154–169.

Kochanek, K.D., Murphy, S.L., Anderson, R.N. & Scott, C. (2004). Deaths: final data for 2002. *National Vital Statistics Report, 53,* 1–116.

Krieger, N. (1990). Racial and gender discrimination: risk factors for high blood pressure? *Social Science and Medicine, 30,* 1273–1281.

Krieger, N., Rowley, D.L., Herman, A.A., *et al.* (1993). Racism, sexism, and social class: implications for studies of health, disease, and well-being. *American Journal of Preventive Medicine, 96,* 82–122.

Krieger, N. & Sidney, S. (1996). Racial discrimination and blood pressure: the CARDIA study of young black and white women and men. *American Journal of Public Health, 86,* 1370–1378.

Landrine, H. & Klonoff, E.A. (2000). Racial discrimination and cigarette smoking among blacks: findings from two studies. *Ethnicity and Disease, 10,* 195–202.

Leary, M.R. (1990). Responses to social exclusion: social anxiety, jealousy, loneliness, depression, and low self-esteem. *Journal of Social and Clinical Psychology, 9,* 221–229.

Leary, M.R. (2001). Towards a conceptualization of interpersonal rejection. In M.R. Leary (ed.), *Interpersonal Rejection* (pp. 3–20). New York: Oxford University Press.

Leary, M.R. (2005). Varieties of interpersonal rejection. In K.D. Williams, J.P. Forgas & B. von Hippel (eds), *The Social Outcast: Ostracism, Social Exclusion, Rejection, and Bullying (pp. 35–51).* New York: Cambridge University Press.

Leary, M.R., Kowalski, R.M., Smith, L. & Phillips, S. (2003). Teasing, rejection, and violence: case studies of the school shootings. *Aggressive Behavior, 29,* 202–214.

Leary, M.R., Tambor, E.S., Terdal, S.K. & Downs, D.L. (1995). Self-esteem as an interpersonal monitor: the sociometer hypothesis. *Journal of Personality and Social Psychology, 68,* 518–530.

Leary, M.R., Twenge, J.M. & Quinlivan, E. (2006). Interpersonal rejection as a determinant of anger and aggression. Personality and Social Psychology Review, *10,* 111–132.

Lee, B.A., Farrell, C.R. & Link, B.G. (2004). Revisiting the contact hypothesis: the case of public exposure to homelessness. *American Sociological Review, 69,* 40–63.

Lee, Y.T. & Ottati, V. (1995). Perceived in-group homogeneity as a function of group membership salience and stereotype threat. *Personality and Social Psychology Bulletin, 21,* 610–619.

Levine, J.M. (1989). Reaction to opinion deviance in small groups. In P.B. Paulus (ed.), *Psychology of Group Influence* (2nd edn; pp. 187–231). Hillsdale, NJ: Lawrence Erlbaum Associates.

Levine, R.S., Foster, J.E., Fullilove, R.E., *et al.* (2001). Black-White inequalities in mortality and life expectancy, 1933–1999: implications for healthy people 2010. *Public Health Reports, 116,* 474–483.

Lewin, K. (1948). *Resolving Social Conflicts*. New York: Harper.

Lewinsohn, P.M., Rohde, P. & Seeley, J.R. (1993). Psychosocial characteristics of adolescents with a history of suicide attempt. *Journal of the American Academy of Child & Adolescent Psychiatry, 32,* 60–68.

Lewontin, R.C. (1972). The apportionment of human diversity. In T. Dobzhansky, M.K. Hecht & W.C. Steere (eds), *Evolutionary Biology* (Vol. 6; pp. 381–386). New York: Appleton Century Crofts.

Link, B.G. & Cullen, F.T. (1986). Contact with the mentally ill and perceptions of how dangerous they are. *Journal of Health and Social Behavior, 27,* 289–303.

Link, B.G. & Phelan, J.C. (2001). Conceptualizing stigma. *Annual Review of Sociology, 27,* 363–385.

Maass, A., Cadinu, M., Guarnieri, G. & Grasselli, A. (2003). Sexual harassment under social identity threat: the computer harassment paradigm. *Journal of Personality and Social Psychology, 85,* 853–870.

MacDonald, G. & Leary M.R. (2005). Why does social exclusion hurt? The relationship between social and physical pain. *Psychological Bulletin, 131*, 202–223.

Major, B. & Eccleston, C.P. (2005). Stigma and social exclusion. In D. Abrams, M.A. Hogg & J.M. Marques (eds), *The Social Psychology of Inclusion and Exclusion* (pp. 63–687). New York: Psychology Press.

Major, B. & O'Brien, T. (2005). The social psychology of stigma. *Annual Review of Psychology, 56*, 393–421.

Makas, E. (1993). Getting in touch: the relationship between contact and attitudes toward people with disabilities. In M. Nagler (ed.), *Perspectives on Disability* (pp. 121–136). Palo Alto, CA: Health Market Research.

Marcus, D.K. & Askari, N.H. (1999). Dysphoria and interpersonal rejection. A social relations analysis. *Journal of Social and Clinical Psychology, 18*, 370–384.

Marmot, M.G. (2005). Social determinants of health inequalities. *The Lancet, 365*, 1099–1104.

Marmot, M.G., Adelstein, A.M. & Bulusu, L. & OPCS. (1984). *Immigrant Mortality in England and Wales 1970–78: Causes of Death by Country of Birth*. London: HMSO.

Marques, J.M., Abrams, D., Paez, D. & Hogg, M.A. (2001). Social categorization, social identification, and rejection of deviant group members. In M.A. Hogg & S. Tindale (eds), *Blackwell Handbook of Social Psychology: Group Processes* (Vol. 3; pp. 400–424). Oxford: Blackwell.

Marques, J., Abrams, D., Paez, D. & Martinez-Taboada, C. (1998). The role of categorization and in-group norms in judgments of groups and their members. *Journal of Personality and Social Psychology, 75*, 976–988.

Marques, J., Abrams, D. & Serôdio, R.G. (2001). Being better by being right: subjective group dynamics and derogation of in-group deviants when generic norms are undermined. *Journal of Personality and Social Psychology, 81*, 436–447.

Marques, J.M. & Paez, D. (1994). The "black sheep" effect: social categorization, rejection of in-group deviates, and perception of group variability. *European Review of Social Psychology, 5*, 37–68.

Marques, J.M. & Yzerbyt, V.Y. (1988). The black sheep effect: judgemental extremity towards in-group members in inter- and intra-group situations. *European Journal of Social Psychology, 18*, 287–292.

Mays, V.M., Cochran, S.D. & Barnes, N.W. (2007). Race, race-based discrimination, and health outcomes among African Americans. *Annual Review of Psychology, 58*, 201–225.

McCord, C. & Freeman, H.P. (1990). Excess mortality in Harlem. *New England Journal of Medicine, 322*, 1606–1667.

McLaren, S., Jude, B., Hopes, L.M. & Sherritt, T.J. (2001). Sense of belonging, stress and depression in rural-urban communities. *International Journal of Rural Psychology, 2*, www.rural-psych.com.

McLaughlin-Volpe, T., Aron, A., Wright, S.C. & Lewandowski, G.W., Jr (2005). Exclusion of the self by close others and by groups: implications of the self-expansion model. In D. Abrams, M.A. Hogg & J.M. Marques (eds), *The Social Psychology of Inclusion and Exclusion* (pp. 113–134). New York: Psychology Press.

Mendoza-Denton, R., Purdie, V., Downey, G. & Davis, A. (2002). Sensitivity to status-based rejection: implications for African-American students' college experience. *Journal of Personality and Social Psychology, 83*, 896–918.

Mize, J. & Ladd, G.W. (1988). Predicting preschoolers' peer behavior and status from their interpersonal strategies: a comparison of verbal and enactive responses to hypothetical social dilemmas. *Developmental Psychology, 24*, 782–788.

MMWR. (2005). Health disparities experienced by black or African Americans—United States. *Morbidity and Mortality Weekly Report, 54*, 1–3.

Morris, J. (2001). Impairment and disability: constructing an ethics of care that promotes human rights. *Hypatia, 16*, 1–16.

Moscovici, S. (1976). *Social Influence and Social Change*. London: Academic Press.

Nazroo, J.Y. (2003). The structuring of ethnic inequalities in health: economic position, racial discrimination, and racism. *American Journal of Public Health, 93*, 277–284.

Nemeth, C., Rogers, J. & Brown, K. (2001). Devil's advocate vs. authentic dissent: stimulating quantity and quality. *European Journal of Social Psychology, 31*, 707–720.

Nemeth, C.J. & Staw, B.M. (1989). The tradeoffs of social control and innovation within groups and organizations. In L. Berkowitz (ed.), *Advances in Experimental Social Psychology* (Vol. 22; pp. 175–210). New York: Academic Press.

Noel, J.G., Wann, D.L. & Branscombe, N.R. (1995). Peripheral in-group membership status and public negativity towards out-groups. *Journal of Personality and Social Psychology, 68,* 127–137.

Ostrove, M.J., Adler, N.E., Kupperman, M. & Washington, A.E. (2000). Objective and subjective assessments of socioeconomic status and their relationship to self-rated health in an ethnically diverse sample of pregnant women. *Health Psychology, 19,* 613–618.

Parliamentary Office of Science and Technology. (2007). *Ethnicity and Health.* Report by the Parliamentary Office of Science and Technology. Retrieved from www.parliament.uk/documents/upload/postpn276.pdf.

Peres, Y. (1971). Ethnic relations in Israel. *American Journal of Sociology, 76,* 1021–1047.

Pettigrew, T. & Tropp, L. (2006). A meta-analytic test of intergroup contact theory. *Journal of Personality and Social Psychology, 90,* 751–783.

Pickett, C.L., Bonner, B.L. & Coleman, J.M. (2002). Motivated self-stereotyping: heightened assimilation and differentiation needs result in increased levels of positive and negative self-stereotyping. *Journal of Personality and Social Psychology, 82,* 543–562.

Pickett, C.L. & Brewer, M.B. (2001). Assimilation and differentiation needs as motivational determinants of perceived in-group and out-group homogeneity. *Journal of Experimental Social Psychology, 37,* 341–348.

Postmes, T., Spears, R. & Cihangir, S. (2001). Quality of decision making and group norms. *Journal of Personality and Social Psychology, 80,* 918–930.

Reicher, S.D. (1996). Social identity and social change: rethinking the context of social psychology. In W.P. Robinson (ed.), *Social Groups and Identities: Developing the Legacy of Henri Tajfel* (pp. 317–336). Oxford: Butterworth-Heinemann.

Riordan, C. & Ruggiero, J. (1980). Producing equal-status interracial interaction: a replication. *Social Psychology Quarterly, 43,* 131–136.

Roberts, E.M. (1997). Neighborhood social environments and the distribution of low birthweight in Chicago. *American Journal of Public Health, 87,* 597–603.

Roberts, E.M. (1999). Socioeconomic position and health: the independent contribution of community socioeconomic context. *Annual Review of Sociology, 25,* 489–516.

Rollins, J.H. (1973). Reference identification of youth of differing ethnicity. *Journal of Personality and Social Psychology, 26,* 222–231.

Rothgerber, H. (1997). External intergroup threat as an antecedent to perceptions of in-group and out-group homogeneity. *Journal of Personality and Social Psychology, 73,* 1206–1212.

Rowley, S.J., Sellers, R.M., Chavous, T.M. & Smith, M.A. (1998). The relationship between racial identity and self-esteem in African-American college and high school students. *Journal of Personality and Social Psychology, 74,* 715–724.

Rudat, K. (1994). *Black and Minority Ethnic Groups in England: Health and Lifestyles.* London: Health Education Authority.

Rumbaut, R.G. (1994). The crucible within: ethnic identity, self-esteem, and segmented assimilation among children of immigrants. *International Migration Review, 28,* 748–794.

Rushton, J.P. (1995). *Race, Evolution, and Behavior: A Life-history Perspective.* New Brunswick, NJ: Transaction.

Sander Thompson, V.L. (1996). Perceived experiences of racism as stressful life events. *Community Mental Health Journal, 32,* 223–233.

Schachter, S. (1951). Deviation, rejection and communication. *Journal of Abnormal and Social Psychology, 46,* 190–207.

Schmitt, M.T. & Branscombe, N.T. (2001). The good, the bad, and the manly: threats to ones prototypicality and evaluations of fellow in-group members. *Journal of Experimental Social Psychology, 37,* 510–517.

Schmitt, M.T. & Branscombe, N.T. (2002). The meaning and consequences of perceived discrimination in disadvantaged and privileged social groups. *European Review of Social Psychology, 12,* 167–200.

Schmitt, M.T., Branscombe, N.R., Kobrynowicz, D. & Owen, S. (2002). Perceiving discrimination against one's gender group has different implications for well-being in women and men. *Personality and Social Psychology Bulletin*, *28*, 197–210.

Schmitt, M.T., Spears R. & Branscombe, N.R. (2003). Constructing a minority group identity out of shared rejection: the case of international students. *European Journal of Social Psychology*, *33*, 1–12.

Schuetz, A. (1944). The stranger: an essay in social psychology. *American Journal of Social Psychology*, *49*, 499–507.

Shneidman, E. (ed.) (1993). *A Conspectus of the Suicidal Scenario*. New York: Guilford.

Simon, B. & Brown, R.J. (1987). Perceived intragroup homogeneity in minority-majority contexts. *Journal of Personality and Social Psychology*, *53*, 703–711.

Simon, B. & Klandermans, B. (2001). Politicized collective identity: a social psychological analysis. *American Psychologist*, *56*, 319–331.

Skinner, E.A. (1992). Perceived control: motivation, coping, and development. In R. Schwarzer (ed.), *Self-efficacy: Thought Control of Action* (pp. 91–106). London: Hemisphere Publishing Corporation.

Smith, G.D., Neaton, J.D., Wentworth, D., *et al.* (1998). Mortality differences between black and white men in the USA: contribution of income and other risk factors among men screened for the MRFIT. *The Lancet*, *51*, 934–939.

Smith, A. & Williams, K.D. (2004). R U there? Effects of ostracism by cell phone messages. *Group Dynamics: Theory, Research and Practice*, *8*, 291–301.

Social Exclusion Unit. (2001). *Preventing Social Exclusion*. Report by the Social Exclusion Unit. Retrieved from www.cabinet-office.gov.uk/seu/index.htm.

Sommer, K.L., Williams, K.D., Ciarocco, N.J. & Baumeister, R.F. (2001). When silence speaks louder than words: explorations into the interpersonal and intrapsychic consequences of social ostracism. *Basic and Applied Social Psychology*, *83*, 606–615.

Spanier, G.B. & Casto, R.F. (1979). Adjustment to separation and divorce: an analysis of 50 case studies. *Journal of Divorce*, *2*, 241–253.

Spears, R., Doosje, B. & Ellemers, N. (1997). Self-stereotyping in the face of threats to group status and distinctiveness: the role of group identification. *Personality and Social Psychology Bulletin*, *23*, 538–553.

Stasser, G., Stewart, D.D. & Wittenbaum, G. (1995). Expert roles and information exchange during discussion: the importance of knowing who knows what. *Journal of Experimental Social Psychology*, *31*, 244–265.

Steele, C.M. (1997). A threat in the air: how stereotypes shape intellectual identity and performance. *American Psychologist*, *52*, 613–629.

Stephan, W.G. (1987). The contact hypothesis in intergroup relations. In C. Hendricks (ed.), *Group Processes and Intergroup Relations* (pp. 13–40). Newbury Park, CA: Sage.

Stott, C.J., Hutchison, P. & Drury, J. (2001). 'Hooligans' abroad? Inter-group dynamics, social identity and participation in collective 'disorder' at the 1998 World Cup Finals. *British Journal of Social Psychology*, *40*, 359–384.

Swim, J.K., Hyers, L.L., Cohen, L.L. & Ferguson, M.J. (2001). Everyday sexism: evidence for its incidence, nature, and psychological impact from three daily diary studies. *Journal of Social Issues*, *57*, 31–53.

Tajfel, H. & Turner, J.C. (1979). An integrative theory of intergroup conflict. In W.G. Austin & S. Worchel (eds), *The Social Psychology of Intergroup Relations* (pp. 33–47). Monterey: Brooks/Cole.

Tajfel, H. & Turner, J.C. (1986). The social identity theory of intergroup behavior. In S. Worchel & W.G. Austin (eds), *Psychology of Intergroup Relations* (pp. 7–24). Chicago: Nelson Hall.

Taylor, J. & Jackson, B. (1990). Factors affecting alcohol consumption in black women. Part II. *International Journal of Addiction*, *25*, 1415–1427.

Towl, G., Snow, L. & McHugh, M. (eds) (2002). *Suicide in Prisons*. Leicester: British Psychological Society.

Tropp, L.R. & Pettigrew, T.F. (2005). Relationships between intergroup contact and prejudice among minority and majority status groups. *Psychological Science*, *16*, 951–957.

Turner, J.C. (1991). *Social Influence.* Milton Keynes: Open University Press.

Turner, J.C., Hogg, M.A., Oakes, P.J., *et al.* (1987). *Rediscovering the Social Group: A Self-catego-rization Theory.* Oxford and New York: Blackwell.

Turner, M.E., Pratkanis, A.R., Probasco, P. & Leve, C. (1992). Threat, cohesion, and group effectiveness: testing a social identity maintenance perspective on groupthink. *Journal of Personality and Social Psychology, 63,* 781–796.

Turner, R.N., Crisp, R.J. & Lambert, E. (2007). Imagining intergroup contact can improve intergroup attitudes. *Group Processes and Intergroup Relations, 10,* 427–441.

Twenge, J.M., Baumeister, R.F., DeWall, C.N., *et al.* (2007). Social exclusion decreases prosocial behavior. *Journal of Personality and Social Psychology, 92,* 56–66.

Twenge, J.M., Baumeister, R.F., Tice, D.M. & Stucke, T.S. (2001). If you can't join them, beat them: effects of social exclusion on aggressive behavior. *Journal of Personality and Social Psychology, 81,* 1058–1069.

Twenge, J.M., Catanese, K.R. & Baumeister, R.F. (2002). Social exclusion causes self-defeating behavior. *Journal of Personality and Social Psychology, 83,* 606–615.

van Knippenberg, D. & Haslam, S.A. (2003). Realizing the diversity dividend: exploring the subtle interplay between identity, ideology, and reality. In S.A. Haslam, D. van Knippenberg, M.J. Platow & N. Ellemers (eds), *Social Identity at Work: Developing Theory for Organizational Practice* (pp. 61–80). New York: Psychology Press.

Walsh, A., Beyer, J.A. & Petee, T.A. (1987). Violent delinquency: an examination of psychopathic typologies. *Journal of Genetic Psychology, 148,* 385–392.

Warburton, W.A., Williams, K.D. & Cairns, K.D. (2006). When ostracism leads to aggression: the moderating effects of control deprivation. *Journal of Experimental Social Psychology, 42,* 213–220.

Wells-Petry, M. (1993). *Exclusion: Homosexuals and the Right to Serve.* Washington: Regnery Gateway.

Werth, J.L. & Lord, C.G. (1992). Previous conceptions of the typical group member and the contact hypothesis. *Basic and Applied Social Psychology, 13,* 351–369.

Williams, D.R. (1995). African American mental health: persisting questions and paradoxical findings. *African American Research Perspective, 2,* 2–6.

Williams, D.R. (1997). Race and health: basic questions, emerging directions. *Annals of Epidemiology, 7,* 322–333.

Williams, D.R. & Jackson, P.B. (2005). Social sources of racial disparities in health. *Health Affairs, 24,* 325–334.

Williams, D.R., Spencer, M.S. & Jackson, J.S. (1999). Race, stress, and physical health: the role of group identity. In R.J. Contrada & R.D. Ashmore (eds), *Self, Social Identity, and Physical Health* (pp. 71–100). New York: Oxford University Press.

Williams, K.D. (2001). *Ostracism: The Power of Silence.* New York: Guilford.

Williams, K.D. (2007). Ostracism. *Annual Review of Psychology, 58,* 425–452.

Williams, K.D., Cheung, C.K.T. & Choi, W. (2000). Cyber ostracism: effects of being ignored over the internet. *Journal of Personality and Social Psychology, 79,* 748–762.

Williams, K.D. & Sommer, K.L. (1997). Social ostracism by one's coworkers: does rejection lead to loafing or compensation. *Personality and Social Psychology Bulletin, 23,* 693–706.

Williams, R.M. (1947). *The Reduction of Intergroup Tension.* New York: Social Science Research Council.

Wood, W., Lundren, S., Ouellette, J.A., *et al.* (1994). Minority influence: a meta-analytic review of social influence processes. *Psychological Bulletin, 115,* 323–345.

Wright, S.C. (2001). Strategic collective action: social Psychology and social change. In R.J. Brown & S.L. Gaertner (eds), *Blackwell Handbook of Social Psychology: Intergroup Processes* (pp. 409–431). Oxford: Blackwell.

Wright, S.C., Aron, A., McLaughlin-Volpe, T. & Ropp, S.A. (1997). The extended contact effect: knowledge of cross-group friendships and prejudice. *Journal of Personality and Social Psychology, 73,* 73–90.

Yuker, H.E. (1988). The effects of contact on attitudes toward disabled persons: some empirical generalizations. In H.E. Yuker (ed.), *Attitudes Toward Persons with Disabilities* (pp. 262–278). New York: Springer Publishing Company.

Yzerbyt, V.Y., Castano, E., Leyens, J-P. & Paladino, M-P. (2000). The primacy of the in-group: the interplay of entitativity and identification. *European Review of Social Psychology, 11,* 257–296.

Zadro, L., Williams, K.D. & Richardson, R. (2004). How low can you go? Ostracism by a computer lowers belonging, control, self-esteem, and meaningful existence. *Journal of Experimental Social Psychology, 40,* 560–567.

CHAPTER 4

Stigma and Exclusion in Healthcare Settings

Elizabeth Mason-Whitehead and Tom Mason

University of Chester, United Kingdom

ABSTRACT

Stigma has its origins in our experiences of difference. The anxiety and personal hurt that is experienced by a person who is labelled as stigmatised is associated with the embarrassment, shame and disapproval of those in society who are regarded as "normal". Whilst stigma and discrimination feature large in our wider societies, we tend not to regard healthcare settings as places where discrimination occurs. This chapter provides an overview of stigma and social exclusion within healthcare settings and how these experiences can arise, be maintained and ultimately cause pain and hurt to all those involved. The way forward is through the development of Government policies, professional development and a more informed public debate.

INTRODUCTION

One of the first initiatives that the UK New Labour government launched in 1998 following their election in 1997 was the Social Exclusion Unit. This unit is staffed by personnel from both the civil service and front-line people with experience of tackling the problem of social exclusion. Although it began its remit on the three main issues considered to lead to social exclusion: (a) truancy and school exclusions, (b) sleeping rough and (c) poor housing, they have now widened their operation into many areas of social life including healthcare. This remit suggests that the problems of social exclusion are, indeed, deeply entrenched in society as well as being highly complex. Social exclusion, as well as its close companion stigma, is rife throughout our social structures and we should not be overly surprised that they exist within the healthcare services themselves. Although healthcare, as a concept, functions to serve the people and is based on equity and inclusiveness by the fact that it is operationalised, in policy and in practice, it is vulnerable to

Multidisciplinary Handbook of Social Exclusion Research. Edited by D. Abrams, J. Christian and D. Gordon.
© 2007 John Wiley & Sons, Ltd.

the vagaries of these influences. This chapter outlines some of the areas within healthcare that have been reported to engage in stigmatisation and social exclusion strategies, either consciously or subconsciously derived (see also Gordon, Chapter 11; Millar, Chapter 1). It further highlights government concerns and policies relating to exclusion in a healthcare setting, provides an overview of some of the theories surrounding exclusion and stigma, and suggests interventions and recommendations for the future.

STIGMA AND SOCIAL EXCLUSION: ITS IMPACT

Stigma has its roots in individual and group "differences". The pain and emotional hurt experienced by the stigmatised person is linked to others' pity, fear, disgust and disapproval of this difference, whether that difference is one of personality, physical appearance, illness and disability, age, gender or sexuality. Stigma can also be defined as an attribute that serves to discredit a person or persons in the eyes of other (Franzoi, 1996). Attitudes towards these discreditable attributes vary through time, so for example the stigmatising impact of being an "unmarried mother" has gradually lessened over the past few decades. Stigma is also culturally defined, and variation is evident in the ways in which particular attributes are either accepted or otherwise between culturally diverse groups. Healthcare provides examples of how politically correct terminology has entered the vocabulary, partly as an attempt to demonstrate acceptance of differences; hence we now refer to "gender realignment" instead of "sex change", and "Down's Syndrome" instead of "mongol". Changes in vocabulary and the passage of time, however, cannot fully eradicate stigma and alter complex cognitive behavioural aspects of stigmatising attitudes. Indeed, when defining issues of "deviancy", healthcare provision and medical diagnosis can shape and promote images of stigma bearers. For instance, blindness may be defined in terms of the impact on people's personality and psychological adjustment rather than a technical handicap which can be compensated for by acquiring new techniques.

The impact of stigmatising attitudes on the stigmatised individual can vary in form and intensity. Much of the behaviour, however, towards the stigmatised serves to emphasise "difference", and thus there are forms of discrimination and prejudice which can be identified on the interactions between the "normal" and the "discredited" (Goffman, 1990). Discrimination and prejudice in any form serve to separate and exclude individuals from society and from many of the benefits of society, such as equitable access to services like housing, education, health and social support. Discrimination in this way is a form of social exclusion.

At an individual level, the impact of stigma and social exclusion can be devastating, leading to low self-esteem, poor social relationships, isolation, depression and self-harm. Groups as well as individuals can be stigmatised and prejudicial behaviour towards them based on race, sexual orientation, culture and religious belief is experienced at an individual as well as a group level. One of the largest potentially stigmatised groups is that of the "kingdom of the sick" (Sontag, 1978). The impact of stigma on those individuals who are already coping with acute or chronic health problems can be profound, and we hope that this chapter will serve to raise, and provide some insight into the experience of stigma and social exclusion for people affected by physical and mental health problems.

CONTEXTUAL FRAMEWORK

As we noted earlier, there appears to be a very distinct human capacity to form groups, and in forming such groups certain social structures become apparent (Simmel, 1950). For example, a group identity is formed by which individual members can distinguish themselves from others (Hughes, 1945). This identity is underpinned by a set of values and normative prescriptions that govern the rules of behaviour for that particular group. Within the context of mixed marriages, for example, if a group values the belief that they are more likely to end in divorce, they should be discouraged. Such prescriptive rules may manifest themselves as banning their children from mixing with, or dating, others from different ethnic/cultural backgrounds, or may incorporate stigmatising strategies of ridiculing, devaluing and dismissive commentary. These latter strategies are employed by many members of a particular in-group who denigrate and disregard those in the out-group (Redfield, 1960). This can be seen when children form groups in the school setting as much as it can be seen in national racist humour that disparages other national groups (Coleman, 1961). It is also manifest with teenage pregnancy.

The major function of these stigmatising strategies is to establish the "them and us" principle according to Foucault (1973). The complex interpretation of this principle is beyond the scope of this book, but suffice to say that it is concerned with establishing those deemed within a value structure which is considered good and in favour, and those considered bad and out of favour (Foucault, 1973). This principle, once established, allows for any amount of stigmatisation and social exclusion, which is then justified and sanctioned by the prejudiced view that distinguishes the difference: i.e. "them and us". Few better examples of this principle, although extreme ones, are found than in the extermination of many millions of people throughout history under the name of ethnic cleansing. Although we would reiterate that these are extreme examples, they typically begin with the same stigmatising processes as do the street gangs, the playground bullies and the workplace cliques. The difference is merely one of degree.

The final context that we wish to mention here concerns the social pressures that are wielded not only to exclude certain individuals from the in-group but also to include chosen members (also see Hutchison, Abrams & Christian, Chapter 3). Peer group pressure is a well-known social phenomenon that is employed to compel people to conform to a set of values. To create the feeling that a person belongs to, or is identified or associated with, a particular group is a powerful mechanism of communication, and can be as effective in rewarding conformist behaviours as well as punishing "aberrant" ones. Once established as a member of any particular in-group, it is often difficult for individuals to extricate themselves from that group or to change group thinking. In short, the group socialisation process becomes a self-reinforcing circuit of control. In the healthcare setting, this can lead to all manner of disturbing actions towards vulnerable groups, such as those witnessed in the numerous inquiries into allegations of abuse. For example, there are reports concerning abuse by staff in learning disability hospitals (for example, HMSO, 1972), and reports on the killing of patients by registered practitioners (for example, the Beverly Allitt Report: HMSO, 1994). What these examples share is a belief in being a member of an "in-group" with the power to stigmatise or socially exclude others.

Healthcare Contexts and Stigma/Prejudice/Social Exclusion

These examples of stigma and its impact on or within healthcare systems have mainly identified specific situations or problems which are potentially observables. However, there are more subtle processes which are not so directly observable, but which nevertheless impact on and relate to the partial or impartial provision of healthcare. These issues originate from healthcare's tendency to focus on illness and the prevention of illness which are suggested here as being the origins of stigmatising processes. Supporters of the biomedical model may push forward the medical profession's knowledge as the only right explanation, using language to bolster these ideas—"doctor knows best", "a little knowledge is a dangerous thing"—so that these ideas are seen as the only "reality" and others find it difficult to disagree (Berger & Luckmann, 1966). Furthermore, health professionals frequently, but mistakenly, think that lay health beliefs "are at best watered down versions of proper professional medical knowledge (i.e. no more than old wives tales)" (Stainton Rogers, 1991, p. 42).

However, it is important to recognise that biomedicine is only one of many differing explanations. Illness itself is merely a matter of definition, which could be illustrated by the following:

> The fracture of a septuagenarian's femur has, within the world of nature, no more significance than the snapping of an autumn leaf from its twig: the invasion of the human organism by cholera germs carries with it no more the stamp of 'illness' than does the souring of milk by other forms of bacteria. . . . (Sedgwick, 1982)

That is, illness is only what it means to the individual and its implication for the person themselves is socially defined. There may be a number of explanations ("sub-universes of meaning") which compete with each other, both within society and within the individual (Berger & Luckmann, 1966). Therefore, it is imperative that lay beliefs are recognised and that both illness and health should be seen as normality and, consequently, as being within a normal person's control (Dingwall, 1976), such that healthcare professionals are not viewed as the only source of knowledge.

Healthcare professionals must be challenged to take account of these lay beliefs, which may differ—even within an individual—according to the particular event and time point within their life. People choose from a range of conflicting attitudes, and this choice depends upon situational demands, mood and perceived importance at that moment. People are endeavouring to "create order out of chaos, and moment to moment make sense of their world and the cacophony" (Rogers, 1991, p. 58). Consequently, when healthcare professionals are trying to explain (as they are charged to do) what factors have contributed to a person's illness and to discover what will enable them to recover, they must examine personal accounts. This is starkly apparent in those who have recently suffered a stroke—where it is the person's own ideas of what will help them to get better and what will happen to them in the future that determine their short- and long-term feelings of well-being.

It is increasingly apparent that we need a system which allows people to be recognised as having their own ideas and opinions, which may or may not be directly in line with medical philosophies; as having their own ways of motivating themselves; and as needing to be allowed some choice and also some control over their own bodies, treatments and futures.

Taking into account people's own ideas and aspirations poses a challenge to healthcare professionals who have developed in a society which encourages conformity. There are strong expectations of participation in healthcare treatments (e.g. rehabilitation, medication, alterations in lifestyle, etc.) and strong penalties for non-participation (e.g. smokers being refused coronary artery bypass operations). Yet what we are suggesting is that healthcare professionals should be able to operate in a non-judgemental way, responding to people's individual needs. However, at present, few mechanisms are in place to equip staff with these skills, either during their training or even after they qualify. Until suitable mechanisms are identified and instigated, the stigmatising nature of healthcare will be potentiated by the very people who should be educating others to take non-judgemental accounts of difference and diversity.

For example, healthcare professionals are in a unique position with regard to those who have recently acquired a disability and social problems. The attitudes of staff cannot only determine how the person with the new problems feels about themselves, but also how others react to their problem. It is foolish to expect that these staff know instinctively how to react to particular situations or people. It is therefore imperative to develop the ability of staff to reflect on their own attitudes and prejudices in order to minimise them and to develop strategies to overcome them and, in turn, to tackle social issues with appropriate levels of responsibilities.

Furthermore, the inability to provide individualised care and the protestation of stigmatising attitudes are compounded and exacerbated by the healthcare system itself. Resources are allocated based not on the requirements of individuals themselves, but on the needs of whole groups which can further compound exclusion in poorer areas. People are thus, by necessity, labelled as having a specific problem in order to be judged in need of a particular type of care or treatment. Any move to avoid labelling people may result in non-allocation of services.

Government Concerns and Social Exclusion

The Independent Inquiry into Inequalities in Health Report (the Acheson Report: Acheson, 1998) is one of the most significant expressions and statements of concern regarding social exclusion that is experienced in Britain today. This report has become the benchmark for understanding, first, the nature of social inequalities in Britain, and second, the manner in which future analysis, research and policy formulation should be undertaken. It argues that the scientific evidence indicates that the adopted socio-economic model is the most appropriate, and highlights three layers of health determinants that are dependent upon each other: first, the individual lifestyle which is concerned with cultural constrictions and socialised behaviours; second, social and community networks as a form of peer groups pressure; and third, general socio-economic and environmental conditions. Acheson goes on to argue that the main areas for increased scrutiny and developmental consideration are:

- policies that are likely to have an impact on health inequalities
- a high priority being given to health of families with children
- further steps to improve the living standards of poor households

What we see here is a focus on the accepted relationship between individual action, social networks and economic conditions. These, argues Acheson, can combine to form either a positive way forward or, if negatively coalesced, a downward spiral of conditions of poor health. The Social Exclusion Unit (SEU), subsequent to the Acheson Report, continues to promote and evaluate research and put forward recommendations to impact on policy. Examples of this are the *Truancy and Social Exclusion Report* (Social Exclusion Unit, 1998) and the *Teenage Pregnancy Report* (Social Exclusion Unit, 1999a). Both of these reports deal extensively with their issues and form platforms for further policy expansion, and they are an excellent source of evidence to support practice development.

Stigma and exclusion can affect different members of the population in different ways. Below we outline four examples of current issues in healthcare which may be associated with exclusion and stigma.

Teenage Pregnancy

Teenage pregnancy in the UK remains a significant health, social and economic issue. Unlike many European countries, the UK has not managed to significantly reduce the numbers of young women under the age of 18 becoming pregnant. Indeed, more teenage young women become pregnant in Britain than anywhere else in Europe, although teen conception rates are falling (Health Statistics Quarterly, Spring 2007). The statistics published by the Health Statistics Quarterly (May, 2005), show that the teenage pregnancy rate for under 18 in England fell to 42.3 conceptions per 1,000 girls in 2003. However, between 2002 and 2003, the teenage pregnancy rate in girls aged between 13 and 15 years rose from 7.9 to 8.0 conceptions per thousand. Studies suggest that this increase in teenage pregnancies may be due to teenagers' ignorance, low expectations regarding education or future employment, or having a disadvantaged childhood—all of which are symbolic of a general neglect (Social Exclusion Unit, 1999b). New government interventions are seeking to address this. As part of their scheme to tackle social exclusion and child poverty, the government aims to reduce teenage conceptions by 50% and to have 60% of teenage mothers in education, training or employment by 2010, in order to reduce their potential for social exclusion from society by being poor.

Teenage pregnancies are disproportionately seen in ethnic minorities within the UK and it has been suggested that sexual health services are not always geared towards ethnic minority groups (Social Exclusion Unit, 1999b). Teenage pregnancy has different issues for different cultural groups and whilst in some it is readily accepted (and even welcomed), in others it is seen as negative, damaging, discreditable and dishonourable. It is this latter, and larger, group that we are concerned about here as they are often stigmatised and become socially isolated (Whitehead, 2001). Teenagers who become pregnant often feel the "wrath" of their families, can be ostracised and may even be shunned completely by their parents. Shame, anger and blame may cause a breakdown of family ties and there are numerous reports of a "loss of face" for parents in this situation. Certainly, teenage pregnancy is a life-changing situation, obviously for the young mother, possibly for the father and maybe for the grandparents. By necessity, there will be changes to the teenager's social life, which may lead to a breakdown in social networks and relationships and this can quickly lead to social isolation. The stigma associated with teenage pregnancy can be profound with badness and immorality being attributed to the teenager (Whitehead, 2001). A study conducted in the United States concluded that two out of five adolescents reported that they felt stigmatised by their pregnancy compared with their non-stigmatised peers.

The stigmatised adolescents were more likely to say that they had considered having an abortion, were afraid to tell their parents that they were pregnant, felt that they had been abandoned by the fathers, and felt that teachers and parents thought their pregnancy was a mistake (Wiemann *et al.*, 2005).

Teenage pregnancy can be both a cause and a consequence of social exclusion (Social Exclusion Unit, 1999b). The government has acknowledged the potential social exclusion faced by teenage mothers in terms of disrupting their education and leaving them isolated from society. Yet it has also been suggested that a dislike of school may be a risk factor for teenage pregnancy, with children who feel alienated by school perceiving pregnancy as inevitable or as more positive than continuing to study (Bonnell *et al.*, 2003). The notion of helping young mothers to remain included is thought to have health-promoting benefits and support for young mothers is one way by which to make young mothers remain feeling socially included (McLeod, Baker & Black, 2006). Such support may come from various sources, including parents, healthcare workers and the government. However, some teenage mothers, who are frequently unsupported by their child's father, often also lose the support of peers, friends and family, and become even more isolated. A government pilot housing support scheme for teenage mothers has been introduced which, although it may alleviate societal concerns about young girls becoming pregnant for the council housing benefits subsequently bestowed upon them, may in fact further the girls' exclusion from society as a whole (Kidger, 2004). While well intended, the notion of increasing young mothers' education and employment implies that full-time mothering, a practice which is perceived favourably in mothers with a partner/spouse to support them, is not a valid choice for teenage mothers (Kidger). Thus, these mothers are faced with the stigma of being "bad" mothers if they go out to work and do not stay at home with their children, or "bad" citizens for not being part of society (Kidger, 2004). The exclusion faced by young mothers thus appears to be multifaceted.

Finally, healthcare problems can arise because of the tension between deciding to have an abortion versus raising a child, as the teenager bears the brunt of massive social pressures associated with this. The decision is never an easy one and factors such as perceived social support, wanting to have a child, being in a relationship with the baby's father, religion, expectations about motherhood and the teenager's age at conception can all influence the decision (Pope, Adler & Tschann, 2001). Young teenage pregnant women are often viewed as lacking in morals and considered both weak willed and blameworthy. There is often a pressure for teenagers to take responsibility for their actions and follow through with the consequences of their behaviour by raising their child (Tabberer *et al.*, 2000). A comprehensive qualitative research project into teenage pregnancy conducted for the Joseph Rowntree Foundation in 2000 suggests that impartial advice for teenagers is lacking as that they often feel isolated and make a rushed decision regarding their pregnancy (Tabberer *et al.*, 2000). Opinions and values of parents and the community about motherhood and abortions are important in decision making, particularly regarding the negative connotations surrounding abortion (Tabberer *et al.*, 2000). Yet young girls' families often decide to step back from the decision-making process, and there is frequently a lack of support from a boyfriend or partner, which means that young girls are often left to make a decision based on their own values and the community in which they live thus furthering their isolation (Tabberer *et al.*, 2000). As Tabberer and colleagues point out, this is often a community in which "teenage pregnancy is highly visible and abortion is invisible" (p. 27). High conception rates found in teenagers from more deprived backgrounds are paired with low abortion rates (Bradshaw, Finch & Miles, 2005) suggesting that interventions regarding inclusion need to be targeted at teenage mothers from such areas. Thus, we can see a complex relationship between cultural diversity, normative prescriptions and traditional mores that underpin the teenage pregnancy and both family and societal pressures.

Involuntary Childlessness

For those who have had children relatively easily, both planned and unplanned, it may be difficult to appreciate the full extent of the range of emotions that can be felt by those desperate for a child. Those readers who may have had a child following a lengthy period of trying will be readily familiar with the deep disappointment of each menstruation followed by the aching anticipation with each cycle. Certainly, for those trying for a child we can empathise with the joy of success. As Blythe and Moore (2001) put it, "in pronatalist societies i.e. virtually all known cultures, married couples are expected both to want and to have children, and motherhood is seen as a defining characteristic of women" (p. 217). Those that deviate from this cultural norm may become stigmatised. Blythe and Moore (2001) prefer to use the term involuntary childlessness rather than infertility, which has negative social connotations, as Roget's Thesaurus would indicate i.e. "barren", "fruitless", "impotent", "incompetent" and "sexless", to name but a few. Given this it is not surprising that social exclusion may well occur. The Human Fertilisation and Embryology Authority (HFEA) recently published data based on treatment carried out between April 2003 and 31 March 2004. According to the published data, 29,688 women underwent in vitro fertilisation (IVF) treatment in the UK resulting in 8,251 successful births. The average success rate for women undergoing IVF treatment using fresh eggs in the UK is 28.2% for under 35 years of age, 23.6% aged between 35 and 37, 18.3% aged 38 to 39, and 10.6% aged 40–42. Around 1% of all births are the result of IVF and donor insemination. Early (failed) attempts at becoming pregnant may well be concealed and hidden from family and friends. However, as time passes, social comments may well be heard regarding the absence of the "patter of tiny feet", and whilst ostensibly light-hearted they apply an element of social pressure that can only be at best unhelpful. The exclusion felt by couples who are in this situation has been recognised by those involved in their care and treatment (Layrea, 1986; Pearson, 1992). Appleton (1990) identified that a root cause for such stigmatisation felt by childless couples was that the structure of society is based upon the family unit and we are constantly reminded of family activities such as shops filled with family consumables. The effects of stigmatisation can lead to marital difficulties, divorce and in some societies this can extend to ostracism. Appleton (1990) also advises us to remember that we are treating "people who are infertile" rather than "infertility". A qualitative research study from the United States revealed that the infertility experienced by women was a transformational process in which they mourned the loss of their reproductive function, parenting roles, felt stigmatised and excluded from not being able to fulfil their societal roles (Gonzalez, 2000). The consequences of male infertility have been investigated by Nachtigall et al. (1997) who conclude that the father's perception of stigma may adversely affect the father–child relationship.

After a period of time during which all manner of "old wives tales" and popular "remedies" may have been attempted, the couple may decide to seek the assistance of "scientific" medicine. Whilst previously medicine could offer very little in this domain over recent years, with the advent of new treatments for infertility there is now more "hope" for such couples. However, this "hope" or belief in medical technology may well be part of the stigmatisation process as for many; successes are at worst illusory and at best a medical success and not a personal one. Furthermore, as Whiteford and Gonzalez (1995, p. 36) argued, "the very process of medical intervention further stigmatises women and devalues them for any accomplishments outside of reproduction. Once into the process of medical intervention, the woman's identity as a person is all too often determined by the outcome of the medical intervention, her ability to reproduce". The problem is similar for infertile males who up until the recent development of intracytoplasmic sperm injection had to rely on donor insemination, which was felt to be tantamount to a quasi-adulterous intruder resulting in a quasi-illegitimate child (Blythe & Moore, 2001). The potential for the role of healthcare professionals, and certainly medical "science" of the time, to be part and parcel of the stigmatisation process of the infertile male is clearly apparent (Blythe, 1999).

The process of IVF is not as "inclusive" as it might be. Success rates and IVF services offered vary from one NHS Primary Care Trust (PCT) to another and the number of IVF treatment cycles offered to patients is not standardised across health authorities, despite guidelines from the National Institute for Health and Clinical Excellence (NICE, 2004). These state that all patients are entitled to three cycles of IVF treatment on the NHS (Sinclair, 2007). Following on from the NICE guidelines, the Secretary of State for Health maintained that by 2005 every PCT would offer at least one cycle of treatment, yet this is not currently the case. Indeed, approximately 75 % of all IVF patients currently pay for their own treatment (Henderson, 2007). In order to manage their budgets, some PCTs reduce their IVF treatment services which results in different levels of IVF treatment options available across PCTs. Thus, within the UK, there are some areas in which IVF is not provided at all on the NHS, while in other areas three IVF treatments are offered. This disparity of treatment creates inequality and the resultant "postcode lottery" may mean patients consider moving in order to obtain free NHS treatment, to which they are entitled. Patients' IVF treatment on the NHS is thus dependent upon the postcode of their GP. In addition, there are eligibility (or exclusion) criteria which patients must meet in order to be permitted IVF treatment, about which there are similar inconsistencies across PCTs. Variety in the IVF treatments offered depending on the patients' age, partners' age, previous children, single women, smoking and same sex couples is also found (British Fertility Society; Kennedy *et al.*, 2006). As an example, another criterion which further excludes this group is Body Mass Index (BMI). In some PCTs, treatment is only offered to women with a BMI of less than 30, while other PCTs implement a different BMI cut-off point. Overweight women may be less likely to conceive and less responsive to fertility drugs than women with a BMI of 19–29, yet the British Fertility Society recognises this inequality in unfertile groups and proposes that this be increased to include otherwise healthy women with a BMI of less than 36 (Kennedy *et al.*, 2006). Inconsistent treatment approaches lead to treatment inequality within the UK, with some patients being disad-vantaged simply due to where they reside.

Breastfeeding

Breastfeeding, that most natural and commonly occurring event, is at first sight an unlikely target for stigmatisation and social exclusion. Unicef (2006) can claim to have some success in their breastfeeding initiatives, with the greatest improvements being in Latin America and the Caribbean. The Unicef initiatives focus on the proper initiation of breastfeeding in maternities and hospital and supportive legislation. The 8% increase in exclusive breast-feeding has been estimated to have reduced infant mortality by more than one million, decreased fertility by 600,000 births and saved countries billions of dollars in unneeded breast milk substitutes. Unicef also report that the global statistics continue to rise. Breast-feeding in public is not stigmatised in most parts of Africa, Asia and Scandinavia but is so in the UK (Smale, 2001). Furthermore, this author claims that "in England, breastfeeding appears to be less tolerated the further from London one moves" (Smale, 2001, p. 235). In a survey about infant feeding conducted in 2005, 76% of UK mothers reported at least some breastfeeding of their infants (Bolling, 2005). Breastfeeding was found to be more likely in mothers reporting a higher level of education, those with managerial and profes-sional occupations, those over the age of 30, and those having their first child (Bolling, 2005). Breastfeeding rates have continued to rise in the UK since 1990 (Bolling, 2005), yet despite guidelines about the positive effects of breastfeeding for both mother and child, still not all mothers choose to breastfeed. This decision is sometimes made for health reasons, but society also plays a role in mothers' decisions to breastfeed. Common reasons for choosing to breastfeed include the benefits to the baby's health and convenience, while reasons for not breastfeeding include making it possible for others to feed the baby and not liking the idea of breastfeeding (Hamlyn et al., 2000). Furthermore, mothers' peer group can also influence their decision to breastfeed (Hamlyn et al., 2000) suggesting implicit pressures to "conform". Moreover, mothers may feel pressured to breastfeed, with pressure to do so often reportedly coming from midwives (Hamlyn et al., 2000).

Largely a question of cultural differences, there are different responses to breastfeeding from different social groups. For example, there are reports that 79% of restaurants would *allow* breastfeeding as long as there were no complaints (Modern Midwife, 1993). The important phrase being *to allow* the mother to breastfeed, which highlights all manner of tensions between right and wrong, natural and unnatural, place and event, visible and hidden, and so on. The fact that mothers would be unlikely to experience being complained about if they were bottle-feeding highlights the fact that it is more about revealing the breast, or more intimately the nipple, rather than the feeding (Smale, 2001). However, this is not to discount a deeper psychoanalytical interpretation regarding the act of a breast being suckled and its relation to the sexual connotations in adult life—perhaps beyond the scope of this chapter. What is important for us here is that mothers who are breast-feeding may be subject to an array of stigmatising approaches from both society at large and healthcare professionals in particular. A study carried out in Alabama (USA) dem-onstrated that the belief that mothers should not breastfeed their babies in public is not confined to an older and more conservative generation. This research involved high school and college students. The findings showed that although there were positive attitudes towards breastfeeding, less than half the students thought that breastfeeding should take place in public (Forrester, Wheelock & Warren, 1997).

There are numerous accounts that the main area, outside of the home, for breastfeeding was the ladies lavatory (Smale, 2001) and it is interesting, in fact Smale calls it outrageous, "that it should be relegated to the area set aside for the elimination of waste products" (p. 235). That this naturally occurring bodily fluid which gives life to the growing child, in an act that few object to in the animal kingdom and which is highly recommended by the medical profession, should receive such public condemnation, is extraordinary. The expression that "breast is best" appears to butt against "but only in private places". In this, Smale argues, the healthcare professional may be unaware of the tension, which leaves the mother open to stigma and some element of being socially excluded. Further to this, whilst the healthcare promotion is concerned with valuing breast milk over powdered milk, for those choosing the latter there is a huge "medical scientific" pressure as well as social pressures to accept the former. Clearly this, in itself, produces a stigma for those choosing the bottle over the breast.

Substance Abuse

Substance abuse is an increasing problem in many societies and by its nature leads to heightened stigma and social exclusion. Substance abuse is defined as "the continual misuse of any mind altering substance which severely interferes with an individual's physical and mental health, social situation and responsibilities" (Nursesnetwork, 2004). Despite the individualistic nature of this definition, the major concern is with its impact on the social fabric. Some addictions have corollaries that impact on society, especially when that dependence cannot be supported by adequate funds. The drive to satisfy an addiction can overcome social values leading to violence and crime, which in turn can impinge on both the individual and the wider society. A Swedish study examined the relationship between substance misuse and stigma. The researchers concluded that the process of stigma within this context was a process of social control amongst family and friends, decisions by social and health agencies, governments and policy (Room, 2005). Other studies have shown that the social accommodation of "sensible" recreational drug use is becoming more commonplace in UK societies, but that the accommodation of this illegal activity is never likely to be completely achieved (Parker, 2005). Despite its illegality, cultural acceptance of illicit drug use also seems to be increasing thanks in part to its portrayal by the media (Parker). The recreational use of cannabis within UK society has become largely normalised and substance use as a recreational activity, part of the clubbing or "going out" scene, is becoming more commonly accepted within society (Parker). Yet there is still an important divide between people who use drugs recreationally and those who become dependent on them.

Substance abuse is more likely in unemployed individuals and equally it makes finding employment difficult (Coulthard et al., 2002). A survey conducted in 2000 on 8,580 adults aged 16–74 living in private housing in the UK found that being young, male, non-married, unemployed, in financial difficulty and living in rented accommodation were common factors in those with drug dependence (Coulthard et al., 2002). Substance abuse or dependence is related to the prevalence of stressful life events and a lack of support. Such stresses may include financial insecurity, homelessness and unemployment; factors which may make individuals feel alienated and excluded from society as a whole. In turn, substance abuse can further exclude these individuals from society, and interventions need to be undertaken regarding their inclusion. It is hard to infer the direction of causality and whether drug use brings about the exclusion and stigma or vice versa. Drug use is common in people who have been in trouble with the police (Coulthard et al., 2002). Breaking the law implies deviating from societies' conventions and may make people feel excluded or separate from society as a whole. Such feelings of exclusion may lead people to drug taking, broadening their separation from society.

The impact of substance abuse on healthcare can be seen on two levels. First, we can see its impact on the individual, and second, we can observe the implications for service delivery. In terms of the former, the impact on the healthcare of the individual, it is often the case that patients are unaware of the damage that it causes until it is "too late". In terms of service delivery, it is clear that there is a financial implication in setting up and running rehabilitation services. There is also a drain on existing healthcare services as substance abusers become in need of health services. Access to these services, however, can be difficult as substance abusers can be viewed negatively as they have self-inflicted their harm and can be devalued for not having sufficient will power. They may also be viewed as not being deserving of healthcare services, particularly in relation to scarce organs for transplant operations. This is seen in relation to the debate on tobacco smokers and cessation issues in lung transplants and bypass grafts as well as in liver transplants for alcoholics (recently George Best). Although we may baulk at the thought of healthcare professionals holding such values—or at least making decisions based on those values— they, in fact, do hold them, or more accurately *some* do and believe that it is right to do so. Thus, we have a growing awareness that there are limitations to healthcare services in relation to our personal lifestyles and the choices that we make.

THEORISING EXCLUSION WITHIN THIS DOMAIN

In the move towards the acceptance of a certain form of behaviour, a specific physical characteristic is dependent upon the development of a society's cultural heritage. For example, historically, the Greek sponge divers accept and value deformity that is caused by high water pressure when diving in deep waters for their sponges. This may be determined by key historical and social landmarks creating the values of that society. The origins of such stigmatisation lie in the group feeling threatened by an individual, or a number of individuals, who are perceived to disunite, undermine and contaminate the larger society (also see Hutchison, Abrams & Christian, Chapter 3). Such reactions commonly arise from a fear of the unknown and the unfamiliar. This is clearly a sociological area of study, but it also has strong links with both social psychology and anthropology. The historical development will be dealt with in an overlapping style, reflecting their emergence from a number of perspectives.

DEVIANCE

One explanation for exclusion in this manner is to examine the role of group and individual behaviour. Stigma is not an isolated sociological concept but one that is more closely wrapped up with many other aspects of the human condition, leading to prejudices and marginalisation. These often produce derogatory identification terms such as deviance, which, like stigma, is a fluid concept and, again, one that changes over time. Therefore, deciding what is deviant and what is not is a process that can only be defined by a particular society at a given point in its social development. Deviance may be considered a form of social behaviour, as defined by that group for their purposes and function. It is the social group itself that defines its norms and decides what forms of behaviour lie outside of those regulatory frameworks. In its relationship with stigma, deviance is most closely associated with Goffman's concept of "moral behaviour" (Goffman, 1990). For example, when society chooses to stigmatise on moral grounds it is actually making a statement regarding what it believes to be considered deviant. As deviant behaviour is culturally relative, that which is considered to be deviant to one culture may not have the same structural components as in another. For example, marriage for 13-year-old girls among the Muslims of Pakistan is an accepted, and welcomed, cultural practice. In Britain this is not accepted, and marriage is illegal until the age of 16.

Durkheim and Deviance

The significance of the French sociologist Emile Durkheim's (1858–1917) work on deviance lies in the influence he was to have on later sociologists. Taken as a whole, Durkheim's sociological work may be considered nothing less than the construction of what later philosophers would call "a scientific research programme". This can be said to have three central components: (a) a "hard core" comprised of metaphysical beliefs; (b) an intermediary "protective belt" of positive and negative heuristics; and (c) outlying theories for numerous sub-disciplines which make empirical statements, predictions and interpretations of differentiated sectors of the real world. In short, Durkeim produced a sociological research programme that had the central components of the natural scientific method and ensconced sociology alongside such other procedural sciences. His notion of deviance is closely linked to social and religious community and, although he earlier believed that social malaise was responsible for the condition of deviance, he came to feel that society itself had lost its moral code, thus isolating individuals and marginalising them as deviants. What is important is that this "positioning" of deviance is, at one level, the responsibility of the individual and, at another, the fault of society which is reflective of our contemporary British community and its reaction to what it considers to be deviance.

Symbolic Interactionism

Durkheim's positivist methodology was constantly striving to demonstrate that sociology should be acknowledged as an empirical science as governed by natural laws, although later thinkers in sociology field believe that this was a fruitless endeavour. Symbolic Interactionism originates from a particularly fertile and exciting time in American sociology, which can be located in the early "Chicago School". The Chicago School, particularly in the inter-war years, can boast a number of prominent Symbolic Interactionists such as George Herbert Mead, Charles Cooley, Howard Becker and Erving Goffman (Burns, 1992). The concept of Symbolic Interactionism rests on one individual being able to imagine the social role of another, and on our ability to imagine ourselves as acting in other social roles. Furthermore, the reflexive adoption of the role of the other will depend upon our capacity for an internal dialogue with ourselves regarding what the constituent parts of that role may be. Herbert Blumer and others have analysed the complexities of this reflexive process, and the three main principles of Symbolic Interactionism, as put forward by Blumer are:

- Human beings act towards things on the basis of the meaning that things have for them.
- These meanings arise out of social interaction.
- Social action results from a "fitting together of individual lines of action".

Thus there is a close relationship between the individual, the group and the wider social context in which they operate. Outside of this, a deviation leads to the production of stigma (Blumer, 1956).

Labelling Theory

The importance and relevance of Howard Becker rest on his contribution to the study of deviance and his formulation of labelling theory. Unlike many of his predecessors, Becker's approach to deviance was not put forward as a pure theoretical concept but rather as a dynamic force which occurs within a framework of sociological interaction. In this context, deviance is a product of the social world and the effect of the operationalisation of the values, and their meaning, in which Symbolic Interactionism is concerned. In terms of social exclusion, the following extract from Becker's *Perspectives on Deviance: The Other Side* (Becker, 1963) outlines the relationship between the labelling of deviance and the social group which is applying it.

> Social groups create deviance by making the rules whose infraction constitutes deviance, and by applying those rules to particular people and labelling them as outsiders. From this point of view, deviance is not a quality of the act the person commits, but rather a consequence of the application by others of rules and sanctions to an 'offender'. The deviant is one to whom that label has successfully been applied: deviant behaviour is behaviour that people so label. (Becker, 1963, p. 3)

Thus we can see the concepts of labelling theory and stigma as being highly relevant to the healthcare settings of today in which many conditions are seen as deviant forms of behaviour. As labelling theory is constructed around how relationships are formed by the influences of society and specific groups within that community, this is a particularly relevant perspective for understanding the role of healthcare workers in contemporary practice.[1]

Erving Goffman

Contemporary sociological analysis of stigma and social exclusion has its origins in the work of Erving Goffman (1922–1982), who in turn was influenced by others such as Durkheim. When the first edition of his work on *Stigma: Notes on the Management of Spoiled Identity* was published in 1963 (Goffman, 1990), both the academic and the lay reader were for the first time provided with a comprehensive sociological map of the concept of exclusionary techniques. Although an absolute definition of stigma is difficult to encapsulate, the following attempt by Goffman is an excellent starting point from which to base further sociological exploration.

> While the stranger is present before us, evidence can arise of his possessing an attribute that makes him different from others in the category of persons available, for him to be, and of a less desirable kind—in the extreme a person who is quite

---

[1] Labelling theory also has implications for social identification and the ways in which an individual might subsequently construct his/her self-concept (Tajfel & Turner, 1979, 1986). For example, within the context of healthcare, one might adopt the role of a patient, and this might in turn inform underlying intentions and motivate health promoting behaviours (for discussion of group dynamics, see Hutchison, Abrams & Christian, Chapter 3).

thoroughly bad, or dangerous, or weak. He is thus reduced in our minds from a whole and usual person to a tainted discounted one. Such an attribute is a stigma. (Goffman, 1990, p. 53)

This extract focuses Goffman's understanding of stigma from the viewpoint of society and shows how the individual can socially emerge as different. His concern with understanding how and why some members of society choose to stigmatise a particular social group is important in understanding the reasons for the stigmatising process. A notable achievement of this work is that it provokes the reader, irrespective of their sociological background, to critically consider the dynamics of stigma from either an experiential or a theoretical perspective. The value of this is that it is a proven framework for generating research and analysis on the attitudes of society towards marginalised individuals and groups. The significance of Goffman's analysis is that it has remained a text of shared identification and meaning for people across many societies, and pivots on personal accounts and lived experiences of being and feeling, excluded. There are a significant number of vignettes in Goffman's text that are personal experiences from stigmatised individuals, and these personal accounts ground the book in the lifeworld of the marginalised "other". Deeply rooted in Goffman's work is his identification of moral career as an emergent concept within the creation of difference and the shared learning experiences of particular stigmatised individuals within a wider marginalised group. Goffman highlights the following example:

> This illustration is provided by a homosexual in regard to his becoming one: I met a man with whom I had been at school. He was of course, gay himself, and took it for granted that I was too. I was surprised and rather impressed. He did not look in the least like the popular idea of a homosexual, being well built, masculine and neatly dressed. This was something new to me. Although I was perfectly prepared to admit that love could exist between men. I had always been slightly repelled by the obvious homosexuals whom I had met because of their vanity, their affected manner and careless chatter. These, it now appeared formed only a small part of the homosexual world, although the most noticeable one . . . (Goffman, 1990, p. 53)

Edward Jones and His Co-authors

Another influential historical contribution comes from Edward Jones and his colleagues whose work post-dates Goffman by 20 years. Our own book is enhanced by the diverse disciplines of those authors who also have the benefit of the work of Goffman, and also of other writers since his classical work was published. Jones et al.'s Social Stigma: The Psychology of Marked Relationships (1984) has made a significant contribution to the research and subsequent understanding of the nature and social impact of stigmatised individuals. Edward Jones, as the editor of the book, wrote:

> [We] intend to focus in this book on a particular category of social relationships— those in which one participant has a condition that is at least potentially discrediting. We shall be concerned with the cognitive and affective underpinnings of such relationships and with the behavioural problems they entail. We shall also be concerned with the course and development of such relationships over time. (Jones et al., 1984, p. 6)

We can see from this focus that Jones et al.'s main concern was the impact of the stigmatising condition on the mental state of the person concerned, and the overall impact that this was to have on their functioning in the wider society. This is of central concern for healthcare workers who often interface with such persons and have a role to play in understanding its wider influence on social and behavioural problems. This fundamental contribution which emanates from the work of Jones and his colleagues can be located under the rubric of affective psychology. In this, the personal experiences of marginalised individuals are very much associated with emotional feelings of depression, anger and humiliation.

In this historical development the contributors, representing many disciplines, examine stigma and social exclusion from broad perspectives, with Jones's overall analysis being concerned about social relationships that involve at least one person who is vulnerable to being labelled as deviant and thus being stigmatised. Thus the significant value of Jones's contribution is the relationship between societal values and the perceptions of the marginalised individual as a devalued person. Therefore, it is the feeling of stigma as perceived by vulnerable individuals which in this context deals with the personal responses of fear, anger, worthlessness, depression, etc. The emotional impact of these engendered feelings, whether or not explicitly evoked by the society response to the stigma, is implicitly felt as a corollary of those social expectations. The result of this, according to Jones *et al.*, is the development of mental strategy to deal with the social implications of the stigma. These he terms the *six dimensions* of (a) concealability, (b) course, (c) disruptiveness, (d) aesthetic qualities, (e) origin and (f) peril. We can now look at these dimensions in a little more depth.

Since Jones, others continue to work in this area, for example, one such theorist is Graham Scambler, who identified and explored the notion of felt stigma. He revealed that some subjects experience shame, which was intensely felt by those who have a stigmatising condition and furthermore, he identified the oppressive fear of what he termed "enacted stigma" (Scambler, 1984). The anticipation of stigma is particularly relevant in Scambler's work with people who have epilepsy, where they may anticipate the stigma of having a convulsion. We argue that such "anticipation" can be applied to other situations such as the stigma of someone who has a facial disfigurement and their apprehension in meeting others.

Two significant essays, both from the United States, have given the experience of stigma a new focus for the 21st century. Major and O'Brien's contribution (2005) has skilfully united the sociology of Goffman (1963) and the psychology of Jones *et al.* (1984), together with new theories and ideas that penetrate areas of stigma which many people may feel uncomfortable in discussing. For example, the authors draw upon the work of Crocker and Major (1989), Major, Quinton and McCoy (2002), and Major, Kaiser and McCoy (2003) to expose the experience of how stigmatised groups may cope with their encounters with negative outcomes. The authors argue that a way of coping with such threat to their self-esteem is by blaming the outcome on discrimination rather than themselves. To blame the event on the discrimination serves the purpose of protecting the self-esteem and moves it to the external cause, namely, the prejudice of others. This discussion highlights the complex relationship between the stigmatised and those responsible for the stigma, illustrating that there is not a simple paradigm of the good victim and the evil perpetrator. It may be that this debate suggests that we are at a delicate stage in our present understanding of stigma (also see Hutchison, Abrams & Christian, Chapter 3).

Also, Keusch, Wilentz and Kleinman (2006) place stigma high on the global agenda in factors affecting health, but they call for a new science of stigma. Their rationale for such a move is "the recognition of the enormous personal, social and still unmeasured economic toll of stigma, and the absence of a conceptual framework or an evidence base for interventions, are driving a movement to reinvent a science of stigma" (p. 526). The idea that we should have a science of stigma will be a long time coming for some theorists and clinical practitioners, for others however, the notion that stigma has not been replaced by consensus is one that they may debate (Sumner, 1994).

CONCLUSIONS AND RECOMMENDATIONS

Recognising and acknowledging the existence of stigma in society as well as in healthcare settings is the first step towards addressing a complex problem, which has profound implications for all those concerned. The evidence is overwhelming that shows that people in society who are marked by a "difference" can suffer the devastation of prejudice and isolation (see Hutchison, Abrams & Christian, Chapter 3). The consequences of social exclusion lie in the difficulties faced by someone reintegrating into society following a stigmatising illness or surgery.

It is undoubtedly an awesome challenge for all of us who wish to contribute to transforming a state of exclusion into inclusion, whether this "state" is that of an individual group or community. A multi-agency approach, which means involving everyone who has been affected by social exclusion, is one of many ways of approaching this challenge. This would ensure that the "voice" of every interested party is heard including the victims, carers, health professionals and policy makers. Ideally, the perpetrators of stigma and social exclusion should be part of this multi-agency approach, but the reality is that this may not be possible.

We have put forward a number of ideas that can be incorporated into a policy statement which seeks to overcome stigma and social exclusion. These are not exhaustive as there are many more, they are merely suggested as a prompt to provoke creative discussion.

Five Ideas for a Social Inclusion Policy:

(a) Equable and collaborative approach to the policy.
(b) To ensure the policy informs and educates.
(c) To ensure the policy develops awareness.
(d) Address specific "differences" in the policy.
(e) Reflect, review and respond to the public's reaction to the policy.

Working towards a society which is more socially inclusive is one of the greatest challenges presented to contemporary society. For those working in healthcare settings, they have the additional challenge of protecting some of the most vulnerable people in our communities; those who cannot speak for themselves and those who are dependent upon others for their care. On this basis we put forward the argument that healthcare settings are communities with characteristics that in some way set them apart from the rest of society. "They are places where vulnerable, injured, damaged and hurt members of society intersect with professional people, whose purpose is to aid, assist and care for them" (Mason & Mason-Whitehead, 2006, p. 116). It is with this sentiment in mind that we conclude by stating that stigma research and scholarly activities can only have any value when their findings are applied to enhancing practices that strive to reduce stigmatisation in health care settings.

REFERENCES

Acheson, D. (1998). *Independent Inquiry into Inequalities in Health Report*. London: The Stationery Office.

Appleton, T. (1990). Counselling, care in infertility: the ethic of care. *British Medical Bulletin*, *46*(3), 842–849.

Becker, H. (1963). *Perspectives on Deviance: The Other Side*. Toronto: Macmillan.

Berger, P. & Luckmann, T. (1966). *The Social Construction of Reality*. London: Allan Lane.

Blumer, H. (1956). *Symbolic Interactionism—Perspectives on Method*. Englewood Cliffs, NJ: Prentice Hall.

Blythe, E. (1999). Secrets and lies: barriers to the exchange of genetic origins information following donor assisted conception. *Adoption and Fostering*, *23*(1), 49–59.

Blythe, E. & Moore, R. (2001). Involuntary childlessness and stigma. In T. Mason, C. Carlisle, C. Watkins & E. Whitehead (eds), *Stigma and Social Exclusion in Healthcare*. London: Routledge.

Bolling, K. (2005). *Infant Feeding Survey 2005: Early Results. Prepared for The Information Centre for health and social care and The UK Health Departments by BMRB Social Research.* The Information Centre, UK. Retrieved from www.ic.nhs.uk, accessed 23/3/07.

Bonnell, C.P., Strange, V.J., Stephenson, J.M., *et al.* (2003). Effect of social exclusion on the risk of teenage pregnancy: development of hypotheses using baseline data from a randomised trial of sex education. *Journal of Epidemiology and Community Health*, *57*, 871–876.

Bradshaw, J., Finch, N. & Miles, J.N.V. (2005). Deprivation and variations in teenage conceptions and abortions in England. *Journal of Family Planning, Reproduction and Health Care*, *31*(1), 15–19.

Burns, T. (1992). *Goffman*. London: Routledge.

Coleman, J.S. (1961). *The Adolescent Society*. New York: Free Press.

Coulthard, M., Farrell, M., Singleton, N. & Meltzer, H. (2002). *Tobacco, Alcohol and Drug Use and Mental Health*. Office for National Statistics Report. Retrieved from http://www.statistics. gov.uk/downloads/theme_health/Tobacco_etc_v2.pdf, accessed 24/3/07.

Crocker, J. & Major, B. (1989). Social stigma and self-esteem: the self-protective properties of stigma. In B. Major & T.O. O'Brien (2005). The social psychology of stigma. *Annual review of psychology*, *56*, 393–421.

Dingwall, R. (1976). *Aspects of Illness*. London: Martin Robertson.

Forrester, I.T., Wheelock, G. & Warren, A.P. (1997). Assessment of students' attitudes towards breastfeeding. *Journal of human lactation*, *13*(1), 33–37.

Foucault, M. (1973). *The Birth of the Clinic: An Archaeology of Medical Perception*. London: Tavistock.

Franzoi, S.L. (1996). *Social Psychology*. London: Brown & Benchmark.

Goffman, E. (1963). *Stigma—Notes on the Management of Spoiled Identity*. London: Penguin.

Goffman, E. (1990). *Stigma—Notes on the Management of Spoiled Identity* (3rd edn). London: Penguin.

Gonzalez, L.O. (2000). Infertility as a transformational process; a framework for psychotherapeutic support in infertile women. *Issues in Mental Health Nursing*, *21*(6), 619–633.

Hamlyn, B., Brooker, S., Oleinikova, K. & Wands, S. (2000). *Infant Feeding 2000: A Survey Conducted on Behalf of the Department of Health, the Scottish Executive, the National Assembly for Wales and the Department of Health, Social Services and Public Safety in Northern Ireland*. London: The Stationary Office.

Health Statistics Quarterly. (Summer 2005). Report: conceptions in England and Wales, 2003.

Health Statistics Quarterly. (Spring 2007). Report: teenage conceptions by small area deprivation in England and Wales, 2001–2002. Retrieved from http://www.statistics.gov.uk/downloads/ theme_health/hsq33web.pdf, accessed 22/3/07.

Henderson, M. (2007). Childless couples to face new IVF hurdle. Retrieved from http://www. timesonline.co.uk/tol/news/uk/health/article1610453.ece, accessed 5/4/07.

HMSO. (1972). *Report into Conditions at Farley Hospital*. London: HMSO.

HMSO. (1994). *The Allitt Inquiry: Independent Inquiry Relating to Deaths and Injuries on the Children's Ward at Grantham and Kesteven General Hospital During the Period February to April 1991*. London: HMSO.

Hughes, E.C. (1945). Dilemmas and contradictions of status. *American Journal of Sociology, March*, 353–359.

Jones, E.E., Farina, A., Hastorf, A.H., *et al*. (1984). *Social Stigma, The Psychology of Marked Relationships*. New York: W.H. Freeman.

Kennedy, R., Kingsland, C., Rutherford, A., *et al*. (2006). Recommendations from the British Fertility Society for national criteria for NHS funding of assisted conception. *Human Fertility, 9*(3), 181–189, or available from http://www.fertility.org.uk/news/documents/HumanFertilitypaper. pdf, accessed 23/3/07.

Keusch, G.T., Wilentz, J. & Kleinman, A. (2006). Stigma and global health: developing a research agenda. *The Lancet, 367*(9509), 525–527.

Kidger, J. (2004). Including young mothers: limitations to New Labour's strategy for supporting teenage parents. *Critical Social Policy, 24*(3), 291–311.

Layrea, M.G. (1986). Infertility a social stigma? *Kenya Nursing Journal, 14*(2), 5–9.

Major, B., Kaiser, C.R. & McCoy, S.K. (2003). It's not my fault: when and why attributions to prejudice protect self-esteem. *Personality and Social Psychology Bulletin, 29*, 772–781. In B. Major & L.T. O'Brien (2005). The social psychology of stigma. *Annual Review of Psychology, 56*, 393–421.

Major, B. & O'Brien, L.T. (2005). The social psychology of stigma. *Annual Review of Psychology, 56*, 393–421.

Major, B., Quinton, W.J. & McCoy, S.K. (2002). Antecedents and consequences of attributions to discrimination: theoretical and empirical advances. In M.P. Zanna (ed.), *Advances in Experimental Social Psychology* (pp. 251–330). San Diego, CA: Academic.

Mason, T. & Mason-Whitehead, E. (2006). The social construction of stigma. In M. Bendall & B. Howman (eds), *Decoding Discrimination* (pp. 94–123). Chester: Chester Academic Press.

McLeod, A., Baker, D. & Black, M. (2006). Investigating the nature of formal social support provision for young mothers in a city in the North West of England. *Health and Social Care in the Community, 14*(6), 453–464.

Modern Midwife. (1993). *Men's Attitudes to Breastfeeding*, Editorial, November–December, 7, 4.

Nachtigall, R.D., Tschann, J.M., Quiroga, S.S., *et al*. (1997). Stigma, disclosure, and family functioning among parents of children conceived through donor insemination. *Fertility and Sterility, 68*(1), 83–89.

NICE. (2004). Fertility: assessment and treatment for people with fertility problems guide. Retrieved from http://www.nice.org.uk/page.aspx?o=CG011, accessed 24/3/07.

Nursesnetwork. (2004). *Substance Abuse*. Retrieved from www.nursesnetwork.co.uk/medicine/psychiatrics/, accessed 16/03/2004.

Parker, H. (2005). Normalization as a barometer: recreational drug use and the consumption of leisure by younger Britons. *Addiction Research and Theory, 13*(3), 205–215.

Pearson, L.H. (1992). The stigma of infertility. *Nursing Times, 88*(1), 36–38.

Pope, L.M., Adler, N.E. & Tschann, J.M. (2001). Postabortion psychological adjustment: are minors at increased risk? *Journal of Adolescent Health, 29*, 2–11.

Redfield, R. (1960). *The Little Community*. Chicago: University of Chicago Press.

Room, R. (2005). Stigma, social inequality and alcohol and drug use. *Drug and Alcohol Review, 24*(2), 143–155.

Scambler, G. (1984). *Sociology as Applied to Medicine*. London: Bailliere Tindall.

Sedgwick, P. (1982). *Psychopolitics*. London: Pluto.

Simmel, G. (1950). *Sociology*. New York: Free Press.

Sinclair, K. (2007). *IVF 'Postcode Lottery' Continues*. Retrieved from http://www.ivf.net/content/index.php?page=out&id=2560, accessed 22/3/07.

Smale, M. (2001). The stigmatisation of breastfeeding. In T. Mason, C. Carlisle, C. Watkins & E. Whitehead (eds), *Stigma and Social Exclusion in Healthcare*. London: Routledge.

Social Exclusion Unit. (1998). *Truancy and Social Exclusion*. London: Social Exclusion Unit.

Social Exclusion Unit. (1999a). *Review of the Social Exclusion Unit*. London: Social Exclusion Unit.

Social Exclusion Unit. (1999b). *Teenage Pregnancy*. London: Social Exclusion Unit.

Sontag, S. (1978). *Illness as Metaphor*. London: Allen Lane.

Stainton Rogers, W. (1991). *Explaining Health and Illness: An Explanation of Diversity*. London: Harvester Wheatsheaf.

Sumner, C. (1994). *The Sociology of Deviance—An Obituary*. Buckingham: Open University Press.

Tabberer, S., Hall, C., Prendegrast, S. & Webster, A. (2000). *Teenage Pregnancy and Choice. Abortion or Motherhood: Influences on the Decision*. York: York Publishing Services Ltd.

Tajfel, H. & Turner, J.C. (1979). An integrative theory of intergroup conflict. In G.W. Austin & S. Worchel (eds), *The Social Psychology of Intergroup Relations*. Monterey, CA: Brooks Cole.

Tajfel, H. & Turner, J.C. (1986). The social identity theory of intergroup behaviour. In S. Worchel & W. Austin (eds), *Psychology of Intergroup Relations*. Chicago: Nelson-Hall.

Unicef. (2006). 'Facts and Figures' Retrieved from http://www.unicef.org/programme/breasfeeding//facts.htm, accessed 19/05/06.

Whitehead, E. (2001). Teenage pregnancy: on the road to social death. *International Journal of Nursing Studies*, *38*, 437–446.

Whiteford, L. & Gonzalez, L. (1995). Stigma: the hidden burden of infertility. *Social Science and Medicine*, *40*(1), 27–36.

Wiemann, C.M., Rickert, V.I., Berenson, A.B. & Volk, R.J. (2005). Are pregnant adolescents stigmatised by pregnancy? *Journal of Adolescent Health*, *36*(4), 352.

CHAPTER 5

Homelessness and Social Exclusion

David Clapham

Cardiff University, United Kingdom

ABSTRACT

This chapter examines the links between homelessness and social exclusion at a number of levels. The first is a comparison of the discourses that have framed public policy in both areas. It is argued that the discourses share common contested concepts of "deserving" and "undeserving", and embrace ambiguous and potentially conflicting elements of structure and action. These ambiguities are reflected in the following discussion of the links between social exclusion and homelessness at the individual level and mean that the questions of whether homeless people are also socially excluded and vice versa do not have clear answers. The paper argues that the dichotomy between agency and structure that characterises the policy discourses is also reflected in academic debate. However, the paper examines approaches to "homelessness pathways" and "new poverty" that offer potential to overcome this problem by examining the interactions between the two phenomena in a holistic and dynamic way. Finally, the paper engages with definitions of policy success by bringing together threads of discussion in the paper to argue for a definition of policy success that focuses on the outcomes favoured by the individuals concerned, rather than on "objectively defined" outcomes.

INTRODUCTION

Homelessness and social exclusion are often considered together in policy and academic debates in Britain. People who sleep on the streets or *rough sleepers* as they are sometimes known, are often held up as the epitome of social exclusion. They are seen as people who are so cut off from society that they have no roof over their heads and cannot enjoy the type of life that most people take for granted. Therefore, it is nott surprising that one of the first reports of the Government's social exclusion unit was on *rough sleeping* and the drive to get people *off the streets* was one of the first elements of the Labour Government's strategy for combating social exclusion.

Multidisciplinary Handbook of Social Exclusion Research. Edited by D. Abrams, J. Christian and D. Gordon.
© 2007 John Wiley & Sons, Ltd.

The aim of this chapter is to examine the links between homelessness and social exclusion. The discussion is confined to Britain. This is because the discourses that structure public policy differ between countries. However, the framework of analysis presented here is relevant to any country and there may be clear resonances in the policy debates. Therefore, readers interested in other countries may still find the discussion of value.

The analysis will take place on three levels, reflecting the many ways in which the phenomena are linked. The first level of the analysis is an examination of the discourses of social exclusion and homelessness that have framed policy debate. Policy discourses usually contain a definition of the problem, a story of causation and a view of appropriate policy responses. It is argued that both discourses are ambiguous and contested with a division between what are termed minimalist and maximalist conceptions. Therefore, the discourses share many things in common such as a recurring concern with categories of deserving and undeserving, and an ambiguity between the influence of structural causes and individual behaviour.

The second level is that of individuals. This chapter will examine whether there is an overlap between those who are socially excluded and those who are homeless. The discussion looks at the issues from two directions. Are socially excluded people more likely to become homeless? And are homeless people socially excluded? Of course, the answer to these questions depends on the discourses and their inherent definitions of the phenomena. The paper explores some of the meanings embedded in the different definitions by examining a number of homelessness situations that people may find themselves in, and discussing, whether these would be defined as social exclusion. For the purposes of the discussion, social exclusion is seen as the absence of social inclusion, which is broken down into civic, economic, social and interpersonal inclusion. This analysis highlights the ambiguous nature of the discourses and the complex impact of policy responses. In particular, the discussion focuses on the problematic but vital element of interpersonal inclusion. Some policy interventions aimed at combating other elements of exclusion may exacerbate interpersonal exclusion by making it difficult for people to mix with those they choose. This situation highlights the *top down* nature of definitions of social exclusion and the key issue of voluntary exclusion. Should the aim of policy be to move people out of certain defined situations or to give them more control over their lives?

The third level of analysis in the paper is that of academic discourse and study of both homelessness and social exclusion. It is argued that research has mirrored the policy discourses in being driven by the dichotomy between agency and structure. This leads some research to focus on the characteristics and actions of the people concerned and other studies to consider the structural constraints. There is little work that attempts to examine the interaction between individuals and their context. The paper focuses on two frameworks that do examine both aspects. These are the pathways approach to homelessness and the *new poverty* approach to poverty research. A way forward is examined in academic study of both homelessness and social exclusion by arguing for a method of analysis that incorporates structural and agency elements and is holistic and dynamic.

Finally, adoption of the proposed framework highlights the issue of appropriate policy objectives. The paper concludes with an argument for treating the control that individuals can exercise over their circumstances as the main aim of policy, rather than seeking to achieve the absence of an objectively defined state of social exclusion or homelessness.

DISCOURSES OF SOCIAL EXCLUSION AND HOMELESSNESS

Like all policy discourses, those of social exclusion and homelessness include basic assumptions about the nature of the relevant phenomenon, its causes and appropriate policy responses. It is argued that the discourses share many common features. They are contested and ambiguous. They contain understandings of who is "deserving" and "undeserving" of help that have their roots deep in the history of social policy. Further, both discourses have an underlying ambiguity and contradiction between agency and structure that underlies much of the dispute over definitions and policy prescriptions.

The discourse of homelessness has been the subject of much debate and dispute. Jacobs, Kemeny and Manzi (1999) refer to the difference between minimalist and maximalist discourses of homelessness. Minimalist discourses tend to define homelessness in narrow terms as just consisting of rough sleepers. Within this context, the implicit cause of homelessness is held to be the personal shortcomings of the homeless people themselves, and so policy needs to be oriented towards changing the behaviour of homeless people once their immediate problem has been alleviated. It is also perceived to be important to make a distinction between those deserving and not deserving of aid. For example, those who are perceived as bringing the homeless situation on themselves through inappropriate behaviour such as getting into mortgage arrears and being repossessed cannot be helped for fear of being seen to create incentives that would encourage others to follow voluntarily. Likewise, some people, such as single people, are considered able to take responsibility for themselves and help for them would undermine work incentives. Where help is provided it needs to be conditioned on the acceptance of behavioural norms such as actively seeking work, or undertaking training designed to increase the chances of gaining employment.

In contrast, the maximalist discourse includes a wide variety of situations in its definition of what constitutes homelessness. At its extreme it can include all those without appropriate housing. The cause of homelessness is perceived as the structural forces of the provision and regulation of housing and social services by the state. Therefore, people are said to be homeless because there is not enough affordable housing, or welfare benefits are not generous enough, or some people fall through the welfare net. The policy prescriptions include helping people without restriction, or need to prove lack of personal guilt, and concentration on the wider policy issues such as the provision of the appropriate amount of affordable housing.

Jacobs, Kemeny and Manzi (1999) see the recent history of state policy towards homelessness in Britain as being the result of the playing out of the forces supporting these competing discourses. For example, the homelessness legislation of 1977 was a major victory for the supporters of the maximalist discourse, because it gave homeless people the right to help. It saw the appropriate response to homelessness as the provision of accommodation, which implies that the problem is a shortage of affordable housing and the difficulties of access to it that disadvantaged people may have. However, the legislation was only passed because of compromises made with supporters of the minimalist discourse. Therefore, the issues of vulnerability, local connection and intentionality were included. These reduced the scope of the rights that had been given and introduced the idea that some people were the agents of their own misfortune and did not deserve to be helped. Thus, the legislation was an uneasy compromise between the two discourses and it has been amended many times since with the balance of advantage swinging one way and the other (see Somerville, 1999). However, Evans (1999) shows that the 1977 legislation achieved its aims in that she found no difference in housing need between those housed under the statutory homelessness procedures and those denied accommodation. The difference was whether they were considered to be "deserving" or "undeserving". In general, the deserving group traditionally consists of women with dependent children, mostly in single parent families. Their status as deserving was challenged in legislation in 1996 that sought to restrict their rights to housing (Somerville, 1999). Under both the 1977 and 1996 legislation, the undeserving group has largely been comprised of young single people who are considered to be work-shy, or at least likely to be influenced by supposed disincentives to work held to be inherent in the provision of support.

At present, the coverage of the legislation is wider than in 1977 and the scope of the restrictive vulnerability and intentionality clauses has been reduced. In particular, young people have seen their rights extended considerably. However, there is now a twin concern both with the provision of accommodation and with support for individual homeless people. The support has two dimensions with emphasis both on the provision of appropriate services to homeless people and on the appropriate behaviour of the recipient. Hutson (1999) argues that many young people do not ask for the support and they often view it as not being related to their own lives and priorities. Hutson (1999) gives examples of young people denied shelter in hostels because they are considered to be unlikely to benefit from the support provided. Clearly, the emphasis on support is based on professional and political views of what should be provided based on the policy discourse, rather than on the wishes and the definitions held by the young people of their situation.

The discourse of social exclusion is similarly contested and, therefore, contains ambiguous elements. All seem to include the multiple and compound nature of disadvantage and the difficulty of breaking what is seen as the enduring nature of disadvantage (Gordon, Chapter 11). One strand (one could label this the maximalist conception of social exclusion) emphasises the processes that exclude disadvantaged people. These are usually focused around the perceived powerlessness of excluded people to be able to influence public organisations to get appropriate levels of state support. They are seen as slipping through the welfare net through no fault of their own. For example, socially excluded homeless people do not get the health services they need. The reason being that such NHS services are not oriented towards people with no fixed address. Therefore, the solution lies in the reform of health services to improve access and to make them more sensitive to the needs of the prospective users. Another example is the social exclusion of particular neighbourhoods with a concentration of disadvantaged people. The perceived solution is the regeneration of these areas by public organisations to improve facilities. However, this is to be done in a way that listens to and is accountable to the views of residents who are, therefore, empowered by being given an opportunity to express their voice.

The second strand (the minimalist) focuses more on the behaviour of the excluded people themselves. An extreme example of this approach is the *underclass* discourse expounded by Charles Murray (1989). According to Murray, the problems of social exclusion are perceived to be the result of inappropriate cultures that pattern and influence subsequent behaviour. Important aspects are attitudes towards family and work, and State policy is also implicated in the problem inasmuch as it reinforces this inappropriate behaviour through reward. For example, if an unmarried teenage girl becomes pregnant, she is given priority access to council housing, thus it is seen as creating an incentive for perceived irresponsible behaviour as well as undesirable household forms (Morgan, 1998).

Other versions of this emphasis in the discourse are reflected in the *tough love* type approaches to young people that make help conditional on respect for particular codes of behaviour. The premise of such approaches is that young people are at least partly responsible for their own social exclusion (they exclude themselves from society because of their perceived inappropriate behaviour.)

As with homelessness, the emphasis in both discourse and policy has swung between the two positions. At present, in the UK, there seems to be a balance with both aspects present in the discourse and policy. Although this may seem to be sensible in practice, it leads to an ambiguity in the concept. How can you satisfactorily define social exclusion when its meaning is changing and elastic? How can you use it as a guide for policy when two different and contradictory policy approaches can both be justified under the discourse?

There is substantial similarity between the social exclusion and homelessness discourses. Both are ambiguous and contested. Both have minimalist and maximalist interpretations that contain opposing and contradictory explanations of the phenomenon—its causes and solutions. Both have led to policies that contain divergent and sometimes contradictory elements. Both contain elements of concern with individual behaviour and the structural forces that shape that behaviour without ever stipulating the balance between them and how these relate together. Given this, we attempt to draw—below—some of these links.

HOMELESS PEOPLE AND SOCIAL EXCLUSION

In their review of the links between homelessness and social exclusion, Clapham and Evans (2000) argue that there is a strong relationship between homelessness and the range of disadvantages that are usually associated with social exclusion. However, they argue that the links are complex, with homelessness being a consequence of social exclusion, as well as creating it. It is clear that social disadvantage is one predisposition of homelessness. Of course, this does not mean that all disadvantaged people become homeless. Nevertheless, disadvantaged people are over-represented in those classified as homeless. For example, Clapham and Evans (2000) show that members of black and minority ethnic groups are more likely than white people to become homeless. Similarly, lone parents, young people leaving care, ex-prisoners and those in poverty are more likely to become homeless. These categories are not mutually exclusive and some people suffer a number of disadvantages; however, not all disadvantaged people become homeless and there needs to be a trigger that impacts on the housing situation. This may be relationship breakdown that forces a move out of existing accommodation, or a young person being thrown out of the family home or spending time in prison when existing accommodation arrangements are lost. A key contributing factor to homelessness seems to be the lack of support from family, or a partner that makes it harder to overcome short-term obstacles.

The relationship between homelessness and disadvantage can be a difficult one to disentangle because of the lack of a clear direction of causality. For example, many homeless people suffer from health problems, both physical and mental. Between one third and one half of rough sleepers suffer from mental health problems and the great majority of these were ill before they became homeless (Craig *et al.*, 1993). A large proportion of rough sleepers have a serious drug or alcohol problem (Clapham & Evans, 2000). Although for some people their health problems are a contributing factor towards their homelessness, there is also little doubt that the experience of homelessness contributes towards these problems. Even if some people had no health problems before they became homeless, they are likely to experience them when they become homeless. This is particularly true of rough sleeping, where the physical privations of cold and damp and lack of sanitary facilities are in addition to the, often difficult, mental health impacts of the experience of homelessness.

An example of the physical and mental impact of problems is of people who experience mortgage arrears and are threatened with homelessness by being repossessed. Nettleton *et al.* (1999) found that many people who had been repossessed found the experience one of the most traumatic of their lives. Many people felt a lack of control over their situation. Mortgage debts arose for a variety of reasons which sometimes occurred together and which in many cases people felt powerless to alter. In some cases, wives were left by their husbands and then discovered the debts that had been incurred. Increases in mortgage payments and service charges were sometimes coupled with reduced earnings in employment or unemployment. Along with the lack of control went uncertainty as people did not know what would happen to them and where they would live. The loss of the home brought profound emotional responses in many people such as a mixture of anger, bitterness and hurt, mixed with feelings of inadequacy and failure. People reported a loss of social status and identity related to assuming the identity of homeless person or renter rather than owner. Self-esteem and confidence were also affected and many people suffered strained personal relationships and poor health.

There is substantial evidence that socially excluded people are more likely to become homeless, but some homeless people are not previously socially excluded. The complex nature of the relationship between the two phenomena means that it is useful to assess whether homeless people are necessarily socially excluded.

There are many definitions of social exclusion as shown earlier. An interesting way of looking at the social exclusion position of homeless people is by adopting the categorisation put forward by Commins (1993) and discussed in Berghmann (1995). The analysis is based on the idea that social exclusion is the absence of social inclusion. In defining social inclusion, the analysis follows the lead of Marshall (1950) in his categorisation of citizenship rights. Marshall posited the existence of civil, political and social rights. The basis of social inclusion is said to be civic, economic, social and interpersonal integration. By civic integration is meant the ability to participate equally in the democratic system. A simple example of this may be the ability to be accepted on the electoral register. Economic integration is seen simply as having employment and consequently being able to pay one's way. Social integration means being able to avail oneself of the social services provided by the state. Interpersonal integration means having family and friends, and the social networks to provide care, companionship and moral support when needed. Therefore, social exclusion can be said to be the lack of any one of these elements.

Are homeless people socially excluded through a lack of integration in these elements? Before tackling this question, it is necessary to refer back to the contested nature of the definitions of homelessness considered earlier. Homelessness has many definitions and so to illustrate the issue, a number of different situations will be taken that are sometimes (but not always) considered to constitute homelessness. The first situation is the rough sleeper on the streets who is almost always considered to be homeless. The second is the resident of a hostel for homeless people. This person may be considered to be homeless, but government policies have been aimed at moving people off the streets and into hostels so a resident would not count if homelessness was considered to be just rough sleeping. The final example is someone living in an overcrowded household. A person in this category would not necessarily count as homeless under existing legislation, but under wider definitions of the concept can be considered not to have a satisfactory home.

To be a rough sleeper, without a fixed address, may mean the lack of civic inclusion as the person is unlikely to be able to register to vote as the basis of civic duty. It is also very difficult to gain employment and experience economic inclusion without a fixed address. Social inclusion may also be problematic for rough sleepers who may be unable to access social provision. For example, it has been shown that rough sleepers have major problems in accessing GP health services that are the gatekeepers to other health provision, despite many having substantial health difficulties (Pleace & Quilgars, 1997). Clearly, the lack of a fixed abode is a severe obstacle to access to many aspects of life. The final element is interpersonal integration and here the position is more difficult to assess. The issue is the extent to which rough sleepers are "at home on the streets" by which is meant whether they are with friends and feel secure and appreciated by their peers. They may be part of a group that offers its members interpersonal support, but is itself excluded from the wider society. This situation raises many issues about the nature of inclusion and its relationship to integration. Barry (2002) raises questions about the status of voluntary exclusion. In other words, if a rough sleeper chooses to integrate with friends on the streets and, as a consequence, erodes the ties between them and the wider society, is it correct to classify them as socially excluded? As Barry (2002) points out, the concept of social exclusion carries the assumption that it is "a bad thing" to be avoided. However, if people are actively choosing to segregate themselves, is this always problematic?

The hostel dweller may be able to access political enfranchisement as well as employment. Many hostels provide substantial support to enable homeless people to access employment opportunities through training, advice and counselling. Hostel residents may also find it possible to access social services if the hostels are working in partnership with other organisations as most attempt to do. However, interpersonal inclusion may be difficult as some hostels can be threatening places and a resident may be with strangers whom one would not necessarily choose to live with (Hutson, 1999). There seems little attempt in hostels to enable the resident to build up social links with people living outside, or to have the space to be able to exercise family obligations or pursue a "normal" family life. And many hostels are single sex so that families may be split up when they become homeless.

The person in the overcrowded household may have access to civic, economic and social inclusion, although they are perhaps less likely to be plugged into social services than the hostel dweller who may be brought to the attention of the providers of state services. It is possible for the overcrowded household to be unknown to public authorities and, therefore, not to receive the services to which they may be entitled. The presence of interpersonal integration may depend on factors such as the status of the neighbourhood and the impact of the situation on self-esteem and confidence. If the overcrowded household lives in an area with a concentration of disadvantaged people, then they may be disadvantaged in terms of access to employment and other private and public facilities because of any stigma attached to the area. Their reaction to this could take a number of forms (Dean & Hastings, 2000). They may find common cause with fellow residents and unite to counter a negative image. In this way they may find integration into the local community, despite exclusion from the wider society. Alternatively, the low regard of outsiders may undermine confidence and self-esteem, and be reflected in a withdrawal from social interaction with neighbours and may be an influence on family pressures and possible disintegration. In such situations, personal inclusion is not achieved.

These examples are given to show how difficult it is to assess whether a homeless person is socially excluded. The answer may depend on the type of homelessness experienced as well as the particular aspect of exclusion considered. It may also depend on the resources and attitudes of the individual concerned and their personal circumstances. Not all individuals react in the same way to similar circumstances, and the personal reaction to their situation may be an important factor in influencing the possibility of social exclusion as the above have shown. However, the reported analysis draws attention, in particular, to the difficulties of achieving interpersonal integration. In some instances, it is evident that interventions designed to eliminate homelessness, such as moving a rough sleeper into a hostel, may overcome some elements of exclusion whilst making others worse.

ACADEMIC DEBATES

Academic discourse on homelessness has followed the structure/agency divide that has characterised political discourse (Clapham, 2003). For example, in their review of research on homelessness among single people in Britain, Fitzpatrick, Kemp and Klinker (2000) point to the common perception that the distinction between individual and structural explanations is generally perceived as "a useful starting point" (p. 19). Despite their use of the dichotomy between individual and structural explanations of homelessness in reviewing existing research, Fitzpatrick, Kemp and Klinker (2000) quote Neale (1997) in arguing that this dichotomy is overly simplistic, and that no sharp distinction can be made between the two sets of factors. The implication is that both sets of factors are important in causing homelessness and that the interactions between them are complex. However, there has been a distinct lack of a coherent framework in which to examine the nature of these interactions. This is perhaps not surprising given the importance and ubiquity of this dichotomy in social science. However, there has been increasing interest in the interaction between individual action and structural forces as shown, for example, in the work of Giddens (1984).

One framework that has been used to examine homelessness is that of a homelessness pathway (Clapham, 2003). The concept of a homelessness pathway has been used by Fitzpatrick (1999) in her study of homeless young people in Glasgow. She criticised the static nature of much research on homelessness and sought to shed light on the dynamic nature of the experience of homelessness of many people. She also sought to provide a holistic framework by placing the housing pathways of young people in relation to other pathways such as the transition from education to employment. Another focus was the relationships between family members and the young person which could influence the process of leaving home and the help received when attempting to live independently. The research technique used was the biographical interview in which subjects were asked to recount their biography. This was coupled with an (only partially successful) attempt to trace the subjects a year later and to undertake follow-up interviews to shed light on the changes in their position over time. From this research, Fitzpatrick was able to criticise the prevailing view of a downward spiral of homelessness and to identify six particular types of homelessness pathway. These varied according to geographical location (whether in the city centre or in the local area studied), degree of entry to *official* homelessness agency facilities (such as hostels) and the stability of the young person's housing situation.

Another use of a pathways framework was undertaken by Anderson and Tulloch (2000). They defined a homelessness pathway as a description of "the route of an individual or household into homelessness, their experience of homelessness and their route out of homelessness into secure housing" (Anderson & Tulloch, 2000, p. 11). From their review of the research evidence, Anderson and Tulloch identified 23 different general pathways into and out of homelessness divided according to the stage in the life course. Five were associated with young people, 11 with adults and seven with people in later life. The descriptions of these generalised pathways included the trigger factors and the experience of homelessness in terms of the physical location of the individual (for example, a hostel or sleeping rough). Some pathways included a route out of homelessness, but many did not. Interestingly, a limited account was provided outlining the interaction between homeless people and the policy mechanisms they encountered. Descriptions include outcomes from dealings with the mechanisms of statutory homelessness procedures, and barriers to accessing housing because of a record of rent arrears.

Both research studies are valuable starting points in using the pathways framework. The strengths of Fitzpatrick's work were the focus on the voices and perceptions of the young people themselves as they constructed their own situation, and the dynamic and holistic nature of the framework used. Both studies use the concept of a pathway in homelessness research to overcome drawbacks of other approaches. For example, they emphasise the dynamic nature of homelessness, showing that homeless people move in and out of homelessness, in some cases a number of times. The diversity of the experiences of homelessness has also been stressed.

However, the research could have been developed further to make the most of the pathways framework. The pathways approach was relatively untheorised and not related to a wider literature. This meant that the large amount of information collected in each case was described rather than analysed. In particular, Fitzpatrick describes the individual biographies and identifies the wider structural factors involved, but does not relate the two. The analysis followed the usual method of describing structural factors as constraints, and treating them independently from the biographical factors. Therefore, little light was shed on the interactions between agency and structure. When confronted with the individual biographies and the pathways identified, the focus is on the behaviour of the individual and not on the structural factors which may have influenced this. Although it is clearly not the wish of the authors, the impact is to reinforce the minimalist conception of homelessness. These drawbacks can be overcome through the incorporation of an analysis of the impact of discourses and their relationship to the reality constructed by homeless people. To show the importance of this, it is necessary to focus on the theoretical underpinning of the pathways approach.

The most developed exposition of the pathways approach is given in Clapham (2002, 2005). The approach is based on social constructionism, but combines this with the concept of structuration (Giddens, 1984) that sees social practices having both an agency and a structural dimension. Social structures are seen as being produced and reproduced by human agency at both the individual and institutional level where they serve both to constrain and enable action. Clapham (2002) defines a housing pathway as "patterns of interaction (practices) concerning house and home, over time and space" (p. 63). The pathway of a household is the continually changing set of relationships and interactions which it experiences over time in its consumption of housing. This includes changes in social relations as well as changes in the physical housing situation.

It is assumed that households undertake what Giddens calls "life planning" in a search for identity and self-fulfilment. Housing is a key element in this. King (1996) argues that housing should be seen as a means to an end rather then an end in itself. "It (housing) is a means of fulfilment that allows other human activities to take place" (King, 1996, p. 22). Housing can also be an important source of identity. Taylor (1998) makes the distinction between categorical and ontological identity. Categorical identity is concerned with the labels which are ascribed to us by ourselves and society. An example would be the category of socially excluded or homeless person which brings with them a set of discourses which ascribe their relation to the wider society. This is in addition to categories of social class, gender, ethnicity, sexuality, disability, age and so on. Ontological identity is how these are forged by individuals into a coherent sense of self-identity. Categorical identity is a key concept because of its mediating position between society and the individual. That is, the category of "homeless person" carries with it the discourses of homelessness outlined earlier that are expounded in political debate and in the media. These discourses can influence the way that other people perceive homeless people as well as the way that homeless people perceive themselves and their situation.

Within the pathways framework, homelessness is conceived as an episode or episodes in a person's housing pathway. Previous research has been concerned with the construction of personal biographies of individuals in order to elucidate their *assumptive worlds*. The pathways approach examines the relationships between these assumptive worlds and the societal discourses that influence and shape them.

Research on social exclusion has largely focused around issues of definition and measurement of the concept (see for example, Hills, Le Grand & Piachaud, 2002; Room, 1995). There has been some analysis of the changing status of households over time. For example, Barnes (2005) and Burchardt, Le Grand and Piachaud (2002) found that only a few people were socially excluded over a period of time.

One element of research has the potential to link to the pathways approach, while at the same time offering the same benefits of linking the agency and structure dimensions. This tradition of research finds its roots in the concept of *new poverty*, put forward by Leisering and Walker (1998). Within the *new poverty* framework, the assumption is that poverty is dynamic in nature and evidence is given of the way that households move in and out of poverty over time. In other words, poverty is seen as an episode or episodes in a household's earnings pathway, just as homelessness can be seen as an episode in a housing pathway. As in homelessness research, this can lead to a fruitful examination of the factors that trigger a poverty episode and those that can enable a household to move out of poverty. This research focus is similar to that in homelessness where there has been considerable research on the immediate causes of homelessness, and on the interventions that can help to bring an episode to a conclusion.

However, the dynamic focus of the new poverty approach needs to be combined with an analysis of the structures that frame individual action. Otherwise the approach can easily lead to an overemphasis on individual action without examining the discourses that influence the way that people think and act and the opportunities open to them.

INTEGRATING PATHWAYS

The analysis of homelessness using the housing pathways approach, and the dynamic approach to poverty have much in common and can be effectively combined to form a useful aid to understanding the phenomena of homelessness and social exclusion. It was shown earlier that the two phenomena are related at the level of the individual. People defined as socially excluded are more likely to suffer homelessness; also many homeless people would be defined as socially excluded. Therefore, what is being considered are related aspects of the life of some individuals. The pathways framework emphasises the need to adopt a holistic approach to the understanding of a person's housing situation. It is necessary to understand the related employment and family pathways with their impact on income in order to understand the changing housing situation. Decisions that individuals make may take into consideration both their income and housing circumstances. Such decisions impact on these and other aspects of their life. As we have shown earlier, the discourses that frame these decisions have many similarities and are closely related. For all these reasons, homelessness and social exclusion are inextricably linked phenomena that need to be examined together and the pathways approach offers a way of doing this.

The pathways approach demands a different emphasis in terms of research method. The research needs to employ ethnographic, or biographic methods to understand the meaning of individuals and households and the conscious aspects of behaviour. However, the unconscious meanings and actions also need to be explored bearing in mind the constraints and opportunities which structure them and are reproduced by them. Also, the structures themselves need to be analysed.

There are a number of elements of an analysis of pathways, but not all of these need to be included in any one empirical research study. Indeed, it would be very difficult to design and implement research which did undertake all elements simultaneously. Therefore, concentration on some aspects of the whole is usually necessary, although it must be stressed that all of the elements need to be in place for a full understanding of pathways. One of the strengths of the approach is that it draws attention to the importance of a comprehensive analysis. The emphasis on meaning and the wide-ranging nature of many discourses means that the pathways approach tends towards holistic forms of understanding. Many positivist research studies look for partial explanations of phenomena by examining the influence of one or a small number of variables in what is called a nomothetic explanation. In contrast, an idiographic approach attempts to develop as complete an explanation as possible. Therefore, concepts need to be derived which are holistic, enabling all the factors which influence meaning and behaviour to be related together. Where research constraints mean that only a nomothetic analysis is possible, there needs to be a framework in place where partial pieces of the jigsaw can be related to the rest of the picture.

Research on pathways needs to be able to capture the meanings held by households and others, whilst incorporating an awareness of the importance of interaction and the dimension of time. It is a difficult task to choose research tools which meet all of these criteria.

Many of the current widely used research tools in housing analysis are positivist, thus not being "adequate at the level of meaning" (de Vaus, 2001, p. 11) and are cross-sectional in design, thus limited in their approach to the time dimension (for a full discussion of the pathways research approach, see Clapham, 2004).

ASSESSING PUBLIC POLICY

Both homelessness and social exclusion are fields where there is very active public policy intervention. These interventions are shaped by the dominant discourses that were considered earlier. Effectiveness of these interventions is usually judged by criteria within the discourses. For instance, intervention in homelessness is judged by whether an individual remains homeless. Similarly, the effectiveness of social exclusion policies is judged by the extent to which they result in people becoming socially included. There are a number of problems with this approach. The major problem is the contested and ambiguous status of the key concepts in the discourses. The discussion earlier highlighted how the "official" definition of homelessness has changed over time, and is contested by pressure groups representing homeless people. Is someone living in a hostel homeless? Similarly with the concept of social exclusion, it was argued earlier that the concept has a number of dimensions, and it is not always clear how someone becomes socially included. Is a person who has a job, but is socially isolated, socially excluded?

A further problem is caused by the dynamic nature of the two phenomena. A person may be in a hostel one night, but be on the streets intermittently. Alternatively, someone may move rapidly in and out of employment and their income level may change from week to week. At what point is success achieved? The difficulty is in taking a view at one point in time of a complex, dynamic process, where outcomes can change quickly and erratically.

The usual policy approach also defines success on the basis of externally defined criteria which stems from the "top down" nature of the discourses. For example, we have seen that a person may be defined as being homeless and socially excluded if they are on the streets, but may not be so if they are in a hostel. However, the person concerned may view their situation differently and may feel more at home and more socially included on the streets.

One definition of homelessness is that a person does not feel *at home*. This is a very subjective state that may vary considerably between individuals. Research on the meaning of home has shown a wide range of factors that can constitute home and substantial variations between individuals as to what home means to them (for a review, see Clapham, 2005). In the same way social exclusion may be defined in different ways by different people because of its relationship to desired lifestyles. In other words, what people may choose to be included within may vary. In many situations, the *objective* view of homelessness and social exclusion may coincide with that of the person concerned, but in other situations it may not. It is possible to envisage circumstances where policy intervention designed to alleviate homelessness and social exclusion may make the situation as defined by the individual worse (i.e. a person forced to enter a hostel against his/her will). Some definitions of social exclusion stress the powerlessness of individuals and their inability to make the choices that others may be able to make. Therefore, it seems counterproductive to make policy interventions that reduce power by overruling the wishes of the individuals concerned.

The pathways approach opens up another way of assessing success in policy intervention. Rather than focusing on destinations, whether measured in terms of housing situation or income or disadvantage, it is possible to focus on processes. The central focus of this application is the control that individuals have over their circumstances.

CONTROL

Housing policy has been focused on the achievement of certain outcomes, or housing circumstances usually defined in terms of an externally assessed concept of housing quality. This is the case in the policy field of homelessness where there has been a continuing focus on what can be *objectively* defined as constituting a home. It is increasingly difficult to sustain these definitions when housing is a means to an end rather than an end in itself. The importance of housing is to enable people to pursue self-fulfilment and self-esteem through the ability to sustain a valued identity and lifestyle. Therefore, the meaning which people ascribe to their own housing situation is a key factor. In these circumstances, the scope of housing policy is reduced when compared with the modern era. The state cannot hope to understand the meanings which housing will have to individual households. As King (1996, p. 185), argues, the job of the state is ". . . to equalise opportunities for self-creation and then leave people alone to use or neglect their opportunities".

The issue of perceived control is a vital one. In the area of community care of older people, Heywood, Means and Oldman (2002) argue that the positive choice of residential care brings satisfaction as does control over the form of domiciliary services. There is an interesting parallel here with research on the impact of housing on health. Byrne *et al.* (1986) found that the self-reported health status of tenants living in unpopular or difficult to let housing was worse than that of tenants living in identical house types in more popular areas. This could either be explained by the lack of choice of less healthy tenants resulting in them being concentrated in the less popular areas, or it could be that their perception of their situation was crucial in influencing their health status. The latter view is supported by research by Woodin, Delves and Wadhams (1996) which showed that the rehousing of tenants from an unpopular estate led to an increased sense of well-being and a reduction in demand for medical services. They argued that the higher morale of tenants meant that they were better able to deal with problems. The importance of factors such as mastery and self-esteem in influencing health was stressed by Macintyre *et al.* (2000). They found that the most important factors in predicting health and psychological outcomes were age, self-esteem and income.

Further, Giddens' (1994) idea of *regenerative welfare* encompasses forms of State intervention which aim to reinforce people's self-esteem and identity, and enable them to exercise choice in pursuing their own lifestyle and, the notion of a housing pathway (Clapham, 2002, 2005), gives a framework for judging the effectiveness of social interventions. It is difficult to define a successful outcome in terms of specific housing destinations, because identity and self-esteem may be reinforced in many different housing circumstances depending on the meanings held and lifestyle adopted by different households. It is more in keeping with the idea of regenerative welfare for the appropriate judgement to be the extent to which intervention enables households to take charge of their own housing pathway by exercising choice and independence. A major task of housing policy is to find a way of operationalising the concept of personal control in a way that can be used as an indicator of the success of homelessness policy. Taking the overall aim of homelessness policy to be the growth of personal efficacy and self-esteem could radically change the major thrust of policy.

The policy criteria of control and self-esteem also fit well with some discourses of social exclusion. It has already been noted that social exclusion has a strong subjective dimension. Many definitions of the concept emphasise the importance of powerlessness that can be interpreted as being a lack of control. It can be argued that control and self-esteem lie at the heart of issues about the ability of people to achieve integration. This may particularly apply to the difficult issues of personal integration. As with homelessness it could be argued that the key to dealing with social exclusion is to empower individuals through increasing their self-esteem and enabling them to take charge of their circumstances.

CONCLUSION

The chapter has argued that homelessness and social exclusion are linked at many levels and have many similarities. The policy discourses share common features and are both disputed and ambiguous. The individuals labelled as homeless or socially excluded are often the same people as the discourses sometimes cover different aspects of the same personal situation.

The major issue that has created ambiguity and dispute in the policy discourses and has dominated academic study of the two phenomena is the balance between agency and structure. Discourses differ in the primacy they attach to personal agency and structural forces in the causation of the situation and the policy solutions. Academic research has focused either on the structural issues, or the personal circumstances, and has not found a way of effectively combining the two aspects in a coherent analysis.

The chapter puts forward the pathways framework as a way of achieving an integration of agency and structure dimensions. The idea has been used in the analysis of homelessness and it builds on dynamic approaches to the study of *new poverty*. The approach provides a way forward in academic research, but it also highlights a different way of planning and evaluating policy. It is argued that the primary aim of policy should be to put individuals in control of their own circumstances rather then focusing on particular end states or destinations.

REFERENCES

Anderson, I. & Tulloch, D. (2000). *Pathways Through Homelessness: A Review of the Research Evidence*. Edinburgh: Scottish Homes.

Barnes, M. (2005). *Social Exclusion in Britain: An Empirical Investigation and Comparison with the EU*. Aldershot: Aldgate Publishing.

Barry, B. (2002). Social exclusion, social isolation and the distribution of income. In J. Hills, J. Le Grand & D. Piachaud (eds), *Understanding Social Exclusion* (pp. 13–29). Oxford: Oxford University Press.

Berghmann, J. (1995). Social exclusion in Europe: policy context and analytical framework. In G. Room (ed.), *Beyond the Threshold: The Measurement and Analysis of Social Exclusion* (pp. 10–28). Bristol: Policy Press.

Burchardt, T., Le Grand, J. & Piachaud, D. (2002). Degrees of exclusion: developing a dynamic multi-dimensional measure. In J. Hills, J. Le Grand & D. Piachaud (eds), *Understanding Social Exclusion* (pp. 30–43). Oxford: Oxford University Press.

Byrne, D., Harrison, S., Keithley, J. & McCarthy, P. (1986). *Housing and Health*. Aldershot: Gower.

Clapham, D. (2002). Housing pathways: a post modern analytical framework. *Housing, Theory and Society, 19*, 57–68.

Clapham, D. (2003). Pathways approaches to homelessness research. *Journal of Community and Applied Social Psychology, 13*, 1–9.

Clapham, D. (2004). Housing pathways – a social constructionist research framework. In K. Jacobs, J. Kemeny & T. Manzi (eds), *Social Constructionism in Housing Research*. Aldershot: Aldgate.

Clapham, D. (2005). *The Meaning of Housing*. Bristol: Policy Press.

Clapham, D. & Evans, A. (2000). Social exclusion: the case of homelessness. In A. Anderson & D. Sim (eds), *Social Exclusion and Housing: Context and Challenges*. Coventry: Chartered Institute of Housing.

Commins, P. (ed.) (1993). *Combating Exclusion in Ireland 1990–94: A Midway Report*. Brussels: European Commission.

Craig, T., Hodson, S., Woodward, S. & Richardson, S. (1993). *Off to a Bad Start: A Longitudinal Study of Homeless Young People in London*. London: Mental Health Foundation.

Dean, J. & Hastings, A. (2000). *Challenging Images: Housing Estates, Stigma and Regeneration*. Bristol: Policy Press.

de Vaus, D. (2001). *Research Designs in Social Research*. London: Sage.

Evans, A. (1999). Rationing device or passport to social housing? The operation of the homelessness legislation in Britain in the 1990's. In S. Hutson & D. Clapham (eds), *Homelessness: Public Policies and Private Troubles* (pp. 133–154). London: Continuum.

Fitzpatrick, S. (1999). *Young Homeless People*. Basingstoke: Macmillan.

Fitzpatrick, S., Kemp, P. & Klinker, S. (2000). *Single Homelessness: An Overview of Research in Britain*. Bristol: Policy Press.

Giddens, A. (1984). *The Constitution of Society*. Cambridge: Polity Press.

Giddens, A. (1994). *Beyond Left and Right*. Cambridge: Polity Press.

Heywood, F., Means, R. & Oldman, C. (2002). *Housing and Home in Later Life*. Buckingham: Open University Press.

Hills, J., Le Grand, J. & Piachaud, D. (eds) (2002). *Understanding Social Exclusion*. Oxford: Oxford University Press.

Hutson, S. (1999). The experience of homeless accommodation and support. In S. Hutson & D. Clapham (eds), *Homelessness: Public Policies and Private Troubles* (pp. 208–225). London: Continuum.

Jacobs, K., Kemeny, J. & Manzi, A. (1999). The struggle to define homelessness: a social constructionist approach. In S. Hutson & D. Clapham (eds), *Homelessness: Public Policies and Private Troubles* (pp. 11–28). London: Continuum.

King, P. (1996). *The Limits of Housing Policy: A Philosophical Investigation*. London: Middlesex University Press.

Leisering, L. & Walker, R. (eds) (1998). *The Dynamics of Modern Society: Poverty, Policy and Welfare*. Bristol: Policy Press.

Macintyre, S., Kearns, A., Ellaway, A. & Hiscock, R. (2000). *The Thaw Report*. Glasgow: University of Glasgow.

Marshall, T. (1950). *Citizenship and Social Class*. Cambridge: Cambridge University Press.

Morgan, P. (1998). An endangered species. In M. David (ed.), *The Fragmenting Family: Does It Matter?* (pp. 68–99). London: Institute for Economic Affairs.

Murray, C. (1989). Underclass; a disaster in the making. *Sunday Times*, 26 November.

Neale, J. (1997). Theorising homelessness: contemporary sociological and feminist perspectives. In R. Burrows, N. Pleace & D. Quilgars (eds), *Homelessness and Social Policy* (pp. 35–49). London: Routledge.

Nettleton, S., Burrows, R., England, J. & Seavers, J. (1999). *Losing the Family Home: Understanding the Social Consequences of Mortgage Repossession.* York: Joseph Rowntree Foundation.

Pleace, N. & Quilgars, D. (1997). Health, homelessness and access to health care services in London. In R. Burrows, N. Pleace & D. Quilgars (eds), *Homelessness and Social Policy.* London: Routledge.

Room, G. (ed.) (1995). *Beyond the Threshold: The Measurement and Analysis of Social Exclusion.* Bristol: Policy Press.

Somerville, P. (1999). The making and unmaking of homelessness legislation. In S. Hutson & D. Clapham (eds), *Homelessness: Public Policies and Private Troubles* (pp. 29–57). London: Continuum.

Taylor, D. (1998). Social identity and social policy: engagements with post modern theory. *Journal of Social Policy*, 27(3), 329–350.

Woodin, S., Delves, C. & Wadhams, C. (1996). *Just What the Doctor Ordered.* London: London Borough of Hackney.

CHAPTER 6

Education and Social Exclusion

Peter Hick

Manchester Metropolitan University, United Kingdom

and

John Visser and Natasha MacNab

University of Birmingham, United Kingdom

ABSTRACT

This chapter offers an overview of educational research related to issues of social exclusion. Educational research in this field critiques, responds to and informs the developing policy context, and this theme is present throughout the chapter. We begin by exploring the varied, changing and at times contested meanings of some key terms, through the development of a range of understandings of "social exclusion" and "inclusion" in education. The chapter focuses on disciplinary exclusion from school, and goes on to consider hidden forms of exclusion from school and the consequences for social exclusion beyond schooling. This leads to a discussion of issues affecting young people who are not attending school, and those who are missing from any form of educational provision.

Social exclusion can also be understood as a process that has its origins within schools and the educational system. We discuss issues of streaming and the segregation of students who are seen as presenting challenges through their behaviour, within so-called "Learning Support Units". Pressures on schools to internally differentiate pupils by ability are widely thought to impact on equality issues. These are explored in relation to key groups of pupils: those from Black and Minority Ethnic Communities, children who are "looked after" by local authorities, children experiencing mental distress and those identified as having special educational needs within mainstream schools. The chapter concludes by highlighting the tensions between the standards and inclusion agendas in New Labour policy and questioning how far further reforms are likely to impact on structural inequalities.

INTRODUCTION

"Education, education and education" were famously the top three priorities for New Labour under Tony Blair. Yet despite 10 years of policy initiatives, combined with significant levels of investment, substantial inequalities persist in both educational attainment, and more broadly in social inequality. In a recent review of progress in tackling social

Multidisciplinary Handbook of Social Exclusion Research. Edited by D. Abrams, J. Christian and D. Gordon.
© 2007 John Wiley & Sons, Ltd.

exclusion (Social Exclusion Task Force, 2006), the government highlights their claims for success, yet recognises the scale of the challenge involved in meeting their stated goals in this area. A recent review by the Centre for Analysis of Social Exclusion at the LSE, of the evidence on the impact of policies towards poverty, inequality and social exclusion under New Labour (Joseph Rowntree Foundation, 2005), suggests that progress has been limited. For example, they found that the level of child poverty is still above the European average, and that large social class differences remain in education: "overall improvements in . . . educational achievement have sometimes left the most disadvantaged lagging even further behind".

It is widely recognised amongst educationalists that there remains a tension at the heart of New Labour education policy, between the drive to raise standards and the goal of promoting educational inclusion (Dyson, Gallannaugh & Millward, 2003). Equally, schools are increasingly being posited as a site for generating social transformation; yet the most disadvantaged communities served by schools in challenging circumstances, are sometimes seen as contributing to the process of social exclusion, through a "poverty of aspiration". A key weakness of this understanding of social exclusion is a downplaying of the impact of poverty and material disadvantage. There is a conflation with characteristics imputed to individuals; these are seen as increasing risk factors or conferring personal resilience to adverse circumstances. However, it is material disadvantage that moulds the social framework within which the "risk and resilience" discourse is played out, in real life in schools and communities. The experience of the National Evaluation of the Children's Fund (Edwards *et al.*, 2006) suggests that strategies aimed at building individual resilience, should be understood in the context of the need to address the levels of material disadvantage that are likely to be experienced by children at risk of social exclusion.

Social inequality needs to be included in any definition of social exclusion and the way in which people can be excluded from "opportunities, choices and life chances" (p. 1) needs to be acknowledged. In 1997, the Social Exclusion Unit (SEU) was established to tackle "the social, economic and educational causes of disaffection and alienation" (Vulliamy & Webb, 2003, p. 45). Social exclusion has been described by the New Labour government as:

> A shorthand term for what can happen when people or areas suffer from a combination
> of linked problems such as unemployment, poor skills, low incomes, poor housing,
> high crime, bad health and family breakdown. (SEU, 2001, para. 1.2, 2001)

The SEU recognised that this definition is ambiguous and that many other dimensions of exclusion could be added; these problems are deemed as related and mutually reinforcing, and it is acknowledged that they can combine to create a complex and fast-moving vicious cycle (Daniels, 2004). Through a combination of poverty, family conflict, poor educational opportunities and poor services, government has suggested that many young people find their lives on a trajectory characterised by underachievement and social exclusion (SEU, 2000). Furthermore, government highlight "poor" educational achievement as contributing significantly, so that "people who have had problems at school are more likely to become socially excluded" (SEU, 2001).

SOCIAL EXCLUSION AND INCLUSION IN EDUCATION

The frequency of use of the term "inclusion" in education has grown rapidly over the last 15 years, and with it the range of meanings associated with the term (Ainscow, Farrell &

Tweddle, 2000). It is a vague term, open to an assortment of understandings and interpretations within a range of contexts, usually resting on a set of values embedded within
a community and a range of practice (Fletcher-Campbell, 2001). In the UK, the prominence given to inclusion by the New Labour government since 1997 has given particular
impetus to this development. "Inclusion" has increasingly come to mean different things
to different people, reflecting the range of contexts, purposes and interests involved in
constructing these meanings (Thomas & Loxley, 2001). Surveying the literature now, it
is clear that there is no single, universally agreed meaning of the term "inclusion" (Slee,
2004). One useful approach is to describe the range of understandings of inclusion in the
research literature, rather than to prescribe another "new" definition (Booth and Arinscow,
1998). This involves "mapping" the major schools of thought and streams of research in
inclusive education over the last 15 years, together with the definitions and conceptions
of inclusion they both reflected and developed (Clough, 2000; Lunt & Norwich, 1999).
The influence on policy making of these approaches, can be traced through the range of
definitions used by UK government departments and agencies.

The following diagram serves to illustrate these issues:

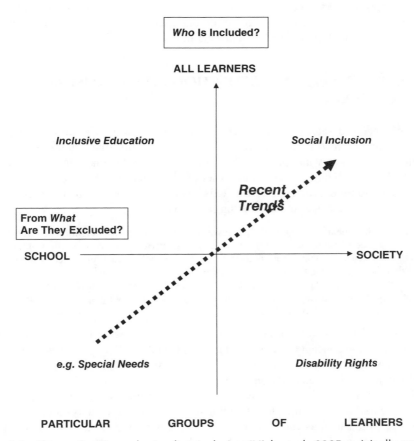

Figure 6.1 Perspectives in understanding inclusion (Hick *et al.*, 2005; originally proposed
by Alan Dyson)

Figure 6.1 highlights a general direction of development in approaches to understanding inclusion. The diagram suggests a process of movement from, for example, an initial focus on the inclusion of learners with disabilities, to a wider focus on all learners at increased risk of exclusion or marginalisation from schooling; and from a specific concern with exclusion from school, to a broader concern with exclusion from participation in society beyond school. The figure highlights two dimensions of difference in meanings of inclusion: on the one hand *who* is being included? And on the other hand, from *what* are they being excluded?

The lower left quadrant "the inclusion of learners with disabilities in mainstream schools" could be characterised as a "special needs" perspective. This is allied with a "disability rights" perspective, which advocates the inclusion of people with disabilities in society as a civil right. A concern with developing the capacity of mainstream schools to include not only learners with disabilities but all those learners who may be vulnerable to marginalisation or excluded from education can be described as an "inclusive education" approach. A perspective based on extending this approach to inclusion in society beyond mainstream schooling can be labelled as "social inclusion" and is represented in the upper right quadrant.

This process can be used to map the major streams of research, exemplified by the work of particular researchers; together with associated conceptions and definitions of inclusion. Alternatively, it can be used to locate definitions used by government departments and agencies, together with policy and programme initiatives.

UNDERSTANDINGS AND DEFINITIONS OF INCLUSION AND EXCLUSION

There is often considerable overlap and mutual influence between the various perspectives represented in Figure 6.1; this "mapping" process also illustrates areas of interaction between research, policy and practice. For example, one influential stream of research is exemplified in the "Index for Inclusion", a set of materials for school self-evaluation and development (Booth & Ainscow, 2000). This has led to the development of some widely disseminated approaches to understanding inclusion:

> Inclusion in education involves the processes of increasing the participation of students in, and reducing their exclusion from, the cultures, curricula and communities of local schools. Inclusion involves restructuring the cultures, policies and practices in schools so that they respond to the diversity of students in their locality. Inclusion is concerned with the learning and participation of all students vulnerable to exclusionary pressures, not only those with impairments or those categorised as having special educational needs. (Booth & Ainscow, 2000, p. 12)

The notion of "barriers to learning and participation" is presented in this perspective as an alternative to the concept of "special educational needs" (SEN). This reflects a development from a within-child, individual deficit approach towards a focus on institutional and societal barriers to inclusion and on taking action to change them. This trend is evident in the language adopted in a series of key policy initiatives by the UK government. For example, one of the three principles of the Inclusion Statement in the National Curriculum (QCA, 1999), described as essential to developing a more inclusive curriculum, involves "overcoming potential barriers to learning". The statutory Inclusion Guidance (DfES,

2001a) defines inclusion as "a process by which schools and LEAs develop their cultures, policies and practices to include pupils [and] actively seek to remove barriers to learning". The recent SEN strategy document (DfES, 2004a) is itself entitled "Removing Barriers to Achievement".

A number of recent research projects have refined the detailed approach described in the "Index for Inclusion" to focus on the *outcomes* of inclusive learning: presence, participation and achievement. This development offers a practical definition of inclusion that reflects the importance of "measuring what we value". This approach has recently been adopted by the Audit Commission (2002) in their review of SEN provision in mainstream schools, and in the Manchester Inclusion Standard:

> *Presence* is concerned with where learners are educated, and whether they attend regularly and arrive punctually. All schools and settings should enable children, young people and adults to receive their education in a mainstream setting as far as possible. Presence is about admissions, attendance, exclusions and the use of withdrawal from class. *Participation* is concerned with the quality of learners' educational experiences. Learners' own views should therefore form an essential part of any judgement made about the quality of their participation. *Achievement* is concerned with learner outcomes across the whole curriculum, both inside and outside the classroom. (Manchester City Council, 2004)

As noted previously, this chapter addresses broader issues of social exclusion and education, rather than adopting a narrower focus on the inclusion in mainstream schools of children with disabilities. However it is worth noting that, contrary to the impression given in sections of the media, there has been only a marginal change in the proportion of children with Statements of SEN placed in mainstream schools since the introduction of the Statutory Inclusion Framework in 2001 (OFSTED, 2004). Indeed, English law at present does not give an unfettered right to inclusion in mainstream schools; instead, it places a "duty" on local authorities to educate young people with SEN (Visser & Stokes, 2003). Under section 1 of the Special Educational Needs and Disability Act (DfES, 2001b), local authorities have a "duty" to educate children with SEN in mainstream schools, provided that:

- other children's education is not adversely affected (and that reasonable measures have been taken to prevent this);
- parents are in agreement (although a local authority can place a child in a mainstream school if a special school is not appropriate).

DISCIPLINARY EXCLUSION

At the core of the literature on inclusion is the issue of how to reconcile the seemingly opposing principles of increasing, on the one hand school attainment and on the other inclusion. Evans and Lunt (2002) note that the obvious divergence in government policy between the "standards" and "league tables" debate and the "inclusive schools" discourse make it challenging for schools to become more inclusive. Armstrong (2005) notes the ambiguous and contradictory nature of current policies on inclusive education indicating that there is an assumption that "to be 'just', the education system must accommodate children whose individual disadvantages place them at risk of exclusion" (p. 141). The competitive pressures within and across schools have led some to argue that schools need to maximise their league table position and consequently their market advantage (Sparkes, 1999); and that this fosters an environment in which "hard to manage" or challenging pupils are more likely to be excluded. There has been widespread debate about "troubled" and "troublesome" behaviour which appears to place the needs of these pupils in conflict with the needs of an academically successful and well-disciplined school (McCluskey, 2006). Permanent exclusion from school has been linked to wider exclusion from society (Hayton, 1999) and can result in long periods without education (Audit Commission, 1999; Commission for Racial Equality, 1996; Department for Education, 1995), underachievement and diminished employment prospects (SEU, 1998). During the last decade and a half, concern over the numbers of young people excluded from school has been a key feature of educational policy (DfEE, 1999a, 1999b; SEU, 1998).

Reasons for Exclusion

In most cases, disciplinary exclusion is viewed as the last resort following a range of measures to support pupils in improving their behaviour, particularly for "vulnerable groups" such as looked-after children and those with SEN, for whom every effort should "be made to intervene early and prevent behaviour reaching the threshold for exclusion" (DfES, 2006a, p. 61, para. 5.35). Gordon (2001) however, argues that in many cases permanent exclusion is often not the only remaining option and OFSTED (1996) and Osler, Watling and Busher (2001) argue that it is frequently adopted as a school management tool. Generally, the most common reason given for permanent exclusion from school is physical or verbal violence, followed by disruption and other misconduct. Exclusion on the grounds of disruptive behaviour is one of the most overt forms of rejection by a school of its pupils, and for many young people increases the probability of their social exclusion (Munn & Lloyd, 2005). However, it would appear that there are usually additional reasons behind the one that is recorded. Tensions in pupil–teacher relationships have been highlighted; behaviours seen as challenging and rejecting of teacher authority, such as verbal abuse, have been noted as underlying reasons behind those officially recorded (Gordon, 2001). Berridge et al. (2001) and Vulliamy and Webb (2001) note that exclusion is a social process; often there are discrepancies in the way schools respond to certain behaviours and Osler, Watling and Busher (2001) note that the biggest factor influencing whether a pupil is likely to be excluded from school is the particular school s/he attends.

Numbers of Exclusions

Despite government targets (SEU, 1998) that aimed to reduce the overall number of permanent exclusions by one third by 2002, official exclusion figures have steadily risen, with fluctuations in the intervening years. The number of recorded permanent exclusions quadrupled from 2,900 in 1990/91 to 12,665 in 1996/97, with some reductions during the period 1997–2000 (DfEE, 1999c; Harris, Eden & Blair, 2000). There were 9,135 recorded permanent exclusions from primary, secondary and special schools during 2000/01 (DfES, 2002). During 2002/03, there were 9,290 permanent exclusions from primary, secondary and all special schools of which 7,432 were from secondary schools (DfES, 2004b). By 2004/05, the number of children and young people permanently excluded from school was 9,400—8,070 of these from secondary schools (DfES, 2006a). The "Truancy and School Exclusion" Report (SEU, 1998) highlighted varying exclusion rates from schools serving similar catchment areas:

> Some schools are so anxious to avoid exclusion that they incur some danger to them-selves as institutions, to staff and pupils. Others are only too ready to exclude. A few are irresponsibly profligate in the use made of exclusion, devaluing it as a sanction. (SEU, 1998, p. 2)

The report also indicated that exclusions had increased for a number of reasons, including:

- poor acquisition of basic skills;
- limited pupil aspirations;
- social and family risk factors;
- poor pupil relationships with teachers;
- pressures on schools to increase academic standards;
- publication of school performance tables;
- inappropriate curricula for those who have "fallen behind" in class;
- lack of training for teachers in handling behaviour difficulties.

However, others (Beckmann & Cooper, 2004) point to the post-1988 educational environment, with its emphasis on the achievement of government-led standards, leading to what McNess, Broadfoot and Osborn (2003) call a "performance model" of education. As a result, a school worried about its public image or position in league tables may be more likely to resort to fixed-term, permanent or "unofficial" exclusions.

Unofficial Exclusions

Besides the official categories of exclusion, the literature makes reference to unofficial exclusions (Daniels *et al.*, 2003; Osler, Watling & Busher, 2001; SEU, 1998; Vulliamy & Webb, 2001), whilst others indicate that data can be manipulated or distorted by schools (Visser & Stokes, 2003; Vulliamy & Webb, 2001). Daniels *et al.* (2003) found that head teachers were at times resorting to "informal" exclusions, in an attempt to avoid financial penalties and meet national targets. These "unofficial" exclusions may include "managed transfers" which fall outside official recording systems. This usually involves persuading or encouraging parents to move their child to another educational institution, in lieu of a threatened exclusion. Thus the move is presented as beneficial to the parents and pupil and the school's league table image is safeguarded (Vulliamy & Webb, 2001). DfES sees a move of this kind, when done through official means, as an opportunity:

> to enable the pupil to have a fresh start in a new school. The head teacher may ask another head teacher to admit the pupil. This should only be done with the full knowl-edge and cooperation of all the parties involved, including the parents, governors and the LA, and in circumstances where it is in the best interests of the pupil concerned. (DfES, 2006a, http://www.teachernet.gov.uk/wholeschool/behaviour/exclusion/guidance/part1/)

Yet the consequences of such a move may be unknown to parents and children. Osler, Watling and Busher (2001) indicate that these unofficial exclusions can hamper parents' and carers' rights to confront the school, and may lead to longer-term problems for children, their parents and schools.

School Exclusion and Social Consequences

The literature refers to a link between school exclusion and crime (Audit Commission, 1996, 1999; Bracher, Hitchcock & Moss, 1998; Osler *et al.*, 2001, Parsons, 1999; Rutter, Giller & Hagell, 1998; Vulliamy & Webb, 2001). This link has been noted in the "Truancy and School Exclusions Report" by the SEU (1998) which commented on a clear link between children not attending school and crime, stating that "many of today's non-attenders are in danger of becoming tomorrow's criminals and unemployed" (p. 3). The Audit Commission (1996) found that 42% of offenders of school age who were sentenced in the youth courts have been excluded from school. Berridge *et al.* (2001) conducted a retrospective policy that looked at data on excluded young people between the years 1988 and 1998. Out of 263 cases examined, Berridge *et al.* (2001) found that:

- 85 had no recorded offences prior to, or following, permanent exclusion from school;
- 117 had no recorded offences prior to permanent exclusion but had a record of offending following permanent exclusion;
- 47 had recorded offences before and after permanent exclusion;
- 14 had recorded offences before but not after.

However, we concur with Berridge *et al.* (2001) in their caution against adopting a one-dimensional approach to analysing links between school exclusion, crime and social exclusion. These complex issues are explored in more detail elsewhere in this volume (see Hale & FitzGerald).

YOUNG PEOPLE NOT ATTENDING SCHOOL

What are the alternatives for those young people who may be at risk of social exclusion or have become marginalised from school? It has been recognised by government, for a number of years, that for some pupils, a range of alternative settings for their education should be available, and this is an element of the DfES Behaviour and Attendance Strategy (DfES, 2006a). An alternative educational environment could be offered while the pupil is still on school-roll or after they have been excluded, offering a wider range of options. Schools and Local Authorities (LAs) should have a number of strategies to address behaviour which may lead to exclusion (DfES, 2006a) and head teachers:

> should be able to refer pupils identified at risk of exclusion, to alternative or additional provision to meet their individual needs, which could include working in partnership with other agencies. (DfES, 2006a)

The range of alternative provision identified includes schools, Pupil Referral Units (PRUs), voluntary or community organisations, private sector providers, and further education colleges or work experience placements. Any relevant information about the pupils, including an assessment of needs, should be passed on to the LA (DfES, 2006a, para. 171). The Elton Report, for example, proposed:

> that ordinary schools should do all in their power to retain and educate all the pupils on their roll on-site. However, we recognise that in the case of a small number of pupils this may be difficult, and in some cases impossible. (Department of Education and Science, 1989, p. 152, para. 6.39)

The Programme of Action (DfEE, 1998) indicated that for some pupils, especially those described as experiencing "social, emotional and behavioural difficulties" (SEBD), alternative provision has an important function. However, the literature indicates that there is often a long waiting period before a child is placed (Berridge et al., 2001), exacerbating their isolation.

Further Education has become one element of the Government's drive for "social inclusion" and "widening participation" and is seen as an important means of engaging the disengaged in education and training (Crossan et al., 2000; Gallacher et al., 2000). Providing alternative curricula which could allow achievement to flourish, has been greeted as a potential means of assisting in the engagement and interest of pupils who may have experienced failure at school. In spite of the Government's rejection of the Tomlinson Report (DfES, 2004d), the benefits that some pupils could have in more mature, adult environment were noted:

> the larger 'disaffected but in touch' group which comprises approximately 20 % of 14–16 year-olds have been shown to respond to a range of initiatives which often share the characteristics of taking them out of school . . . into work-related settings (e.g. FE college, workplace). (DfES, 2004d: p. 94, para. 244)

Children and Young People Missing from Education

One severe form of social exclusion that is sometimes overlooked is the experience of young people who go missing from the education system. There is a danger that some young people excluded from school may become increasingly marginalised (MacNab, Visser & Daniels, 2007), and ultimately lost to education altogether. NACRO (2003), the crime reduction charity, define "the missing" as those children and young people who have not been on any educational register in the previous 6 months.

It has been suggested that this cohort have not gained from recent government policies on inclusion, and are often invisible on government agendas (Broadhurst, Paton & May-Chahal, 2005). Children and young people who are "missing" are missing out on, as well as missing from, the education which aims to equip them with abilities that assist them in life (Visser, Daniels & MacNab, 2005). Visser, Daniels and MacNab (2005) point out that children who go missing, can include children who have had poor learning experiences; those who have experienced bullying and racial harassment in school; those who are labelled as a troublesome pupil; together with young people who have been permanently excluded from school. A sizeable proportion of children and young people missing, they indicate, are likely to have social, emotional and behavioural difficulties. However, there is a lack of data for identifying other needs amongst those who are missing, because the trajectory of a missing young person is often complicated.

There are many circumstances in which children can go missing from education and thus suffer very high degrees of social exclusion, amongst them:

- families for whom education is not a priority and thus do not register their child(ren);
- a lack of knowledge or unhelpful encounters with educational systems, which can discourage families from engaging;
- a lack of information on pupils or poor tracking systems in place during the transfer from school to alternative settings;
- those reluctant to re-engage after being out of education for a long duration (Visser, Daniels & MacNab, 2005).

Defining who "the missing" are, is part of the difficulty in trying to quantify the numbers who are missing. Since they are missing, these young people will not be on any database, therefore how does one calculate something which is not there? OFSTED (2003) indicate:

> The best estimate—and it is an estimate—is that there were 10,000 15 year olds missing from school rolls in England in 2002. (p. 48, para. 158)

Others state that the figure may be much higher. NACRO (2003), for example, imply that the figure may be between 50,000 and 100,000 when looking across all key stages.

Recent policy initiatives (DfES, 2002) have attempted to address the issue of the "missing". Every Child Matters (2004) and DfES (2002) have attempted to ensure that by 2005, systems would be in place in each LA to identify and track children missing from education or those deemed "at risk" of going missing from education. Using the "Identification, Referral and Tracking Guidance", LAs had to identify an individual who would be responsible for collating information on children and young people identified as missing from education and providing appropriate support for them. DfES (2006b) reported that most LAs have systems in place to track children identified as missing, although many LAs noted that having systems in place did not always mean that the systems were working.

SOCIAL EXCLUSION WITHIN SCHOOLS

Streaming

The principle of streaming pupils by ability in schools, a dominant ideology in the postwar period, became progressively unpopular in England from the 1970s. With a move away from the 11+ examination, there was a parallel shift from the streaming agenda, towards classes being structured by mixed-ability settings. Yet over the past 10 years or so, DfEE (1997), OFSTED (1998) and individual schools have reassessed the question of setting or streaming pupils according to their achievement levels (Hallam, Ireson & Davies, 2004). This has partly been in response to the standards agenda and is seen as a means of raising achievement. Streaming pupils by ability and achievement has garnered much debate and questions about the effectiveness of streaming and its consequences for social inclusion continue.

There are two main types of grouping primary school pupils by ability within schools:

• streaming—separating pupils into groups by global ability and teaching them in the same class for all subjects;
• setting—separating pupils into different groups by ability for individual subjects.

The most common type of grouping is "within-class" where the teacher sets ability groups within the class (DfES, 2006c).

One of the negative effects of setting is the potential for stigmatisation and damage to a pupil's self-esteem, itself a form of social exclusion within school. According to Gamoran (2002), there are two main problems associated with setting and streaming. The first relates to inequalities for particular groups of learners; when teachers separate pupils by achievement levels they are also predisposed to separate by race/ethnicity, and by social class. Secondly, differences in achievement levels of pupils in different classes tend to become exacerbated over time. Hallam, Ireson and Davies (2004) highlight primary school pupils' perceptions and experiences of being grouped by ability. They found that pupils were aware of the function of setting, and that the majority supported the policy in their school. The pupils interviewed in Hallam et al.'s study (2003) stated that the main advantage of ability grouping was having their work set at appropriate levels, while the main disadvantage was the stigmatisation of lower ability pupils. There is a need therefore, to carefully consider the effects that setting may have on pupils as this may affect "their performance, their perceptions of themselves as learners, and on their lifelong view of education and schooling" (Davies, Hallam & Ireson, 2003, p. 58).

Learning Support Units

One strand of the DfES "Excellence in Cities" programme was the development of designated units within secondary schools to meet the needs of pupils whose behaviour is perceived as presenting particular challenges. These "Learning Support Units" are an integral part of government policy to increase inclusion by improving behaviour and attendance, promoting:

> a whole-school behaviour and attendance inclusion policy that should reflect inclusive philosophy and practice as defined in Every Child Matters: Change for Children . . . and are designed to meet the needs of pupils who may have any number, or combination of challenges to their learning. (DfES, 2005, p. 1)

OFSTED in their report "Evaluation of the impact of learning support units" (2006) revealed that all of 12 units inspected were successful in improving the behaviour and attendance of their pupils. OFSTED (2006) define successful units as those that combine teaching and pastoral care. However, in some units, it was found that:

reintegrating pupils to mainstream classes was not always successful, either because pupils had not learnt to cope or because mainstream teachers did not have strategies to manage the reintegrated pupils effectively. (OFSTED, 2006, p. 2)

SOCIAL EXCLUSION AND PARTICULAR GROUPS OF LEARNERS

Within the excluded population, certain groups of children are disproportionately represented. For example, there are an unequal proportion of particular minority ethnic groups and of children "looked after" by local authorities. Osler, Watling and Busher (2001) note that ethnicity, gender, socio-economic status and SEN can all have an impact on the likelihood of being excluded from school. Around 80% of those excluded are male (DfES, 2002; Hayden & Dunne, 2001; OFSTED, 1996; SEU, 1998) and there is an over-representation of children with statements of SEN (DfEE, 1999a; Osler *et al.*, 2001).

Pupils from Black and Minority Ethnic (BME) Communities

DfES (2005) has confirmed that there continues to be a disproportionate level of disciplinary exclusion of pupils from some minority ethnic groups. Black Caribbean boys who are identified as having SEN are particularly vulnerable to being excluded from school (Hick, 2005). Figures show that the highest exclusion rate by ethnic group was for Black Caribbean pupils, at 37 per 1,000, over three times the rate of White pupils excluded (Babb, Martin & Haezewindt, 2004). In 2003/04 around 25 in every 10,000 pupils of mixed ethnic origin were permanently excluded from school—similar to figures for excluded Black pupils (29 in every 10,000—twice that for White pupils). Approximately 7 in every 100 pupils of Black or Mixed ethnic origin were excluded for a fixed period in 2003/04. This compares with almost 5 in every 100 pupils of White ethnic origin (DfES, 2005). However, there was a sharp decline from 1997/8 (76 per 1,000) for Black Caribbean exclusions, while figures for others in Black and ethnic minority communities remained relatively stable (Babb, Martin & Haezewindt, 2004). The evidence shows that some schools exclude at much higher rates than others with comparable populations, and suggests that those that exclude more children tend to exclude disproportionately more BME children (Osler, 1997; Blair, 2005).

In what ways are children from BME communities still missing out in terms of SEN? The DfES recently started collecting data on individual pupils' attainment, using particular categories of ethnicity and SEN. A preliminary analysis of the first year's data (DfES, 2005, p. 2) highlights a number of key findings, for example:

- Permanent exclusion rates are higher for Travelers of Irish Heritage, Gypsy/Roma, Black Caribbean, Black Other and White/Black Caribbean pupils.
- Black Caribbean and Black other boys are twice as likely to have been categorised as having behavioural, emotional or social difficulty as White British boys.
- Pupils with English as an additional language are slightly less likely to be identified with SEN and are less likely to be classified as having a specific learning difficulty [e.g. dyslexia]. However they are more likely to have an identified speech, language or communication need.

- Pakistani pupils are two to five times more likely than White British pupils to have an identified visual impairment or hearing impairment.
- Gypsy/Roma pupils and Travelers of Irish Heritage have very low attainment through Key Stage assessments and also have much higher identification of SEN.

These findings are based on SEN identified by schools, a process called "School Action Plus", or by local authorities, through "Statements" of SEN. In order to understand how a process of institutional racism can lead to an over- or under-identification of SEN in BME communities, we need to recognise the role of SEN categories in an administrative process for rationing resources.

How does it happen that children from some BME communities are discriminated against, or treated less favourably, when their teachers are typically not racist? One important strand of explanation focuses on White teachers' interpretations of Black pupils' cultural characteristics. For example, the incorrect reading of Black pupils' body language, attitude and clothing (Blyth & Milner, 1993; Gillborn, 1999; Majors, Gillborn & Sewell, 1998; Osler & Hill, 1999); responses to Black pupils' questioning of teachers' judgements (Osler, Watling & Busher, 2001); the "over-masculinising" of Black boys' identities, together with negative racial stereotyping of Black pupils (Appiah & Chunilal, 1999; Wright et al., 1998, Wright, Weekes & McGlaughlin, 1999); have all been proposed as factors underlying the disproportionate number of excluded Black pupils. However, this discussion needs to be understood in the context of a more general account of issues of race and social exclusion (see Percival, Chapter 9).

Looked-after Children

Children who are looked after by local authorities are viewed as another group at greater risk of social exclusion (see Jackson, Chapter 7). DfES describe them as a:

> disadvantaged group who have very low average levels of attainment, often related to frequent changes of school because their care placements change. (DfES, 2003, para. 3.14)

The SEU Report "A Better Education for Children in Care" (SEU, 2004a) focused on the marginalisation of these children. It found that a "significant minority—around one in four—are educated in non-mainstream settings or at home" (p. 4). The report suggested five reasons why looked-after children may be less likely to succeed in education:

- Their lives are characterised by instability.
- They spend too much time out of school.
- They do not have sufficient help with their education if they fall behind.
- Primary carers are not expected or equipped to provide sufficient support and encouragement for learning and development; and
- They have unmet emotional, mental and physical health needs that impact on their education (p. 3).

Additionally, SEU (2004a) noted a number of underlying factors adversely affecting the education of looked-after children, including staff and skills shortages, structures that prevent joined-up working, and poor management and leadership (p. 3).

Looked-after children are excluded from school at a disproportionately high rate: 0.9% of looked-after children were permanently excluded in 2004/5 compared with 0.1% of all children (DfES, 2006d). Circular 13/94, "The Education of Children Being Looked After by Local Authorities" and "Care Matters: Transforming the Lives of Children and Young People in Care" (DfES, 2006d) highlighted the vulnerability of this group of children, and called for understanding to be exercised when looked-after children are at risk of exclusion. The Statutory Guidance on the Duty on Local Authorities to Promote the Educational Achievement of Looked After Children under Section 52 of the Children Act 2004 states:

> it is important to be especially sensitive in relation to exclusions where looked after children are concerned. Every practicable means should be tried to maintain the child in school. (DfES, 2004c, p. 13, para. 41)

Pupils with SEN

Exclusion rates of pupils with Statements of SEN are also very high; figures show that they were nine times more likely to be excluded from school than those with no SEN in 2002/3. Some children do experience difficulties in learning, and parents and teachers may seek to identify them as having SEN in order to access additional resources for them. SEN are defined in relative terms: a child's needs are "special" if they require more support than is usually available to other children (DfES, 2001a). But how much is more? In practice this can vary between schools, and between local authorities, influenced by local policies, resources and patterns of provision, together with levels of social disadvantage. There may be variations between schools in the level of needs they support within their own resources, and when accessing outside agencies as "School Action Plus". The legal definition of SEN, however, is not based on an objective, uniformly applied measurement or diagnosis of "need". It is important to understand that the various categories of SEN are assigned to individual children through a social process. For example:

> At what point does the disaffection and underachievement of a Black Caribbean boy at a secondary school, who is increasingly resisting schooling (possibly as a result of what he sees as a racist experience), become an emotional or cognitive need, recognised as a special educational need meriting necessary additional resources organised by the SENCo [SEN Coordinator]? (Gerschel, 2003, p. 53)

A "social model" of disability describes SEN categories such as "moderate learning difficulties", or "behavioural, emotional or social difficulties", together with medical diagnoses such as ADHD (Attention Deficit Hyperactivity Disorder) as labels that serve to pathologise children (Oliver, 1990). Attention is thus focused on individual children's difficulties rather than on how well schools support them, or on social disadvantage. The way in which individual differences between children are defined, so that some are categorised as having "special educational needs", is essentially socially constructed (Thomas & Loxley, 2001). Categorisation often depends on our reading of what is "normal" behaviour. Assessment tools such as IQ (Howe, 1997) tend to reflect social and educational inequalities, based on social class and ethnicity.

Pupils Experiencing Difficulties with Mental Health

The Health Advisory Service (HAS) report "Together We Stand" (HAS, 1995) highlighted that Directors of Education should regard mental health provision as a "significant responsibility" (HAS, 1995, p. 9). Cole, Daniels and Visser (1999) highlight the connection between some pupils' neglected mental health needs and disaffection from school (see also Cole *et al.*, 2002). Furthermore Cole and Visser (2000) have noted the link between poor quality of child and adolescent mental health services (CAMHS) and school exclusions.

The educational policy focus on young people experiencing mental health difficulties could be said to reflect the OFSTED framework for inspecting inclusion in schools (OFSTED, 2000). The literature has established links between mental health and issues of social exclusion including youth crime, early pregnancy, truancy and violent behaviour. Saxe and Cross (1997) assert that only a small proportion of pupils in need of mental health services receive them, particularly in non-mental health settings such as schools.

The Mental Health Foundation (2001) indicates the importance of schools in helping to promote children's mental health. They comment that primary schools in particular, should do more to identify and support children at risk of developing mental health problems. The Report recommends that:

- Every school should identify a mental health co-ordinator to develop practice promoting children's mental health and provide a link to specialist mental health services;
- All teachers within mainstream schools should have ongoing training on child development issues including mental health difficulties; and on straightforward school-based work with children at risk of developing mental health problems;
- OFSTED inspections should additionally take account of the emotional development of children and assess schools on their ability to work effectively with children with emotional and behavioural problems.

In order to reduce social exclusion, schools need to play their part in promoting better mental health for children and young people (Young Minds, 2002). This requires the development of more "practical teaching resources to challenge the stigma surrounding mental health from an early age through schools" (SEU, 2004b, p. 7).

CONCLUSIONS

Inclusion and social exclusion have been at the core of New Labour's education policies for the last decade. Yet, despite the positive policy initiatives implemented by the government in recent times (for example Sure Start, and Excellence in Cities), there is little evidence so far to indicate their wider impact on social inequality. Subsequent policies and guidance documents affirm the government's commitment to at least the rhetoric of the inclusion agenda. The literature grapples with the contradictions between the standards agenda and inclusion policies and the "tensions" at the centre of any debate about exclusion and inclusion (Fletcher-Campbell, 2001). According to Fletcher-Campbell (2001), these tensions arise from the following issues:

- efficiency, economy and resources;
- the needs of pupils;
- the choices, aspirations and beliefs of various stakeholders, for example LEAs, teachers and parents (p. 75).

Yet government see these policies as complementary rather than contradictory (Croll & Moses, 2000); the Cabinet Office (2002) state that "social inclusion has never been that far away from the Excellence Agenda" (p. 1). Dyson, Gallannaugh and Millward (2003) state that the inclusion agenda is complicated by two factors: the difficulties in defining the term inclusion and the government's drive for standards and excellence in schools, which many see as diametrically opposed to a social inclusion agenda. They warn against being pessimistic arguing that if there were to be even a "small moderation of standards-based policies and a limited strengthening of the supportive factors some real differences could become apparent" (pp. 14–15).

However, it seems unlikely that a refinement or intensification of current policy initiatives related to social exclusion, will in themselves be sufficient to overcome the structural social inequality and child poverty that arguably underpins persistent inequalities in educational attainment. A significant redirection of social resources towards more directly addressing poverty and material disadvantage would arguably be a prerequisite for more fundamental progress in tackling social exclusion. In education, a wholesale shift away from selective and competitive pressures on schools, towards a more comprehensive, egalitarian distribution of resources and opportunities, would equally form a basis for a more inclusive education system.

REFERENCES

Ainscow, M., Farrell, P. & Tweddle, D. (2000). Developing policies for inclusive education: a study of the role of local education authorities. *International Journal of Inclusive Education, 4*(3), 211–229.

Appiah, L. & Chunilal, N. (1999). Examining school exclusions and the race factor. The Runnymede Trust Briefing Paper.

Armstrong, D. (2005). Reinventing 'inclusion': New Labour and the cultural politics of special education. *Oxford Review of Education, 31*(1), 135–151.

Audit Commission. (1996). *Misspent Youth: Young people and Crime.* London: HMSO.

Audit Commission. (1999). *Missing Out: LEA Management of School Attendance and Exclusion.* Retrieved from www.audit-commision.gov.uk

Audit Commission. (2002). *Special Educational Needs: A Mainstream Issue.* London: Audit Commission.

Babb, P., Martin, J. & Haezewindt, P. (2004). *Focus: Social Inequalities.* London: T.S.O.

Beckmann, A. & Cooper, C. (2004). 'Globalisation', the new managerialism and education: rethinking the purpose of education in Britain. *Journal for Critical Education Policy Studies, 2,* 2. Retrieved from http://www.jceps.com/?pageID=article&articleID=31

Berridge, D., Brodie, I., Pitts, J., *et al.* (2001). The independent effects of permanent exclusion from school on the offending careers of young people. RDS Occasional Paper 71, London: Home Office.

Blair, M. (2005). The education of black children: why do some schools do better than others? In M. Nind, J. Rix, K. Sheehy & K. Simmons (eds), *Curriculum and Pedagogy in Inclusive Education.* Abingdon: Routledge Falmer.

Blyth, E. & Milner, J. (1993). Exclusion from school: a first step to exclusion from society? *Children and Society, 7*(3), 255–268.

Booth, T. & Ainscow (Eds.) (1998). *From Them to Us: an International Study of Inclusion in Education*. London: Routledge.

Booth, T. & Ainscow, M. (2000). *Index for Inclusion*. Bristol: Centre for Studies on Inclusive Education.

Booth, T. & Ainscow, M. (2002). *Index for Inclusion: Developing Learning and Participation in Schools*. Bristol: Centre for Studies on Inclusive Education.

Bracher, D., Hitchcock, M. & Moss, L. (1998). The process of permanent exclusion and implementation of "fresh start" programmes. *Educational Psychology in Practice*, *14*(2), 83–92.

Broadhurst, K., Paton, H. & May-Chahal, C. (2005). Children missing from school systems: exploring divergent patterns of disengagement in the narrative accounts of parents, carers, children and young people. *British Journal of Sociology of Education*, *26*(1), 105–119.

Cabinet Office. (2002). *Understanding Criterion 6 Assessor, Charter Mark*. Retrieved from http://www.cabinetoffice.gov.uk/chartermark/downloads/doc/Understanding_criterion_six.doc

Clough, P. (2000). Routes to Inclusion. In P. Clough & J. Corbett, *Theories of Inclusive Education: a Students' Guide*, section 1, pp. 1–34. London: Paul Chapman.

Cole, T., Daniels, H. & Visser, J. (1999). Child and adolescent mental health from an educational perspective. In M. Kerfoot & R. Williams (eds), *Strategic Approaches to Planning and Delivering CAMHS*. Oxford: Oxford University Press.

Cole, T., Sellman, E., Daniels, H. & Visser, J. (2002). *The Mental Health Needs of Children with Emotional and Behavioural Difficulties in Special Schools and Pupil Referral Units*. London: Mental Health Foundation. Retrieved from www.mentalhealth.org.uk

Cole, T. & Visser, J. (2000). *Review of Provision for Pupils with EBD*. Report for Telford and Wrekin and Shropshire LEAs, University of Birmingham.

Commission for Racial Equality. (1996). *Exclusions from School: The Public Cost*. London: CRE.

Croll, P. & Moses, D. (2000). *Special Needs in the Primary School*. London: Cassell.

Crossan, B., Field, J., Gallacher, J. & Merrill, B. (2000). Further education and social inclusion: understanding the processes of participation. In A. Jackson & D. Jones (eds), *Researching 'Inclusion'* (pp. 67–73). Boston: University of Nottingham, SCUTREA.

Daniels, H. (2004). Cultural historical activity theory and professional learning. *International Journal of Disability, Development and Education, 51*(2), 185–200.

Daniels, H., Cole, T., Sellman, E., *et al.* (2003). Study of Young People Permanently Excluded from School. DFES Research Report 405, London.

Davies, J., Hallam, S. & Ireson, J. (2003). Ability groupings in the primary school: issues arising from practice. *Research Papers in Education, 18*(1), 45–60.

Department for Education. (1995). *National Survey of Local Education Authorities' Policies and Procedures for the Identification and Provision for Children who are out of School by Reason of Exclusion or Otherwise*. London: DFE.

Department for Education and Employment (DfEE). (1997). *Excellence in Schools*. London: HMSO.

Department for Education and Employment (DfEE). (1998). *LEA Behaviour Support Plans*. Circular 1/98. London: DfEE.

Department for Education and Employment (DfEE). (1999a). *Social Inclusion: Pupil Support*. Circular 10/99. London: DfEE.

Department for Education and Employment (DfEE). (1999b). *Social Inclusion: the LEA Role in Pupil Support*. Circular 11/99. London: DfEE.

Department for Education and Employment (DfEE). (1999c). *Statistical First Release*. SFR 10/1999, 28 May 1999. Retrieved from www.dfee.gov.uk/statistics

Department of Education and Science. (1989). *Discipline in Schools (Elton Report)._London: HMSO.

Department for Education and Skills (DfES). (2001a). *Inclusive Schooling—Children with Special Educational Needs*. London: DfES.

Department for Education and Skills (DfES). (2001b). *Special Educational Needs and Disability Act 2001*. London: The Stationery Office Limited.

Department for Education and Skills (DfES). (2002). *14–19: Extending Opportunities, Raising Standards: Summary*. London: DfES.

Department for Education and Skills (DfES). (2003). *Every Child Matters*. London: DfES.

Department for Education and Skills (DfES). (2004a). Removing Barriers to Achievement. *London: DfES*.

Department for Education and Skills (DfES). (2004b). *Permanent Exclusions from Schools and Exclusion Appeals, England 2002/2003 (Provisional)*. London: DfES.

Department for Education and Skills (DfES). (2004c). *Statutory Guidance on the Duty on Local Authorities to Promote the Educational Achievement of Looked After Children Under Section 52 of the Children Act 2004*. London: DfES.

Department for Education and Skills (DfES). (2004d). *Curriculum and Qualifications Reform Final Report of the Working Group on 14–19 Reform (The Tomlinson Report)*. London: DfES.

Department for Education and Skills (DfES). (2005). *Ethnicity and Education: The Evidence on Minority Ethnic Pupils*. London: DfES.

Department for Education and Skills (DfES). (2006a). Improving Behaviour and Attendance: Guidance on Exclusion from Schools and Pupil Referral Units. *London: DfES. Retrieved from http://www.teachernet.gov.uk/wholeschool/behaviour/exclusion/guidance/*

Department for Education and Skills (DfES). (2006b). *Children Missing Education: Experiences of Implementing the DfES Guidelines*. London: DfES.

Department for Education and Skills (DfES). (2006c). Primary Pupils' Experiences of Different Types of Grouping in School: The Benefits and Disadvantages of Grouping by Ability. *Retrieved from http://www.standards.dfes.gov.uk/research/themes/pupil_grouping/primary_grouping/benefits_disadvantages*

Department for Education and Skills (DfES). (2006d). *Care Matters: Transforming the Lives of Children and Young People in Care*. London: DfES.

Dyson, A., Gallannaugh, F. & Millward, A. (2003). *Understanding and Developing Inclusive Practices in Schools*. Economic and Social Research Council UK grant LI39251001.

Edwards, A., Barnes, M., Plewis, I., *et al.* (2006). *Working to Prevent the Social Exclusion of Children and Young People: Final Lessons from the National Evaluation of the Children's Fund*. Research Report RR734. London: DfES.

Evans, J. & Lunt, I. (2002). Inclusive education: are there limits? *European Journal of Special Needs Education, 17*(1), 1–14.

Every Child Matters (2004). *Identifying and Maintaining Contact with Children Missing or At Risk of Going Missing from Education*. LEA/0225/30 July 2004. Available on-line at: http://www.everychildmatters.gov.uk/ete/childrenmissingeducation/

Fletcher-Campbell, F. (2001). Issues of inclusion: evidence from three recent research. studies. *Emotional and Behavioural Difficulties, 6*(2), 69–89.

Gallacher, J., Crossan, B., Field, J. & Merrill, B. (2000). Education for all? Further education, social inclusion and widening access. Report from the project *New Entrants to Education* for Scottish Executive. Centre for Research in Lifelong Learning, Glasgow Caledonian and Stirling Universities.

Gamoran, A. (2002). *Standards, Inequality & Ability Grouping in Schools*. University of Wisconsin-Madison, CES Briefings.

Gerschel, L. (2003). Connecting the disconnected: exploring issues of gender, 'race' and SEN within an inclusive context. In C. Tilstone & R. Rose (eds), *Strategies to Promote Inclusive Practice*. London: Routledge Falmer.

Gillborn, D. (1999). Fifty years of failure: 'race' and education policy in Britain. In A. Hayton (ed.), *Tackling Disaffection and Social Exclusion: Education Perspectives and Policies*. London: Kogan Page.

Gordon, A. (2001). School exclusions in England: children's voices and adult solutions? *Educational Studies, 27*(1), 69–85.

Hallam, S., Ireson, J. & Davies, J. (2004). Primary pupils' experiences of different types of grouping in school. *British Educational Research Journal, 30*(4), 515–533.

Hallam, S., Ireson, J., Lister, V. & Andon Chaudhury, I. (2003). Ability grouping practices in the primary school: a survey'. *Educational Studies, 29*(1), 69–83.

Harris, N., Eden, K. & Blair, A. (2000). *Challenges to School Exclusion*. London: Routledge.

Hayden, C. & Dunne, S. (2001). *Outside, Looking in: Children's and Families' Experiences of Exclusion from School*. London: The Children's Society.

Hayton, A. (ed.) (1999). *Tackling Disaffection and Social Exclusion: Education Perspectives and Policies*. London: Kogan Page.

Health Advisory Service. (1995). *Together We Stand—the Commissioning, Role and Management of Child and Adolescent Mental Health Services*. London: HMSO.

Hick, P. (2005). Still missing out: minority ethnic communities and special educational needs. In B. Richardson (ed.), *Tell It Like It Is: How Our Schools Fail Black Children*. Stoke: Trentham.

Hick, P. with Ainscow, M., Dyson, A., *et al.* (2005). *Inclusive Learning with ICT: Report of a Research Project for BECTA*. Manchester: University of Manchester.

Howe, M.J.A. (1997). *IQ in Question: The Truth about Intelligence*. London: Sage.

Joseph Rowntree Foundation. (2005). *Policies towards Poverty, Inequality and Exclusion since 1997: JRF Findings 15*. York: Joseph Rowntree Foundation. Retrieved from http://www.jrf.org.uk/knowledge/findings/socialpolicy/0015.asp, accessed 28/05/07.

Lunt, I. & Norwich, B. (1999). *Can Effective Schools be Inclusive Schools?* London: Institute of Education.

MacNab, N., Visser, J. & Daniels, H. (2007). Desperately seeking data. *Journal of Research in Special Educational Needs*, 7, 3.

Majors, R., Gillborn, D. & Sewell, T. (1998). The exclusion of black children: implications for a racialised perspective. *Multicultural Teaching*, *16*, 3.

McCluskey, G. (2006). *Exclusion from School—What Does It Mean to Pupils?* CREID Briefing. Edinburgh: The University of Edinburgh Printing Services.

McNess, E., Broadfoot, P. & Osborn, M. (2003). Is the effective compromising the affective? *British Educational Research Journal*, *29*(2), 243–257.

Manchester City Council (2004). *The Manchester Inclusion Standards*. Manchester: Manchester City Council.

Mental Health Foundation. (2001). *"I Want to Be Your Friend . . . But I Don't Know How" Whole School Approaches to Children's Mental Health*. London: MHF.

Munn, P. & Lloyd, G. (2005). Exclusion and excluded pupils. *British Educational Research Journal*, *31*(2), 205–221.

NACRO. (2003). *Missing Out*. London: NACRO.

OFSTED. (1996). *Exclusions from Secondary Schools, 1995–6*. HMCI Report. London: The Stationery Office.

OFSTED. (1998). *Setting in Primary Schools*. London: OFSTED.

OFSTED. (2000). *Evaluating Educational Inclusion: Guidance for Inspectors and Schools*. HMI 235. London: OFSTED.

OFSTED. (2003). *Key Stage 4: Towards a Flexible Curriculum*. London: OFSTED.

OFSTED. (2004). *Special Educational Needs and Disability: Towards Inclusive Schools*. London: OFSTED.

OFSTED. (2006). *Evaluation of the Impact of Learning Support Units*. London: OFSTED. Retrieved from www.OFSTED.gov.uk

Oliver, M. (1990). *The Politics of Disablement*. London: Macmillan.

Osler, A. (1997). *Exclusion from School and Racial Equality*. London: C.R.E.

Osler, A. & Hill, J. (1999). Exclusion from school and racial equality: an examination of government proposals in the light of recent evidence. *Cambridge Journal of Education*, *29*(1), 33–62.

Osler, A., Watling, R. & Busher, H. (2001). *Reasons for Exclusion from School*. School of Education, University of Leicester, DfEE.

Osler, A., Watling, R., Busher, H., *et al.* (2001). *Reasons for Exclusion from School*. Research Report RR244. London: DfEE.

Parsons, C. (1999). *Education, Exclusion and Citizenship*. London: Routledge.

QCA (1999). *The National Curriculum: Handbook for Primary Teachers in England: Key Stages 1 and 2*. London: Stationery Office for DfEE & QCA.

Rutter, M., Giller, H. & Hagell, A. (1998). *Antisocial Behaviour by Young People*. Cambridge: Cambridge University Press.

Saxe, L. & Cross, T. (1997). Interpreting the Fort Bragg Children's Mental Health Demonstration Project: The cup is half full. *American Psychologist*. 1997 May 52(5): 553–556.

Slee, R. (2004) Inclusive education: a framework for school reform. In V. Heung and M. Ainscow (Eds.) *Inclusive Education: A Framework for Reform*. Hong Kong Institute of Education.

Social Exclusion Task Force. (2006). *Reaching Out: An Action Plan on Social Exclusion*. London: HM Government.

Social Exclusion Unit. (1998). *Truancy and School Exclusion*, Cm 395. Retrieved from www.cabinet-office.gov.uk/seu

Social Exclusion Unit. (2000). *National Strategy for Neighbourhood Renewal: a framework for consultation*. London: Cabinet Office (Social Exclusion Unit), on-line at: http://achive.cabinetoffice.gov.uk/seu/publication847e.html?did=48

Social Exclusion Unit. (2001). *Preventing Social Exclusion*. Retrieved from http://www.cabinetoffice.gov.uk/seu/publications/reports/html/pse/pse html/01.htm

Social Exclusion Unit. (2004a). *A Better Education for Children in Care*. London: Office of the Deputy Prime Minister.

Social Exclusion Unit. (2004b). *Mental Health and Social Exclusion*. London: The Office of the Deputy Prime Minister.

Sparkes, J. (1999). Schools, education and social exclusion. London School of Economics, CASE paper 29.

Thomas, G. & Loxley, A. (2001). *Deconstructing Special Education and Constructing Inclusion*. Buckingham: Open University Press.

Visser, J., Daniels, H. & MacNab, N. (2005). Missing: children and young people with SEBD. *Emotional and Behavioural Difficulties*, 10(1), 43–54.

Visser, J. & Stokes, S. (2003). Is education ready for the inclusion of pupils with emotional and behavioural difficulties: a rights perspective? *Educational Review*, 55, 65–75.

Vulliamy, G. & Webb, W. (2001). The social construction of school exclusion rates: implications for evaluation methodology. *Educational Studies*, 27(3), 358.

Vulliamy, G. & Webb, W. (2003). Reducing school exclusions: an evaluation of a multi-site development project. *Oxford Review of Education*, 29(1), 33–49.

Wright, C., Weekes, D. & McGlaughlin, A. (1999). Gendered-blind racism in the experience of schooling and identity formation. *International Journal of Inclusive Education*, 3(4), 293–308.

Wright, C., Weekes, D., McGlaughlin, A. & Webb, D. (1998). Masculinised discourses within education and the construction of black male identities amongst African-Caribbean youth. *British Journal of the Sociology of Education*, 19, 1.

Young Minds. (2002). *Schools Must Promote Mental Health to Reduce Social Exclusion:* Young-Minds Briefing on the Review of OFSTED's Framework, *Inspecting Schools*. Retrieved from http://www.youngminds.org.uk/briefings/02_06_01.php

CHAPTER 7

Care Leavers, Exclusion and Access to Higher Education

Sonia Jackson
University of London, United Kingdom

ABSTRACT

Children who spend time in public care, particularly in adolescence, are at especially high risk of social exclusion as adults, even taking account of the extremely deprived families from which they originate. Research on long-term outcomes is limited due to lack of follow-up and loss of contact between care leavers and local authorities. However, there is much evidence of their over-representation among disadvantaged groups of all kinds.

The declared aim of the UK care system is to improve life course outcomes for children separated from their families, but clearly it fails to do so at present. This chapter argues that one of the most important factors in this failure is the low priority given to education in the past, with the vast majority of children in care leaving school with no qualifications. The gap in attainment between "looked-after" children and the school population has remained extremely large despite very active attempts by government to reduce it.

After briefly outlining the historical background, this chapter goes on to review research over the past 20 years on leaving care and education. There have been few studies of children in care who are educationally successful. However, the chapter describes the *By Degrees* project which tracked 129 students with a care background through their university degree courses. This study has important implications for practice and underlines the need for fundamental changes in the care system if we are to reduce substantially the social exclusion currently experienced by the majority of young people who have been "looked after" in public care.

INTRODUCTION

Children who are separated from their families and looked after in foster homes or in residential care, are at high risk of social isolation in childhood and social exclusion as

Multidisciplinary Handbook of Social Exclusion Research. Edited by D. Abrams, J. Christian and D. Gordon.
© 2007 John Wiley & Sons, Ltd.

adults. Studies of the most disadvantaged groups in British society all find that they include a high proportion of individuals who have spent periods in local authority care (Jackson *et al.*, 2002; Simon & Owen, 2006). For example, almost half of the inmates in UK young offenders' institutions have been in care as children and at least a quarter of all adult prisoners.

Additionally, surveys of homeless people suggest that between 20–30 % of people sleeping rough, in hostels or sheltered accommodation, are those who have been through the care system, or care leavers (Centrepoint, 2004; Stephens, 2002). Psychiatric units and drug and alcohol rehabilitation centres similarly report a high proportion of patients with a "care" background. This trend is further substantiated with evidence from numerous studies that have found that girls in care are at higher risk of becoming teenage mothers than those from other populations (Brodie, Berridge & Beckett, 1997; Corlyon & McGuire, 1997, 1999; Social Exclusion Unit, 1999). Biehal *et al.* (1995) found that one in four of their sample of female care leavers aged 16–18 was a parent or pregnant. Likewise, Broad's (2001) survey of young women in or leaving care in Manchester reported an even higher figure: 45 % were pregnant or already had a child (Broad, 2005).

An analysis of longitudinal data from the age 30 sweep of the 1970 British Birth Cohort looked at 20 outcomes associated with social exclusion and found highly significant differences on 16 of them between those who had ever been in care and the general population (Feinstein & Brassett-Grundy, 2005). Thus, there is a wealth of evidence from many different sources of a strong association between having been in care as a child and social exclusion in adulthood. While the poor outcomes of a childhood in public care are no longer disputed, there remains a long-running debate about the reasons why. The majority of children in care come from families who suffer severe deprivation (Bebbington & Miles, 1989), so the question is: are they simply following the same trajectory as would have been expected if they had remained in their families of origin? And, in addition, given that children are only removed from their homes in extreme circumstances, most of them will have suffered serious abuse and neglect, with long-term effects on their social, emotional and cognitive development before being removed. Is their tendency to replicate the problems of their parents to be attributed to the social background from which they originate or to their experiences in care? While we might be able to address these questions, what seems clear is that the British care system as at present constituted does not operate to improve the life chances of those who enter it to any significant extent, although that is the explicit aim of the UK Government (Department for Education and Skills, 2002; Department of Health, 1998a).

In this chapter, I suggest that one of the key factors in the social exclusion of people with a care background is their lack of educational qualifications, and furthermore, the low priority given to their education by "corporate parents" within the care system, which can be contrasted with the high level of concern displayed by *real* parents of children who do not find themselves in care.

HISTORICAL BACKGROUND

The present system of substitute care for children whose parents are unable or unfit to look after them dates from the Children Act 1948. This was designed to implement the recommendations of the Curtis Report (1946) which had exposed the appalling conditions in which children at the time were kept. They might live in workhouses, little changed since the days of Oliver Twist, or be herded together in large, impersonal institutions run by charitable organisations. Alternatively, they could be boarded out with little protection against ill-treatment or exploitation.

Under the 1948 Act, every local authority was obliged to set up a Children's Department, headed by a Children's Officer, who would have personal responsibility for all children in the area looked after away from home. Twenty years later these departments were absorbed into the new structure set up by the 1971 Social Services Act, bringing together childcare, adult services and mental health into a single local authority Social Services Department. It was not the spirit of the 1971 Act that all social workers should immediately take on the tasks of former specialists, but that was how it was interpreted at the time. The result was a disastrous loss of expertise, most seriously being the knowledge of child development, a consistent factor emerging from the numerous child abuse inquiries that took place over the next 30 years (Reder, Duncan & Gray, 1993).

Most major reforms of the child welfare system in the UK can be traced to the publicity surrounding such events (Butler & Drakeford, 2003; Jackson, 2006). At the time of writing, another organisational change is in progress which will to some extent bring back the old children's departments, though with a much more integrated approach. Following the report of the Victoria Climbié enquiry (Laming, 2003), the Government published a Green Paper, *Every Child Matters* (2003). This was then followed by the Change for Children programme, under which all local authorities are to appoint Directors of Children's Services, with responsibility for education as well as children in care or "in need". Those appointed so far—in most cases—have a background in education, which could be seen as a positive development, although there have been some suggestions that the interests of children in care, being such a small minority, might be overlooked (Hayden, 2005).

This chapter goes on to discuss the characteristics of the care system and the children and families who make use of it, in particular how far the social exclusion of adults with a background in care can be attributed to failures in the service as opposed to pre-care factors. It continues by reviewing the evidence from studies of care leavers, including the small minority who succeed in education and go on to university.

TYPES OF FACILITY

Two features of the system set up by the 1948 Act were to have far-reaching effects. One was the strong preference for foster care over children's homes. This was somewhat paradoxical considering that the fundamental reform of the child care system had been set in train by the death of a foster child, Dennis O'Neill, at the hands of his foster father (Monckton Report, 1945). However, the Curtis Report (1946) argued that what children most needed when they could not live with their parents was *the personal element* (p. 146), which could best be provided in a family environment rather than in an institution. Partly for this reason, as well as because of its lower cost, foster care has continued to be the placement of choice right down to the present day. The result is that, contrary to the popular conception that being in care means living in a children's home, the great majority of children in care are in foster families. This is very different from the situation in European countries like Denmark and Germany where more than half of children and young people separated from their birth families are in group residential care (see Table 7.1). The implications of this contrast are discussed later.

The second crucial decision was to give central responsibility to the Home Office, and later to the Department of Health, creating a complete split between care and education, which continued until 2003 when children's services were transferred to the Department for Education and Skills (Parker, 1990). The rift which developed between the two services would inflict immense damage on successive generations of children in care and was a key factor, as I shall show in this chapter, in their future social exclusion (Jackson, 1987).

WHO IS IN CARE?

Routine statistics have been collected on children in care for over 30 years and published annually in the form of National Statistics. From this information, it is possible to trace some cyclical movements in the care system. For example, until the 1950s relatively few children were boarded out and most were accommodated by religious and charitable organisations in large institutions, described at the time as *mouldering bastions* (Packman, 1975). During the 1960s, the local authorities gradually took over their traditional functions and almost all residential care came to be provided in the statutory sector. However, in the late 1970s, local authorities began to close children's homes to save money, and to place as many children as possible in foster homes, a trend that continued for the rest of the century (Berridge & Brodie, 1998).

However, there continued to be a need for residential placements for children presenting with extremely difficult behaviour, for sibling groups, and for others who are considered hard to place in foster homes, such as children with disabilities and those from minority ethnic backgrounds or of mixed parentage. The shortfall of places resulted in a rapid expansion of the independent and private sector, often charging very high fees for placements. This skewed local authority budgets for children's services, concentrating resources on a small number of young people perceived as problematic and diverting them from the ordinary needs of the majority of children in care. More recently the same process has occurred in relation to foster care, with the shortfall in mainstream local authority foster homes producing a rapid growth in private fostering agencies, paying better rates to carers at high cost to local authorities.

During the post-war years, there was a steady stream of legislation concerning children living away from home, most of it consolidated in the Children Act 1989. This Act continues to provide the legal framework for local authority care. The Act introduced a new terminology, designed to make the system be seen as more supportive and less punitive. The term in care now technically refers only to children who are subject to a court order. Other children are accommodated or "looked after" by the local authority. Although both these groups are still referred to by the legal term "looked-after children" in local authority plans and policy statements, in care has slipped back into general currency, including government documents. The terms are used interchangeably in this chapter, though, in fact, the legal distinction persists.

Two further important pieces of legislation that have the potential to influence the social inclusion of children in care are the Children (Leaving Care) Act 2000, which is discussed further below, and the Children Act 2004. The latter included, for the first time, a specific duty on local authorities to promote the educational attainment of children they look after.

Numbers of Children In Care

At any one time, the number of children in care under 18 in the UK is about 79,000 and 60,000 of them are in England (DfES, 2005). However, this is not a static population; almost 100,000 children pass through the care system in the course of a year. About half return to their parents or relatives after a short period and may never have another care episode. Almost nothing is known about this group of children, although it is likely that they are drawn from a very disadvantaged population and may be similar in other respects to those who remain in care. A further group of children, about 10 %, are subject to a care order but are allowed to live at home with a parent or parents under supervision. Of the remainder, 68 % are placed with foster families, including 12–20 % who live with relatives or friends (Broad, 2001) and 13 % are in residential units or schools of various kinds. Some foster families are quite large and some residential homes extremely small, with only two or three children. The main difference is that in a foster placement, the adults live on the premises and provide care on a full-time basis in their own home, whereas in residential units, the staff work on a shift system and usually live elsewhere (Cairns, 2004).

Outcomes for Children In Care

During the 1980s, the rising numbers and escalating costs of children in care caused the Department of Health, in the interests of economy and efficiency, to set up a working party of leading researchers to consider the question of measuring outcomes, something never previously attempted (Parker *et al.*, 1991). The working party conducted a comprehensive review of research and concluded that the poor outcomes of substitute care could be attributed to three main factors: (a) the lack of any means of linking inputs—the services provided—to results, in the form of increased well-being for the child; (b) the absence of any one person to oversee all aspects of the child's care experience; and (c) the failure of caregivers to behave in the way ordinary parents do to safeguard and promote their child's development. The aim was originally intended to provide an instrument by which researchers could assess the outcomes of care, however, the work was increasingly dominated by the concerns of the Department of Health, and in turn became an elaborate administrative system designed to be acceptable to social workers and their managers.

The result was the production of the age-related Assessment and Action Records (AARs), which formed the core of the tool. The criteria though, were related to deficits in care identified by previous research and covered seven domains: health, education, identity, family and social relationships, emotional and behavioural development, social presentation and self-care skills. The system had the potential to provide valuable new evidence on outcomes but there was extreme political pressure to avoid this, and the proposal to include an assessment at 18 years or the point of leaving care was firmly rejected. The idea of including objective measures of educational attainment was also resisted by civil servants on the grounds that it might be discouraging to the children or seem critical of their carers.

Both the pilot research leading up to the launch of the Looking After Children (LAC) system (Parker *et al.*, 1991; Ward, 1995), and later studies highlighted social workers' neglect of education and ignorance of the most basic facts about children's schooling. The critical points had already been identified as shortcomings by previous research (Fletcher-Campbell & Hall, 1990; Jackson, 1987, 1989). In many cases, for example, the sections of the AARs on education were simply left blank, confirming the impression that social workers considered school and education not their business, although there was some evidence that when used as intended the system could bring about improvements (Skuse & Evans, 2001).

USING STATISTICS TO IMPROVE SERVICES

In contrast to the previous Government's unwillingness to hear bad news about the low attainment of children in care, the Labour Government elected in 1997 laid great emphasis on the collection of statistical information and its use to drive up standards (DfES & DoH, 2002). This was an important innovation, because until then published tables of statistics were regarded as inert data and the idea of using them as an instrument of social policy was quite new (Simon & Owen, 2006). Local authorities were now required to make returns on a whole range of measures, providing hard evidence of the shortcomings in the care system already well known to practitioners. This applied both to outcomes from care, such as educational attainment, and features of the care system itself, particularly its instability and the large number of different placements experienced by many children (Jackson & Thomas, 2001). Under the Personal Social Services Performance Assessment Framework (PAF), the Government sets targets for improvement and the results are published in the annual Autumn Performance Reports, enabling local authorities to compare their own record with that of other similar authorities with the aim of raising questions about current policy and practice if necessary.

As part of the *Modernising Social Services* initiative (Department of Health, 1998b), the Government set specific targets for *improving the life chances of children* in care. These included increasing the proportion of care leavers obtaining educational qualifications, reducing youth offending and the under-18 conception rate, and improving health care for "looked-after" children. The main target for care leavers was clearly intended to reduce their risk of social exclusion by "improving the level of education, training and employment outcomes for care leavers aged 19 so that levels of this group are at least 75 percent of those achieved by all young people in the same area by 2004" (Department of Health and Department for Education and Skills, 2003). If this target had been reached, it would have resulted in many fewer 19 year olds, who had been in care, considered to be "NEET"—not in education, employment or training—but most local authorities fell far short of it.

Although it was already well documented that the attainment of children in care fell below that of the general school population, the published statistics revealed for the first time, with shocking clarity, the enormous gap in achievement and the inadequacy of previous attempts to reduce it. The key statistical measure was the proportion of children looked after at 16 years who obtained passes at A*–C grades in the first national public examination, the General Certificate of Secondary Education (GCSE). The most recent figures show only a very small improvement over 3 years, from 5 to 8 % of looked-after children obtaining five good GCSE passes, compared with 53 % of all children (DfES, 2005). Almost half had no qualifications of any kind, compared with only 5 % of the whole school population; and only 52.9 % managed to achieve the minimum target of one or more GCSE or GNVQ passes at grades A*–G. Their employment prospects are, therefore, extremely limited: 21 % are unemployed after leaving school, compared with 7 % of young people generally, and the jobs they do find are low paid and insecure. One study of care leavers found that 80 % of the sample were unemployed and living on welfare payments 2 years after leaving care (Broad, 2005).

EVIDENCE ON SOCIAL AND FAMILY BACKGROUND

In Britain, more than in some other countries, public child care is the very last resort and a cause of shame to families who are forced to make use of it (Colton et al., 1997). Consequently, even among those at the lowest socio-economic level and with multiple problems, only a small minority have children in care, although they may well make use of informal family arrangements to provide care when parents are unable to do so. Evidence from the 1958 National Child Development study and later from the 1970 cohort study consistently showed that children in care were overwhelmingly drawn from severely disadvantaged backgrounds (Bebbington & Miles, 1989; St. Claire & Osborn, 1987). For many years, it was argued that negative outcomes for this population were all that could be expected and the care system could not therefore be held responsible. During the 1990s this view was increasingly challenged, particularly by the growing body of evidence on what happened to young people at the point of leaving care and afterwards, although Berridge (2007) has asserted that sociological evidence supports the former postion.

RESEARCH ON LEAVING CARE AND BEYOND

There is a serious lack of outcome data on care leavers, because until 2001 local authorities had no obligation to keep in touch with young people who had been in their care once a court order ended, or when they were considered old enough to live independently. Although the official age of leaving care has always been 18, it gradually became conflated with the end of compulsory schooling, so that more and more children were discharged from care at 16 or 17, and were left to fend for themselves with minimal support (Action on Aftercare Consortium, 1996). Some of them drifted back to their families, although these arrangements tended to break down quite quickly, according to research by the Dartington Social Research Unit (Bullock, Gooch & Little, 1998). The majority attempted to survive on welfare benefits, living in council flats in run-down areas or squats. Still worse off were the young people described as "homeless, skill-less adolescents", who were typified by almost constant movement and chaotic lifestyles (Bullock, Gooch & Little, 1998, p. 191).

A series of small-scale research studies all demonstrated that most care leavers could look forward to a constrained and poverty-stricken life. As already mentioned, young women were likely to become pregnant, or already have a child by the time they left care. Boys were at high risk of committing offences and being drawn into the criminal justice system (see Chapter 8—Crime). Both were vulnerable to sexual exploitation and drug and alcohol misuse (Jackson *et al.*, 2000; Williams *et al.*, 2001). Lacking budgeting, home-making, self-care and negotiating skills, these vulnerable young people were ill-equipped to cope with independent living, and they were expected to do so at a far earlier age than would be normal for others of their age. Support from the local authority would quickly run out leaving many of them homeless and unemployed.

Reports on the extent to which these young people were being failed by social services had begun to appear in the 1980s (Stein & Carey, 1983), and research over the next 15 years followed a similar pattern. Stein and his team of researchers, based first at Leeds and then at York University, produced a series of reports spelling out the deprivations suffered by care leavers and the failure of services to meet their needs (Biehal *et al.*, 1995; Stein, 2002, 2004). Their findings were supported by London-based studies in the early 1990s (Garnett, 1992), and by surveys of the services which were gradually developing both in the voluntary and statutory sectors to try to improve the situation (Broad, 1998). It was pointed out that for children in care the transition to adulthood was *accelerated and compressed* instead of taking place gradually over several years, as it does for young people living in their own families (Stein, 2002).

Most of this evidence was drawn from projects designed to help young people in difficulties and it could be argued that it was biased towards negative findings for that reason. However Broad (2005) surveyed a random sample of care leavers and found little change by comparison with studies carried out 10 years earlier. The majority of young people in his study were living cheerless and constricted lives, lacking the most basic forms of support.

Research on the Education of Children In Care

A consistent pattern emerging from all the above studies was the very high proportion of young people leaving care and education with no qualifications of any kind. The link with their high level of unemployment and low income in adult life was obvious, but for a long period it seemed to be regarded by social workers as inevitable, and more emphasis was placed on equipping young people to claim welfare benefits than on tackling the cause of the problem. Most research on "looked-after" children focused on issues of placement breakdown, relationships between children and carers, or contact with birth families (Jackson, 2000). Although more and more children were in foster homes, research attention tended to be fixed on residential care (Sinclair, Gibbs & Wilson, 2004). This was partly because of recurrent scandals about physical and sexual abuse in children's homes (Levy & Kahan, 1991; Utting, 1997; Waterhouse, 2000). Most of the reports mentioned in passing the lack of attention to education in the homes and the fact that in many of them few, if any, of the residents were attending school, but it was not their main focus.

The importance of education for children in care was very slow to be recognised, and was even disputed on the grounds that paper qualifications were less important for them than "life skills". This view was first challenged in a paper commissioned by the Social Science Research Council [predecessor to the Economic and Social Research Council (ESRC)], which attributed the low attainment of children in care primarily to the division at both administrative and professional levels, between care and education, and to the low priority given to school and education by social workers (Jackson, 1987). The ESRC used the report to commission two further studies. One by the Oxford-based research group, led by Anthony Heath, remains the only comparative research on the educational attainment of children in care and children from a similar socioeconomic background who stay in their own homes. Unlike most social work research, it employed standardised tests of reading, vocabulary and mathematics, and used statistical techniques to compare a group of 58 children receiving social work services but not in care, with a group of 49 children in long-term stable foster care. The fostered children were found to be doing even less well than those living with their birth families, and much less well than those in the general school population. Retested at annual intervals over 3 years, they had made some progress but the gap between their attainment and the average level remained the same. In the first report of their findings, the authors claimed that the results showed that the low attainment of children in care could be attributed to their families of origin and earlier adversity rather than their care experience (Heath, Colton & Aldgate, 1989). In later publications, they responded to criticism by saying that if children in care were to catch up with others, "greater than average educational inputs would be required" (Heath, Colton & Aldgate, 1994). A further important finding of this study was that low attainment among the fostered children was not, as is still often claimed, related to behaviour problems (Colton & Heath, 1994).

The other study funded under this initiative was by the National Foundation for Educational Research (NFER) and its emphasis and conclusions were very different. It consisted of a survey of local authorities, a questionnaire survey of over 400 children in care and 20 detailed case studies. It located the problem in the failure of education and social services to work together rather than the characteristics of the children or their families (Fletcher-Campbell & Hall, 1990). Many of the other findings of this illuminating study have been repeated over and over again in subsequent research, for example, the failure to engage foster parents as partners, the low priority given to school attendance, the instability of care placements, and the narrow conception of education held by social services personnel. "The idea that education could contribute to meeting the personal needs of many children in care . . . was not so much rejected as not entertained" (Fletcher-Campbell & Hall, 1990, p. 160). Fletcher-Campbell went on to survey the education support services which had been set up by some social services departments to try to address the issues raised by the NFER study (Fletcher-Campbell, 1997). This report concluded that such services had done something to bridge the education/care divide and were highly valued by social workers, teachers and carers. It was not possible, however, to show that they had actually raised attainment among children in care or care leavers.

Considering that this is now acknowledged to be such an important issue, it is striking how little high-quality research exists on the subject. Most studies have consisted of introducing measures to address the perceived deficits in services and evaluating the results, not in terms of attainment outcomes, but by attempting to measure changes in subsidiary indicators such as school attendance, number of exclusions, bullying, attitudes of professionals, availability of study support and facilities, and young people's views. The National Children's Bureau, which received funding from the Gatsby Foundation to support projects in three local authorities, was able to show marked improvements in some of these areas, but partly because of the small numbers of children involved, no statistically significant effects on levels of achievement. Key factors appeared to be a strong commitment from senior management, Project Lead Officers to coordinate the work and continually stress its importance, and supportive care placements giving high priority to educational progress, not simply attending school (Harker *et al.*, 2004; Jackson & Sachdev, 2001).

PARTICIPATION IN HIGHER EDUCATION

Is it possible to show that improving educational outcomes would reduce the levels of social exclusion experienced by people who have been in care? Research by the Centre for the Wider Benefits of Learning has shown that this certainly applies to the general population, and that the greatest benefits are experienced by those who progress to post-secondary education (Jackson, Ajayi & Quigley, 2003), but does it hold true for care leavers? There has been very little research on the small minority of care leavers who could be considered educationally successful. We do not even know with any certainty how many children in care continue in education beyond the compulsory school leaving age. Under the Children (Leaving Care) Act 2000 (CLCA), local authorities are now expected to keep in touch with those formerly in their care up to the age of 21, but have lost contact with up to a third of them by the time they reach 19. At that point, they are required to make a return to the DfES on how many are not in education, training or employment (NEET), but the three categories are not differentiated so that we do not know how many are still in full- or part-time education.

The participation rate in any form of higher education is very low: estimates vary between 1 and 5 %, compared with 43 % in the general population (Jackson, Ajayi & Quigley, 2005; SEU, 2003). There are two small-scale retrospective studies of adults who spent all or part of their childhood in care, both comparing a group who succeeded in accessing further or higher education with a group who did not.

The first study, Jackson and Martin (1998), attempted to verify the link between educational failure and quality of life for people who had been in care as children. A sample of 38 people formerly in care was matched by age, gender, ethnicity and care experience with a second group who had obtained fewer than five GCSE or O level passes. They found highly significant differences in outcomes for the two groups despite their similar families of origin. Most of the less successful group could be described as socially excluded in terms of unemployment (73 %), having periods of homelessness or living in poor quality social housing, early parenthood, welfare dependency and alcoholism; 18 % of the men were serving custodial sentences. The "high achievers" by contrast, were all in employment, most owned their homes or lived in privately rented accommodation, the majority were in stable relationships and none had been involved with the criminal justice system.

The second study, based in Scotland, focused on risk and protective factors affecting a group of ex-care adults with a wide age spread, comparing nine individuals who had accessed higher education with a similar group who had not (Mallon, 2005; Mallon, 2007). The interesting feature of this research was that, through detailed examination of case studies, the researcher was able to separate out and enumerate pre-care, in-care and post-care risk factors. Pre-care factors were similar for both groups. Post-care risk factors for the non-higher educated group tended to be psychosocial with fewer instances of social pathology or exclusion than expected from previous research. In-care risk factors far outnumbered pre- and post-care factors. Resilience and positive outcomes from adverse beginnings were strongly associated with educational success. As a qualitative study, this can only be indicative. However, it does provide further evidence to challenge the view that children bring their problems with them into the care system, and that the care experience is at worst neutral. Like the Jackson and Martin subjects (1998), Mallon's successful respondents had had to overcome numerous obstacles during their time in care, and most had received very little help.

Care Leavers in Higher Education: the *By Degrees* Study

In 1999 a British charitable foundation, the Frank Buttle Trust, commissioned a 5-year longitudinal study of care leavers entering higher education, *By Degrees: From Care to University*. Participation in higher education only became a practical possibility for more than a handful of care leavers with the enactment of the Children (Leaving Care) Act 2000 (CLCA). This addressed some of the obstacles identified by Jackson and Martin (1998), notably lack of financial support and accommodation during university vacations. Under the CLCA, local authorities were required to provide personal and financial support to young people who had been in their care, subject to eligibility, up to the age of 24 if they were in full-time education.

The *By Degrees* study aimed to recruit 50 young people in three successive years who had been in care at the age of 16 and had conditional or confirmed offers of a university place. The first cohort, entering university in 2001, was tracked through their complete degree course and the year after graduation. The second group was followed for their first 2 years and the third cohort for 1 year. The aims of the project were:

- to identify ways of increasing the participation of young people in care in higher education;
- to enable them to make the most of their time at university and to complete their courses successfully;
- to provide information for local authorities on the financial, practical and emotional support needed by care leavers to achieve similar educational outcomes to those of young people in the general population;
- to document their experience of university; and
- to raise awareness among higher education institutions of the particular needs of this group of students.

Method

The research participants were recruited through local authority 'leaving care' teams, and lead officers for the education of children in care, and were all volunteers, so it is not possible to know with any certainty to what extent the sample was representative. However, the Frank Buttle Trust, which raised the funds for the research, offered grant aid to students in need from a care background, and although this was not conditional on participation in the study, it provided an incentive to local authorities to make nominations. The authorities who did not make nominations, usually explained that they had no care leavers planning to go on to higher education in that year. The original plan was to limit the number of nominations from each authority, but this proved unnecessary due to the small numbers involved. It is likely, therefore, that a high proportion of young people going to university from care in the years 2001–2004 were included in the study.

All those who agreed to take part were contacted by one of the three researchers who recorded factual data and arranged a first interview. This was a semi-structured life story interview in a place chosen by the participant and often lasted up to 3 hours. The interviewees were encouraged to tell the story of their experiences in their birth family, at school and in care in their own words, as well as their first impressions of university life (Jackson *et al.*, 2003). The researchers prompted only to keep the narrative flowing, for clarification and to ensure that all the required areas were covered. More structured interviews were carried out with participants at approximately 6-month intervals over the course of the project, in addition to many telephone contacts, two focus groups and several social events. Some of those who initially volunteered to take part in the study failed to obtain the required grades or decided not to take up their places for other reasons. However, 129 students were interviewed and remained in contact with the researchers until the end of the project and publication of the final report, *Going to University from Care* (Jackson, Ajayi & Quigley, 2005).

Findings

Characteristics of participants

Women outnumbered men in all three cohorts, which reflects that fact that girls tend to do better than boys academically and are also more inclined to take part in research studies. Girls are also more likely than boys to be placed in foster homes as opposed to residential units. One young woman explicitly attributed her academic success to never having been in a children's home which she described, from her observation of other children in care, as "being thrown on the educational scrapheap". Only one participant had gone from residential care to university, and he had nothing good to say about it.

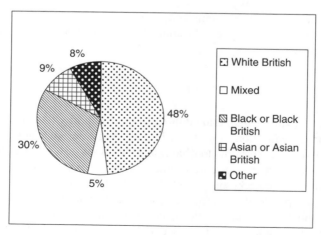

Figure 7.1   Ethnicity of *By Degrees* participants

A high proportion of participants came from minority ethnic backgrounds as shown in Figure 7.1. This was particularly marked in the third cohort, students entering higher education institutions in 2003. Among this group, 40 % had been born overseas and 16 % had come to the UK as unaccompanied asylum-seekers. The majority of Black participants in the study were of African rather than Caribbean origin, with a scattering of refugees from other countries.

Family background

There was no evidence that these young people had suffered fewer adversities before coming into local authority care than other children in the care population. With some exceptions among the asylum-seekers, the majority of birth parents had no educational qualifications and, if employed, were in low-paid, manual occupations. Very few of the participants had been living with both natural parents before coming into care.

The general picture presented by accounts of their birth families was one of extreme volatility, with many house moves, changes of partners, new people joining or leaving the household, constant turmoil and upheaval. Domestic violence and physical or sexual abuse were a feature of many accounts. Many participants described traumatic incidents arising from their parents' mental illness or drug and/or alcohol addiction.

The reasons for admission to care were very similar to those given for the care population in official statistics (DfES, 2005) and are shown in Figure 7.2. In Cohort 1, entering university in 2001, 78 % of the participants had suffered abuse by parents or step-parents, even if this was not stated as the main reason for care. Coming into care, although emotionally devastating for some, had often provided their first experience of security and predictability.

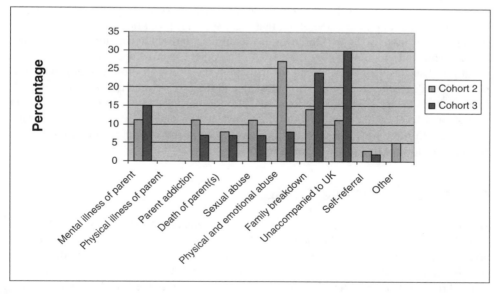

Figure 7.2   Reasons for admission to care

THE CONTRIBUTION OF CARE

The majority of participants had spent over 5 years in care, so their care experience could take some credit for their educational success. Despite many criticisms of the way they had been looked after, almost all acknowledged that they would not have got to university if they had remained with their birth families. This was less true of those who had come from overseas, of whom the majority said that their parents had impressed on them the importance of education and had given them support and encouragement up to the time of their separation. Once in care, most respondents cited their foster families as a major source of motivation and support, which usually continued throughout their university careers (Jackson & Ajayi, 2007).

Support from Local Authorities

The Children (Leaving Care) Act 2000 was implemented in October 2001, so it applied to Cohorts 2 and 3, but not to the first group to take part in the study. It is an open question how far the Act has improved prospects for care leavers (Broad, 2005), but for these young people at least, there is no doubt that it made a big difference. At the time when the first group started university, few local authorities had any formal policies on the support of care leavers in higher education, and simply doled out small sums of money in an arbitrary way. A survey of local authorities carried out at that point discovered very wide variations in the level of financial support provided, and a lack of awareness that they had a duty to provide vacation accommodation and other forms of support (Jackson, Ajayi & Quigley, 2003). A second survey 3 years later was able to report considerable progress, although almost all ex-care students still felt under constant financial pressure. When this meant they had to work long hours in supermarkets or bars to support themselves, it seriously interfered with their academic work (Jackson, Ajayi & Quigley, 2005). It is all the more remarkable, therefore, that the overall drop-out rate, at 10 %, was below the national average of 14 %. Moreover, it was almost entirely accounted for by the first cohort, who were not covered by the CLCA. The others seemed determined to continue whatever obstacles they encountered. At the end of the study, all those who had not completed their degree courses were still studying and the rest were either working or travelling. Asked about their expectations for the future, most envisaged themselves in professional level employment, owning their own homes and possibly starting a family. In contrast to their educationally unsuccessful peers in the care population, the risk of social exclusion for this group seemed remote.

CRITIQUE OF RESEARCH BASE

Despite the great improvement in the statistical information available about children in care since 1998, there are still large gaps in the research base and much of our information comes from small-scale studies which may not be representative. Due to the difficulties of gaining access to research subjects and their high mobility, it is quite likely that those in most difficulty are not included in research samples so that the findings underestimate the proportion of children in care and care leavers who are most vulnerable and marginalised and fail to record their experiences (Wigfall & Cameron, 2006). The extent of social exclusion among those who have been in care may, therefore, have been underestimated.

With the exception of the *By Degrees* study, there is a great shortage of longitudinal data. We have snapshots about outcomes for young people at the point when they should have sat GCSEs and immediately after their 19th birthday (except for the one in three with whom social workers have lost contact), but no information about what happens to them between those two points. There is evidence of the over-representation of people who have been in care in offenders' institutions, drug and alcohol rehabilitation centres and homelessness projects, but no statistical data on what proportion of care leavers are homeless, commit offences or become teenage parents. Some very important issues, such as the prevalence of mental health problems or self-harming, are not covered at all.

The other major weakness of research on children in care, in general, and their education in particular, is its limited frame of reference. It seems to operate entirely within its own boundaries, as if children in care were a different species from others. So, for example, it very seldom draws on disciplines other than social work or, to a limited extent, sociology. Research on the education of children in care completely ignores the extensive literature on educational underachievement or the influence of home background on attainment. Although there is much talk of listening to young people and involving them in decision making (e.g. Thomas, 2000), this is often tokenistic and rarely attempts to address the more fundamental identity issues that are discussed in the widening participation literature. Yet the complex institutional, structural and cultural practices that contribute to educational exclusions and inequalities are highly relevant to our continued failure to close the gap in educational attainment between children in care and the general population (Archer, Hutchings & Ross, 2003). The literature on widening participation has repeatedly concluded that identities are central to understanding deeply embedded feelings of (not) belonging in university (or other educational) spaces (Archer & Leathwood, 2003; Burke, 2002). This raises important questions about the ways that children in care construct their identities as learners and how this influences their educational choices and decisions. Yet these issues are barely touched on in the discussion of the attainment and behaviour of children in care.

Another weakness is the inward-looking nature of most research on children in care, which is almost entirely UK-focused. Relatively poor educational attainment and underachievement feature in many other English-speaking countries as well as the UK, especially the United States and Australia and the issues are very similar (Cashmore, Paxman, & Townsend, 2007; Casey Family Services 2005; Pecora *et al.*, 2003; Elze *et al.*, 2005). There is also much to learn from other European countries that adopt a different approach, particularly to residential care, and appear more successful in creating a stable, stimulating educational environment for children living away from home as well as managing a far more gradual and individualised transition to adulthood (Petrie & Simon, 2006).

PRACTICE IMPLICATIONS

There have been numerous attempts to translate research findings on the education of children in care and the needs of care leavers into practice. The first joint DfES/DoH guidance on the education of looked-after children incorporated most of the recommendations arising from research up to that point as well as the Who Cares? Trust action project, *Equal Chances* (DfES & DoH, 2000). The Social Exclusion Unit (SEU) report, *A Better Education for Children* in care (2003) made a series of recommendations and incorporated numerous examples of local good practice, though it was unable to show that any of them led to measurable improvements in attainment. The DfES has issued extensive Guidance after consultation on the new duty to promote educational attainment in the Children Act 2004. The *By Degrees* report concludes with 47 recommendations relating to central and local government, foster and residential care, and higher education institutions (Jackson, Ajayi & Quigley, 2005). Some professional groups, such as educational psychologists, have a clear view of the problems and how they might be overcome (Jackson & McParlin, 2006). Will all this activity lead to genuine improvements in looked-after children's educational opportunities and a reduction in their risk of social exclusion in adulthood?

It would be too pessimistic to suggest that the legislation and policy initiatives of the last 8 years will have no effect at all, but they are battling against deeply embedded attitudes and problems in the care system which have proved extremely resistant to change. All of these were already identified in the 1980s: indeed many were discussed in the Curtis Report (1946). They include the instability of placements, the lack of interest of social workers in education, the difficulty for children of engaging fully in school amid the turmoil of their lives, the unsympathetic attitude of some schools, and the stigmatisation and bullying that many looked-after children experience. Of all these, the most fundamental problem is the quality of the care environment.

Even those children who are lucky enough to have only one or two stable placements are likely to be cared for by people who have very limited education themselves, and are not in a position to act as effective advocates for the children they look after or to understand and help them actively with their school work. The situation in group homes is even worse, since residential care is treated as a last resort, with a succession of very disturbed and unhappy children mostly staying for short periods. There is little opportunity to form relationships and in most residential units the staff are preoccupied with maintaining control rather than fostering the children's personal and educational development. Petrie and Simon (2006) show from their comparison of children's homes in England with those in Denmark and Germany how group living can be a positive experience for both staff and residents. However, this would require a transformation in attitudes, funding, expectations, and above all in staff status, recruitment and training. We would probably need to create a completely new graduate profession, on the lines of the French psycho-educateur, or the German or Danish pedagogue, sometimes translated in English as *life-space worker*.

Table 7.1 Proportions of children in residential placements in Scotland and England, Denmark and Germany

	National population (millions)	Young people in social care, looked after in institutions	Per cent of all children in care
Scotland and England	55.1	7,485	12
Denmark	5.3	8,187	54
Germany	82.2	82,000	59

CONCLUSION

In this chapter, I have pointed to evidence that children looked after by local authorities are at higher risk of social exclusion in adulthood than any other group of children in British society. Many different factors contribute to this outcome, but I suggest that by far the most important is their extremely low level of educational attainment and lack of qualifications, which makes it almost impossible for them to find stable or rewarding employment. A few individuals manage to find other routes to success via sport, the arts, pop music or entrepreneurship, but they are a tiny minority. For most, the idea of this kind of achievement is a deceptive mirage, sometimes promoted by well-meaning social workers as a kind of compensation for educational failure.

Statistics on educational attainment continue to show a steady decline with age, until by age 16, GCSE results comparing children in care with others show a difference of 45 percentage points. This gap has hardly changed since educational statistics began to be collected. It is too early to tell if the transfer of children's services from the Department of Health to the Department for Education and Skills or more generally the Government's Change for Children programme will have any impact on this long-standing problem. So far most of the efforts to raise school performance have bypassed children in care, or even had the effect of further disadvantaging them. Schools controlling their own admissions policies and ambitious to raise their standing in the league tables are often very resistant to providing places for children in care who they perceive as potential troublemakers and low achievers. The result, as the *By Degrees* research showed, is that looked-after children are rarely enrolled in schools where a high proportion of students achieve good examination results and go on to university. Only four of the participants in that study attended secondary schools in the top range of the league tables.

Organisational changes in the past have often failed to deliver the expected benefits for children. It may be that changes at ground level would have more impact and that educational research has more to tell us than studies focused on social care. The evidence is extremely consistent that the most important influence on educational attainment is not the personal qualities of the child, but the educational qualifications of parents and the interest they take in their children's schooling. A first step to combating the social exclusion of people who have been in care is to ensure that as children they are looked after day-to-day by adults who are well educated themselves and value and promote their education in the broadest sense.

ENDNOTE

Since this chapter was written there have been important policy developments relating to the education of children in care in the UK, especially in England. In October 2006 the government published a Green Paper, *Care Matters: Transforming the Lives of Children and Young People in Care*, which, for the first time acknowledged the clear link between poor educational outcomes and diminished life chances for children in care (DfES, 2006). The Secretary of State in his foreword described it as "inexcusable and shameful" that "the care system seems all too often to reinforce (this) early disadvantage rather than helping children to successfully overcome it" (p. 3). Following extensive consultation, raising educational attainment was made a central plank of the programme for improvement and new legislation set out in the subsequent White Paper, *Care Matters: Time for Change* (DffS, 2007), which included a raft of new measures, and innovative ideas, many of which will become statutory. These include appointing a "virtual headteacher" in every area, with responsibility for overseeing the educational progress of all children in care, giving looked after children the right to attend high-performing schools even when they are already full, giving social workers more control over budgets, providing enhanced training and career opportunities for foster carers, ending abrupt cutoff points for leaving care and giving young people the opportunity to stay longer in foster placements, as well as, more controversially, introducing the idea of independent social work practices to provide services for children and exploring the concept of social pedagogy as a basis for residential work. *The White Paper showed signs of moving away from exclusive reliance on examination passes as an indication of progress and developing a broader view of education encompassing social skills and community engagement with a strong emphasis on giving children in care access to a wide range of cultural, artistic and sporting activities.*

The Frank Buttle Trust followed up the *By Degrees* project by establishing a Quality Mark for universities which have developed a comprehensive policy for recruiting, retaining and supporting students with a background in local authority care. Many more UK higher education institutions now recognise the need to increase participation of children in care, and the number applying for, and being awarded the Quality Mark is growing rapidly.

It is unlikely that any of these initiatives will end the social exclusion of children and young people in care in the short term, but at least there are more hopeful signs of movement in the right direction than at any time in the past.

Acknowledgements

The *By Degrees* research was funded by a consortium of charitable bodies corrdinated by the Frank Buttle Trust in addition to the Department for Education and Skills. Thanks also to the Calouste Gullbenkian Foundation UK for support at the pilot stage and KPMG for funding the dissemination of findings.

REFERENCES

Action on Aftercare Consortium. (1996). *Too Much Too Young: The Failure of Social Policy in Meeting the Needs of Care Leavers.* Ilford: Barnardo's.

Archer, L., Hutchings, M. & Ross, A. (2003). *Higher Education and Social Class: Issues of Exclusion and Inclusion.* London and New York: Routledge Falmer.

Archer, L. & Leathwood, C. (2003). Identities, inequalities and higher education. In L. Archer, M. Hutchings & A. Ross (eds), *Higher Education and Social Class: Issues of Exclusion and Inclusion.* London and New York: Routledge Falmer.

Bebbington, A. & Miles, J. (1989). The background of children who enter local authority care. *British Journal of Social Work, 19*(5), 349–368.

Berridge, D. (2007). Theory and explanation in child welfare: education and looked after children. *Child and Family Social Work, 12*(1), 1–10.

Berridge, D. & Brodie, I. (1998). *Children's Homes Revisited.* London: Jessica Kingsley.

Biehal, N., Clayden, J., Stein, M. & Wade, J. (1995). *Moving On: Young People and Leaving Care Schemes.* London: HMSO.

Broad, B. (1998). *Young People Leaving Care: Life after the Children Act 1989.* London: Jessica Kingsley.

Broad, B. (ed.) (2001). *Kinship Care: The Placement Choice for Children and Young People.* Lyme Regis, Dorset: Russell House Publishing.

Broad, B. (2005). *Improving the Health and Well-being of Young People Leaving Care.* Lyme Regis, Dorset: Russell House Publishing.

Brodie, I., Berridge, D. & Beckett, W. (1997). The health of children looked after by local authorities. *British Journal of Nursing, 6*(7), 386–391.

Bullock, R., Gooch, D. & Little, M. (1998). *Children Going Home: The Re-unification of Families.* Aldershot: Ashgate.

Burke, P.J. (2002). *Accessing Education: Effectively Widening Participation.* Stoke-on-Trent: Trentham Books.

Butler, I. & Drakeford, M. (2003). *Social Policy, Social Welfare and Scandal: How British Public Policy is Made.* Basingstoke: Palgrave Macmillan.

Cairns, B. (2004). *Fostering Attachments: Long-term Outcomes in Family Group Care.* London: British Agencies for Fostering and Adoption.

Casey Family Services. (2001). *The Road to Independence: Transitioning Youth in Foster Care to Independence.* New Haven, CT: Casey Family Services.

Cashman, J., Paxman, M. & Townsend, M. (2007). The educational outcomes of young people 4–5 years after leaving care, an Australian perspective. *Adoption & Fostering* (Special Issue on Education) *31*(1), 50–61.

Centrepoint. (2004). *Youth Homelessness Statistics.* London: Centrepoint.

Colton, M., Casas, F., Drakeford, M., *et al.* (1997). *Stigma and Social Welfare; An International Comparative Study.* Aldershot: Avebury.

Colton, M. & Heath, A. (1994). Attainment and behaviour of children in care and at home. *Oxford Review of Education, 20*(3), 317–328.

Corlyon, J. & McGuire, C. (1997). *Young Parents in Public Care: Pregnancy and Parenthood among Young People Looked After by Local Authorities.* London: National Children's Bureau.

Corlyon, J. & McGuire, C. (1999). *Pregnancy and Parenthood: The Views and Experiences of Young People in Public Care.* London: National Children's Bureau.

Curtis Report. (1946). *Report of the Care of Children Committee.* Official Report cmnd 6922. London: HMSO.

Department for Education and Skills. (2006). *Care Matters: Transforming the Lives of Children and Young People in Care.* London: DfES (Green Paper).

Department for Education and Skills. (2007). *Care Matters: Time for Change.* London: DfES (White Paper).

Department for Education and Skills & Department of Health. (2000). *Guidance on the Education of Children and Young People in Care.* London: DfES & DoH.

Department for Education and Skills (DfES) & Department of Health (DoH). (2002). *Education Protects: Collecting and Using Data to Improve Educational Outcomes for Children in Public Care.* London: DfES and DoH.

Department of Health. (1998a). *Quality Protects Circular LAC (1998) 28.* London: DoH.

Department of Health. (1998b). *Modernising Social Services,* cmnd 4169. London: HMSO.

Department of Health (DoH) & Department for Education and Skills (DfES). (2003). *Social Services Performance Assessment Framework Indicators 2002–2003.* London: DoH.

Elze, D.E., Auslander, W.F., Stiffman, A. & McMillen, C.(2005). Educational needs of youth in foster care. In G.P. Mallon & P.C. McHess (eds), *Child Welfare for the 21st Century: A Handbook of Practices, Policies and Programs.* New York: Columbia University Press.

Feinstein, L. & Brassett-Grundy, A. (2005). *The Lifecourse Outcomes for Looked After Children: Evidence from the British Cohort Study 1970.* London: Institute of Education.

Fletcher-Campbell, F. (1997). *The Education of Children Who Are Looked-After.* Slough: National Foundation for Educational Research.

Fletcher-Campbell, F. & Hall, C. (1990). *Changing Schools? Changing People? The Education of Children in Care.* Slough: National Foundation for Educational Research.

Garnett, L. (1992). *Leaving Care.* London: National Children's Bureau.

Harker, R., Dobel-Ober, D., Berridge, D. & Sinclair, R. (2004). *Taking Care of Education*. London: National Children's Bureau.

Hayden, C. (2005). More than a piece of paper? Personal education plans and 'looked after' children in England. *Child and Family Social Work*, 10, 343–352.

Heath, A., Colton, M.J. & Aldgate, J. (1989). The educational progress of children in and out of care. *British Journal of Social Work*, 19(6), 447–460.

Heath, A., Colton, M.J. & Aldgate, J. (1994). Failure to escape: a longitudinal study of foster children's educational attainment. *British Journal of Social Work*, 24(3), 241–259.

Jackson, S. (1987). *The Education of Children in Care*. Bristol: University of Bristol School of Applied Social Studies.

Jackson, S. (1989). Education of children in care. In B. Kahan (ed.), *Child Care Research, Policy and Practice*. London: Hodder & Stoughton.

Jackson, S. (2000). Raising the educational achievement of looked-after children. In T. Cox (ed.), *Combating Educational Disadvantage: Meeting the Needs of Vulnerable Children*. London: Falmer Press.

Jackson, S. (2006). Looking after children away from home: past and present. In E. Chase, A. Simon & S. Jackson (eds), *In Care and After: A Positive Perspective*. London: Routledge.

Jackson, S. & Ajayi, S. (2007). Foster care and higher education. *Adoption & Fostering, 31*(1), 62–72.

Jackson, S., Ajayi, S. & Quigley, M. (2003). *By Degrees - The First Year: From Care to University*. London: National Children's Bureau.

Jackson, S., Ajayi, S. & Quigley, M. (2005). *Going to University from Care*. London: Institute of Education.

Jackson, S., Feinstein, L., Levacic, R., *et al.* (2002). The costs and benefits of educating children in care. CLS Cohort Studies Working Paper No. 4. Retrieved from http://www.cls.ioe.ac.uk/Cohort/Publications/mainpubs.htm

Jackson, S. & McParlin, P. (2006). The education of children in care. *The Psychologist, 19*(2), 90–93.

Jackson, S. & Martin, P.Y. (1998). Surviving the care system: education and resilience. *Journal of Adolescence, 21*, 569–583.

Jackson, S. & Sachdev, D. (2001). *Better Education, Better Futures: Research, Practice and the Views of Young People in Care*. Ilford: Barnardo's.

Jackson, S. & Thomas, N. (2001). *What Works in Creating Stability for Looked After Children?* (2nd edn). Ilford: Barnardo's.

Jackson, S., Williams, J., Maddocks, A., *et al.* (2000). *The Health Needs and Health Care of School Age Children Looked After by Local Authorities*. Report to the Wales Office of Research and Development. Swansea: University of Wales.

Laming, H. (2003). *The Victoria Climbié Inquiry: Report of an Inquiry by Lord Laming* (cm 5730). London.

Levy, A. & Kahan, B. (1991). *The Pindown Experience and the Protection of Children: the Report of the Staffordshire Child Care Inquiry*. Stafford: Staffordshire County Council.

Mallon, J. (2005). Academic underachievement and exclusion of people who have been looked after in local authority care. *Research in Post-compulsory Education, 10*(1), 83–103.

Mallon, J. (2007). Returning to education after care: protective factors in the development of resilience. *Adoption & Fostering, 31*(1), 106–117.

Monckton Report. (1945). *Report on the Circumstances which Led to the Boarding-Out of Dennis and Terence O'Neill at Bank Farm, Minsterley, and the Steps Taken to Supervise their Welfare* (cmd 6636). London: HMSO.

Packman, J. (1975). *The Child's Generation*. Oxford: Blackwell and Robertson.

Parker, R. (1990). *Away from Home: A History of Child Care*. Ilford: Barnardo's.

Parker, R., Ward, H., Jackson, S., *et al.* (eds) (1991). *Assessing Outcomes in Child Care: The Report of an Independent Working Party Established by the Department of Health*. London: HMSO.

Pecora, P.J., Williams, J., Kessler, R.C. & Morello, S. (2003). *Assessing the Effects of Foster Care: Early Results from the Casey National Alumni Study*, accessed 9 September 2005. Retrieved from www.casey.org/Resources/Publications/NationalAlumniStudy.htm

Petrie, P. & Simon, A. (2006). Residential care: lessons from Europe. In E. Chase, A. Simon & S. Jackson (eds), *In Care and After: A Positive Perspective*. London: Routledge.

Reder, P., Duncan, S. & Gray, M. (1993). *Beyond Blame: Child Abuse Tragedies Revisited*. London: Routledge.

St. Claire, L. & Osborn, A.F. (1987). The ability and behaviour of children who have been in care or separated from their parents. *Early Child Development and Care*, *28*(3), 187–354.

Simon, A. & Owen, C. (2006). Outcomes for children in care: what do we know? In E. Chase, A. Simon & S. Jackson (eds), *In Care and After: A Positive Perspective*. London: Routledge.

Sinclair, I., Gibbs, I. & Wilson, K. (2004). *Foster Carers: Why They Stay and Why They Leave*. London and New York: Jessica Kingsley.

Skuse, T. & Evans, R. (2001). Directing social work attention to education: the role of the looking after children materials. In S. Jackson (ed.), *Nobody Ever Told Us School Mattered*. London: British Agencies for Adoption and Fostering.

Social Exclusion Unit. (1999). *Teenage Pregnancy*. London: Social Exlusion Unit.

Social Exclusion Unit. (2003). *A Better Education for Children in Care*. London: Social Exclusion Unit.

Stein, M. (2002). Leaving Care. In D. McNeish, T. Newman & H. Roberts (eds). *What Works for Children? Effective services for children and families*. Buckingham: Open University Press.

Stein, M. (2004). *What Works in Leaving Care?* (2nd edn). Ilford: Barnardo's.

Stein, M. (2006). Research Review: young people leaving care. *Child and Family Social Work*, *11*, 273–279.

Stein, M. & Carey, K. (1983). *Leaving Care*. Oxford: Blackwell.

Stein, M. & Wade, J. (2002). *Helping Care Leavers: Problems and Strategic Responses*. London: Department of Health.

Stephens, J. (2002). *The Mental Health Needs of Homeless Young People. Bright Futures: Working with Vulnerable Young People*. London: The Mental Health Foundation.

Thomas, N. (2000). *Children, Family and the State: Decision-making and Child Participation*. Basingstoke: Macmillan.

Utting, W. (1997). *People Like Us: The Report of the Review of the Safeguards for Children Living Away From Home* (official report). London: The Department of Health and The Welsh Office.

Ward, H. (ed.) (1995). *Looking After Children: Research into Practice*. London: HMSO. Department of Health 1998 Quality Protects.

Waterhouse, R. (2000). *Lost in Care: Report of the Tribunal of Inquiry into the Abuse of Children in Care in the Former County Council Areas of Gwynedd and Clwyd since 1974*. London: The Stationery Office.

Wigfall, V. & Cameron, C. (2006). Promoting young people's participation in research. In E. Chase, A. Simon & S. Jackson (eds), *In Care and After: A Positive Perspective* (pp. 152–168). London: Routledge.

Williams, J., Jackson, S., Maddocks, A., *et al.* (2001). Case-control study of the health of those looked after by local authorities. *Archives of Disease in Childhood*, *85*(4), 280–285.

CHAPTER 8

Social Exclusion and Crime

Chris Hale and Marian FitzGerald
University of Kent, United Kingdom

ABSTRACT

This chapter explores different notions of "social exclusion" and questions the British government's overall approach to the problem on two main grounds. One is that it has tended to define the problem in terms of its symptoms rather than its causes; and the other is its over-reliance on getting people into paid work as the solution. Employment will not of itself ensure that people are able to participate in today's society in a meaningful sense; and the impact of changes in the labour market on crime pose long-term challenges which governments have tended to overlook. Instead, many of the criminal justice policies pursued by the present British government have actively contributed to social exclusion. They have reflected both the government's commitment to being tough on crime (rather than on the causes of crime) and the premium it has attached to measurable indicators of performance. Together these have eroded the scope for discretion within the criminal justice system, resulting in unprecedented rates of incarceration and the criminalization of young people in particular. However, the impact has not fallen evenly across the population. It has fallen disproportionately on sections of society (including minority communities) who already had a heightened risk of social exclusion in the first place.

INTRODUCTION

Social exclusion is one of the buzz-ideas in the New Labour lexicon. Along with community, the third way and the mantra "Tough on crime; Tough on the causes of Crime", social exclusion was a central plank of New Labour's policy initiatives following their landslide election victory in 1997. In his first speech, the Prime Minister (Blair, 1997a) was talking of the need to tackle the existence of ". . . an underclass of people cut off from Society's mainstream, without sense of shared purpose" through ". . . reforming welfare so that government helps people to help themselves and provides for those who can't rather than trying to do it all through government", and by ". . . encourag(ing) people like single mothers who are anxious to work but unable to do so to get back into the labour market". In the same speech Mr Blair announced that the first budget would be the "Welfare to

Multidisciplinary Handbook of Social Exclusion Research. Edited by D. Abrams, J. Christian and D. Gordon.
© 2007 John Wiley & Sons, Ltd.

Work Budget" from the "Welfare to Work" government. The importance they attached to the need to combat social exclusion was reflected in the launch of the Social Exclusion Unit (SEU) (henceforth referred to as "the Unit") at the end of the same year. In his speech announcing its formation, Blair (1997b) saw social exclusion as a joined up problem, citing ". . . failure at school, joblessness, crime—(that) are interwoven together", thereby necessitating joined-up solutions which would now be co-ordinated by the Unit.

DEFINING SOCIAL EXCLUSION

Lacking from the outset, however, was a clear *definition* of what was actually meant by the term "social exclusion". As the previous paragraph illustrates, when the Unit was set up the concept of exclusion was described in terms of its symptoms; and the policies for tackling it were based on a set of assumptions about the interrelated processes which produced it. In 2005, though, David Milliband was to make a speech as the newly appointed minister responsible for the Unit in which he tried to grapple with some of these complexities, but cited as a definition that coined by researchers at the London School of Economics (LSE). Yet this definition also tends to focus on symptoms and effects, as follows:

> An individual is socially excluded if a) he or she is geographically resident in a society but b) for reasons beyond his or her control, he or she cannot participate in the normal activities of citizens in that society, and c) he or she would like to so participate. (Milliband, 2005)

Inasmuch as definitions such as these refer to crime at all, they tend to treat it merely as a symptom of social exclusion. However, the relationship between the two is more complex than the simple formulation "social exclusion causes crime". The general neglect of the process that result in social exclusion has made it possible to ignore key questions about the extent to which the government's response to crime may, of itself, actually exacerbate the problem. We argue that, while there is little evidence that criminal justice policies have much direct impact on the overall level of crime, the response of the criminal justice system to engagement in criminal or disorderly and antisocial behaviour *by* the socially excluded may nonetheless, have a significant indirect influence on the exclusionary processes already at work.

Combating Exclusion

Current strategies to tackle crime contribute to social exclusion in a number of different ways. Most obviously, the focus of much policing activity is on groups who are "at risk" of exclusion; and where an intensification of this activity leads, in turn, to more punitive punishment this creates problems of social exclusion in its own right. Such problems include the labelling and stigmatisation of offenders. This stigmatising has been aggravated by recent moves to tackle disorder through the use of Antisocial Behaviour Orders (ASBOs) which have led to people being excluded, and also to behaviour that was previously tolerated becoming criminalised. Meanwhile, the numbers sentenced by the courts increased by 12 % over New Labour's first 7 years in power; but, in the case of young people aged 10–17, the increase was 22 %.

Thus, there is an inherent tension within New Labour's strategy where a "populist puni-tive" approach to crime and punishment leads insistently towards harsher punishment; and the rhetoric of tough on crime drowns out the more positive aspects of the social inclusion strategy, such as measures to meet government's targets for reducing child poverty and make better provision for early years education. Instead, by generating larger numbers of offenders, the "tough on crime" strategy measures pose additional difficulties in trying to reintegrate young offenders. At the same time the approach also criminalises larger sections of the excluded communities which tend disproportionately to produce such offenders in the first place. While criminal justice statistics are not routinely available on the basis of socio-economic status or neighbourhood, ethnic data are. The experience of the more disadvantaged ethnic minorities may serve as a surrogate measure for dis-advantaged groups more generally, especially where (like the poorer ethnic minorities) they also live in disadvantaged, high crime areas (also see Chapter 9, Social Inclusion: Race and Ethnicity). In 2003, the overall rate of incarceration for British males was 2.5 per thousand whereas over 10 out of every thousand black men were in prison (see further below).

Moreover, the role of crime in producing social exclusion extends also to the victims of crime since victimisation is not distributed randomly. Rather, people living in poor neighbourhoods and those who are already socially excluded have higher probabili-ties of being victims of crime, so crime adds to their experience of social exclusion in this sense too. However, changes in policing in England and Wales, and particularly the increased role for private policing, have exacerbated the problem, inasmuch as the latter have the potential to deny security and reassurance to the poorest and most excluded seg-ments of society. The strategies adopted in private policing and surveillance of private property such as shopping centres, retail and leisure complexes, and cultural centres add to the systematic exclusion of the ". . . undesirable or disobedient" (Wakefield, 2005, p. 529).

This chapter therefore begins by looking at a broad range of conceptions of social exclusion. In the light of this, we then look at the relationship between social exclusion and crime—as defined in terms of those offences that are of popular concern to the public, politicians and the media, but excluding crimes, for example, of pollution, corporate crime or violations of health and safety laws (despite the fact that these arguably cause as much or more social harm). We explore this relationship between crime and exclusion from two perspectives. First we look at the broad range of economic factors which are implicated in social exclusion in general. Then, we explore factors that are linked to the dispropor-tionate involvement in crime of people who are socially excluded (not only as perpetrators but also as victims). Second, we examine, more specifically the impact on social exclusion of government responses to crime. The chapter concludes by drawing out some of the challenges the government faces if it is effectively to reconcile its approach to tackling crime with its commitment to reducing social exclusion.

Social exclusion is a concept that originated in the debates in French Social Policy and developed to be a central concern within the European Union, as discussed by Gordon (Chapter 11) and Millar (Chapter 1). From here the concept has ". . . found its way from continental Europe into an abundance of discourses, text and book titles in Britain" (Bowring, 2000, p. 307), this edition adding to the profusion. Importantly, however, the term used by the French was *insertion* rather than "exclusion" to describe issues surround-ing crime. The concept of insertion has its roots in the republican tradition of social soli-darity (Silver, 1994), and its connotations are far more positive than that of exclusion. That is, it places the emphasis on what people need in order to realise their aspirations to be *included* in society, and it assumes a collective will that provision should be made to this end. It avoids implicitly stigmatising the beneficiaries of such measures, whereas the term "exclusion", even when it is used sympathetically, always carries some risk of labelling.

As the concept was adopted through Europe, the discourses around it became adapted to reflect individual national histories and concerns such that EU policy documents show ". . . a curious amalgam of a liberal Anglo-Saxon concern with poverty and a more conservative, continental concern with moral integration and social order" (Levitas, 1998, citing Room, 1995). As Levitas (2005, p. 22) notes the English New Labour discourse uses a much narrower interpretation of the concept than that implied by the notion of "solidarity" and, of particular relevance to our own arguments, is the emphasis it places on the importance of paid work in overcoming social exclusion.

It is true that the government's Social Exclusion Unit acknowledges that broader dimensions are involved than employment alone, and its general statements have consciously striven to avoid any implications of blame. Social exclusion is a shorthand term for what can happen when people or areas suffer from a combination of linked problems such as unemployment, poor skills, low incomes, unfair discrimination, poor housing, high crime, bad health and family breakdown (Social Exclusion Unit, 2004, p. 4).

> social exclusion has complex and multidimensional causes and consequences, creating deep and long-lasting problems for individual families, for the economy and for society as a whole. It can pass from generation to generation: children's life chances are strongly affected by their parents' circumstances such as their income and the place they live (Social Exclusion Unit, 2004, p. 1).

These multiple facets of social exclusion were reflected in the keynote speech of the minister responsible to oversee the unit in 2005. While avoiding any appearance of blaming those excluded, he also strongly emphasised the need for excluded people to *choose* to take up the opportunities provided by the government, to overcome their disadvantages, and stressed that to provide these opportunities would in future:

> . . . . require services that offer deals to users—extensions of rights and support conditional on fulfilling certain responsibilities. This can be a way of ensuring increasing state responsibilities is matched by personal responsibility. (Milliband, 2005)

The specific issues on which the Unit has focused are significant in this context; rather than starting with an overall analysis of the causes of exclusion and the processes at work (see earlier discussion), as Levitas (2004) points out, they have instead mainly targeted groups whose behaviour is seen as problematic. The overriding impression is of trying to control groups that are disruptive of the social order for the benefit of the majority—or, put more starkly—to allay the concerns of the majority by managing more effectively the minorities they see as threatening their interests.

Wider Context

Of course, it is not necessary to turn to continental European discussions of social exclusion for a more nuanced appreciation of its wider dimensions. In his classic 1979 study,

Poverty in the United Kingdom, Peter Townsend refined the notion of poverty by basing his analysis instead on the concept of relative deprivation (Townsend, 1979), whereas poverty had hitherto been discussed in studies and policy documents in terms of some level of subsistence income. Thus, while he never actually uses the term "social exclusion", poverty as defined by Townsend is to do with the lack of resources that prevents people from being able to be involved in the normal life of society. In other words, poverty is what excludes people from participating in full citizenship (also see discussion in Chapter 11, Gordon).

Importantly, for our purposes, this analysis means that tackling the problem is not just a matter of ensuring people are in paid work, but that they have the wherewithal to participate socially in ways which are taken for granted by most people. Such activities would include participating in leisure activities, buying birthday presents, having the ability to communicate with others and generally maintaining a standard of living which does not fall so far below that of their neighbours (or workmates or classmates) that they are marked out and stigmatised.

As many authors have noted (Bowring, 2000; Young, 2002), one of the aspects that has made this concept attractive to commentators is this multidimensionality. Townsend's approach is better able to capture the nature of deprivation in post-industrial societies than terms such as (financial) poverty or marginalisation; and, in particular, it enables us to take on board the exclusionary impact of labelling or social stigmatisation. As we shall argue this is particularly relevant in discussing aspects of the relationship between crime and social exclusion.

In addition to differences over the conceptualising of exclusion, more disagreement arises about the causes of social exclusion, with explanations lying broadly either at the individual or the structural level. John Veit-Wilson characterises these approaches as "weak" and "strong" conceptions of social exclusion which differ in their notion of agency—that is in whether they see the problem as one which is self-imposed or socially imposed. Additionally, Young (2002) makes a further distinction within the structural models of social exclusion. He posits three basic positions:

1. The individual is to blame for lack of motivation and being reliant on the state welfare system. The classic exemplar of this approach is Charles Murray in his writings on the underclass comprised of work-shy young men and teenage single mothers content to get by on welfare payments and petty crime.
2. The system has failed in that there has been "... a sort of hydraulic failure ... to provide jobs". This leads to social isolation through the lack of positive (male) role models and job opportunities. Young cites the work of Chicago sociologist William Julius Wilson as an exemplar of this approach.
3. The final position sees the active rejection of the underclass by society following the downsizing and restructuring of the economy and particularly the manufacturing sector. The workless are stigmatised and there is a stereotyping of the underclass as criminogenic and with severe alcohol and drug problems.

There are similarities between the three positions identified by Young, and the discourses set out in the typography by Levitas (1998, 2005). Levitas describes a moral underclass discourse (MUD), a social integrative discourse (SID) and a redistributive discourse (RED) (see Table 8.1).

Table 8.1   Levitas's Typology of Exclusion

Process	Exclusion type
MUD	Cultural—lacking normal citizenship participation—synonymous with Murray's underclass of welfare dependents with thieving young men and single mothers.
SID	Workforce—inequality between types of workers—participation or not in paid work. Levitas notes this tends to obscure inequalities between paid workers and to ignore gender, class and ethnic differences within the Labour Market and, the focus on paid work also ignores the importance of unpaid work and its gendered distribution.
RED	Power—Young's third position of active rejection focusing on the processes that produce inequality and implying the need for a radical reduction of inequalities and a redistribution of power and resources to tackle the problem.

Social Exclusion and Crime

Based on the above, we hold that social exclusion consists of a lack of opportunity to participate not only economically but also socially and politically relative to others. Those who are socially excluded have accounted for a very high proportion of the individuals who are processed through the criminal justice system in every age. Currently we would argue the following:

1. The present structure of the labour market, and the factors which have shaped this, have had a particular impact on social exclusion and thereby also on recorded crime. In this context, the emphasis placed by the government on employment as the main route out of social exclusion (and by inference a means of reducing crime) is misconceived and may in some instances be counterproductive.
2. Related to this, economic participation itself cannot be conceived of only in terms of income but also of expenditure. Recent developments in relation to patterns of consumption need to be taken into account as well; for these have had an impact on social exclusion and levels of crime in their own right.
3. Recent developments in criminal justice policy have themselves directly contributed to the process of social exclusion; so, ironically, these may also come to be seen not as the solution to crime but as part of the problem.

THE ROLE OF THE LABOUR MARKET

While social exclusion is multi-causal, one significant factor in producing postmodern forms has been the globalisation of the world economy, and the shift in production from the high labour cost markets of the developed economies to the developing nations. This has led to dramatic changes in the domestic labour market with shifts in employment from traditional manufacturing industries to service industries which have also had significant but largely neglected implications for levels and patterns of crime.

This perspective does not deny the possibility of individual-level choice—such that one person may become a persistent offender while another who is apparently similarly disadvantaged may never have offended at all (see Beinart *et al.*, 2001; FitzGerald, Stevens

& Hale, 2004, for discussions of risk and protective factors in juvenile offending). As reflected in the ministerial pronouncements with regard to social exclusion cited above, the tradition of looking beyond individual-level explanations tends to focus immediately on the issue of employment. However, any notion that employment *per se* is the antidote to criminality would always have been wildly oversimplistic, and we argue that this is truer than ever in the context of the changes in the domestic labour market referred to above. The impact of change has further been exacerbated by other economic developments which have been occurring in parallel with them and which are, in some respects, directly linked.

The idea that crime might be related to economic marginalisation has long been reflected in proverbial insights such as *The devil makes work for idle hands* or *Poverty is the mother of crime*. The first suggests that work (in the sense of gainful employment) is important in preventing crime. In part, this is because it provides a structure which means that people who might be inclined to commit crime are otherwise occupied, but also by inference because those who do not work lack self-discipline and may therefore also be more susceptible to the seductions of crime (Katz, 1988). The second maxim suggests that poverty causes crime—that the poor will be more likely to be criminal—as those lacking in material resources may be forced into illegal behaviour to provide their daily bread. Having less to lose than the better off, they may additionally be less afraid of the consequences if their offending is discovered. Both propositions, as with the media and political discourse noted above, tend to ignore the crimes of the rich—including the crimes of the idle rich; and they also ignore the issue of victimisation, focusing exclusively on the propensity of those who are economically marginalised to *commit* crime. However, their influence can be seen implicitly in the way much writing on the relationship between the economy and crime has focused narrowly on employment rather than on the central issue of economic marginalisation.

In this section we present a brief review of the work on the relationship between economic marginalisation and recorded crime. By definition, this means focusing on research concerned with those crimes that are predominantly perpetrated by the poor, such as muggings, burglary, theft of and from motor vehicles, benefit fraud, violence and disorder. Even though the Home Office (2005b) have estimated the total costs of crime to individuals and households in 2003/2004 as £32.2 billion, including the costs of the criminal justice system, the cost of fraud to British business in the same year was estimated at £72 billion. However, it is also important to highlight that the poor are also very disproportionately at risk of being victims of many of these same crimes (see further below), and the complex interrelationship between the two types of experience is such that it is misleading to conceive of "crime" *only* in terms of offending (see for example, Hope, 2000, 2003). Although we can only briefly look here at some of the more significant recent work in this area, most, if not all, criminological theories can be read as predicting that the overall number of crimes committed tends to increase with economic marginalisation (for an excellent review see Box, 1987). The impact of this has also fallen hardest on those who are already victims of this marginalisation. Thus, Trickett *et al.* (1995) have also shown that during the 1980s, a decade when the long-term trend to greater equality of wealth, income and opportunity was rapidly reversed, inequality of victimisation also became more marked.

Crime and its relationship to poverty reappeared in the last decades of the 20th century as part of a politically right-wing response to the perceived failings of the welfare state. Cushioned by the welfare state so that they become "welfare dependent", many were unable to stand on their own two feet. Within criminological debate this became known by the label Right Realism (also part of the approach to social exclusion characterised by Levitas as MUD), and saw crime as related to a wider range of social problems, but ascribed all of them to individual characteristics rather than the result of any structural factors. Criminality was voluntaristic, committed by individuals with no self-control who choose crime as well as unemployment and poverty, and who could collectively be described as constituting an "underclass".

Particularly relevant here is the work of Charles Murray, echoing Victorian notions which divided the poor into the "deserving" and the "undeserving" on similar criteria. The important distinguishing characteristic of the underclass is not simply that they are poor, but that they are not respectable.

For Murray and his supporters, the underclass has three main characteristics: illegitimacy, violent crime and economic inactivity. Society essentially is segregated between, on the one hand, those who uphold traditional values of hard work, sobriety and family; and on the other, the underclass, the morally weak who are unemployed, involved in crime, drug addiction, have illegitimate children raised by single mothers living on welfare. Murray sees this as a matter of choice. To encourage the right choices to be made the solution is to reduce welfare payments. The problem of crime in Murray's view is that increasing numbers of young men are being brought up without positive male role models, and are avoiding the civilising institutions of marriage, family and work preferring to live on welfare or illegal activities. Murray sees the habitual criminal as a classic member of the underclass living off the mainstream society without contributing to it. Indeed the definitive sign that an underclass has developed is that ". . . large numbers of young healthy, low income males *choose* not to take job" (italics added) (Murray, 1990, p. 15). The keyword here is of course "choose" since Murray believes that as well as unemployed workers who are actively seeking work, there is a large group of "economically inactive" some of whom have opted not to work. (Also see Clapham, Homelessness and Social Exclusion, Chapter 5.)

The notion of the underclass is not unique to Murray, but is clearly reflected in some depictions of the "socially excluded", some of which are central to much of New Labour thinking. The terms are different, but the people who Murray would include in his underclass are the same as those who are regarded as socially excluded, as the symptoms of social exclusion include not just poverty but also political and spatial exclusion. The socially excluded, though, are denied access to ". . . information, medical provision, housing, policing, security etc." (Young, 2002); and these factors interact and reinforce each other to the extent that those who experience the exclusion are denied the chance to participate fully as citizens; and this tends to imply that the issue is a structural problem rather than the fault of the individual.

In effect, these notions of the underclass and the socially excluded are simply two variants of the same phenomenon, corresponding to Veit-Wilson's weak and strong versions of social exclusion (Byrne, 1999; Veit-Wilson, 1998). In the first instance, it is personal deficiencies which prevent full participation in society. The dysfunctional members of the underclass have chosen their lot, and must be "encouraged" to participate in the low-wage labour market of poor quality work by attacking the dependency culture encouraged by the welfare state. While the "strong" version sees the problems at the structural level, Young (2002) discerns two approaches within this distinguishing a "passive" and active version.

The passive version of social exclusion is most notably illustrated in the work William Julius Wilson (Wilson, 1987, 1996), who sees the problems resulting from the failure of the system to provide jobs leading to ". . . . 'social isolation' wherein people lose not so much the motive to work but the capacity to find work because of lack of positive role models coupled with a spatial isolation from job opportunities" (Young, 2002, p. 458). The second emphasises the active rejection of the underclass by society. In a story that should by now be familiar it stresses the ". . . downsizing of industry, the stigmatization of the workless and the stereotyping of the underclass as criminogenic and drug-ridden with images that are frequently racialised and prejudiced" (Young, 2002, p. 458).

In a classic study, Field (1990) used consumer expenditure as an indicator of economic activity, and controlling for a wide range of socio-demographic, criminal justice and environmental factors showed that property crime increased in periods of economic downturn. Conversely, he showed that violent crime tended to increase in periods of economic prosperity (see Hall & Winlow, 2004, for an interesting discussion of the night-time economy, binge drinking and violent crime). These findings were confirmed by related econometric modelling in Pyle and Deadman (1994) and Hale (1998). For our purposes, a more interesting approach is to look at the implications for crime of broader labour market changes in the period since 1945, since these we would argue are relevant to our ideas of social exclusion. Hale (1999) argues that since 1945 the UK economy, and particularly its labour market, has undergone fundamental changes in this period. There has been:

1. a shift in employment from the manufacturing to the service sector
2. a increase in part-time employment and an accompanying increase in numbers employed in temporary and untenured jobs
3. a shift in the patterns of employment from men to women

A dual labour market has developed with a primary or core sector and a secondary or peripheral sector. The primary sector consists of skilled workers usually working full-time for large organisations with good employment and benefit rights. On the other hand, those in the secondary sector are either unemployed or have a high propensity to be unemployed at some time. They have low skills, and when working, low wages. They are more likely to be employed part-time and have few rights to benefits with regard to sickness, holiday or pensions. The secondary sector is characterised by high labour turnover among the least skilled workers. For those at the margins:

> Employment in the 1990s has become far more unstable. The penalties attached to job loss, jobless duration, and the reduced wages on return have risen. Hence the secondary labour market has become far riskier. However this new insecurity has been concentrated on a minority for whom jobs for life will become the stuff of legends.
> (Gregg & Wadsworth, 1995, p. 89)

In his empirical analysis, Hale (1999) concentrated on deindustrialisation, the shift from manufacturing to service sector jobs. This general approach was linked to the work of Allen and Steffensmeier (1989), on the relationship of youth crime to the quality of jobs available, and to that of Carlson and Michalowski (1994) which focuses on deindustrialisation and crime. Allen and Steffensmeier show that for juveniles it is the availability of employment that matters, whereas for young adults it is the quality of employment that is important, part-time work with low pay leads to higher rates of property crime.

Braithwaite, Chapman and Kapuscinski (1992) looked at the impact of the increased participation of women in the labour market on crime in Australia. They contend that increased female employment may lead to increased crime in a patriarchal society if appropriate measures are not introduced to ". . . 'take up the slack' in the traditional female role of guardianship" (Triggs, 1997). The mechanisms they identify for this link between crime and female employment include

- Supervision—women in traditional roles (a) guard their own homes and those of neighbours during the day and (b) look after children who if unsupervised are more likely to be both offenders and victims.
- Opportunity and motivation—women in the labour force may have more opportunity to commit crime; conversely their motivation might decrease. Victimisation of working women might increase if they are out more or if domestic tensions increase. Conversely of course domestic tensions might decrease if the household economic situation improves via female wage contribution.

Similar results, using USA data may, be found in Witt and Witte (1998) and for the UK in Hale (1999). Hansen (2003) argues that increased female participation in the labour market is likely to have had two effects. First, increasing the supply of labour will tend to lower wage rates. Second, given that the increased employment of women is mainly in part-time unskilled work, this increased supply is likely to increase male unemployment. This will particularly be the case amongst young, less well-educated men most likely to commit property offences. Using cross-section data from England and Wales, she shows that areas with higher rates of female labour force participation are likely to have higher levels of recorded crime. We do not argue here that women should be excluded from paid employment. We do, however, suggest that one of the unintended consequences of attempting to combat social exclusion by encouraging people to seek paid work has been to weaken the informal social ties that bound communities together.

This is important because central to New Labour's strategy of combating social exclusion, and hence being tough on the causes of crime, is entry into work. Any work is better than no work, and of course unpaid work is not proper work. The focus has been on persuading the unemployed and excluded back to work with a stick-and-carrot approach by offering retraining programmes but also threatening to cut benefits on the basis of the unfair burden they are imposing on "taxpayers" (i.e. those in work). Thus, Milliband's 2005 speech appears to put them on notice that they must take greater responsibility for improving their own lot, announcing that the government intends to look at:

> . . . . how funding can become more preventative and progressive. People experiencing poverty, disadvantage and social exclusion *cost the taxpayer a large amount*. For instance, around £30 billion is spent each year on income support, Jobseeker's Allowance, housing benefit, and Council Tax Benefit. (emphasis added)

However, the evidence that work per se is not the answer and that poorly paid work, part-time work with little security and sense of worth do not reduce crime in the long run was reviewed above. As Currie (1998) has shown, inclusionary policies that focus on work as the mechanism where work involves long and inflexible hours serve to undermine the family and community and hence weaken rather than strengthen social control. Also, Hale (2005) suggests that such policies have been coupled with a political emphasis on being tough on crime that has increased rather than decreased social exclusion by pushing crime and disorder to the margins of society.

ECONOMIC PARTICIPATION AS CONSUMERS

Field's study cited above already points to the relationship between the economic cycle, consumption and patterns of crime. Both patterns of consumption and the context in which they take place, though, have been rapidly changing since Field was writing. The ways they have done so have actively contributed to social exclusion and are reflected in the crime figures. In large measure, the marked upward trends in recorded crime since the Second World War (Figure 8.1) have been related both to increased affluence and to the changes in the labour market referred to above.

Overall, standards of living in Britain have risen markedly over the last 20 years. This is illustrated by the fact that total domestic consumption rose in real terms by 278 % between 1984 and 2004. Within these estimates, the rises were more pronounced for expenditure on services than for goods, but there were also higher increases in the consumption of durable and semi-durable goods than in non-durable goods. As people have had more disposable money to spend, they have spent it on the products of the service sector, sustaining and increasing demand for what could not in any traditional sense be described as essential goods and services (i.e. basic food, clothing and shelter). Instead money has been available to be spent on leisure pursuits (including in the rapidly growing night-time economy referred to above in relation to the link between drinking and the rise in violence), and on a range of goods which reflects the pace of technological change both in the number of new goods on offer and, importantly, the rate at which each version was displaced by the next. In this context, built-in obsolescence and/or the felt need to own the latest model, have acted as a further stimulus to sustain and increase the demand which, in turn, helped keep the economy buoyant.

For the purposes of the present chapter, particularly important developments have taken place in relation to electronic media, including communications and the increasing availability of portable equipment related to this, especially in the more recent period, as Figure 8.2 illustrates. Effectively, those who do not have access to these types of commodity are excluded from important new forms of communication which are rapidly coming to be taken for granted by the majority of the population.

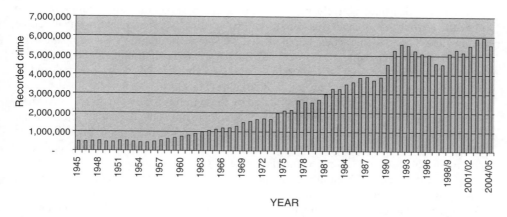

Figure 8.1   Total recorded crime: England and Wales

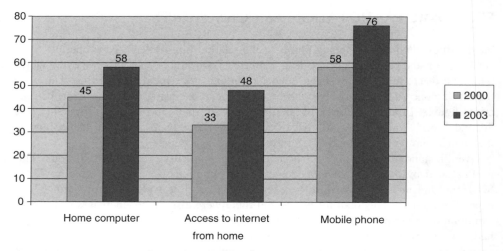

Figure 8.2   Proportion of population owning selected consumer durables (and related trends in communication, Great Britain 2000 to 2003)
Source: National Statistics, 2004.

Meanwhile, however, the increases in disposable income which have fed the market for these types of goods and services have not occurred evenly. Since 1997, the Labour government has actively taken steps to arrest the cycle of rising poverty among the most disadvantaged sections of society. For example, the introduction of the national minimum wage in 1998, and a range of measures to reduce child poverty, including increases in universal Child Benefit and Income Support rates for children, the introduction of the Child Tax Credit scheme and children's bonds, practical support measures such as Sure Start have been implemented. Leaving aside questions about the extent to which such measures have been successful, the economic polarisation which began in the 1990s has nonetheless persisted almost unabated since New Labour came to power (National Statistics, 2005; Figure 5.13). The differential in people's ability to participate as consumers has persisted for these reasons also. Those who are least well placed have nonetheless been enabled to consume beyond their means by the increasing availability of credit facilities. Such abilities have actively been promoted by an expanding and profitable niche within the service sector such that the difficulties originally experienced by such people have in many case been further compounded by the accumulation of significant debt. According to the Department of Trade and Industry, "more than half of those who are over-indebted have incomes of less than £7,500 a year; families with children, and in particular lone parent families, are most at risk." (DTI, 2005).

Young people have been especially affected by these trends for two main reasons. First, the commercial success of many of these developments has depended on juvenile markets—whether in the context of leisure pursuits or in the development of electronic goods, including video games and devices for downloading films and music and replaying them in portable format. Second, while the range of goods and services available to them has rapidly increased, differentials in the purchasing power of young people have almost certainly widened at a faster rate than in the population at large.

Set against this backdrop, there is increasing pressure from central government for young people to stay on in education past the statutory school leaving age of 16. However, this has resulted in ever larger numbers remaining financially dependent on their parents and, making them more susceptible to use credit. According to the 2001 Census, 38% of 16–24 year olds were economically inactive and, 28% of those classified as economically active, were full-time students. Ironically, this policy appears to run counter to the philosophy that economic self-sufficiency through paid employment is the antidote to social exclusion; and it has had direct implications for young people's purchasing power in this increasingly important juvenile market, where fashion is inordinately important and a failure to keep up with the latest trend can itself be exclusionary—or worse. A key consideration for young people, in the context of street crime, has been that not having the "right" accessories could make them a target for bullying (FitzGerald, Stockdale & Hale, 2003; see also further below). An increasing minority of these young people are also living in households headed by a lone parent. By 2004 the proportion of dependent children in this situation had reached 24% compared with 18% in 1992 and these households, on average, are twice as likely to be in poverty as other households with dependent children (National Statistics, 2005; tables 2.4 & 5.20).

For these reasons, it is not surprising that the sudden rapid rise in personal robbery since 2000 was driven largely by the theft of mobile phones by young people. The problem seemed to be most acute in areas where the numbers of young people living in poverty were highest but where they also had access (or exposure) to others whose capacity to consume was much greater. The motive of offenders was not exclusively, to gain personal possession of these goods. Rather, the interplay between the pressures to consume in particular ways and an increasing inability to do so legitimately were creating a growing and lucrative juvenile market for stolen goods (FitzGerald, Stockdale & Hale, 2003; Hallsworth, 2005; Smith, 2003).

The government's draconian response to the problem in the form of the Prime Minister's Street Crime Initiative of 2002 is analysed in detail in a joint inspectorate report (HMIC, 2003). A recurrent theme of the report is the question of whether the resources devoted to meeting the target set by the Prime Minister for reducing street crime were sustainable (and, by inference, justifiable). Although the target was duly met, the underlying factors which produced the problem in the first place remained. That is, that while measures were effectively taken to render stolen mobiles unusable, their place was already being taken on young people's Christmas lists by other new gizmos.[1] By the first quarter of 2005–6, there had been a rise of 4% in recorded robberies over the same period in 2004–5 and there was an even larger rise (11%) in the following quarter (Kara & Upson, 2006).

In parallel with these developments in people's ability to consume and their patterns of consumption, important changes have also been taking place in the context in which they consume. In particular, a major growth area in the service sector in recent years has been the growth of the private security industry. The British Security Industry Association (BSIA) website (http://www.bsia.co.uk/industry.html) indicates that while in 1983 it had 71 members with 51,800 employees with annual turnover of £499 million by 2004 it had 541 members, employing 118,400 with turnover of £4,261 million. The BSIA estimated that in total 600,000 people were employed in the private security industry and the total turnover in the sector was over £5 billion.

---

[1] It is no coincidence that the first major surge in the growth of street crime occurred in the first quarter of 2000—that is, immediately after Christmas 1999.

A large part of this growth has been in the policing of two major sites of consumption —leisure venues and shops. The former include pubs and clubs which feature significantly in the growth of the night-time economy and where the role of private security has been the subject of considerable scrutiny—not least in the work of Dick Hobbs and his co-workers (Hobbs *et al.*, 2003). The latter have received less attention, but their role too has become increasingly important with the expansion in the numbers of shopping malls and out-of-town retail parks as an alternative to the traditional high street. They are of particular interest for our purposes in terms of the power exercised by those responsible for policing them to exclude certain types of people. This was exemplified in May 2005 with the ban imposed in one large retail centre on people wearing hoods—a move which was spontaneously endorsed by the Deputy Prime Minister when he first heard of it in a radio interview, and which was then formally backed by the Prime Minister himself later that day.

The implications for social exclusion of this expansion of private security are profound when considered in the light of Wakefield's observation that:

> Urban space in Britain has been privatised to such an extent that most sectors of the population now regularly spend time in publicly accessible spaces controlled by private interests. (Wakefield, 2005)

Importantly, with specific reference to the policing of retail complexes, she refers back to Stenning (1988) in noting that:

> For the commercial user of private security, any policing strategy must be proven cost-effective, since a business will not adopt a security solution more costly than the problem. In general, therefore, corporations will seek to prevent a loss rather than try to recover the loss after it has occurred, and to change the situation in which any problems occur rather than to draw on the slow and costly criminal justice process in pursuit of sanctions. Thus, private security personnel, and the security hardware that they have at their disposal (such as radio communication and closed circuit television (CCTV) technology), have become fundamental to the successful governance of such territories, *enabling a pre-emptive approach to security* in contrast with the reactive style of state police agencies. (Wakefield, 2005; emphasis added)

That is, shopping malls and other major retail developments now regularly attract a very wide section of the public over extended periods on a scale which has few other contemporary parallels. As such, they may be seen as prime sites for mass social participation. This gives added significance to the power of private policing agencies to exclude a minority of the population in order to pre-empt their committing crime. At the same time, it also means that such people will be even more disproportionately represented among those who spend time in the diminishing number of publicly accessible spaces which fall directly under the control of the police service proper who, in turn, are the main gate-keepers of the criminal justice system.

THE ROLE OF THE CRIMINAL JUSTICE SYSTEM IN SOCIAL EXCLUSION

As the preceding sections have illustrated, the processes at work in producing social exclusion are multiple and complex. This has added considerably to the challenge of tackling the causes of crime with which they are closely interrelated. It has, therefore, proved easier for the Government to be seen to be living up to the other half of its original promise, focusing on being tough on crime rather than claiming credit for trying to tackle the causes. Since 1997, this approach has been reflected in a succession of specific measures (including the creation of around 1,000 new offences by the end of 2005) and in a rhetoric of punitiveness which, ironically, may have further contributed to the processes of social exclusion. Their impact can be seen at the point of entry to the criminal justice system through to its furthest point, in the figures for the prison population. Meanwhile, other steps were being taken, which would actively increase the stigma attached to convictions and which were likely further to increase their exclusionary potential.

An important ingredient of the Labour Party's recipe for winning power after nearly 20 years in opposition was to be seen as the party of law and order. Although recorded crime overall was falling in the 1990s, the party's strategists had breathed new political life into the issues with the discovery of the antisocial behaviour agenda. In office, many of the new offences they created were concerned with antisocial behaviour; and they also instigated a battery of measures for tackling the problem, including giving additional powers to the police and providing for the courts to impose ASBOs. These were civil law remedies, but breaching their conditions would be a criminal offence. The orders were used only sparingly at first; but ministers, particularly during their second period in office, placed considerable emphasis on increasing their number and many police forces responded accordingly. The number had risen from 323 in the whole of 2001 to 1,826 for the first three quarters of 2004 and, much of this rise was achieved by the use of "bolt-on" ASBOs, which the police could ask courts to impose in addition to a sentence for a substantive offence (Burney, 2005).

Inevitably much of the impact of the antisocial behaviour agenda (which also included provision for the imposition of curfews and the exclusion of individuals from certain areas) fell on people who were disproportionately likely to frequent public space. As the previous section illustrates, these were disproportionately likely to come from sections of the population who were already excluded to a greater or lesser degree, and they were bound to include young people who typically have always been most likely to spend time together on the streets, in part, because they are least likely to have the money to buy their way into privatised leisure venues. Thus, Campbell, evaluating the first generation of ASBOs, found that nearly 60% were on people aged under 21 and that; "in the 60 percent or so of cases where information was available, there was a high proportion where some mitigating factor appeared to have contributed to their behaviour. Almost a fifth had a drug abuse problem and a sixth a problem with alcohol. Problems with school were also common, with many being either temporarily or permanently excluded, or noted as having learning disabilities" (Campbell, 2002, p. 17).

In the case of those with drug and alcohol problems, this obviously begged important questions about the availability of the type of help they would need if they were to be able to avoid repeating the offending behaviour. However, breaches of ASBOs more generally were high, running on average at around 40% (Burney, 2005), and this was as true of young people as it was of adults. In addition to the range of new offences for which young people could now be prosecuted this de facto increased their chances of going into adulthood with a criminal record where their counterparts in previous generations might have behaved in exactly the same ways but would have grown out of this behaviour without formally coming to the notice of the criminal justice system at all.

Two further policy developments added to these risks. One arose in the context of the new juvenile justice system set up by law in England and Wales in 1998, the details of which were announced in a government White Paper entitled "No More Excuses"

(Home Office, 1997). In addition to delivering on this implied promise of that no act of youth offending would in future be allowed to evade the system, the system was itself based (like many of the policy innovations of the time) on a managerialist approach, which regularly assessed its performance according to a battery of measures linked to a proliferation of targets and "indicators". The combined effect was to formalise all interventions with young people, making it less possible for those coming into contact with the system for the first time to be given a second chance without any stain on their record. The other was the dispensation publicly to "name and shame" juveniles in cases of antisocial behaviour, even though their anonymity continued to be guaranteed in all other cases (including those involving serious offences), other than in the most exceptional circumstances.

Thus, while there was an overall increase of 12 % in the numbers of people sentenced by the courts between 1997 and 2004, the figure for the 10- to 17-year-old age group rose by 22 % (Home Office, 2005a). Insight into the types of offending where this net-widening is occurring has started to become apparent in the annual statistics for the new juvenile justice system. These were first published for the financial year 2002–2003, and by the following year they showed an increase of 7 % in the numbers of young people being supervised by Youth Offending Teams (YJB, 2004). However, this rise was not spread evenly across all offence categories; it was driven by much higher than average increases in four particular offence categories. Three of these already appear to be directly related to the criminalisation of antisocial behaviour. The numbers convicted of criminal damage had risen by 13 %, with an increase of 15 % in the case of both public order and violence against the person, but the largest increase was in breaches of statutory orders, an increase of 36 %.

Meanwhile, at the furthest end of the criminal justice system, by 2002 the prison population had already exceeded the highest of the Home Office estimates for 2005 (according to the projections when Labour came to power in 1997). The rise over this period was not directly attributable to any explicit policy directive or new legislation and the influence of the Sentencing Guidelines Council was yet to be seen at the time of writing, since its first set of guidelines was issued only in December 2004. Also, the rise occurred over a period when, according to the government, crime was actually falling and the police detection rates were showing no sign of increasing. That is, there is no single, obvious explanation for the rise in the prison population; but the following trends will all have contributed.

The increase in "summary" (or less serious offences) sentenced between 1997 and 2004 was slightly larger than the proportionate increase in indictable offences (25 % compared to 22 %). However, the former—which are tried and usually sentenced in magistrates' courts—are nearly three times as numerous as the more serious indictable offences, which can only be tried by judges at the Crown Court. Over this period, in addition to this significant increase in the intake to the criminal justice system at the lower end of the scale of seriousness, there was also a larger increase in the numbers of summary offences which resulted in a custodial sentence compared to indictable offences. The fact remains that custody is very much more common in the case of the more serious (indictable) offences; but for these it rose by 11 % over the period compared with an increase of 20 % in the case of summary offences. The overall rise in the prison population was strongly influenced by the increase in the average length of sentence imposed by the Crown Court. Yet over this period judges' overall use of custody did not increase, but actually fell

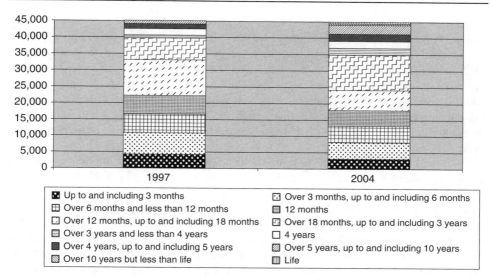

Figure 8.3 Custodial sentences imposed by the Crown Court in 1997 and 2004

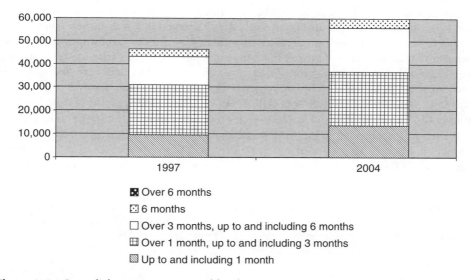

Figure 8.4 Custodial sentences imposed by the magistrates' courts in 1997 and 2004

slightly as a proportion of all sentences (albeit by less than one percentage point) (see Figure 8.3).

By contrast, at the same time, the magistrates' courts were making much greater use of their powers to impose custodial sentences. The increase here was in the imposition of short sentence, so, while the judges were adding to the prison population by tying up prison places for longer, the magistrates contributed to its expansion by sentencing increasing numbers of people convicted of less serious crimes to custody for periods of less than 3 months (see Figure 8.4).

The reasons why judges imposed longer sentences while magistrates became more inclined to reach for the custodial option are not fully apparent. They may include the fact that sentencers were simply reflecting the more punitive political climate in which they were operating. However, the government's legislative hyperactivity also provided them with an ever-expanding menu of sentences (and an unfamiliar range of agencies who would deliver them). It has, therefore, been suggested anecdotally that one unintended and unconscious effect of this was that sentencers were simply more likely to fall back on the options they were familiar with—and that custody was the most obvious of these.

The Social Exclusion Unit itself rang alarm bells about the wider implications of this rise in imprisonment in a report on reducing prisoner reoffending in 2002 (Social Exclusion Unit, 2002). Being in custody is itself de facto exclusionary; but the fact of having been in prison is additionally exclusionary, and it may further undermine offenders' chances of gaining legitimate employment. Arguably, this situation will have been exacerbated by the government's creation in 2002 of the Criminal Records Bureau. Although the Bureau's main emphasis is on providing safeguards where individuals may be working with children, its remit effectively gives a wide range of employers the right to check whether anyone has a criminal record before deciding to hire them.

Here again, though, the impact of these developments may fall disproportionately on particular sections of the population who are already at greatest risk of social exclusion. That is, groups who are already significantly disadvantaged in terms of their employment prospects and related earning potential will already be further handicapped. A higher proportion of their adult males are in prison at any one time (see earlier discussion), and in addition a significant employment penalty attaches to the fact that many more of their potential wage earners have criminal records. As such policies that, however unintentionally, exacerbate these disadvantages will directly increase the social exclusion of these groups. The impact of criminal justice policies on black communities in the United States is already well established in the American literature, and has been described as "Malign Neglect" in Michael Tonry's book of the same name (Tonry, 1995) (see also Clear, 1995; Clear et al., 2003). It would appear that Britain is now following suit. The increase in the

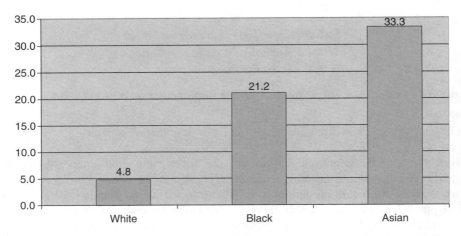

Figure 8.5 Increase in numbers of male prisoners by ethnic group from 1997 to 2003 (British nationals only)

total number of British male prisoners between 1997 and 2004 masks very much higher rises for both black groups and for Asians (see Figure 8.5). Likewise, the figures for Asians (that is, people with origins in the Indian subcontinent: Indians, Pakistanis and Bangladeshis) provide a further important illustration of the disproportionate impact of more punitive sentencing on groups who are already the most disadvantaged. For Indians, whose overall socio-economic profile is similar to, and in some respects, better than that of the "white" population, the increase was no higher than average. In the case of the very deprived Pakistani and Bangladeshi groups, though, the rise was 47 %.

DISCUSSION AND CONCLUSIONS

While New Labour has accepted the arguments that social exclusion is a structural problem, it has nevertheless adopted policies that tend to blame the victim by locating solutions at the individual level. Its Social Exclusion Unit (SEU), set up in 1997, has looked to tackle a wide range of issues including deprived neighbourhoods, unemployment, drug use, teenage pregnancy, truancy, school exclusion—a list of the classic symptoms of social exclusion. It has stressed the interconnectedness of the problems and demonstrated the need for "joined-up" solutions across government departments. The Unit is clear that social exclusion is a major factor in both crime and fear of crime, and that in turn, these are part of the interlinked facets of the problem (Social Exclusion Unit, 2001). Whilst acknowledging the (global) economic and social changes that have taken place. The Unit see the problem of crime and social exclusion as related to issues of socialisation and lack of control in young people related to poor parenting, and inadequate schooling together with drug and alcohol abuse. That is, having first identified the problems at a structural level the emphasis, as Matthews and Young (2003) point out, shifts to solutions based on an implicit control theory.

It is, of course, arguable that governments are limited in their ability to tackle the latter-day manifestations of strain especially where these stem, for example, from global factors leading to restructuring of the labour market. It might also be politically unthinkable for governments of whatever political persuasion, however committed they might be to redistribution, to make available many of the things people now consider "essential" for their full participation in society. They do, however, exercise choices over policy developments that may make things better or worse in this context. While some of the steps they have taken have been designed to militate against social exclusion (or, at least, to alleviate its impact), others have actively exacerbated the problem.

During their second term in office, 2001–2005, the New Labour government discovered a further policy agenda, social cohesion, which at first sight appears simply to be a variant on the original notion of "social exclusion" but which gives it a more positive spin. However, the goal of "social cohesion" was coined directly in response to disturbances in a number of northern towns in Britain involving young Asians of Pakistani origin. An essential driver of the "social cohesion" agenda has been a new found political concern to ensure that different ethnic groups are thoroughly "integrated" into British society. Yet, at the same time, the government continued relentlessly to pursue criminal justice policies which, as we have illustrated, were already having the opposite effect.

The evidence we have set out in this chapter suggests that the government cannot hope to address the problems of social exclusion, and still less attain its goal of social cohesion unless it is prepared to take a radically different approach to criminal justice policy.

Ironically, this would not require major new thinking; and it would almost certainly be cost-effective since it would reduce bureaucracy as well as the need for significant new investment to house a growing prison population. It would, however, require this—and any other future—government to find the courage to change tack in several important ways. They would need to begin by recognising that the criminal justice system of itself has little influence on crime trends over the long term, but that it can exacerbate the problem of crime if it actively contributes to the process of social exclusion. Based on that premise, governments should give a lead to criminal justice practitioners by signalling that increasing imprisonment represents failure on the part of the criminal justice system. Additionally, they should themselves set an example by applying rigorous self-discipline over the creation of new offences. Finally, they should also abandon their current attempts to micromanage the system by obsessively assessing its "performance" on the basis of input measures that attach a premium to the use of formal sanctions. Instead, they should restore appropriate professional discretion to those working in the system on the clear understanding that this is to be exercised equitably, and that the output measures on which their performance will henceforth be judged will include the contribution made at every stage of the criminal justice process to improving social cohesion.

REFERENCES

Allen, E.A. & Steffensmeier, D.J. (1989). Youth, underemployment, and property crime: effects of the quantity and quality of job opportunities on juvenile and young adult arrest rates. *American Sociological Review, 54*, 107–123.

Beinart, S., Anderson, B., Lee, S. & Utting, D. (2001). *Youth at Risk? A National Survey of Risk Factors, Protective Factors and Problem Behaviour among Young People in England, Scotland and Wales*. London: Communities that Care.

Blair, T. (1997a). Speech at Aylesbury Estate, 2 June 1997.

Blair, T. (1997b). Speech "Bringing Britain Together", 8 December 1997.

Bowring, F. (2000). Social exclusion: limitations of the debate. *Critical Social Policy, 20*(3), 307–330.

Box, S. (1987). *Recession Crime and Punishment*. London: Macmillan.

Braithwaite, J., Chapman, B. & Kapuscinski, C.A. (1992). Unemployment and crime: resolving the paradox, mimeo. American Bar Foundation Working Paper 9201. Chicago, IL.

Byrne, D. (1999). *Social Exclusion*. Buckingham: Open University Press.

Burney, E. (2005). *Making People Behave*. Cullompton, Devon: Willan Publishing.

Campbell, A. (2002). *A Review of Anti-social Behaviour Orders*. Home Office Research Study 236. London: Home Office.

Carlson, S.M. & Michalowski, R.J. (1994). *Structural Change in the Economy, Economic Marginality, and Crime*, mimeo. Western Michigan University.

Clear, T.R. (1995). *Harm in American Penology: Offenders, Victims and Their Communities*. New York: State University of New York Press.

Clear, T.R., Rose, D.R., Waring, E. & Scully, K. (2003). Coercive mobility and crime: a preliminary examination of concentrated incarceration and social disorganization. *Justice Quarterly, 20*(1), 33–64.

Currie, E. (1998). *Crime and Punishment in America*. New York: Metropolitan Books.

DTI. (2005). *Tackling Over-Indebtedness: Annual Report 2005*. Department of Trade and Industry, Department of Work and Pensions, Department of Constitutional Affairs. Retrieved from http://www.berr.gov.uk/files/file18547.pdf

Field, S. (1990). *Trends in Crime and their Interpretation: A Study of Recorded Crime in Post-war England and Wales*. Home Office Research Study No. 119. London: Home Office.

FitzGerald, M., Stevens, A. & Hale, C. (2004). *Review of Knowledge on Juvenile Violence: Trends, Policies and Responses in Europe*. Final Report to the EU. University of Kent.

FitzGerald, M., Stockdale, J. & Hale, C. (2003). *Young People and Street Crime: Research into Young People's Involvement in Street Crime*. London: Youth Justice Board.

Gregg, P. & Wadsworth, J. (1995). A short history of labour turnover, job tenure and job security, 1975–1993. *Oxford Review of Economic Policy, 11*(1), 73–90.

Hale, C. (1998). Crime and the business cycle in post-war Britain revisited. *British Journal of Criminology, 38*(4), 681–698.

Hale, C. (1999). The labour market and post-war crime trends in England and Wales. In P. Carlen & R. Morgan (eds), *Crime Unlimited: Questions for the 21st Century*. Basingstoke: Macmillan.

Hale, C. (2005). The politics of law and order. Chapter 21. In C. Hale, K. Hayward, A. Wahidin & E. Wincup (eds), *Criminology*. Oxford: Oxford University Press.

Hall, S. & Winlow, S. (2004). Barbarians at the gate: crime and violence in the breakdown of the pseudo-pacification process. Chapter 23. In J. Ferrell, K. Hayward, W. Morrison & M. Presdee (eds), *Cultural Criminology Unleashed*. London: Glasshouse Press.

Hallsworth, S. (2005). *Street Crime*. Cullompton, Devon: Willan Publishing.

Hansen, K. (2003). The impact of increasing female labour force participation on male property crime. Paper presented at the British Society of Criminology Conference, Bangor, July.

HMIC. (2003). *Streets Ahead: A Joint Inspection of the Street Crime Initiative*. HM Inspectorate of Constabulary, Social Services Inspectorate, HM Crown Prosecution Service Inspectorate, Magistrates Courts Services Inspectorate, Ofsted, HM Inspectorate of Prisons, HM Inspectorate of Probation. London: Home Office.

Hobbs, D., Hadfield, P., Lister, S. & Winlow, S. (2003). *Bouncers; Violence and Governance in the Night-time Economy*. Oxford: Oxford University Press.

Home Office. (1997). *No More Excuses: A New Approach to Tackling Youth Crime in England and Wales*. Cm 3809. London: HMSO.

Home Office. (2005a). *Sentencing Statistics 2004*. Home Office Statistical Bulletin 15/05.

Home Office. (2005b). *The Economic and Social Costs of Crime against Individuals and Households 2003/04*. Home Office Online Report 30/05.

Hope, T. (2000). Inequality and the clubbing of security. In T. Hope & R. Sparks (eds), *Crime, Risk and Security*. London: Routledge.

Hope, T. (2003). Private security and crime victimisation in the risk society. Paper presented to the Conference "Per Una Societa Piu Sicura: Il Contributo Conovisto dell Informazione Statistica", ISTAT, Rome, 3–5 December 2003.

Kara, M. & Upson, A. (2006). *Crime in England and Wales: Quarterly Update to September 2005*. Home Office Statistical Bulletin 03/06. Home Office.

Katz, J. (1988). *Seductions of Crime: Moral and Sensual Attractions in Doing Evil*. New York: Basic Books.

Levitas, R. (1998). *The Inclusive Society? Social Exclusion and New Labour*. Basingstoke: Palgrave Macmillan.

Levitas, R. (2004). Let's hear it for Humpty: social exclusion, the third way and cultural capital, *Cultural Trends, 13*(2), 41–56.

Levitas, R. (2005). *The Inclusive Society? Social Exclusion and New Labour* (2nd edn). Basingstoke: Palgrave Macmillan.

Matthews, R. & Young, J. (2003). *The New Politics of Crime and Punishment*. Cullompton: Willan.

Milliband, D. (2005). *Social Exclusion: The Next Steps Forward*. Speech to the Centre for Analysis of Social Exclusion. LSE. 29 November 2005. ODPM.

Murray, C. (1990). *The Emerging British Underclass*. London Institute of Economic Affairs.

National Statistics. (2004). *General Household Survey*. London: National Statistics.

National Statistics. (2005). *Social Trends No 35*. Basingstoke: Palgrave Macmillan.

Pyle, D. & Deadman, D. (1994). Crime and the business cycle in post-war Britain. *British Journal of Criminology, 34*, 339–357.

Room, G. (ed.) (1995). *Beyond the Threshold*. Bristol: Policy Press.

Silver, H. (1994). Social exclusion and social solidarity: three paradigms. *International Labour Review, 133*(5/6), 531–578.

Smith, J. (2003). *The Nature of Personal Robbery.* Home Office Research Study 254. London: Home Office.

Social Exclusion Unit. (2001). *Preventing Social Exclusion.* London: Stationery Office.

Social Exclusion Unit. (2002). *Reducing Re-offending by Ex-prisoners.* London: Office of the Deputy Prime Minister.

Social Exclusion Unit. (2004). *Tackling Social Exclusion: Taking Stock and Looking to the Future: Emerging Findings.* London: Office of the Deputy Prime Minister.

Stenning, P. (1988). Corporate Policing: Some Recent Trends. In P. Wiles and J. Shepland (eds) *Business and Crime: A Consultation.* Swindon, Crime Concern.

Tonry, M. (1995). *Malign Neglect: Race, Crime and Punishment in America.* New York: Oxford University Press.

Townsend, P. (1979). *Poverty in the United Kingdom.* Harmondsworth: Penguin.

Trickett, A., Ellingworth, D., Hope, T. & Pease, K. (1995). Crime victimisation in the eighties. *British Journal of Criminology, 35,* 343–359.

Triggs, S. (1997). *Interpreting Trends in Recorded Crime in New Zealand.* New Zealand Ministry of Justice. Retrieved from www.justice.govt.nz/pubs/reports/1997/crime

Veit-Wilson, J. (1998). *Setting Adequacy Standards.* London: Policy Press.

Wakefield, A. (2005). The public surveillance functions of private security. *Surveillance and Society, 2*(4), 529–545.

Wilson, W.J. (1987). *The Truly Disadvantaged.* Chicago: Chicago University Press.

Wilson, W.J. (1996). *When Work Disappears.* New York: Knopf.

Witt, R. & Witte, A.D. (1998). Crime, imprisonment and female labour force participation: a time series approach. *Journal of Quantitative Criminology, 16,* 69–86.

Young, J. (2002). Crime and social exclusion. Chapter 14. In M. Maguire, R. Morgan & R. Reiner (eds), *The Oxford Handbook of Criminology* (3rd edn). Oxford: Oxford University Press.

YJB. (2004). *Annual Statistics 2003–4.* Youth Justice Board of England and Wales.

CHAPTER 9

Social Inclusion: Race and Ethnicity Policies in New Clothes

Greville Percival

Former Head of Research, Commission for Racial Equality

ABSTRACT

This chapter reviews some of the prevailing issues leading to the transition from 1960s multiculturalism into a more complex set of policies outlined in the social inclusion agenda. Within this framework, I argue that there has been limited critical assessment of the strategies designed to deliver race inclusion policies. This, in turn, has led to an increasingly devitalized social infrastructure dependent on public funding and increasingly stifled of initiative and endeavour. I then conclude the chapter with a broad discussion concerning the implications of ethnic identification and theorizing on racial inclusion in 21st century Britain.

INTRODUCTION

In simple terms, social inclusion describes the processes and measures designed to eliminate multiple disadvantage amongst immigrating peoples through a series of initiatives aimed at equalizing opportunities. In this respect, it differs little from policies developed over several decades. However, one main difference is that the social inclusion agenda, compared with other poverty theories, extends central coordination of policy measures to an unprecedented level. Historically, the roots of this all-embracing centralist approach to social policy, which can be seen as paving the way for this rhetoric, can be traced back to the writing of Anthony Crosland (Crosland, 1956). Crosland's significance lay in his belief that people should be able to enjoy life and that the Labour Party had become too long associated with economic decline and austerity. He viewed this austerity as being in direct opposition to the Party's and the ability to participate in society it implicitly carried

Multidisciplinary Handbook of Social Exclusion Research. Edited by D. Abrams, J. Christian and D. Gordon.
© 2007 John Wiley & Sons, Ltd.

with it. Thus New Labour's approach to equality, in many respects, can be seen as sitting within the tradition of revisionist social democracy established by Crosland, and whose view of social democracy has been a particular source of inspiration to the architects of New Labour. For our purposes, however, this discussion is restricted to the current ideology of the Labour government and the ways in which it influences the conceptualization of racial equality in the UK.

As discussed by Millar (Chapter 1) and Gordon (Chapter 11), many of the practical policies of the social inclusion agenda are linked with the objectives promoted across member states of the European Union (EU) following the Lisbon conference in 2000. The conference signified agreement by EU leaders to combat poverty and exclusion amongst immigrant communities in the host society, primarily through immigrants' participation in employment and economic growth schemes of member states (see, Phillimore & Goodson, 2006). The framework outlined at Lisbon fitted well with New Labour's own overall strategy, and provided the further benefit of enabling the New Labour government to make positive statements about being at the heart of the EU. However, the precise means for achieving this ambitious objective – equalizing opportunities – were left to the discretion of the member states. By implication, New Labour was now poised to define the structure and implementation mechanisms to tackle racial inclusion issues directly.

UNDERSTANDING MECHANISMS UNDERLYING "RACIAL EXCLUSION"

As touched on in the introduction of this chapter, the New Labour government's social inclusion agenda was part of a shift in strategy which viewed *wealth creation* emphasized over and above that of *wealth redistribution*. In other words, it signified acceptance by the New Labour Party that its traditional "tax and spend" approach to eliminating deprivation and poverty could no longer be sustained in the changing global environment. It needed a fresh focus to build its social inclusion policy. Therefore, social inclusion policies were inherently linked to national economic growth plans, which were seen as a means of being able to offer increased employment opportunities for minorities (also see, Peattie, Chapter 10).

However, it was not long before this approach was also tempered somewhat with notions of "personal empowerment". The key advantage of adding empowerment to the racial inclusion agenda was that it helped to reshape perceptions of individuals away from that of "victims of society" to enable them to be seen as "agents fully able to participate in society". With agency also came increased personal responsibility for one's own inclusion. This was further promoted when the government suggested that solutions to social *inclusion* required a range of initiatives which addressed deprivation and disadvantage, not least because the social problems were thought of as not necessarily mutually exclusive, but were seen as interlinked and particularly so with employment opportunities.

For example, the "Improving Opportunity, Strengthening Society" strategy, launched in January 2005 was the basis of the Government's commitment to create communities of equality. That is, communities in which every individual, irrespective of their racial or ethnic origin, could potentially experience equal opportunities, rights and responsibilities, enabling them to fulfill their potential (Home Office, 2005). This was followed by initiatives such as 'Fair Cities', a demand-led approach to helping individuals from disadvantaged backgrounds gain employment (Home Office, 2006)—crucially to enhanced participation amongst marginalized subgroups (also see, Peattie, 2007). Programmes such as these were perceived as particularly pertinent in achieving the government's inclusion agenda, as 42% of those falling into "poverty" in the UK are ethnic minorities (SEU, 2006). However, questions have been raised about the success of these programmes, both in terms of reaching employment targets, and also in terms of improving the overall quality of life amongst minority group members.

If we decompose these poverty figures, and focus attention on employment, we see that ethnic minority leavers from "New Deal for Young People" achieve only 78% of the job outcomes of their white counterparts (Select Committee on Education and Employment). These figures are compounded by the fact that ethnic minority group members are less likely to have qualifications than the population as a whole, and there is some disparity amongst subpopulations since some are less likely than others to hold qualifications in general. According to Jobcentre Plus's 2005 review, 46% of the Bangladeshis of working age (those aged 16–64) have no qualifications, making it much more difficult for them to compete for jobs and ultimately fully participate in society (Corkett, 2005). (Also see discussion below concerning the implementation of services for racial inclusion.)

And the pattern of impoverished opportunity applies to achievement levels in education (also see Hick *et al.*, Chapter 6), access and experience with other services, as well as their performance on general well-being outcomes. That is, ethnic minority groups consistently experience disproportionately poor outcomes across a range of well-being indicators. South Asians, for example, are 40% more likely than the general population to contract coronary heart disease, and they are 50% more likely to die prematurely from such conditions. Diabetes is also much more common (up to six times) among South Asians, and can be up to three times more frequently reported among Black African and Black Caribbean populations. Furthermore, several studies exploring access to education and health care amongst minority applicants, such as the groups mentioned here, show that refugees who have not registered for asylum in the UK were not permitted healthcare services other than those classified as an "emergency", unless the conditions exhibited pose a public health risk (Pollard & Savulescu, 2004). Thus, reviewing the evidence of minority group members' access to services, it must be said that at best public services aim to help to counter much of the discrimination within society against people from ethnic minorities. However, ethnic minority groups consistently report worse outcomes with lower levels of satisfaction across a range of different services than their white counterparts do (SEU, 2004). Given that health behaviours underpin ability to compete satisfactorily in job market activities one can question how effective the programmes really are.

DELIVERING SERVICES TO MINORITY COMMUNITIES: AN OVERVIEW OF HOW SERVICES ARE ADMINISTERED

How does the government provide services for racial inclusion? A good starting point for outlining the implementation of public services is a report produced by the Prime Minister's Strategy Unit (2005). In it service delivery mechanisms are critiqued, and the authors identify fundamental shortcomings in the systems for delivery, as well as providing packages of institutional support for deprived areas (i.e. regeneration programmes). Subsequently, these findings were used to inform the design of amended delivery systems, with the aim of fine tuning better practical aid to minority communities. Such practical measures consisted of a wide range of neighbourhood renewal and regeneration programmes known as area-based initiatives (ABIs), and they also included EU funding for tackling deprivation to supplement the range of diverse mainstream public services (i.e. housing, education services). Examples of these new programmes included: "Employment Zones", specialist programmes aimed to provide a fresh approach to job seeking; "Sure Start", pre-school programmes intended to equalise educational opportunities for children from deprived areas; and the "Single Regeneration Budget", aimed at diminishing the gap between those in deprived versus similar non-deprived communities.

The delivery of this raft of programmes was intended to be achieved through national and regional tiers of governance, along with local authorities who also provide a number of additional programmes and mainstream services. At a national level, the Government Offices for the Regions (GOs) act as intermediaries in the chain of delivery, regulating the performance of Local Strategic Partnerships (LSPs), and managing EU funded programmes. At a regional level, Regional Housing Boards (RHBs) draw up regional housing strategies, and Regional Development Agencies (RDAs) coordinate the implementation of economic strategy. A further layer of oversight was included between regional government and local authorities. Such organizing bodies included: Learning and Skills Councils (LSCs), Strategic Health Authorities, Connexions, Police Authorities and Jobcentre Plus. All of these services were designed with the aims (a) of improving the skills of young people, and (b) ensuring that Britain could compete globally at a world class standard.

As noted, the main route of delivery from the end user's perspective has been largely that of local authorities (i.e. Councils). And at the neighbourhood level, it is safe to say that many organizations have offered support to redress apparent gaps in provision offered by their local anthorities. Numerous local charities, community organizations and voluntary groups provide tangible services to minority communities. In general, these often tend to be (a) small groups with minimal staffing, or (b) larger organizations within the community and voluntary sector (CVS). Both types of groups have been widely commissioned to deliver services in accordance with national strategies, as defined by the government's agenda on social inclusion.

EQUALITY COMMISSIONS AND THEIR ROLE

Although services are administered through local and regional providers, the policies they are implementing have been largely overseen by equality commissions. That is, one of the ways in which the Government has implemented its inclusion strategy has been through the Equality Commissions. This action has been accompanied by legislation which required all public bodies to positively develop and implement equality programmes. These programmes cover domains such as: age, gender, religion, ethnicity and now reach across all strands of equality. In 2005, there were three commissions, the Commission for Racial Equality (CRE), the Equal Opportunities Commission (EOC) and the Disability Rights Commission (DRC). Of these commissions, the CRE was the one body designated to oversee issues relating to race and ethnicity, although its responsibilities are presently transferring to the cross-cutting Commission for Equality and Human Rights (CEHR).

Following the development and extension of the Government's social inclusion agenda into all areas of public services, the CRE's approach has been reviewed increasingly in the context of the Government's national strategic priorities for social inclusion. The difficulty facing the CRE has always been that many members of minority communities criticised it for supporting the *status quo* inclusion policies, while at the same time it also faced mainstream criticism whenever it gave forceful expression to its law enforcement activities. As a result, its role has frequently been seen as oscillating between periods in which it pursued formal investigations of racial discrimination, often resulting in the issuing of non-discrimination notices, and periods when it adopted a softer approach encouraging public bodies and employers to develop good practice. What can now be argued is that, with the introduction of legislation to cover multiple areas of equality including age, sexual orientation, disability and religion, race equality can no longer occupy its former advantaged position at the forefront of the equality debate. It is also questionable whether the new body, the CEHR, will gain an influential role in the delivery of the social inclusion agenda.

With the formation of a single equality commission, there has been another marked shift in policy perceptions of social differences. Under the new structure, "multiculturalism" (i.e., celebrating differences) is considered to have a more negative impact, because it sustains *difference* rather than supporting integration into the mainstream or host society. This view was itself reinforced by Trevor Phillips, Chairman of the CRE (and now chair of the CEHR), in his 2005 "Sleepwalking to Segregation" speech. In it he argued the need for a more strongly socially integrated society:

> We already know a lot about what an integrated society looks like. It has three essential features: equality, where everyone is treated equally, has a right to fair outcomes, and no one should expect privileges because of what they are; participation: all groups in society should expect to share in how we make decisions, but also expect to carry the responsibilities of making the society work; and interaction: no-one should be trapped within their own community, and in the truly integrated society, who people work with, or the friendships they make, should not be constrained by race or ethnicity. (Phillips, 2005).

This speech attracted a good deal of attention from policy commentators, who saw it as a stark departure from the traditional position of the CRE, that is to support multiculturism. However what in fact attracted most attention was that the rejection of multiculturalism seemed to signal an adoption of social integration (see, Berry, 1997). This appeared to overturn two decades of public policy by suggesting that "celebrating diversity" was akin to perpetuating differences within and between communities through what Hutchison *et al.* (2007) refer to as optimal distinctiveness, or seeing ones differences as one's strengths. Thus, multiculturalism was considered to have a negative impact because it sustained *difference* rather than supporting integration into the host society. While Phillips used this speech as part of a platform to gain wider support for the CEHR, he also signalled that the "new" social inclusion agenda represents a conceptual transition from the traditional approach. Where disadvantage previously had been tackled by policies that subdued the economic and social forces which acted to heighten discrimination, such measures were now replaced with policies that also address simultaneously the religious and cultural factors which may attenuate ethnic minorities inclusion in mainstream British society.

Ballard's (2001) seminal paper argues that Government policy on racial inclusion, as outlined in a recent Home Office report, is not only internally inconsistent, but fails to address the nature of community responses to the forces of exclusion, and therefore undermines the position of the commissions. Ballard drew attention to the difficulties of implementing the Government's call for a shared "civic identity"—an "overarching" identification for uniting communities through a shared outlook and shared aspirations—while at the same time balancing the Home Office's expressed desire to confront cultural practices that are in conflict with democratic society (inferred as equating to cultural homogeneity). With such opposing perspectives facing the commissions, programme providers and researchers interested in racial inclusion, one can only ask, "What factors might motivate 'shared values' or a 'British Identification' such that we could build interventions around them?"

Theorising About Racial-Community Identification as a Vehicle for Racial Inclusion

There are well-developed literatures exploring many dimensions central to the development of identification presented in sociological, psychological and political science domains. Although these streams of identification are connected with the growing body of literature on racial exclusion, much less is known about minority groups' perceptions of them, or more specifically what factors might lead to "racial community conflict". As a concrete first step, researchers assessing the role of "racial identity" and "community conflict" in Britain have reported that the extent to which people endorse cultural values within individual communities can have a strong effect on lifestyles and attitudes towards host communities (Percival & Forsythe, unpub.). Percival and Forsythe demonstrated that young women of Pakistani heritage reported becoming increasingly resentful of male peers and parental figures exercising control over their lifestyles, seeing this involvement as hindering their own empowerment, participation and social inclusion.

Additionally, a large-scale study conducted across several towns in the North of England prior to the ethnic disturbances that occurred in Bradford in 2002 (Commission for Racial Equality: Percival, 2000), revealed that religious and cultural differences were reportedly seen within and across ethnic communities as major factors contributing to an absence of social cohesion and underpinning many of the feelings of isolation. A key finding from the investigation was that the factors underlying community conflict were experiences of widespread alienation, most notably from institutions as well as from the supposed "social justice" perceived to be bestowed by the institutions themselves. A Ministerial Review Team downplayed the underlying value differences that might be associated with religious and cultural differences, presenting them as distal rather than proximal factors, perhaps because of a reticence to recognise a multicultural rather than integrationist pressure at work (Home Office, 2001b).

To further explore the role of group contact and values within the context of racial and community identification, Choudhury (2004) examined the effect of bringing groups of people together in order for members of each group to develop an influence on one another. This echoes themes developed by Allport in his work on reducing prejudice. Choudhury found, as outlined by Allport almost 60 years ago (Allport, 1954), that positive and cooperative contact between members of previously hostile groups reduces prejudice. Hutchinson *et al.* (Chapter 3) offer a more detailed description, but suffice it to say that according to Allport (1954) beneficial intergroup contact must meet certain conditions. These include (a) the establishment of cooperative and goal-oriented contact under circumstances wherein there is equal status between members of the two groups, and (b) the creation of situations that allow for a personalized interaction and the provision of support by relevant social groups and authorities. Besides these conditions, there are many different aspects of contact that determine its effects on attitude. For example, the quantitative aspects of contact include frequency and duration; the role aspects of contact include both competitive and cooperative activity, as well as superordinate–subordinate role relations; and the social aspects include the presence or absence of a history of conflict and whether or not the contact is based on voluntary involvement (Allport, 1954; also see Abrams & Christian, Chapter 12, Abrams *et al.*, 2005).

With the context of racial inclusion in Britain, Choudhury's 2004 analysis suggests that when considering Anglo-Asian relations, these aspects of intragroup contact need to be facilitated through support services in the community. If such a long-term view of community presence is not adopted, than community tensions will increase, as well as incidences of increased depression, drug issues and relationship breakdown. He notes that this is because many young people are struggling to resolve identity conflicts between their ethnic and Anglo identifications, and group contact is an important part of that process.

Assessments of Structures for Inclusion

How successful have we been at increasing racial inclusion? Little systematic research attention has been paid to assessing the effectiveness of racial inclusion policies or practices in the UK. In part, this may be because there is an inherent lack of clarity in many of the concepts (see, Millar, Chapter 1; Gordon, Chapter 11). But equally it may be, as Bagguley and Hussain (2003) show, that there are overlaps with multiple forms of exclusion, making efforts to tease apart the proximal and distal factors leading to exclusion extremely difficult.

Yet, another plausible explanation could be that exclusion has been conceived of as a single dimension and to take account of relationships on an intergroup level as well as an institutional one would require a more robust framework (Abrams & Christian, Chapter 12). Using this approach, one could suggest that we may be overlooking the possibility that pronounced religious and cultural differences are more of a "defence mechanism" utilized by communities who consider themselves poorly served, both by the institutions of society as well as by more general processes of social change. It is entirely possible that communities which fear a loss of culture and identification do so for a multiplicity of reasons and, in their desire to protect their identity and culture, may well see other communities as a source of potential threat.

Finally, the flaws that have plagued the effective delivery of services, most notably inconsistent funding, might also hinder the evaluation of the outcomes. That is, as we have noted, monies are frequently given to short-term initiatives in which small-scale and short-term work programmes are set up, which lead to discontinuity and hindering inclusion efforts. This implementation problem is further compounded by the fact that delivery agents tend not to use standardized outcome measures. A recent assessment by the National Audit Office (2004) of the NDC Partnerships found 70 separate programmes (known as Area Based Initiatives or ABIs), each with its own regulations and management processes. This in turn has acted as a major obstacle deterring community involvement in service programmes. Thus, one can conclude that the complexity of tackling racial inclusion arises from the fact that it is a complex multidimensional social issue facing our society. Nonetheless focusing on more standardized outcomes, providing longer term funding, and assessing interventions in a timely way will go some way towards tackling the problem.

CONCLUSION

In this chapter, I highlight that while racial exclusion is generally assessed through measures that increasingly view it through the lens of multiple disadvantage, this also ensures that it remains on the periphery of the exclusion agenda. In part, this is a pragmatic problem interwoven with questions about effective service delivery, but it is also tied to funding and evaluation of targets and services. What becomes increasingly clear from the review presented in this chapter, is that we require longer term interventions, which take greater account of the processes underlying exclusion. Additionally, practise efforts should also be balanced with the implementation of longitudinal research programmes, aimed at redressing gaps in our understanding of this multifaceted social issue and leading us towards the goal of having a more racially inclusive society.

REFERENCES

Abrams, D., Hogg, M.A. & Marques, J. (2005). *The Social Psychology of Inclusion and Exclusion*. New York: Psychology Press.

Allport, G.W. (1954). *The Nature of Prejudice*. Reading, MA: Addison-Wesley.

Bagguley, P. & Hussain, Y. (2003). *Conflict and Cohesion: Constructions of 'Community' around the 2001 'Riots'*. Paper presented to the Communities Conference, 18–20 September 2003. Available at http://www.leeds.ac.uk/sociology/people/yhdocs/community's%20paper.doc

Ballard, R. (2002). Race, Ethnicity and Culture. In Martin Holborn (ed.). *New Directions in Sociology*. Ormskirk: Causeway.

Berry, J.W. (1997). Immigration, acculturation and adaptation. *Applied Psychology: An International Review*, 46, 1, 5–68.

Choudhury, S. (2004). Disaffection among British Muslim youth. BBC News online Wednesday, 31 March, 2004.

Corkett, J. (2005). Jobcentre Plus Evaluation: Summary of Evidence. Leeds: Corporate Document Services (for the Department of Work and Pensions).

Crosland, C.A.R. (1956). *The Future of Socialism*. Jonathan Cape, London.

Home Office (2001a). Report CM 5387. Secure Borders, Safe Haven. Integration with Diversity in Modern Britain. Available at http://www.archive2.official-documents.co.uk/document/cm53/5387/cm5387.pdf

Home Office (2001b). Building cohesive communities: a report of the Ministerial Group on Public Order and Community Cohesion. Available at www.communities.gov.uk/publications/communities/publicorder cohesion

Home Office (2005). 'Improving Opportunity, Strengthening Society' strategy. Available from: http://www.communities.gov.uk/index.asp?id=1504860

Home Office (2006). Equality in the job market: Closing the unemployment gap. Available from: http://www.communities.gov.uk/pub/396/RaceEqualityandCommunityCohesionNews Issue1Spring2006_id1502396.pdf

National Audit Office (2004). Report on NDC Partnerships 2004. NRU NM Pathfinder Evaluation 2003/4. Available at http://www.publications.parliament.uk/pa/cm200304/cmselect/cmpubacc/492/49206.htm

Percival, G. (2000). CRE research report (unpublished) of views on equality and diversity amongst a sample of residents in towns in the North of England.

Percival, G. & Forsythe, M. (unpub). *Europe Culture and Identity.* Unpublished research (2003).

Phillimore, J. & Goodson, L. (2006). Problem or opportunity? Asylum seekers, refugees, employment and social exclusion in deprived urban areas, Urban Studies, 43:*10*, 1715–1736.

Phillips, T. (2005). Sleepwalking to Segregation. Commission for Racial Equality Press Release 22 September 2005.

Pollard, A.J. & Savulescu, J. (2004). Eligibility of overseas visitors and people of uncertain residential status for NHS treatment. *British Medical Journal, 329*, 346–349.

Prime Minister's Strategy Unit (2005). Strategic Audit: Progress and challenges for the UK. Available from: http://www.cabinetoffice.gov.uk/strategy/downloads/work_areas/strategic_audit/strategic_audit2.pdf

Select Committee on Education and Employment Third Report. Disadvantaged Job Seekers. http://www.parliament.the-stationery-office.co.uk/pd.cm200001/cmselect/cmeduemp/48/4806.htm#n85

Social Exclusion Unit (2004). *Mental Health and Social Exclusion*, Office of the Deputy Prime Minister: London.

Social Exclusion Unit (2006). *Improving Services, Improving Lives: Evidence and Key Themes.* Office of the Deputy Prime Minister: London.

CHAPTER 10

Business and Social Inclusion

Ken Peattie

Cardiff University, United Kingdom

ABSTRACT

Discussions about business in relation to social exclusion and inclusion usually focus on economically orientated issues relating to the role of businesses in generating wealth and employment, and providing the goods and services that those within society consume. This chapter broadens the discussion out further to demonstrate how the increasing range of roles that businesses play within contemporary society ensures that they are involved in almost every factor contributing to either the causes of, or proposed solutions to, social exclusion. The chapter considers the roles that business plays in generating (and unfortunately sometimes reducing) opportunities for employment, earnings, savings, consumption and the development of connections between individuals and their communities. It also highlights the roles that specific industries such as transport, house building and the media play in shaping society and determining the opportunities that exist for individuals to be, and feel, included.

INTRODUCTION

When business is discussed in relation to social exclusion and inclusion, it is usually with a relatively narrow focus on businesses as generators of wealth and providers of employment. Given that poverty and unemployment are two of the most significant contributors to social exclusion, this is not surprising. These themes also combine to create a further strand of the discussion, with a focus on entrepreneurship and the opportunities that can exist to stimulate the development of new businesses to improve social inclusion in deprived areas where regeneration is needed.

The attention shown to the role of businesses in generating wealth and employment can disguise the extent to which business has a wide-ranging, multifaceted and often subtle influence on social exclusion and inclusion. The products, services and technologies of business have the ability to both reinforce and overcome barriers within and between societies. The strategic and operational decisions of businesses can impact individuals and communities for good or ill, through both deliberate policies, and the unintended

Multidisciplinary Handbook of Social Exclusion Research. Edited by D. Abrams, J. Christian and D. Gordon.

consequences of actions and decisions. The variety of contributions that businesses make to social exclusion and inclusion reflects the multiple roles that businesses play as providers of goods and services; as generators of wealth and employment; as pension providers; as influencers of (and increasingly as partners in) public sector policies and projects; and as part of the communities within which they operate.

The social and environmental impacts of business, the relationship between businesses and their many stakeholders, and the role of businesses as "corporate citizens" are central to two intertwined research streams within the discipline of business and management, of Corporate Social Responsibility (CSR) and Business Sustainability. The contributions that businesses can make to creating more sustainable, more equitable, and more cohesive communities and societies are considerable. However, the proportion of research explicitly dedicated to the role that business plays in social exclusion and inclusion remains disappointing, and it represents a considerable field of opportunity for scholars from business disciplines and from other social sciences for the future.

The term "social exclusion" has been the subject of much discussion and debate that is reflected elsewhere in this book (see Gordon, Chapter 11). Partly, this is because the word "exclusion" implies an active process through which society excludes individuals. In practice, the processes by which an individual becomes disengaged or disconnected from society may involve no deliberate intent, or they may reflect the intention and choices of an individual who wishes to withdraw from society. This can make it more helpful to consider these issues in terms of social engagement and disengagement, particularly from a business perspective. Businesses are rarely involved in deliberately excluding individuals from the rest of society, although in the case of privatised prisons, this forms the very basis of their business.

Burchardt, Le Grand and Piachaud (1999) offer a definition of social exclusion that is helpful when considering the role that businesses play:

> An individual is socially excluded if (a) he or she is geographically resident in a society, and (b) he or she does not participate in the normal activities of citizens in that society. (p. 230)

A key idea within this is "normal activities", and these are defined according to five dimensions of participation in society that constitute "inclusion" (as defined by a variety of authors including Berghman, 1995; Oppenheim, 1998; Walker, 1997). These are defined as:

1. Consumption activity (being able to consume at least a basic level of the goods and services which are considered normal for a particular society);
2. Production activity (engaging in an economically and/or socially valued activity, including paid work, education, volunteering or family care);
3. Savings activity (by accumulating personal savings, pensions entitlements or holding property);
4. Political activity (engaging in some collective effort to improve or protect the social and physical environment); and
5. Social activity (engaging in significant social interaction with family or friends and identifying with a cultural group or community).

The importance of business in the social exclusion/inclusion debate is immediately obvious from this. Businesses produce the goods and services that we consume, they provide many of the pensions that the retired depend upon (either directly through company pensions, or indirectly through investment returns to fund public sector pension schemes), and they are the source of much of the paid and productive work. The accumulation of savings and acquisition of property are each facilitated by major industries, and collective efforts to improve or protect the social and physical environment are increasingly linked to partnerships with, and sponsorship from businesses. In an era when industrialised economies have witnessed the "hollowing out of the state" (Rhodes, 1994), many of the activities aimed at generating inclusion (such as social housing programmes), that would once have been provided entirely through public sector efforts, are now being delivered by the private sector or through public–private partnerships.

It is notable that social activities, although largely concerned with the relationship between individuals and their families, friends and communities are increasingly defined by and related to commercial consumption. In the late 19th century in Britain, the mainstays of many people's social lives beyond the workplace were likely to be the Church, local community institutions (from the local school to the public house), local organisations and events, and the local park and library. In the early 21st century, the mainstays of our social lives are largely provided for by global players in industries dedicated to leisure and hospitality or telecommunications. As Tomlinson (1990) notes, even changes in British laws aimed at preventing public disorder have made it increasingly difficult for large groups of people (legally) to gather together other than at formal, commercialised public events. There is relatively little left to us as individuals, in terms of achieving social inclusion that does not depend upon, or involve in some way, businesses.

THE EVOLVING ROLE OF BUSINESS IN SOCIETY

Businesses are important as both a component of, and an influence on society. The relationship between economic activity, business entities, the structure and nature of society, and instances of social exclusion is an extremely complex one. It has also evolved over time as the relationship between business and society has passed through several eras. The pre-industrial era was characterised by a relatively localised and small-scale approach to production and consumption. Although there was a limited amount of international trade, most people's needs were met by local artisan producers and they would work near to where they lived, and most likely near to where they were born. For most people, production, consumption and socialisation took place within local communities which they could hardly help, but be integrated into (which is not to deny the existence of the many soldiers, sailors, nomadic herdsmen, isolated farmers, itinerant workers or hermits that existed hundreds of years ago, but to view them as the exception, not the rule).

The era of industrialisation allowed for the development of mass production and mass consumption, the growth of "big business", and the increasing separation between producers and consumers and also between the places of work and residence. The growing scale and influence of businesses gave them a much greater ability to contribute to either social exclusion or inclusion. In some cases, very strong and well-integrated communities emerged to serve particular industries, with the communities in the South Wales' valleys that grew to service the needs of the coal and steel industries during the 19th century being perhaps the best-known example. It also led to the development of "company towns" or "model villages" such as the one George Cadbury created at Bourneville, that sought to provide healthy communities with the explicit aim of integrating the workers of a business with other community members. From the point of view of consumption, the 20th century represented an age in which there was an unprecedented democratisation of consumption. By the end of the century, products such as cars, foreign holidays, televisions and washing machines had all come to be viewed as part of the basic necessities of life for the majority of people in industrialised economies, when only a few decades earlier they had represented luxuries enjoyed only by a relatively wealthy elite. During the 20th century, the share of household expenditures in Organisation for Economic Co-operation and Development countries (which represent 30 of the world's wealthiest democracies) dedicated to leisure, education, travel and communication (all forms of consumption with strong potential to increase social inclusion) roughly doubled (Donaghy, Rudinger & Poppelreuter, 2004).

During the latter part of the 20th century, the era of globalisation brought about intense international competition in global markets in many key industries such as electronics, automotive, engineering, chemicals and aerospace. For many communities with strong links to companies in such industries, this led to intense dislocation and "disintegration" as a result of corporate restructuring. This process was famously portrayed in Michael Moore's film *Roger and Me* chronicling the decline of his home town of Flint, Michigan, following General Motors' decision to cease production in what was also their home town. Bynner (1996) notes that over time these transformations in economies and technologies have changed the demands of business for particular skills, and the mix of demand for full-time or part-time working, and between manufacturing and service jobs. Such changes can reduce the opportunities for particular individuals contributing to their social exclusion, and they can also change the nature of work and careers to make them more individualistic. Market globalisation policies have been promoted by governments and institutions with the aim of generating economic growth and supposedly reducing inequalities between nations. In practice, it has also often acted to exacerbate trends within countries towards inequality, polarisation and the reduction of infrastructure through which common citizenship benefits can be delivered (Room, 1999).

The early part of the 21st century sees society within industrialised economies increasingly entering the "Digital Age". This has brought a new technological dimension to the debate about social inclusion and led to the emerging concept of the "Digital Divide". Originally, this was used to denote different levels of access to information and communications technology (ICT) amongst the populations of rich and poor countries. Increasingly, it is now being used to discuss equality of access to the digital economy within societies such as the UK. As access to information, products and public services becomes increasingly dependent upon Internet access, so the danger grows that some individuals will suffer from exclusion. The concern is that inequalities in access to ICT will both create new forms of social exclusion whilst also potentially reinforcing existing patterns of exclusion (Selwyn, 2002).

The Role of Business in Social Exclusion and Inclusion

As well as being a state, social exclusion is also a process involving the loss of social cohesion and the marginalisation of individuals. There are a number of factors that can contribute to a person becoming marginalised and having their access to the "normal" activities and opportunities of society restricted, including:

- age
- employment status
- poverty
- homelessness
- sex
- lifestage (e.g. parenthood or retirement)
- location (relative to both "community" and the means to gain access to their community through transport services or access to ICT)
- ethnic origin or religion
- language
- low levels of literacy or educational attainment
- health and disability
- personality and preferences

For many of these issues such as age, sex, lifestage, ethnic origin, religion and disability, businesses have a legal obligation not to discriminate against individuals in offering them employment opportunities, access to their goods and services, or access to their premises. For other factors such as location, poverty or health, business can assist people to become more socially included as part of their core business through the provision of transport services, affordable products or healthcare products and services. For factors such as homelessness, literacy problems or disability, businesses can also contribute to social inclusion through initiatives such as volunteering programmes, cause-related marketing campaigns or charitable donations.

Social exclusion can relate to places as well as individuals. Oppenheim (1998) identifies a number of features that apply to "poor places", relating to employment opportunities, weak local economies, loss of services (particularly financial services) and higher prices for key purchases such as food and transport. The risk is that poor communities fall prey to a downward spiral in terms of losing people, wealth, services, employment opportunities and business investment. Businesses, as part of communities, can play a role in reversing this process to generate opportunities for their communities as well as themselves, and in the process generate employment opportunities and wealth, and help to develop the social capital of the people they employ.

This chapter explores key aspects of the role that businesses can play in reducing social exclusion and promoting social inclusion, through the insights available from the emerging literature of this relatively new field for research. The focus of this chapter is mainly at a UK national level. Research insights gained from a country like the UK are largely applicable to other liberal market economies, but will need to be applied with caution to countries where the social structure and the nature of the relationship between business and society are significantly different. Although only touched upon briefly, the role that businesses can play at a community level, and also on a global scale, in influencing social inclusion and exclusion are each worthy of at least a chapter, if not a book, in themselves.

BUSINESS, CONSUMPTION ACTIVITIES AND SOCIAL EXCLUSION

Williams and Windebank (2000) highlight that social inclusion through employment and production activity has been the dominant focus of the policy debate about social exclusion in the UK in a way that has overshadowed the role that consumption plays. Gordon *et al.* (2000) sought to map the extent to which some UK adults were excluded from mainstream consumption through being unable to afford the basic "necessities" of life (items which the majority believed all adults should be able to afford, and which they should not have to forego). Their findings suggested that 58% of people lacked none of these items in 1999, but nearly one in four (24%) households could not afford three or more necessities. The most common of these were the ability to:

- save as little as £10 per month (25%);
- take a holiday away from home (18%);
- keep the home in a decent state of decoration (14%);
- have a small amount of money to spend on oneself rather than the family weekly (13%); and replace worn-out furniture or electrical items (both 12%).

It is worth noting that what constitutes a "normal" level of consumption is a relative concept according to the nature of the country and community that an individual lives within. An individual lacking the ability to afford a certain number of such necessities will feel less excluded if they live in a relatively poor neighbourhood than a relatively affluent one.

In some cases, access to particular goods and services is also rendered more difficult or more expensive for less affluent consumers by the pricing structures or billing arrangements of companies. A simple example is the use of coin-fed meters to supply gas or electricity to poorer consumers, resulting in a premium price compared to more affluent consumers who can use direct debit (Allen, 2000). Previous research suggests that poorer households often lack access to credit, or can only access it at "extortionate" rates relative to more affluent households (Kempson & Whyley, 2000). In addition to the affordability of consumption, individuals can find themselves socially excluded because of the relative inaccessibility of consumption and shopping experiences (Williams *et al.*, 2001). With the concentration of retail investment in larger and often out-of-town locations, the most affluent and mobile consumers face increasing levels of choice and variety, whilst the "disadvantaged consumer", faces reduced choice (Eversley, 1990).

The research of Williams and Windebank (2000) demonstrates that people can feel themselves to be excluded, because they cannot afford to buy the goods and services that constitute "normal" consumption in a society; or because they have to use "alternative" channels to access goods and services by relying on friends and family, second-hand shops, car-boot fairs or online auction services such as eBay. "For the disadvantaged shopper, consumer choice is often no choice at all; there is reliance on a dwindling range of stores or use of informal sites where counterfeit, stolen or second-hand goods may be purchased" (Williams & Windebank, 2000). Although there is some evidence of significant differences amongst socio-economic groups (in terms of car ownership, employment status, age and family size) in terms of where they shop, it is not a simple issue of strict segregation in shopping behaviours along socio-economic lines. Williams *et al.* (2001), also found that the past experience of individuals and their emotional reactions to shopping experiences could strongly effect behaviour and, for example, whether or not people patronised small but local shops.

Potential solutions to preventing people becoming excluded as consumers through a lack of access, require a mix of policy innovations and changes to business practices to improve accessibility and affordability. Williams and Windebank (2000, p. 510) suggest a need to "curtail the current purported up-market shift in retailers' trading strategies, encouraged by a retail planning system that discourages 'bargain basement retailing' due to its impact on the 'attractiveness' of shopping centres. This 'cherry-picking' process is resulting in the exclusion of poorer populations". Improving the affordability of products also requires improvements within the financial services industry in terms of the provision of basic financial products and cheap credit to poorer consumers (see for example Leyshon & Thrift, 1995; Kempson, 1996; Kempson & Whyley, 1999).

Research and discussion about the influence of consumption on social inclusion and exclusion have a strong focus on rational economic issues concerning the quantity of consumption and the economic ability of individuals to engage in "normal" consumption practices and patterns. Other perspectives and more cultural dimensions of consumption and its effects are somewhat neglected in comparison to the economics of product afford-ability and accessibility. An alternative perspective is that the consumption of certain products or services may reduce a person's overall level of social inclusion, particularly by reducing their levels of social interaction and activity. Alcohol is one particular product whose consumption can become bound up with problems of stigmatisation, marginalisa-tion and social exclusion (Room, 2005), although the extent to which excessive alcohol consumption is a cause or a symptom of social exclusion will vary amongst individual cases. Similarly, other forms of consumption that can prove addictive, from gambling to computer gaming or Internet usage, can all act to reduce a person's capacity for other forms of social inclusion, even whilst meeting their desires (if not strictly speaking their needs) as a consumer. The idea that affluence and consumption, rather than poverty and deprivation, can cause social exclusion seems counter-intuitive. However, in Japan the phenomenon of *hikikomori*, a form of acute social withdrawal prevalent amongst young men, has emerged in which a lifestyle of home-based consumption leads to self-exclusion from almost all other aspects of society. An exact definition of *hikikomori*, and good data on its prevalence, are both missing, but ". . . there is broad agreement that this illness is a product of the affluence, technology, and convenience of modern Japanese life. Many *hikikomori* spend most of their waking hours on the internet or playing video games, while snacking on food and drink delivered to their homes" (Watts, 2002, p. 1131).

Consumption is also important in the way it is used to construct our sense of identity and "belonging". In reviewing consumer behaviour from a sustainability perspective, Jackson (2005) reviews the different schools of thought within the sociology of consump-tion literature and concludes that: "Whereas in earlier times we were what we did (or sometimes who we knew), in modern society we are what we consume" (p. 30). The role of consumption of material goods goes beyond acting as signals to express our identity, they help to locate and integrate us socially. Douglas and Isherwood (1979) explored the importance of material consumption in providing "marking services", through social rituals (such as festive celebrations or gift giving) which embed individuals in their social group and cement social relations. These maintain social ties, shared meanings and infor-mation flows that help individuals and groups to maintain their social identity in the face of cultural shifts and social shocks.

As Jackson neatly summarises it "We consume not just to nourish ourselves or protect ourselves from the elements or maintain a living. We consume in order to identify our-selves with a social group, to position ourselves within that group, to distinguish ourselves with respect to other social groups, to communicate allegiance to certain ideals. To dif-ferentiate ourselves from certain other ideals. We consume in order to communicate.

Through consumption we communicate not only with each other but with our past, with our ideals, with our fears and with our aspirations. We consume, in part at least, in pursuit of meaning." (p. 33)

The goods and services that businesses market to us, therefore, often seek to appeal directly or indirectly to our sense of solidarity with a particular social group, and perhaps to our fear of social exclusion. Advertising campaigns promoting new mobile phone models on the theme that "Life is full of enough embarrassments, don't let your mobile phone be one of them" tapped into this fear. In a celebrated early essay on fashion, George Simmel (1904) viewed fashion as signifying solidarity and uniformity within social groups (in those days based on class), and that simultaneously and inseparably from creating inclusion, it created the exclusion of all other groups. Such a concept suggests a micro and a macro dimension to the role that consumption can play in relation to concepts of social inclusion and exclusion. Membership of a particular subgroup or subculture, particularly amongst the young, can be signified and intensified by wearing the "right" clothes and accessories or listening to the "right" music (Hunter, 2003). This can simultaneously increase an individual's inclusion within their chosen social group, whilst increasingly setting them apart from mainstream society.

The social significance of particular products can be important for certain groups in terms of creating feelings of social exclusion, not simply in terms of a lack of product availability. Peattie, Jamal and Peattie (2006), in researching into food consumption amongst British Muslim families, found that the lack of availability of Halal food at many venues led to feelings of exclusion and acted to limit their choices in terms of leisure. Similarly young adult Muslims felt that the availability and prevalence of alcohol and the immodest dress adopted at many social venues limited their consumption choices and led to feelings of exclusion. The role played by the availability of products can also have a subtle reinforcing effect in social exclusion. Peattie, Jamal and Peattie (2006) also found that the lack of Halal food available through fast-food outlets led to the opening of specialist Halal outlets within areas with a substantial Muslim population. This tended to reinforce patterns of segregation and acted as a barrier to young Muslims mixing freely with their non-Muslim counterparts.

From a business perspective, addressing issues of social exclusion amongst consumers usually depends upon the identification of business opportunities. On a global scale, this is particularly embodied in the recent discussion of "Bottom of the Pyramid (BOP)" business models that began with the paper by Prahalad and Hart (2002). This posited that the bottom of the (economic) pyramid consists of around four billion people living on less than $2 per day. For over 50 years, public organisations such as the World Bank, aid agencies and national governments have sought to eradicate the global poverty that has created so much social exclusion. Prahalad and Hart's paper uses examples of innovative low-cost business solutions in which those at the bottom of the pyramid are treated as customers and encouraged to become entrepreneurs. The vision is that this will lead to the development of low-margin, high-volume goods and services that will improve living standards and levels of social inclusion whilst also generating profits. This vision, although laudable, poses some difficult questions in relation to:

- the environmental impacts of trying to raise the material standard of living for those at the bottom of the pyramid without reining in the consumption at the top;

- whether the BOP approach is really motivated towards meeting the needs of the poor, or whether it is really about encouraging demand amongst the poor for the products that global corporations market; and
- whether it will simply mean the commercialisation of meeting needs that were previously met on a subsistence basis or through the informal non-monetary economy.

BUSINESS, PRODUCTION ACTIVITIES AND SOCIAL INCLUSION

The relationship between employment opportunities and social exclusion is the subject of another chapter within this book and therefore the central themes of that relationship will not be dwelt upon here (see Houston, Chapter 2). However, it is worth noting that economic priorities and the needs of business are sometimes viewed as being a key motivator behind policies to tackle social exclusion. Levitas (1996) and Byrne (1997) both highlight the extent to which the social exclusion strategy of the UK Government is dominated by issues relating to people's "employability".

The majority of research and writing on social exclusion concentrates on access to the labour market or the quality of employment provided (see for example Atkinson & Hills, 1998, or Brennan, Rhodes & Tyler, 2000). There is a risk in terms of policy making of viewing employment as synonymous with social inclusion (and unemployment as synonymous with exclusion), because there are significant differences in terms of the opportunities that different types of employment provide for social inclusion. Cole (1999) draws a distinction between social inclusion, which is characterised by choice and a degree of control for the individual, and "social insertion" in which people have little control over, or choice about, how they are integrated into the economy.

Although social exclusion is frequently viewed as being synonymous with poverty and unemployment, there are ways in which an individual's employment with a business (or other organisation) can contribute to social exclusion for them or their families. Over time, business has become increasingly international, and this can have profound implications for their employees. At a managerial level there is a long-standing research theme concerning the ability of "ex-patriot" managers within multinational companies to assimilate into the societies of other countries into which they are located (or perhaps more accurately inserted). This research mostly has a business perspective and focuses on the extent to which such postings succeed or fail, and the role of cultural integration of managers and their "trailing" spouses and families. Forster (1997) in reappraising the debate about the success of such postings acknowledges that although failure rates may have been over-emphasised, "there is clear evidence that a higher proportion of staff can struggle in overseas postings and that there are more negative effects on personal and family life than has been previously supposed" (p. 429).

Further down the organisational hierarchy, there are also many industries which depend upon migrant labour and which relocate workers between countries and regions. While large companies are increasingly aware of the need to provide training and support to help expat managers and their families to integrate into new communities, little is done for itinerant or migrant workers. The literature relating to the integration of immigrants does not tend to differentiate between those who migrated in search of a job, and those who migrated because of a job. There is also a difference between those who migrate with their families, who often seek to integrate, and those who leave their families behind. In terms of social exclusion, although there is evidence that migrant workers entering into industrialised economies generate economic benefits for their hosts, they are still "often more resented than loved by the nationals of the receiving countries" (Weinstein, 2002). Such resentment will typically lead to problems with integration and a tendency for populations of migrant labour to stick together.

Although employment has been viewed as a crucial component of social inclusion, it can also be viewed as a barrier to achieving a balance between the different aspects of inclusion. Long working hours and high levels of work-related stress may be viewed as the price necessary to secure an individual's opportunities to engage in production, consumption and savings activities. However, it may also impair their ability to engage in social networks or to be involved in political activities. This issue is often framed rather simplistically as a dichotomy between work and family commitments, and with people forced to make the choice of more stressful work time over more rewarding family time. The reality is more complex, since some people may contribute excessive time at work because they find that more rewarding, and family life more stressful (Hochschild, 1997). What is emerging is a field of research into work–life integration (or work–life balance) in which:

> . . . 'work-life' needs to be framed in a way that allows for the analysis of the perfor-
> mance of key social roles. We propose that this should be considered in terms of a set
> of activities—'work' is one such set but 'family' is not. In addition to working, people
> consume and engage in leisure activities; they devote time to caring for themselves
> (sleeping, eating, exercising) and caring for others (parenting, volunteering, engaging
> in political and/or social activism). Some individuals are engaged in study, most in
> some form of informal social interaction with friends, family or neighbours; some are
> involved as members of voluntary associations that produce civic society; and most
> individuals undertake at least some domestic work or household maintenance . . . pres-
> sures to engage in one activity at the expense of another (for example, if work pressures
> are intense) produce a range of social and economic consequences, including the
> decline of civic engagement, the 'latchkey kid' phenomenon, the decline of commu-
> nity or the rise of GDP. The particular social phenomenon depends on the specific
> societal level pressures and how these are mediated by institutions and individual and
> collective resources. (Reed *et al.*, 2005, pp. 9–10)

As Byrne (1997) points out, there is an irony that the policy debate on social exclusion is so strongly focused on the problems of separation from work, when in practice it can be the nature and demands of the work itself that separate people from other important aspects of, and roles within, society.

BUSINESS, SAVINGS ACTIVITIES AND SOCIAL INTEGRATION

The ability of individuals to be included in normal savings activities mostly depends upon their opportunities to be involved in paid employment, and on some discretionary income remaining after basic consumption needs are met. Although no precise measures of the financially excluded exist, Kempson and Whyley (1999) used data from the *Family Resources Survey* to estimate that around 1.5 million households in Britain (7%) have no mainstream financial products (although this excludes household insurance). A further four million households (19%) enjoy limited use of only one or two financial services.

Those making little or no use of financial services tend to be the young and the old, those in rented accommodation, those receiving state benefits, those without a secure job, and those from ethnic groups who may be deterred by issues of language, culture and religion (Kempson & Whyley, 2000; Kennickell *et al.*, 2000). Kempson (1998) found that 3 out of 10 UK households had no savings, and almost half of those with no financial products (47%) live in one of the 50 most deprived districts and boroughs of England and Wales. Households living in these 50 deprived local authorities are at least six times more likely to have no financial products, compared to those living in the 65 authorities with the least deprived populations (Kempson & Whyley, 1999). The Office of Fair Trading (OFT, 1999) estimates the number of people in Britain without bank and building society current or savings accounts as 6–9% of individuals (2.5–3.5 million people), but with as many as 14% of households having no current account.

In an increasingly cashless society, life can be difficult without access to a bank (or building society) account, and there are concerns that the expansion of "E-cash" will exacerbate the situation for those with access to neither a bank account nor information technology (Christie & Goldie-Scot, 1999). For those on modest incomes and with limited savings, the risk of becoming overdrawn and incurring high charges is a powerful disincentive to operating such an account (Caskey, 2002; Hogarth & O'Donnell, 1999). Consumers without bank accounts may have to pay to have their wages cashed, and they may pay more for services like gas and electricity. Those without bank accounts may be denied access to a range of services for which a bank account or credit card acts as a gateway. Access to short-term credit is an important aspect of managing on a very restricted budget. However, people without a financial history, with inadequate savings, or with problems in their credit record, may find it difficult to obtain credit from mainstream sources (Caskey, 2002).

Another important financial product that some people are excluded from is insurance, with around 2 out of 10 UK households having no home contents insurance (Whyley *et al.*, 1998). Vulnerable consumers are likely to lack household contents insurance and be less able to replace lost things. Risk assessment within the insurance industry has become increasingly sophisticated, and those who live in areas of high crime (who tend to be those who are vulnerable) have to pay higher premiums even though they are likely to be the most in need of insurance.

There are various reasons why individuals become financially excluded. In some cases the industry may restrict opportunities through the controversial practice of "Redlining", in which access to lending (or insurance) is restricted because of the location of a property, rather than because of any characteristics of the borrower or their property. Although this is often associated with race, and particularly with predominantly African-American neighbourhoods in the USA, it is more accurately social exclusion on the basis of "place" rather than race (Aalbers, 2005). Such practices are relatively rare, and few people are actively denied access by financial institutions. Instead, exclusion occurs on the grounds of price, products that are inappropriate to people's needs, and the fact that no one is trying to sell them products (Caskey, 2002). A lack of financial literacy also leads some to self-exclusion, while mistrust of financial institutions, or positive choice encourages others to use alternatives to mainstream sources of finance (Ford & Rowlingson, 1996). However, exclusion is a dynamic process with a substantial minority of households moving in and out of using financial services as their circumstances change (Kempson & Whyley, 1999). These processes may manifest themselves as "finance gaps" whereby individuals and enterprises in disadvantaged areas with less money to start with find it difficult to gain access to credit and financial services more generally (Mayo & Mullineux, 1999).

One important aspect of financial exclusion and inclusion relates to access. Changes in regulation and competition in the financial sector, although increasing access for the majority, have promoted rationalisation and financial exclusion in deprived areas (Leyshon, 1995). This leads to financial exclusion reinforcing patterns of social disadvantage including poor housing, low income and inadequate services in disadvantaged neighbourhoods. Developments in technology and the growth of Internet and telephone banking have increased the range of distribution channels for financial services, and in principle could bring benefits for the vulnerable, but such groups currently have low access to such technology.

The reduction of the bank branch network in poorer areas, brought about by the entry of new institutions into the market using electronic forms of delivery of financial services and the drive of existing operators to reduce costs, also creates difficulties for retail businesses handling cash in those areas. The result can be people going away from a local area to shop, because they have to go elsewhere to access a bank (Mayo *et al.*, 1998). A reduction in retailing demand in areas deserted by financial institutions, in turn, reduces retail presence and property values and ultimately new investment by financial institutions, and the local area without a branch can enter a downward spiral of urban degeneration and decline. Ultimately, the rationalisation of branches in financial institutions may contribute to "cross-cutting and systematic marginalisation from this range of essential private services" for communities (Speak & Graham, 1999, p. 1989). Restructuring in the financial sector can combine with similar trends of withdrawal from the same communities by private services such as energy, telecommunications and food retailing. These trends in combination threaten "to undermine severely the degree to which marginalised urban neighbourhoods can hope to achieve any meaningful degree of . . . inclusion in . . . wider metropolitan life" (Speak & Graham, 1999, p. 1998).

The extent of the problems caused by bank branch closures and other restructuring issues is a subject of some debate. Marshall's (2004) analysis of past research on the reasons behind financial exclusion suggested that despite the branch closures of the last decade, distance from a bank branch was relatively rarely cited as a problem. Even amongst the 15% of the population most distant from a bank branch (that is, more than one mile from a branch in urban areas and four miles from a branch in rural areas), only one in 10 people said they found access to a branch difficult. The main groups experiencing problems were the self-employed working from home, as well as the elderly and those with disabilities.

BUSINESS, POLITICAL ACTIVITIES AND SOCIAL INCLUSION

In the context of political activities such as "engaging in some collective effort to improve or protect the social and physical environment", businesses play a number of roles. Employment within a business leads many individuals into membership of a trade union, and this can be a route by which people become exposed to, and engaged with, specific social and environmental issues. Recent years have seen a revival of interest in the concept of Corporate Social Responsibility (CSR) in which businesses seek to meet the expectations of stakeholders, with the aim of contributing beyond providing products and services to customers and generating profits for shareholders. A number of different aspects of CSR strategies can address social inclusion. Socially responsible pricing can improve opportunities for disadvantaged consumers, and through Fair Trade initiatives can also improve opportunities for disadvantaged producers in poorer countries (Vachani & Smith, 2004). Companies can also make meaningful contributions to social causes that promote inclusion through cause-related marketing programmes (Gourville & Rangan, 2004), and also through involvement in alliances with non-profit organisations (Berger, Cunningham & Drumwright, 2004).

Although associated with large global companies and their desire for social legitimacy and the protection of corporate reputation and brand values, CSR is also being increasingly adopted by smaller companies. For small companies the focus is often on contributing to the local community within which they operate, and on becoming more involved with, and integrated into, the local community (Jenkins, 2004). Employee volunteering programmes, business literacy schemes, sponsorship activities, providing work experience for local school children and serving on local charity boards are all ways in which companies can contribute to local communities and which can directly or indirectly promote social inclusion. Often such efforts are directed through membership of organisations such as *Business in the Community* or *Groundwork*. Employee volunteering programmes are the element of the CSR agenda with the most direct connection to social inclusion, as they directly involve members of the business with local social and environmental issues, and can contribute to the regeneration of disadvantaged communities. *Business in the Community's* "Cares" volunteering programme, for example, engaged with 350 businesses and 300 community organisations, to deliver 100,000 hours of time to communities from 34,927 volunteers during 2003. One of the largest studies of volunteering found that amongst a representative mix of 2,000 UK companies of varying sizes, out of the 348 respondents, around 30% had some form of secondment and/or employee volunteering initiative (Wilson, 1994). In a comprehensive review of research on employee volunteering, Lukka (2000) found that the role of the employer as broker had the potential to engage people with volunteering, and with their communities, in ways that would not otherwise happen.

BUSINESS, LEISURE, SOCIAL ACTIVITIES AND SOCIAL INCLUSION

The dominant view in the debate about consumption and social exclusion equates the inability to engage in "normal" consumption activities for reasons of poverty, isolation or health as contributing to perceptions of social exclusion. A contrary argument is that the nature of "normal" consumption is leading to individuals leading increasingly isolated lives and becoming socially disengaged because of their lifestyles and consumption patterns. Tomlinson (1990), comments on the growing consumption of products such as home entertainments, food delivery services, canned beers, home fitness centres and home banking services which allow people to become ever more private, and the private home to become the focus of people's lives. Commenting on a Henley Centre study of leisure trends, Tomlinson presents a vision of "suitably androgynous figures labouring away at different forms of pleasure: someone typing on the computer keyboard in a study bedroom; someone working out to an exercise tape in a bedroom; . . . someone slumped into the sofa watching the television and someone standing over the hob across from the microwave in the kitchen . . . In their picture of the cellular household at work and play the Henley Centre pundits picture the connoisseur consumer as recluse, and leisure as a specialist monadic activity" (p. 27). He notes that two major leisure-related spending priorities are in home entertainment and foreign holidays, which although "normal" forms of consumption, are both means by which people withdraw from, rather than engage with their own communities and society.

KEY INDUSTRIES FOR INCLUSION

The foregoing discussion has highlighted a number of industries that play a central role in determining patterns of social inclusion and exclusion including financial services, retailing and leisure activities. There are a number of other industries whose component businesses will play an important role in terms of developing a more inclusive society, and with whom policy makers are increasingly seeking to develop partnerships in order to promote a social inclusion agenda.

House Building and Housing

In the housing market, it is possible to differentiate between exclusion *through* housing and exclusion *from* (decent) housing (Cameron & Field, 2000; also see Clapham, Chapter 5). Exclusion through housing does not focus on the lack of access to adequate housing, but rather on the role of housing or the neighbourhood as a causal factor in the generation of other forms of social exclusion, especially from the labour market and civil society: "Social exclusion through housing happens if the effect of housing processes is to deny certain social groups control over their daily lives, or to impair enjoyment of wider citizenship rights." (Somerville, 1998, p. 772).

The issue of housing on the social inclusion agenda is usually focused on homelessness and the provision of affordable housing solutions for those most at risk from social exclusion through poverty (see Clapham, Chapter 5). There are, however, other aspects of the house building business that have an impact on dimensions of social exclusion. Housing design is something that has the potential to influence whether areas of new housing develop a sense of community, and the extent to which residents interact and are able to develop relationships. In some cases, the provision of community facilities or public open spaces is laid down as conditions for house builders to develop land. Less positively, the conversion of existing community facilities such as playing fields or local pubs into housing developments can erode the sense of cohesion and community within an area as a housing "monoculture" emerges.

The way in which housing developments are undertaken also has the potential to contribute to social exclusion or inclusion. Power (2000) suggests that "clean sweep" approaches to urban regeneration in deprived neighbourhoods tend to damage remaining community ties and exacerbate social exclusion. She promotes an alternative focus on micro-initiatives to restore and improve urban neighbourhoods in ways that will secure and sustain existing communities. Similarly, MacFarlane (1997) examined schemes for house building and other construction projects to use local labour, and particularly to take on school leavers and the unemployed, with the aim of providing opportunities and training for them. Such schemes were found to be successful both in terms of contributing to local employment and improving social inclusion, and also in terms of developing a supply of skilled labour for the industry.

Yet, house building is not the only component of the housing industry with the potential to influence social exclusion. The private rental sector also plays an important role, although it tends to receive less attention in the social exclusion literature than public sector housing, even though "in market liberal societies there are many more poor and disadvantaged households in the private rental sector than in social housing and arguably the process of exclusion in the private rental sector is both more complex and deeper in its impacts" (Hulse & Burke, 2000, p. 4). In reviewing the impact of housing rental, Hulse and Burke (2000) noted that the housing rental industry had been far better at meeting the needs of moderate to high income families. Lower income families' risk of social exclusion tended to be compounded by problems with the supply of affordable rentals, and to "problems of insecurity, location amenity, discrimination, lack of support services, and lack of personal and political empowerment" (p. 17). They concluded that those privately renting were effectively "invisible" to policy makers compared to those provided for through social housing.

Transport

As well as the economic ability to engage in "normal" consumption opportunities, individuals can suffer exclusion, because of an inability to physically access normal retail channels through a lack of adequate transport. For those who lack access to a private car, this means access to suitable services from public transport businesses. Although access to physical mobility can be envisaged as simply one amongst a number of dimensions of social exclusion, it tends to have a contributory effect on many of the others (Kenyon, Rafferty & Lyons, 2003). Without access to transport, individuals may find it difficult to access educational or job opportunities, to develop social networks or become involved with community activities or political processes. This tends to most strongly affect those already facing problems such as rural dwellers, residents of poor urban estates, older people, single parents, those with disabilities, the unemployed or those on low incomes (Social Exclusion Unit, 1998). Therefore, social exclusion can be a direct result of lack of mobility, and lack of mobility can exacerbate existing experiences of exclusion. Within the UK, the gradual transfer of responsibility for public transport from the public sector to private businesses has meant that service provision decisions are subject to profit considerations. This can lead to service reduction or withdrawal amongst poorer neighbourhoods which further restricts the opportunities for social inclusion amongst the residents (Speak & Graham, 2000).

From both an academic and public policy perspective, there was relatively little debate about the role of transport in social inclusion that went beyond accessibility for the disabled until the late 1990s. Hine and Mitchell (2001), in reviewing the factors behind "transport disadvantage", note that transport planning has tended to focus on an economic and technical assessment of costs and benefits, combined with an environmental impact assessment. Social impacts of transport infrastructure projects were rarely considered. This changed at the beginning of the new millennium with the publication of the landmark publication, *Social Exclusion and the Provision and Availability of Public Transport* (DETR, 2000) and the consultation exercise launched in 2001 by the Social Exclusion Unit into the links between social exclusion and transport policy.

Although these issues are now being considered from a social policy and transport policy perspective, they are somewhat under-explored from a business perspective. In an age where public transport is increasingly provided by private businesses, the business issues involved in providing transport services to those at risk of social exclusion need to be considered. In many ways, those who lack regular access to a private car are the core market of those providing public transport services, and, therefore, the synergies between running a transport business and providing transport for social inclusion might seem high. There are also examples of other forms of business (particularly retailers such as Tesco or Asda) providing public transport services to help bring customers to them. However, for those running transport services for profit rather than as a public service, they will always face challenges in providing services to those in isolated rural communities.

Media

The media as an industry has an important influence on the social inclusion/exclusion agenda, because the nature of media coverage and exposure tends to determine what is considered "normal". The media also has a profound affect on consumption activities through advertising and consumption-orientated "lifestyle" publications and programmes. The ability of political causes to engage people in political activities is also very dependent on the media coverage and promotion. An event like *Live8*, for example, was as much a media event as a political event.

Media coverage of particular groups can influence attitudes towards them and the degree to which they are accepted by, and integrated into, the rest of society. Widespread, and largely positive, media coverage of the gay community, for example, would appear to have been important in improving the acceptance and integration of gay people within the wider community over the last decade. By contrast, the experience of the Muslim community in the UK appears to have been very different. In 1997, the Runnymede Commission's report *Islamophobia: A Challenge for Us All*, reported that anti-Muslim prejudices in the UK were largely driven by various images and statements that had appeared in the media that promoted a "closed" view of Islam (Runnymede Trust Commission on British Muslims and Islamophobia, 1997). This promoted views of Islam as monolithic, static, sharing little in the way of common values with traditional (Western) British culture, aggressive, undemocratic and supportive of terrorism. These were combined to promote a "clash of cultures" view in which Islam was viewed as an "enemy". Sadly, since 9/11 and the July 2005 bombings in London, news coverage and documentary features have provided further reinforcement for such prejudices. More insidiously, within the entertainment industry, the Islamic fundamentalist has replaced the reclusive megalomaniac or South American drug lord as the villain of choice for TV of film production companies when scripting dramas.

There are other more subtle influences that the media exert on the potential for social inclusion or exclusion among other groups. Advertising and lifestyle programmes can promote a particular consumer lifestyle and material standard of living as "normal", thus creating feelings of exclusion amongst those unable to attain it. Amongst older citizens, the portrayal of their age group in film and TV can influence their own social confidence and willingness to be involved in society. Ginn and Arber (1993), in reviewing research studying the affect of media portrayals on the self-image of older women, found that the tendency of the media to stereotype older women as "obsolete", lacking in commitment and lonely (because they cannot perform the traditional female roles of wife or mother) was absorbed by women who followed the homemaking role in earlier life. Those women whose lifestyles had been less home-centred tended to identify with such stereotypes less and in later life had the confidence to take up voluntary or political activities and maintain their self-identity.

Ironically, positive media coverage of older people can also tend to undermine their confidence. Older people being portrayed as ageing "successfully" in films or television adverts or programmes tend to be portrayed by actors and actresses who are, in reality, actually younger (Kubey, 1980). This "young-old" group is depicted as active and athletic (especially in the USA) primarily as a means of marketing to them as a group of potential consumers (Nussbaum, Thompson & Robinson, 1989). Comparing themselves to what is effectively a falsified reference group can lead older people to feel that they cannot match their own self-image to this young/old portrayal, resulting in the potential for negative self-reference (Biggs, 1993). Positive images of ageing can be as detrimental as negative images, which potentially creates a dilemma for the representation of older people.

Information and Communications Technology

The rise of the "Information Economy" has led to concerns amongst policy makers that the "Digital Divide" will become a new and significant aspect of social exclusion within society, particularly with respect to Internet access (Selwyn, 2002). For example, "Universal internet access is vital if we are not only to avoid social divisions over the new economy but to create a knowledge economy of the future which is for everyone. Because it is likely that the Internet will be as ubiquitous and as normal as electricity is today. We cannot accept a digital divide. For business, or for individuals." (Blair, 2000). Although the process of tackling the digital divide and promoting universal Internet use and access is a central element of government policy, delivering it will strongly depend on the products and services provided by ICT businesses. One key element of this has been Government working with commercial businesses to both bring down the cost of Internet access, and to widen the availability of broadband services.

Care and Healthcare

There are a number of other industries that have an important influence on levels of social exclusion and inclusion for particular individuals, groups or communities. For some individuals, their risk of social exclusion is linked more strongly to their health than to any economic, geographic or cultural factors. Although in the UK, we tend to associate healthcare provision with the public sector, healthcare is also an important sector for commercial businesses. Mackintosh (2003, p. 3), in reviewing the process of commercialisation globally in healthcare across several decades, worries that "Commercialisation—sometimes, discreditably 'sold' as a policy for increasingly equity—has generally acted to embed inequality in new forms". Similarly, for those who have reached retirement as a lifestage, the priorities for achieving social inclusion may alter. Being involved in production activities or savings activities may become less of a priority, whilst being involved in political or social activities may become more significant. The care of elderly people, both within their own homes and within specialised care homes, is an aspect of society in which the commercial sector has become increasingly involved in recent years. It is also an aspect of society whose nature will determine the opportunities for social inclusion in the later stages of life of an increasing number of citizens in the future. (Also, see discussion of healthcare and exclusion, Mason-Whitehead & Mason, Chapter 4)

ENTREPRENEURSHIP, SMALL BUSINESSES AND SOCIAL INCLUSION

Another business-orientated aspect of the social exclusion/inclusion debate relates to opportunities for involvement in business ownership. This can relate to the ability to hold shares in publicly listed companies, or to involvement in the setting up of a business either individually or within a partnership, a co-operative or some other form of collective venture. In the case of share ownership, opportunities are largely determined by individual wealth, education and experience. The process of acquiring shares in companies has been made simpler, more affordable and more accessible through changes to the financial services industry over the past two decades. This has led to a considerable democratisation of share ownership.

For more direct ownership of businesses, entrepreneurship is seen as an important means by which social inclusion can be encouraged. The Treasury produced a review of Enterprise and Social Exclusion (HMT, 1999), which reviewed the potential of entrepreneurship to reduce social exclusion, the evidence concerning business start-ups, and failures within deprived and non-deprived communities, and examined the role played by business support services. Appropriate support mechanisms have been shown to be important in helping those at risk of social exclusion, for example, those from ethnic minorities from becoming involved in entrepreneurship and self-employment (Fallon & Berman-Brown, 2004). In practice, however, starting up businesses is something that is typically undertaken by those who are already socially included. Fielden and Dawe (2004, p. 139), in reviewing research on the role of women in the entrepreneurship and social inclusion debate, note that women are under-represented, and usually if women are discussed within business building context, the focus "tends to be on middle class women, from educated backgrounds, with a family history of business ownership". A range of barriers was found to discourage other women from starting up businesses, including a lack of access to support, finance, premises and childcare, and also more socially constructed barriers relating to a lack of suitable role models, and a relatively male orientation amongst business support services (Fielden *et al.*, 2003; Fielden & Dawe, 2004).

For many of the basic product categories that provide the basics of life, and that are seen as key to the social inclusion of individuals (including water, energy, housing and telecommunications) the providers are typically large companies. However, at a community level, smaller and medium-sized enterprises (SMEs) can play an important part in social inclusion, particularly because they tend to represent the majority of the business community located within the most deprived communities. There has been relatively little attention paid to the role of smaller businesses in promoting social inclusion from both a research perspective, and in terms of practical initiatives to engage SMEs in efforts to promote social inclusion. Joseph (2000) provides a comprehensive review of the part that SMEs can and do play informed by a range of case studies. She concluded that although SMEs in deprived areas were themselves often struggling for survival, it was common to find such companies employing locally, finding ways to help customers afford products, providing work experience and providing materials, facilities or time to support community organisations. At the smallest end of the size scale, another potentially important business contribution to increase social inclusion is the "micro-business", which is often viewed as particularly important in terms of contributing to economic development and social inclusion in rural areas. However, Oughton, Wheelock and Baines (2003), in a study of rural households in Britain and Norway, found that the development of micro-businesses also had the potential to reinforce certain patterns of social exclusion as an unintended consequence.

To achieve greater levels of social inclusion in the future amongst those who currently suffer from some degree of exclusion, part of the solution may lie in developing new and innovative business models. This could be through social enterprises which operate with primarily social rather than financial goals, and who often provide opportunities for skills development and pathways into employment for those in disadvantaged areas (Gray, Healy & Crofts, 2003). Social enterprises typically marry the skills and strategies necessary to address social goals, many of which can contribute to increased social inclusion. Similarly, Local Exchange Trading Scheme (LETS), which provide local grassroots community currency schemes in order to create a cashless trading network for members, were found by Seyfang (2001) to be "successful at delivering new informal employment opportunities to socially excluded groups, boosting their income, and providing a forum for social interaction and community-building." (p. 581).

CONCLUSIONS

The body of research knowledge that exists about the role that businesses play in social inclusion and exclusion is both embryonic and incomplete. It tends to be dominated by a relatively narrow range of issues concentrated around access to consumption opportunities and employment opportunities. It is also held back by a tendency for research contributions to take a relatively polemic stance in which business is seen as largely the cause of, or largely the solution to, social exclusion as a social challenge. Many facets of the role that businesses play in social exclusion and inclusion remain under-researched, and the impact that they have on the nature and quality of social relationships needs to emerge from the shadow cast by the mountain of research dedicated to the economic contribution of business.

Perhaps a more subtle influence that businesses will play in the evolution of policy and thought relating to social exclusion is through the adoption of "business-like" thinking to tackle social issues related to exclusion. One example of this is the growing interest in "social marketing", which seeks to apply the philosophy, tools and expertise of commercial marketing to challenging social issues. The evolution of social marketing has largely concentrated on issues of healthcare such as smoking cessation, healthy diets, exercise promotion and responsible drinking. Geographically it has so far been largely concentrated in the USA, Canada and Australia. However, it is now being adopted more widely in countries like the UK, and applied to an ever-increasing range of aspects of quality of life, and to promoting ways to encourage social inclusion such as literacy programmes. A similar logic has been embraced by the Malaysian Government in promoting a guideline for commercial advertisers in which all commercial advertisements should carry a secondary social message. This has led to some major campaigns to promote ideas like racial harmony and the responsibility of families to remember, visit and care for elderly relatives. The divide between the public and private sectors in the UK is becoming ever more indistinct, and the opportunities for partnership efforts between the two sectors to promote social inclusion represent an important avenue for both practitioners and researchers to explore in future.

Ultimately, we need to develop a more holistic, integrated and multidisciplinary perspective on the role that businesses play in influencing attitudes, behaviours, choices and opportunities within societies and communities and for their different stakeholders. Only then can we better appreciate the complex and often subtle and indirect contributions that businesses can make to social exclusion and inclusion.

REFERENCES

Aalbers, M.B. (2005). Place-based social exclusion: redlining in the Netherlands. *Area, 37*(1), 100–109.

Allen, G.M. (2000). Costs of using prepayment meters for gas and electricity. *Final Report to EAGA Charitable Trust, British Gas Trading and TXU.* Centre for Management under Regulation, University of Warwick.

Atkinson, A.B. & Hills, J. (1998). Exclusion, employment and opportunity. *CASE Paper 4, Centre for Analysis of Social Exclusion.* London School of Economics.

Berger, I.E., Cunningham, P.H. & Drumwright, M.E. (2004). Social alliances company/non-profit collaboration. *California Management Review, 47*(1), 58–90.

Berghman, J. (1995). Social exclusion in Europe: policy context and analytical framework. In G. Room (ed.), *Beyond the Threshold: The Measurement and Analysis of Social Exclusion.* Bristol: The Policy Press.

Biggs, S. (1993). User participation and interprofessional collaboration in community care. *Journal of Interprofessional Care, 7*(2), 151–160.

Blair, A. (2000). *Speech at the Knowledge 2000 Conference,* 7 March 2000. Retrieved from http://www.number-10.gov.uk

Brennan, A., Rhodes, J. & Tyler, P. (2000). The nature of local area social exclusion in England and the role of the labour market. *Oxford Review of Economic Policy, 16*(1), 129–146.

Burchardt, T., Le Grand, J. & Piachaud, D. (1999). Social exclusion in Britain 1991–1995. *Social Policy and Administration, 33*(3), 227–244.

Bynner, J. (1996). *The Use of Longitudinal Data in Social Exclusion.* Paris: OECD.

Byrne, D. (1997). Social exclusion and capitalism: the reserve army across time and space. *Critical Social Policy, 17*(1), 27–51.

Cameron, S. & Field, A. (2000). Community, ethnicity and neighbourhood. *Housing Studies, 15,* 827–843.

Caskey, J.P. (2002). *Bringing Unbanked Households into the Banking System, Centre on Urban and Metropolitan Policy.* Washington, DC: The Brookings Institution.

Christie, I. & Goldie-Scot, D. (1999). E-cash is more interesting than you think: what are the key issues? *European Business Review, 99*(4), 207–210.

Cole, P. (1999). Poverty and social exclusion. In R. Norman (ed.), *Ethics and the Market* (pp. 117–131). Basingstoke: Ashgate.

DETR. (2000). *Social Exclusion and the Provision and Availability of Public Transport*. London: Department of the Environment, Transport and the Regions.

Donaghy, K., Rudinger, G. & Poppelreuter, S. (2004). Societal trends, mobility behaviour and sustainable transport in Europe and North America. *Transport Reviews*, *24*(6), 679–690.

Douglas, M. & Isherwood, B. (1979). *The World of Goods—Towards an Anthropology of Consumption*. London and New York: Routledge.

Eversley, D. (1990). Inequality at the spatial level. *The Planner*, *76*, 13–18.

Fallon, G. & Berman-Brown, R. (2004). Supporting ethnic community businesses: lessons from a West Midlands Asian business support agency. *Regional Studies*, *38*(2), 137–148.

Fielden, S.L. & Dawe, A. (2004). Entrepreneurship and social inclusion. *Women in Management Review*, *19*(3), 139–142.

Fielden, S.L., Davidson, M.J., Dawe, A. & Makin, P.J. (2003). Factors inhibiting the economic growth of female small business owners. *Journal of Small Business and Enterprise Development*, *10*(2), 152–166.

Ford, J. & Rowlingson, K. (1996). Low-income households and credit: exclusion, preference, and inclusion. *Environment and Planning A*, *28*, 1345–1360.

Forster, N. (1997). The persistent myth of high expatriate failure rates: a reappraisal. *International Journal of Human Resource Management*, *8*(4), 414–433.

Ginn, J. & Arber, S. (1993). Ageing and cultural stereotypes of older women. In J. Johnson & R. Slater (eds), *Ageing and Later Life*. London: Sage.

Gordon, D., Adelman, L., Ashworth, K., *et al.* (2000). *Poverty and Social Exclusion in Britain*. York: Joseph Rowntree Foundation.

Gourville, J.T. & Rangan, V.K. (2004). Valuing the cause marketing relationship. *California Management Review*, *47*(1), 38–57.

Gray, M., Healy, K. & Crofts, P. (2003). Social enterprise: is it the business of social work? *Australian Social Work*, *56*(2), 141–154.

Hine, J. & Mitchell, F. (2001). Better for everyone? Travel experiences and transport exclusion. *Urban Studies*, *38*(2), 319–332.

HMT. (1999). *Enterprise and Exclusion*. Report by the National Strategy for Neighbourhood Renewal: Policy Action Team 3. London: HM Treasury.

Hochschild, A.R. (1997). *The Time Bind*. New York: Henry Holt and Company.

Hogarth, J.M. & O'Donnell, K.H. (1999). Banking relationships of lower-income families and governmental trends towards electronic payment. *Federal Reserve Bulletin*, *July*, 459–473.

Hulse, K. & Burke, T. (2000). Social exclusion and the private rental sector: the experiences of three market liberal countries. Paper presented at the ENHR 2000 Conference in Gävle, pp. 26–30, June 2000.

Hunter, J. (2003). Flying-through-the-air magic: skateboarders, fashion and social identity. *Sheffield Online Papers in Social Research*, *7*. Retrieved from www.shef.ac.uk/socst/Shop/7hunter.pdf

Jackson, T. (2005). Motivating sustainable consumption: a review of evidence on consumer behaviour and behavioural change. *Report to the Sustainable Development Research Network*. Retrieved from http://www.sd-research.org.uk/documents/MotivatingSCfinal.pdf

Jenkins, H.M. (2004). A critique of conventional CSR theory: an SME perspective. *Journal of General Management*, *29*(4), 37–57.

Joseph, E. (2000). *A Welcome Engagement: SMEs and Social Inclusion*. London: Institute of Public Policy Research.

Kempson, E. (1996). *Life on a Low Income*. York: York Publishing Services.

Kempson, E. (1998). *Savings and Low Income and Ethnic Minority Households*. London: Personal Investment Authority.

Kempson, E. & Whyley, C. (1999). *Kept Out or Opted Out? Understanding and Combating Financial Exclusion*. Bristol: The Policy Press.

Kempson, E. & Whyley, C. (2000). *Extortionate Credit in the UK*. London: Department of Trade and Industry.

Kennickell, A.B., Starr-McCluer, M., Surette, J.B., *et al.* (2000). Recent changes in the US family finances: results from the survey of consumer finances. *Federal Reserve Bulletin, January*, 1–29.

Kenyon, S., Rafferty, J. & Lyons, G. (2003). Social exclusion and transport: a role for virtual accessibility in the alleviation of mobility-related social exclusion? *Journal of Social Policy, 32*(3), 317–338.

Kubey, R.W. (1980). Television and aging: past, present and future. *The Gerontologist, 20*(1), 16–35.

Levitas, R. (1996). The concept of social exclusion and the new Durkheimian hegemony. *Critical Social Policy, 16*(1), 5–20.

Leyshon, A. (1995). Geographies of financial exclusion: financial abandonment in Britain and the United States. *Transactions of the Institute of British Geographers, 20*, 312–341.

Lukka, P. (2000). *Employee Volunteering: A Literature Review.* London: Institute for Volunteering Research.

Macfarlane, R. (1997). *Unshackling the Poor: A Complementary Approach to Local Economic Development.* York: Joseph Rowntree Foundation.

Mackintosh, M. (2003). Health care commercialisation and the embedding of inequality. Ruig/ Unrisd Health Project Synthesis Paper, United Nations Research Institute for Social Development, Geneva.

Marshall, J.N. (2004). Financial institutions in disadvantaged areas: a comparative analysis of policies encouraging financial inclusion in Britain and the United States. *Environment and Planning A, 36*, 241–261.

Mayo, E., Fisher, T., Conaty, P., *et al.* (1998). *Small is Bankable: Community Reinvestment in the UK.* London: New Economics Foundation.

Mayo, E. & Mullineux, A. (1999). *Show and Tell: A Community Reinvestment Act for the UK.* London: New Economics Foundation.

Nussbaum, F.J., Thompson, R. & Robinson, J.D. (1989). *Communication and Ageing.* New York: Harper and Row.

OFT. (1999). *Vulnerable Consumers and Financial Services: The Report of the Director General's Inquiry.* London: Office of Fair Trading.

Oppenheim, C. (1998). Poverty and social exclusion: an overview. In C. Oppenheim (ed.), *An Inclusive Society: Strategies for Tackling Poverty.* London: Institute for Public Policy Research.

Oughton, E., Wheelock, J. & Baines, S. (2003). Micro-businesses and social inclusion in rural households: a comparative analysis. *Sociologica Ruralis, 43*(4), 331–348.

Peattie, S., Jamal, A. & Peattie, K. (2006). Protecting consumer interests: responsible and inclusive marketing of food to ethnic minority consumers. 35th EMAC Conference, 23–26 May 2006, Athens.

Power, A. (2000). Poor areas and social exclusion, in social exclusion and the future of cities. CASE paper 35, Centre for Analysis of Social Exclusion, London School of Economics.

Prahalad, C.K. & Hart, S.L. (2002). The fortune at the bottom of the pyramid: eradicating poverty through profits. *Strategy and Business, 26*, 1–14.

Reed, K., Blunsdon, B., Blyton, P. & Dastmalchian, A. (2005). Introduction: perspectives on work–life balance. *Labour & Industry, 16*(2), 5–15.

Rhodes, R. (1994). The hollowing out of the state: the changing nature of the public service in Britain. *Political Quarterly, 65*(2), 138–151.

Room, G.J. (1999). Social exclusion, solidarity and the challenge of globalization. *International Journal of Social Welfare, 8*, 166–174.

Room, R. (2005). Stigma, social inequality and alcohol and drug use. *Drug and Alcohol Review, 24*(2), 143–155.

Runnymede Trust Commission on British Muslims and Islamophobia. (1997). *Islamophobia: A Challenge for Us All.* London: Runnymede Trust.

Selwyn, N. (2002). E-stablishing an inclusive society? Technology, social exclusion and UK Government policy making. *Journal of Social Policy, 31*(1), 1–20.

Seyfang, G. (2001). Working for the Fenland dollar: an evaluation of local exchange trading schemes as an informal employment strategy to tackle social exclusion. *Work, Employment & Society, 15*(3), 581–593.

Simmel, G. (1904). Fashion. In D.N. Levine (ed.) (1971) *Georg Simmel on Individuality and Social Forms: Selected Writings.* Chicago: University of Chicago Press.

Social Exclusion Unit. (1998). Bringing Britain together: a national strategy for neighbourhood renewal. Presented to Parliament by the Prime Minister by Command of Her Majesty, September 1998. Retrieved from http://archive.cabinetoffice.gov.uk/seu/publications10db.html?did=113

Somerville, P. (1998). Explanations of social exclusion: where does housing fit in? *Housing Studies*, *13*, 761–780.

Speak, S. & Graham, S. (1999). Service not included: private services restructuring, neighbourhoods, and social marginalization. *Environment and Planning A*, *31*(11), 1985–2001.

Speak, S. & Graham, S. (2000). *Private Sector Service Withdrawal in Disadvantaged Neighbourhoods—Findings*. York: Joseph Rowntree Foundation. Retrieved from www.jrf.org. uk/knowledge/.findings/socialpolicy/230.asp

Tomlinson, A. (1990). Introduction: consumer culture and the aura of the commodity. In A. Tomlinson (ed.), *Consumption, Identity and Style* (pp. 1–40). London: Routledge.

Vachani, S. & Smith, N.C. (2004). Socially responsible pricing: lessons from the pricing of AIDS drugs in developing countries. Centre for Marketing Working Paper No. 04-701, London Business School.

Walker, A. (1997). Introduction. In A. Walker & C. Walker (eds), *Britain Divided: The Growth of Social Exclusion in the 1980s and 1990s*. London: Child Action Poverty Group.

Watts, J. (2002). Tokyo: public health experts concerned about "hikikomori". *The Lancet*, *359*, 1131.

Weinstein, E. (2002). Migration for the benefit of all: towards a new paradigm for economic immigration. *International Labour Review*, *141*(3), 225–252.

Whyley, C., McCormick, J. & Kempson, E. (1998). *Paying for Peace of Mind: Access to Home Contents Insurance for Low-Income Households*. London: Policy Studies Institute.

Williams, C.C. & Windebank, J. (2000). Modes of goods acquisition deprived neighbourhoods. *International Review of Retail, Distribution and Consumer Research*, *10*, 73–94.

Williams, P., Hubbard, P., Clark, D. & Berkeley, N. (2001). Consumption, exclusion and emotion: the social geographies of shopping. *Social & Cultural Geography*, *2*(2), 203–220.

Wilson, A. (1994). *Corporate Giving "It's Your Job to Do Something With It": A Research Report on How and Why Companies Give to Charities*. Ashridge: Ashridge Management Research Group.

CHAPTER 11

History and Development of Social Exclusion and Policy

David Gordon

University of Bristol, United Kingdom

ABSTRACT

This chapter traces the development and use of the concept of social exclusion by policy makers from its French origins in the 1970s until the present day. The concept was adopted by policy makers as a mechanism for resolving conflicting national viewpoints amongst European Union member states on the desirability of an expanded European anti-poverty programme. Social exclusion was also a helpful policy concept for integrating differing philosophical conceptions on the primary purpose of the "Welfare State" into a single European Social Model. The chapter also examines the relatively unsuccessful attempts by United Nations organisations to export the concept of social exclusion to Africa, Asia, the Americas and Oceania.

INTRODUCTION

Social exclusion is a term that is frequently used by policy makers in European Union countries. The idea of social exclusion is derived from French social and economic policy debates on the central importance of solidarity, integration and inclusion as a guiding principal for their social security system. The term was first used by René Lenoir in 1974 in his book *Les exclus Un Francais sur dix*, as a means of referring to people who had been failed by existing state and social networks—such as the poor, disabled people, suicidal people, abused children, drug addicts and so on. Altogether, he cited 10 categories of people who constituted about 10 % of the French population (de Haan, 1998) for Lenoir, the excluded were people who were unable to participate in French society and received little or no help from the French welfare state—they were effectively left out of the system.

Multidisciplinary Handbook of Social Exclusion Research. Edited by D. Abrams, J. Christian and D. Gordon.
© 2007 John Wiley & Sons, Ltd.

The concept of social exclusion was more widely adopted by European policy makers during the 1980s and 1990s, in part as a mechanism for sidestepping the controversy surrounding the continuation of a European Union anti-poverty programme. A number of attempts have been made by various international organisations, such as the World Bank, International Labour Organisation (ILO) and the United Nations Education, Scientific and Cultural Organisation (UNESCO), to export the concept of social exclusion from its European home to other regions of the world. However, these attempts have so far been relatively unsuccessful and so this chapter will first discuss the evolution of social exclusion policies in Europe and then briefly discuss social exclusion policies of United Nations organisations.

SOCIAL EXCLUSION AND EUROPEAN WELFARE STATES

The concept of social exclusion is derived from French republican political philosophy. Within this context the state is often viewed as the embodiment of the "will of the people", yet in practice this can of course be very different. An individual is bound to the larger society by a national consensus so that "separate interests and memberships are reconciled and synthesized into a unitary whole" (Silver, 1995, p. 66). Social exclusion is, thus, viewed as the breaking of the social bond between the society and the individual, which takes place as a consequence of the failure of the institutions that tie the individual to French society. Silver (1995) called this French concept of social exclusion the *Solidarity* paradigm and argues that it is influenced by Durkheimian social thought and Rousseau's social contract philosophy.

The French conceptualisation of social exclusion does not *travel well*, particularly to class-based societies like the UK that have a hereditary monarch as the head of state, and a second legislative chamber made up from members of a hereditary aristocracy and political appointees. The idea that the state is the embodiment of the *will of the people* is untenable in a UK context. In order to understand how the French concept of social exclusion has been used in other European countries, it is first necessary to briefly discuss the primary purpose of welfare states in Europe, as the welfare state is considered by policy makers to be the main guarantor of social inclusion within the European Social Model.

The UK term, "welfare state" is widely used but often ill-defined (Veit-Wilson, 2000). It was "invented" by William Temple, the Archbishop of Canterbury (Briggs, 1994)—possibly based on a translation of the German term *Wohlfahrtsstaat*—and defined as the embodiment of European values by the historian E.H. Carr in an editorial entitled "The New Europe" in *The Times* newspaper on Monday, 1 July 1940:

> Over the greater part of Western Europe the common values for which we stand are known and prized. We must indeed beware of defining these values in purely nineteenth-century terms. If we speak of democracy, we do not mean a democracy which maintains the right to vote but forgets the right to work and the right to live. If we speak of freedom, we do not mean a rugged individualism which excludes social organisation and economic planning. If we speak of equality, we do not mean a political equality nullified by social and economic privilege.

In the 1950s, Richard Titmuss argued that the welfare state was a manifestation "first, of society's will to survive as an organic whole, and secondly of the expressed will of all the people to assist the survival of some people" (Titmuss, 1958). By the 1960s, British sociologist, Dorothy Wedderburn, defined the purpose of the *welfare state* in more narrow *poverty alleviation* terms:

> There is, though, a central core of agreement that the welfare state implies a state commitment of some degree which modifies the play of market forces in order to ensure a minimum real income for all. (Wedderburn, 1965, p. 127)

Similarly, Briggs (2000) argues that it is "a state in which organized power is deliberately used (through politics and administration) in an effort to modify the play of market forces . . ." It does so by first guaranteeing a minimum income irrespective of market situation and then it enables individuals to meet unforeseen events such as sickness and unemployment as well as coping with *foreseen* events like old age. A welfare state should, finally, ensure all inhabitants, without distinction, the best standard available regarding a certain agreed range of social services. Thus, the primary purpose of the welfare state in the UK and other similar countries (such as Ireland) is to alleviate market failures and prevent poverty. Social exclusion in this context is often seen a synonym for poverty and the term is often used interchangeably with poverty by policy makers.

However, in many parts of Europe (Germany and France in particular), the primary purpose of the *welfare state* is not seen as poverty alleviation but social integration. van Kersbergen (1995) has argued that this *corporatist* conception of the *welfare* state and, in particular, the ideology and role of Christian Democratic agendas in Europe has been largely ignored by many welfare state theorists:

> Christian democracy and its impact on social policy performance are conspicuously understudied and often misunderstood phenomena. (van Kersbergen, 1995, pp. 26–27)

Christian Democrats have pursued a specific political project aimed at social integration, class compromise and political mediation between conflicting interest groups. The central goal for Christian Democracy (particularly in Germany) has been class reconciliation and class cooperation to restore the "natural and organic harmony of society" (van Kersbergen & Becker, 2002). Thus, within the German corporatist tradition (Esping-Andersen, 1990), the primary purpose of the welfare state is social integration and social exclusion is often perceived by policy makers as a breakdown of class cooperation and reconciliation.

Insertion and Social Exclusion

In France, the primary purpose of the welfare state is often seen as to prevent social exclusion (*les exclus*) through the reintegration of the *socially excluded* by *insertion* into the labour market and thereby into *responsible* citizenship. However, Thévenet (1989) has suggested that insertion is a broader concept which extends beyond labour market policy and also includes housing provision, community development, health and education.

In 1988, Michel Rocard's socialist government in France introduced the Revenu minimum d'Insertion or RMI (literally a minimum income for insertion) with the aim of ensuring "participation in the life of the community in recognition of the right to citizenship" (Paugam, 1991). The Revenu Minimum d'Insertion requires benefit recipients to sign a *contract of insertion*, agreed between the recipient and the local authorities (*département*) social services.

The pattern of contracts has been characterised as social, professional or economic (Euzeby, 1991). Social insertion refers to the situation of people who are excluded by virtue of social disadvantage, for example, disability or single parenthood. Professional insertion is for people who require some kind of training or preparation for work. Economic insertion is for people who are unemployed but who are in a position to move directly to employment (Spicker, Alvarez Leguizamon & Gordon, 2006).

Thus, it is clear that in Europe the purpose of the *welfare* state and the meaning of social exclusion are often perceived in different ways. In the UK, Ireland and the Nordic countries, social inclusion is often considered primarily in terms of ensuring minimum real incomes for all; whereas, in France and Germany, social inclusion is seen as a prerequisite for ensuring the social integration of all. It is of course both possible and desirable to try to combine these two viewpoints and this is one of the purposes of the European Social Model: a comprehensive safety net covering the whole population can be combined with a more integrated society (Veit-Wilson, 2000). It can be argued that such a combination is a long-term prerequisite for maintaining a welfare state. Empirical research has shown that countries offering extensive income security and welfare services to the middle class are also successful in providing a higher standard for the poor and often have fewer social conflicts (Korpi & Palme, 1998; Nelson, 2003).

EUROPEAN UNION SOCIAL EXCLUSION INITIATIVES

The history of European Union policy initiatives on social exclusion is inextricably entwined with EU anti-poverty policies. In 1961, the Council of Europe adopted a Social Charter which provided a European dimension to the provisions in the United Nations International Convention on Economic, Social and Cultural Rights (ICESCR), such as the right to social security and protection. Although the Social Charter was not legally binding, it did influence subsequent European Union social policies (Hantrais, 1995).

In 1974, a Resolution of the Council of Ministers of the European Community established a Social Action Programme which stated that economic growth should not be seen as an end in itself but should result in improvements in the quality of life of European citizens. As part of the negotiations around the establishment of the Social Action Programme, a proposal for an anti-poverty programme received support (Shanks, 1977), and the first of three European Union Poverty Programmes was agreed by a unanimous vote of the Council of Ministers of the European Community in 1975 (Council Decision 75/458/EEC, 1975). The first Poverty Programme ran from 1975 to 1980, the second from 1980 to 1989 and the third from 1990 to 1994. All three poverty programmes were relatively small scale (Kleinman, 2002). The first programme consisted of just 21 pilot and action projects and the second consisted of 65 action research projects, and together they received 29 million ECUs of funding. The Poverty 3 programme received increased funding of 55 million ECUs and had a more formal structure which included the establishment of an Observatory on National Policies to Combat Social Exclusion (Hantrais, 1995). The Observatory reported annually to the European Commission and its role was to promote social policy analysis and information exchange. The Observatory adopted a rights-based approach which defined social exclusion in terms of access and barriers to the fulfilment of the right to employment, housing and health care (Andersen *et al.*, 1994).

The work of the Observatory and the Poverty 3 programme was influential in promoting the concept of social exclusion (Duffy, 1998).

In 1993, the European Commission proposed a much larger scale programme Poverty 4 with a total budget of 121 million ECUs. However, the objections of a number of *conservative* governments, particularly that of the UK, resulted in the demise of the EU Poverty Programmes. The UK government's position at that time was that poverty did not exist in the UK, and so there was no need for another European Poverty Programme. The argument that poverty no longer existed was set out by John Moore, the UK Secretary of State for Social Security, in his speech on 11 May 1989 at St. Stephen's Club. He claimed that poverty, as most people understood it, had been abolished and that critics of the government's policies were:

> not concerned with the actual living standards of real people but with pursuing the political goal of equality . . . We reject their claims about poverty in the UK, and we do so knowing that their motive is not compassion for the less well-off, it is an attempt to discredit our real economic achievement in protecting and improving the living standards of our people. Their purpose in calling 'poverty' what is in reality simply inequality, is so they can call western material capitalism a failure. We must expose this for what it is . . . utterly false.
> - it is capitalism that has wiped out the stark want of Dickensian Britain.
> - it is capitalism that has caused the steady improvements in living standards this century.
> - and it is capitalism which is the only firm guarantee of still better living standards for our children and our grandchildren.

A senior Civil Servant, the Assistant Secretary for Policy on Family Benefits and Low Incomes at the UK Department of Health and Social Security (DHSS), had made the same point more succinctly when he gave evidence to the House of Commons Select Committee on Social Services on 15 June 1988. He stated "The word poor is one the government actually disputes." (see Gordon & Pantazis, 1997 for discussion). Veit-Wilson (2000) argues that these objections to the existence of poverty were influential for the adoption of the rather nebulous concept of social exclusion by European Union policy makers.

During the discussions on the Maastricht Treaty in the early 1990s, many EU Member States wanted the European Community to have a greater role in social policy. However, at that time, the UK Government objected to any increase in Community powers in this field. Consequently, the social provisions agreed at Maastricht did not become part of the main body of the Treaty but were incorporated as a protocol and an annexed agreement that applied to all Member States except the UK.

In 1997, the Labour Party won the UK General Election and Tony Blair's new government decided to end the British opt-out from the Agreement on Social Policy. It thus became possible to incorporate the agreement into the main text of the Amsterdam Treaty. Articles 136 and 137 of the Amsterdam Treaty, effective since May 1999, extended the European Union's powers to combat poverty and social exclusion and this contributed to the launch of a European social inclusion strategy at the Lisbon summit of the European Council in March 2000.[1] The development of anti-poverty and social inclusion strategies was formalised at the December 2000 Nice summit of the European Council as part of the European Social Agenda. The key objectives are set out in four main groups of aims, which include:

---

[1] http://www.hrea.org/erc/library/hrdocs/eu/Amsterdam-treaty.pdf

1. **Facilitating participation in employment and access by all to resources, rights, goods and services**
   (a) Promoting access to stable employment for all those able to work. Preventing exclusion from work by improving employability.
   (b) Guaranteeing everyone has the resources to live with human dignity.
   (c) Implementing policies that aim to provide access for all to decent housing with adequate basic services.
   (d) Providing access for all to appropriate healthcare.
   (e) Developing, for the benefit of those at risk of exclusion, services facilitating access to education, justice and services (e.g. culture, sport, leisure).
2. **Preventing the risk of social exclusion**
   (a) Exploiting fully the potential of ICT and ensure that no one is excluded.
   (b) Developing policies that seek to prevent life crises that can lead to social exclusion (e.g. debt, homelessness, school exclusion).
3. **Helping the most vulnerable**
   (a) Promoting integration of those with particular integration problems (e.g. people with disabilities).
   (b) Developing comprehensive actions in favour of areas of social exclusion.
4. **Mobilising all relevant bodies**
   (a) Promoting the participation of people experiencing exclusion.
   (b) Mainstreaming the fight against exclusion into overall policy.
   (c) Promoting dialogue and partnership between all relevant public and private bodies.

Given the varied legal frameworks and bureaucratic traditions of European Union countries, it was agreed at the Lisbon European Council (March 2000) that implementation of the strategy to combat poverty and social exclusion should operate via an "open method of coordination" (Ferrera, Matsaganis & Sacchi, 2002). This involves:

- setting objectives
- implementing these objectives through national action plans
- developing common quantitative and qualitative indicators
- monitoring, evaluation and a peer review

In January 2005, the European Union Joint Report on Social Protection and Social Inclusion, outlined seven key policy priorities:[2]

- Increase labour market participation by expanding active policies and ensuring a better linkage between social protection, education and lifelong learning.
- Modernise social protection systems to ensure they are sustainable, adequate and accessible to all.
- Tackle disadvantages in education and training by investing more in human capital at all ages and focusing particularly on the most disadvantaged groups.
- Eliminate child poverty by guaranteeing their education, increasing the assistance given to their families and ensuring that their rights are protected.
- Ensure decent accommodation for vulnerable groups and develop integrated approaches to tackling homelessness.

---

[2] http://europa.eu/scadplus/leg/en/cha/c10622.htm

- Improve access to quality services in the fields of health, social services, transport, and the new information and communication technologies.
- Eliminate sex discrimination and increase the social integration of people with disabilities, ethnic minorities and immigrants.

MEASUREMENT OF SOCIAL EXCLUSION IN EUROPE

In 1975, the European Council adopted a relative definition of poverty in Article 1 of the Decision establishing the first Poverty Programme (also see discussion of Definitions in Millar, Chapter 1). Those in poverty were defined as:

> individuals or families whose resources are so small as to exclude them from the minimum acceptable way of life of the Member State in which they live. (Council Decision 75/458/EEC, 1975). The concept of 'resources' was defined as: good, cash income, plus services from public and private resources. (EEC, 1981)

On 19 December 1984, the European Commission extended the definition of poverty as:

> the poor shall be taken to mean persons, families and groups of persons whose resources (material, cultural and social) are so limited as to exclude them from the minimum acceptable way of life in the Member State in which they live. (EEC, 1985)

This is currently the *official* definition of poverty and social exclusion that is used in the European Union by all 25 member states. The definition is derived from the pioneering research of the British Professor Peter Townsend who argued that poverty could be defined:

> objectively and applied consistently only in terms of the concept of relative deprivation. . . . The term is understood objectively rather than subjectively. Individuals, families and groups in the population can be said to be in poverty when they lack the resources to obtain the types of diet, participate in the activities and have the living conditions and amenities which are customary, or at least widely encouraged or approved, in the society to which they belong. (1979, p. 31)

Building on the earlier work of Townsend, Levitas (2000, 2006) has argued that this concept of social exclusion, in terms of relative deprivation, is the dominant discourse in British critical social policy and she has called it Redistributive Discourse (RED). The central problem in the RED is that the poor lack resources—not just money but also access to public and private services—therefore poverty remains at the core of exclusion. However, the dominant discourse on social exclusion in the policy documents and statements by policy makers in Europe is concerned with social integration (SID). In this Social Integration Discourse (SID), social exclusion is primarily construed as labour market exclusion or lack of paid work, either at an individual or household level (Levitas, 2005). Long-term unemployment and the consequences of economic restructuring were key concerns of the European Observatory on National Policies to Combat Social Exclusion in the 1990s (Room, 1995) and this concern with work remains central to the National Action Plans on Social Inclusion across the EU (Levitas, 2006).

At the Nice Summit in December 2000, EU countries agreed to produce and implement a 2-year (July 2001–June 2003) National Action Plans on Social Inclusion (NAPs/incl)

Table 11.1　Laeken Indicators of poverty and social exclusion adopted by the EU in 2001

Primary Indicators
1. Low income rate after transfers with low-income threshold set at 60% median income, with breakdowns by gender, age, most frequent activity status, household type and housing tenure.
2. Distribution of income, using income quintile ratio.
3. Persistence of low income.
4. Median low income gap.
5. Regional cohesion (measured by variation of employment rates)
6. Long-term unemployment rate
7. People living in jobless households
8. Early school leavers not in education or training
9. Life expectancy at birth
10. Self-perceived health status by income level

Secondary Indicators
1. Dispersion around the 60% median low income threshold using 40%, 50% and 70% median national income
2. Low income rate anchored at a fixed time-point
3. Low income rate before transfers
4. Gini coefficient—income inequality
5. Persistent low income (below 50% median income).
6. Long-term (over 12 months) unemployment share
7. Very long-term (over 24 months) unemployment share
8. Persons with low educational attainment

Note: The Laeken indicators are currently being reviewed (Marlier *et al.*, 2006).

with the aim of promoting social inclusion and combating poverty and social exclusion.[3,4] These detailed plans are a key component of the member states' commitment to make a decisive impact on the further eradication of poverty and social exclusion in Europe by 2010 and these support the EU's aim to be the most dynamic knowledge-based economy in the world, with full employment and increased levels of social cohesion by 2010. With this as a goal, the accurate measurement of poverty and social exclusion is an integral component of this strategy and the Laeken European Council concluded that:[5]

> the establishment of a set of common indicators constitutes important elements in the policy defined at Lisbon for eradicating poverty and promoting social inclusion, taking in health and housing. The European Council stresses the need to reinforce the statistical machinery and calls on the Commission gradually to involve the candidate countries in this process.

During 2001, considerable scientific efforts were made to improve the measurement of poverty and social exclusion (Atkinson *et al.*, 2002) and the newly agreed set of statistics and indicators was a major improvement on previous EU analyses (see Table 11.1).[6] Previous EU studies on poverty had simplistically defined the *poor* as those people living in households with equivalised incomes, or reporting expenditures below half the average in

---

[3] http://europa.eu.int/comm/employment_social/news/2001/oct/i01_1395_en.html
[4] http://europa.eu.int/comm/employment_social/news/2001/jun/napsincl2001_en.html
[5] See http://www.europarl.eu.int/summits/pdf/lae_en.pdf
[6] See http://vandenbroucke.fgov.be/Europepercent20summary.htm for a summary of the Laeken EU poverty and social exclusion indicators and http://www.vandenbroucke.fgov.be/T-011017.htm for discussion.

the country in which they lived (Eurostat, 1990, 1994, 2000; Hagenaars, De Vos & Zaidi, 1994; Mejer & Linden, 2000; Mejer & Siermann, 2000).

Most of the new Laeken indicators of poverty and social exclusion relate either to income or to labour market position, with data to be derived from the European Community Household Panel (ECHP) survey, the harmonised Labour Force Survey (LFS) or the more recent Statistics of Income and Living Conditions (EU-SILC) survey.[7,8] The terminology used to describe what was being measured changed from the more static *low income* to the more dynamic *at risk of poverty* and strong emphasis was placed on the need to disaggregate statistics by age and gender. As well as the primary and secondary indicators, member states are expected to use tertiary indicators that would not need to be comparable at supranational level but would reflect the special circumstances and priorities of different countries.

Table 11.1 shows the 18 indicators of poverty and social exclusion formally adopted by the Employment and Social Policy Council of the European Union in December 2001. They cover four areas: financial poverty, employment, health and education, and will be used by member states in their National Action Plans against Poverty and Social Exclusion (NAPs/incl).

EXTENT OF SOCIAL EXCLUSION/POVERTY IN EUROPE

The European Union is the world's largest economic grouping, and the 25 member countries are amongst the richest in the world in terms of the average amount of Gross Domestic Product (GDP) per person (Figure 11.1). The United States and Japan are the countries which respectively have the largest and second largest economies, however, neither is the richest country in the world as measured by the average amount of GDP per person. Figure 11.1 shows that, in 2004, Luxembourg and Norway both had a larger average GDP per person than the United States and 13 European countries had a larger GDP per person than Japan. Japan's average GDP per person was only slightly greater than the average for the 25 member countries of the European Union.

All European Union member countries have relatively comprehensive welfare states meaning that they redistribute income from men to women, from the *rich* to the *poor* and across an individual's lifespan (i.e. taking income from middle age and redistributing it in childhood and old age via pensions and child/family benefits). Despite the relative wealth of European Union countries, and the redistributive effects of their welfare states, a lack of political will to do more to aid the poor and/or sufficient public support often results in the persistence of high levels of social exclusion in many European countries.

Figure 11.2 illustrates the number of low income/poverty in European countries by calculating the proportion of households with equivalised incomes of less than 60% of the national median household income after social transfers, this is the first Laeken Indicator of Social Exclusion (Table 11.1). In the European Union as a whole (25 countries),

---

[7] The European Community Household Panel (ECHP) was a longitudinal survey with a harmonised questionnaire which was carried out in 15 EU member states between 1994 and 2001.

[8] The Statistics on Income and living Standards (EU-SILC) survey is a harmonised cross-sectional survey designed to replace the ECHP. It started in 2003 in six countries (Belgium, Denmark, Greece, Ireland, Luxembourg and Austria) and will begin in the other EU member countries by 2005. Norway, Iceland, Switzerland and the Acceding and Candidate countries (Bulgaria, Croatia, Romania and Turkey) may also implement the EU-SILC survey.

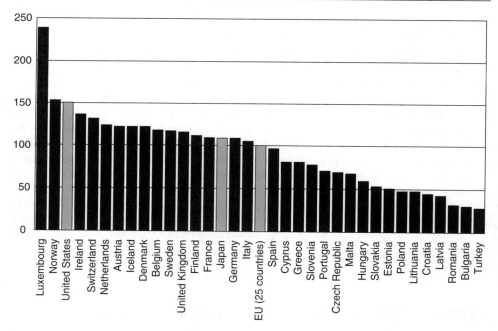

Figure 11.1   GDP per person in 2004 (EU average has been set to equal 100)

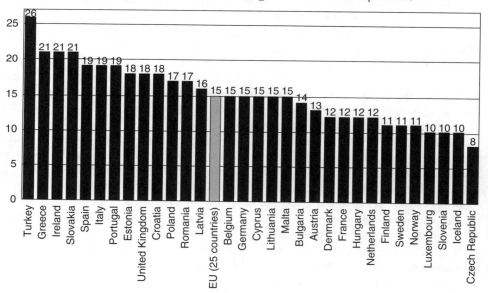

Figure 11.2   At-risk-of-poverty rate in the European Union, 2004
Source: Eurostat (2006).

15% of the population live in households with a relatively low income—they are *at risk of poverty*. The countries with the highest rates of relative income poverty risk considered were Turkey (26%), Greece, Ireland and Slovakia (all 21%) followed by Spain, Italy and Portugal (all 19%). By contrast, the countries with the lowest at risk of income poverty rates were the Czech Republic (8%), Iceland, Slovenia and Luxembourg (all 10%) followed by the Nordic countries of Finland, Sweden and Norway (all 11%).

The extent of the relative risk of income poverty in European countries shows a low correlation with the average GDP per head (Figure 11.2). For example, Ireland, Italy and the United Kingdom all have above EU average GDP per person but also above EU average relative risk of income poverty rates. By contrast, relatively poorer (in terms of GDP per head) but more egalitarian countries like the Czech Republic, Slovenia, Bulgaria and Finland have low at risk of income poverty rates. The countries with the lowest poverty rates are largely those which have either Social Democratic welfare regimes (Esping-Andersen, 1990) or those which had communist governments prior to 1990 but which did not subsequently have sustained periods of governments pursuing neo-liberal economic policies. Those countries with high at risk of income poverty rates are mainly those which have Mediterranean (Matsaganis et al., 2003) or liberal welfare state regimes.

SOCIAL EXCLUSION POLICIES OF UNITED NATIONS ORGANISATIONS

In preparation for the first World Summit on Social Development in 1995 and, given the importance of the role, a number of United Nations organisations attempted to try to apply the European concept of social exclusion to other policy contexts.

United Nations Educational Scientific and Cultural Organisation (UNESCO)

In 1995, UNESCO convened an international symposium entitled "From Social Exclusion to Social Cohesion: Towards a Policy Agenda".[9] The aim was to bring together academics, decision makers and NGOs to review of complex policy issues on the agenda of the Copenhagen Social Summit. The conference made the following recommendations (Bessis, 1995):

- Boosting up community-based social support systems is needed to compensate for the growing ineffectiveness of the welfare state and the fragility of the social sector in many parts of the world.
- To recognise and support community-based social welfare linking to the state sponsored system will create a more caring society that is more sensitive to the needs of the marginalised and the excluded.
- We need new partnerships between government, the market and civil society. The state has the responsibility to enable people to be empowered.
- Social scientists should take part in policy making. They should go beyond the traditional role of only providing data and actively influence policy formulation. Social scientists should devote more attention to providing assessments of programmes and "projects which have failed", and the circumstances and processes which explain this failure and the implications for the society.

---

[9] http://www.unesco.org/most/roskilde.htm

- Important actions against poverty and social inequalities include provision of a "basic income" to all people in society as well as fiscal incentives to employment creation and environmentally benign production systems.
- More effort must be made to hasten the *period of transition* from marginalisation and social exclusion and to protect the vulnerable and disadvantaged of society from the negative effects of social transformations.

There is little evidence to suggest that UNESCO took much notice of these recommendations beyond emphasising social inclusion policies on its first Management of Social Transformations (MOST) programme website entitled *A database of best practices/model projects on poverty and social exclusion*, 1994–2003.[10] However, the second MOST website, set up in 2004, places much greater emphasis on evidence-based policy (the latest social science buzz phrase) and reference to *social exclusion* is given much less prominence.[11]

International Labour Organisation (ILO)

The Geneva-based International Labour Organisation (ILO) made one of the most concerted attempts to export the European idea of social exclusion to countries in the developing world. The ILO commissioned studies and some surveys on social exclusion in Brazil (Singer, 1996), Cameroon (Inack, 1997), India (Appasamy *et al.*, 1996), Mexico (Gordon, 1997), Russia (Tchernina, 1996), Tanzania (Kaijage & Tibaijuka, 1996), Thailand (Phongpaichit *et al.*, 1996), Tunisia (Bedoui, 1995; Bedoui & Ridha, 1996), Venezuela (Cartaya, Magallanes & Domínguez, 1997) and Yemen (Hashem, 1996). Based on these and other work, the ILO produced an international review of social exclusion and anti-poverty strategies (Gore & Figueiredo, 1997).

New social survey data on social exclusion were collected in Tanzania, Yemen and Russia (Kaijage & Tibaijuka, 1996, pp. 7, 118–126 and 182; Hashem, 1996, p. 86; Tchernina, 1996). The ILO reported that:

> All these three studies used survey questionnaires to measure the extent to which the groups pre-identified as socially excluded actually were experiencing multiple deprivations. In designing these surveys, the studies of Russia, Tanzania and Yemen drew more or less systematically on the categories which Peter Townsend used to measure multiple deprivation in his study of Greater London in 1985–86, and adapted them to the different country contexts. (Gore & Figueiredo, 1997, p. 18)

The ILO attempted to measure the social exclusion of pre-identified social groups in three developing countries using a modified version of the questionnaire from the *Charles Booth Centenary Survey of Life and Labour in London* funded by the Greater London Council (GLC) in 1985/86 (Townsend & Gordon, 1989, 1993). Social exclusion, particularly in Russia, was thus conceptualised *as the loss of previously acquired rights and position* (Tchernina, 1996, p. 2) and measured in terms of relative derivation indicators designed to measure poverty as exclusion from the ability to participate in the activities and have the possessions that are considered to be "normal" in a person's society.

---

[10] http://www.unesco.org/most/bphome.htm
[11] www.unesco.org/shs/most

This ILO research project on *the patterns and causes of social exclusion*[12] was funded by the United Nations Development Programme (UNDP) as a contribution to the World Summit for Social Development (Rodgers, Gore & Figueiredo, 1995). It aimed to introduce the concept of social exclusion into the international development debate by extending it beyond its Western European origins. The objective of the project was "to improve the basis of action at local, national, and international levels, aimed at the eradication of poverty and promotion of social integration", by adding a new dimension to anti-poverty policies focusing more sharply on the role of institutions and actors in minimising social exclusion and maximising integration and cohesion (Gore & Figueiredo, 1997).

The ILO argued that the policy implications of the project were twofold. It suggested that the concept of social exclusion could be used to address issues such as social justice in a globalised world and proposed an approach which focused on basic markets, citizenship rights and civil society as the key instruments for the reduction of exclusion and the promotion of social cohesion (Figueiredo & de Haan, 1998). Furthermore, the ILO argued that, even though their research found no single universally accepted strategy or methodology for addressing exclusion, it was possible to identify a number of strategic approaches which had given positive results, particularly in local action. In particular, the ILO highlighted the importance of policies designed to enhance integration, partnership, participation and the spatial targeting approach.[13]

However, there is again little recent evidence of policy makers using the concept of social exclusion in the 10 developing and transition countries studied by the ILO. Since this project concluded in 1997, the ILO has placed greater emphasis on a socio-economic security framework (ILO, 2004). Within the ILO socio-economic security framework, social exclusion is relegated to a relatively minor role and is included only in terms of being the converse of participation. "Security is often linked to three overlapping ideas—participation, agency and empowerment. Participation is seen as the opposite of passivity and social exclusion, agency is seen as the opportunity to make choices on life events, including participation, and empowerment is seen in much the same way" (ILO, 2004, p. 8).

WORLD BANK

The World Bank produces a vast research output and some of this work, particularly in South American countries, has made use of a social exclusion framework for analysis (see Gacitúa-Marió & Wodon, 2001). The concept of *marginality* in Europe is seen by some as synonymous with the concept of social exclusion. For example, the Burnel Report (1989) argued that:

> For some years now we have used the terms 'marginalisation' and 'social exclusion' to denote the severest forms of poverty. Marginalization describes people living on the edge of society whilst the socially excluded have been shut out completely from conventional social norms.

The concept of marginality is also widely used in South America where it has often been understood to result from industrialisation processes and the differences between

---

[12] http://www.ilo.org/public/english/bureau/inst/project/socexcl.htm
[13] http://www.ilo.org/ciaris/ShowIndex.do

traditional and *modern* societies. Some South American authors argued that the marginalisation of *traditional* or *archaic* groups that make up *folk societies* can be overcome by modifying their behaviour patterns—in order to promote *development* and *modernity* which would bridge the gap between both types of societies (Germani, 1973; Spicker, Alvarez Leguizamon & Gordon, 2006). Thus the socially excluded in a South American context often refers to groups of indigenous people whereas in a European context this is much rarer—indigenous populations do not often make up a significant proportion of the socially excluded in any European country.

The World Bank has a United Nations mandate to combat global poverty and for 40 years it has been pursuing what is, basically, the same set of anti-poverty policies (Gordon, 2002; Townsend & Gordon, 2000). These have three elements:

1. broad-based economic growth
2. development of human capital, primarily through education
3. minimum social safety nets for the poor

These policies have been largely unsuccessful. The number of poor people in the world has continued to increase and, in particular, these same policies have resulted in negative consequences in many parts of sub-Saharan Africa, South America and in the countries of the former Soviet Union. In part, they have failed due to a rigid adherence to neo-liberal economic orthodoxy. Joseph Stiglitz—who was Chief Economist at the World Bank and who won the Nobel Prize for Economics for his work on the analyses of markets with asymmetric information—described this orthodoxy as having four stages (Stiglitz, 1998, 2000):

1. **Privatisation**—which tends to raise prices for the poor.
2. **Capital market liberalisation**—which can allow speculators to destabilise countries' economies, as has happened in Asia and South America.
3. **Market-based pricing**—which raises the costs of basic foods and fuel for the poor and has caused rioting, particularly in South America, e.g. Bolivia, Ecuador and, recently, Argentina.
4. **Free trade**—which is governed by World Trade Organisation (WTO) rules that often severely disadvantage poorer countries (Watkins & Fowler, 2002). Despite the advantages of free trade, history has shown that it has often resulted in severe famines and increased poverty (Davis, 2001; UNDP, 1999).

Given the World Bank's history and long-term commitment to these neo-liberal anti-poverty policies, it seems highly unlikely that the recent use of a social exclusion framework in some research reports will result in any significant changes to World Bank policies or practices.

CONCLUSION

The concept of social exclusion is widely used by policy makers in Europe and is certain to continue to be influential in the evolution of social policy amongst European Union member states. A number of United Nations organisations made concerted attempts to export the European concept of social exclusion to developing countries in the run up to and aftermath of the first World Summit on Social Development in 1995. This generated a lot of interesting and productive academic research, but seems to have had limited effects of policy makers in developing countries.

In the European Union, the adoption of the concept of social exclusion seems to have served two main policy functions. Firstly, it provided a mechanism for smoothing over/resolving the differences in the primary purposes of European welfare states (e.g. poverty alleviation in Ireland and social integration in Germany). Secondly, it provided a bureaucratic/diplomatic solution which allowed the continuation of a small-scale European Union programme on poverty during the 1990s in the face of hostility from some governments (particularly the UK Government).

Given these policy functions, it is unsurprising that the concept of social exclusion is somewhat nebulously defined (Pantazis, Gordon & Levitas, 2006). This has led many academics to be highly critical, for example, Else Øyen, the Scientific Director of the Comparative Research Programme on Poverty (CROP) has argued that researchers "are now running all over the place arranging seminars and conferences to find a researchable content in an umbrella concept for which there is limited theoretical underpinning". It is indeed hard to pinpoint any particular policy development or academic advance that has been made possible by the adoption of the concept of social exclusion by the European Union. Most of the policies adopted to combat social exclusion may well have been adopted even if the concept had never achieved widespread use and the European Union had simply continued with its anti-poverty programmes. However, given the political hostility of some "conservative" governments during the 1990s, the EU Poverty 4 programme was never going to receive unanimous approval, therefore the concept of social exclusion was useful in allowing the continuation of an EU wide anti-poverty programme in everything but name.

Niels Bohr, the Danish scientist, is attributed as saying that "prediction is very difficult, especially about the future" and this is as true for policy as it is for physics. However, it seems likely that social exclusion will remain a largely European policy concept which will evolve in European policy documents into the related concept of "social inclusion". This will be a gradual evolution, so the concept of social exclusion will probably persist and continue to be used by policy makers for many years to come.

REFERENCES

Andersen, J., Bruto da Costa, A., Chigot, C., et al. (1994). The contribution of Poverty 3 to the understanding of poverty, exclusion and integration. In *Poverty 3: The Lessons of the Poverty 3 Programme*. Lille: European Economic Interest Group, Animation and Research.

Appasamy, P., Guham, S., Hema, R., et al. (1996). Social exclusion from a welfare rights perspective in India. Research Series, No. 106, Geneva, International Institute for Labour Studies.

Atkinson,. A.B., Cantillon, B., Marlier, E. & Nolan, B. (2002). *Indicators for Social Inclusion in the European Union*. Oxford: Oxford University Press.

Bedoui, M. (1995). *Bibliographie sur l'exclusion dans les pays arabes du Maghreb et du Machreq*. Série Documents de travail No. 80, Geneva, International Institute for Labour Studies.

Bedoui, M. & Ridha, G. (1996). Les politiqu sociale en Tunisie. Série Documents de travail No. 88, Geneva, International Institute for Labour Studies.

Bessis, S. (1995). From social exclusion to social cohesion: towards a policy agenda—The Roskilde Symposium. MOST—Management of Social Transformations: Policy Paper no 2. UNESCO, New York.

Briggs, A. (1994). *A Social History of England*. London: Weidenfield and Nicolson.

Briggs, A. (2000). The welfare state in a historical perspective. In C. Pierson & F.G. Castles (eds). *The Welfare State Reader.* Oxford: Polity Press.

Burnel Report. (1989). *Poverty.* Brussels: European Communities Economic and Social Committee, Economic and Social Consultative Assembly.

Cartaya, V., Magallanes, R. & Domínguez, C. (1997). *Venezuela: exclusion and integration—A synthesis in the building?* Discussion Papers Series No. 90, Geneva, International Institute for Labour Studies.

Council Decision 75/458/EEC (1975, 22 July). Concerning a programme of pilot schemes and studies to combat poverty. 75/458/EEC of 22nd July 1995 (OLJ 99/3430.7.75.)

Davis, M. (2001). *Late Victorian Holocausts.* London: Verso.

de Haan, A. (1998). Social exclusion. An alternative concept for the study of deprivation? *IDS Bulletin, 29*(1), 10–19.

Duffy, K. (1998). Combating social exclusion and poverty: social integration in the European Union. In C. Oppenheim (ed.), *An Inclusive Society—Strategies for Tackling Poverty.* London: IPPR.

EEC. (1981). *Final Report from the Commission to the Council on the First Programme of Pilot Schemes and Studies to Combat Poverty.* Brussels: Commission of the European Communities.

EEC. (1985). On specific community action to combat poverty (Council Decision of 19 December 1984) 85/8/EEC. *Official Journal of the EEC, 2,* 24–25.

Esping-Andersen, G. (ed.) (1990). *The Three Worlds of Welfare Capitalism.* London and Princeton, NJ: Polity Press and Princeton University Press.

Eurostat. (1990). *Poverty in Figures: Europe in the Early 1980s.* Luxembourg: Office for Official Publications of the European Communities.

Eurostat. (1994). *Poverty Statistics in the Late 1980s.* Luxembourg: Office for Official Publications of the European Communities.

Eurostat. (2000). *Income, Poverty and Social Exclusion.* Luxembourg: Office for Official Publications of the European Communities.

Eurostat. (2006). *Structural Indicators.* Luxembourg. Retrieved from http://epp.eurostat.cec.eu.int/portal/page?_pageid=1133,47800773,1133_47802558&_dad=portal&_schema=PORTAL

Euzeby, C. (1991). *Le Revenu Minimum Garanti.* Paris: Editions la Découverte.

Ferrera, M., Matsaganis, M. & Sacchi, S. (2002). Open coordination against poverty: the new EU 'social inclusion process'. *Journal of European Social Policy, 12*(3), 227–239.

Figueiredo, J.B. & de Haan, A. (eds) (1998). Social exclusion: an ILO perspective. Research Series, No. 111, Geneva, International Institute for Labour Studies.

Gacitúa-Marió, E. & Wodon, Q. (2001). Measurement and meaning: combining quantitative and qualitative methods for the analysis of poverty and social exclusion in Latin America. World Bank Technical Paper No. 518., Washington, D.C., World Bank.

Germani, G. (1973). *El Concepto de Marginalidad.* Buenos Aires: Ediciones Nueva Visión, Buenos Aires.

Gordon, S. (1997). Poverty and social exclusion in Mexico. Discussion Papers Series No. 93, Geneva, International Institute for Labour Studies.

Gordon, D. (2002). The international measurement of poverty and anti-poverty policy. In P. Townsend & D. Gordon (eds), *World Poverty: New Policies to Defeat an Old Enemy* (pp 53–80). Bristol: Policy Press.

Gordon, D. & Pantazis, C. (eds) (1997). *Breadline Britain in the 1990s.* Aldershot: Ashgate.

Gore, C. & Figueiredo, J.B. (eds) (1997). Social exclusion and anti-poverty policy: a debate. Research Series, No. 110, Geneva, International Institute for Labour Studies.

Hagenaars, A.J.M., De Vos, K. & Zaidi, M.A. (1994). Poverty statistics in the late 1980's. Research based on Microdata, Luxembourg, Eurostat.

Hantrais, L. (1995). *Social Policy in the European Union.* New York: St. Martins Press.

Hashem, M.H. (1996). Goals for social integration and realities of social exclusion in the Republic of Yemen. Research Series No. 5, Geneva, International Institute for Labour Studies.

ILO. (2004). *Economic Security for a Better World.* Geneva: ILO.

Inack, S. (1997). *L'exclusion sociale au Cameroun.* Genève, Série de Documents de travail No 89, Geneva, International Institute for Labour Studies.

Kaijage, F. & Tibaijuka, A. (1996). Poverty and social exclusion in Tanzania. Research Series No. 109, Geneva, International Institute for Labour Studies.

Kleinman, M. (2002). *A European Welfare State? European Union Social Policy in Context.* Basingstoke: Palgrave.

Korpi, W. & Palme, J. (1998). The paradox of redistribution and strategies of equality: welfare state institutions, inequality, and poverty in the western countries. *American Sociological Review, 63,* 661–687.

Levitas, R. (2000). What is social exclusion? In D. Gordon & P. Townsend (eds), *Breadline Europe: The Measurement of Poverty.* Bristol: Policy Press.

Levitas, R. (2005). *The Inclusive Society: Social Exclusion and New Labour* (2nd edn). Basingstoke: Palgrave Macmillan.

Levitas, R. (2006). The concept and measurement of social exclusion. In C. Pantazis, D. Gordon & R. Levitas (eds), *Poverty and Social Exclusion in Britain* (pp. 123–162). Bristol: The Policy Press.

Marlier, E., Atkinson, T., Cantillon, B. & Nolan, B. (2006). *The EU and Social Inclusion: Facing the Challenges.* Bristol: Policy Press.

Matsaganis, M., Ferrera, M., Capucha, L. & Moreno, L. (2003). Mending nets in the South: antipoverty policies in Greece, Italy, Portugal and Spain. *Social Policy and Administration, 37,* 6.

Mejer, L. & Linden, G. (2000). Persistent income poverty and social exclusion in the European Union. *Statistics in Focus,* Population and Social Conditions. Theme 3—13/2000. Eurostat, Luxembourg.

Mejer, L. & Siermann, C. (2000). Income poverty in the European Union: children, gender and poverty gaps. *Statistics in Focus,* Population and Social Conditions. Theme 3—12/2000. Eurostat, Luxembourg.

Nelson, K. (2003). *Fighting Poverty: Comparative Studies on Social Insurance, Means-Tested Benefits and Income Redistribution.* Edsbruk: Stockholm University.

Pantazis, C, Gordon, D. & Levitas, R. (eds) (2006). *Poverty and Social Exclusion in Britain.* Bristol: The Policy Press.

Paugam, S. (1991). *La Disqualification Socials.* Paris: Presses Universitiaires de France.

Phongpaichit, P., Piriyarangsanan, S. & Treerat, N. (1996). Challenging social exclusion: rights and livelihood in Thailand. Research Series No 107, Geneva, International Institute for Labour Studies.

Rodgers, G., Gore, C. & Figueiredo, J.B. (1995). *Social Exclusion: Rhetoric, Reality, Responses: A Contribution to the World Summit for Social Development.* Geneva: International Institute for Labour Studies.

Room, G. (ed.) (1995). *Beyond the Threshold: The Measurement and Analysis of Social Exclusion.* Bristol: The Policy Press.

Shanks, M. (1977). *European Social Policy, Today and Tomorrow.* Oxford: Pergamon.

Silver, H. (1995). Social exclusion and social solidarity: three paradigms. *International Labour Review, 133*(5/6), 531–578.

Singer, P. (1996). Social exclusion in Brazil. Discussion Paper 94, Geneva, International Institute for Labour Studies.

Spicker, P., Alvarez Leguizamon, S. & Gordon, D. (2006). *Poverty: An International Glossary* (2nd edn). London: Zed.

Stiglitz, J. (1998). More instruments and broader goals: moving towards a post-Washington consensus. WIDER Annual Lecture 2. United Nations University World Institute for Development Economics Research (WIDER), Helsinki. Retrieved from http://www.wider.unu.edu/publications/annual-lectures/annual-lecture-1998.pdf

Stiglitz, J. (2000). What I learned at the world economic crisis. *New Republic,* 17 April 2000.

Tchernina, N. (1996). Economic transition and social exclusion in Russia. Geneva, IILS, Research Series No. 108, Geneva, International Institute for Labour Studies.

Thévenet, A. (1989). *RMI Théorie et Pratique.* Paris: Centurion.

Titmuss, R.M. (1958). *Essays on the Welfare State.* London: Allen & Unwin.

Townsend, P. (1979). *Poverty in the United Kingdom.* Harmondsworth, Middlesex: Penguin Books and Berkeley, California, University of California Press.

Townsend, P. & Gordon, D. (1989). *Low Income Households, Memorandum of Evidence to the House of Commons Social Services Committee*, 579: 45–73. (Also published as Townsend, P. & Gordon, D. (1993). What is enough? The definition of a poverty line. In P. Townsend, *The International Analysis of Poverty* (pp. 40–78). New York, London, Toronto, Sydney, Tokyo, Singapore: Harvester Wheatsheaf.)

Townsend, P. & Gordon, D. (2000). Introduction: the measurement of poverty in Europe. In D. Gordon & P. Townsend (eds), *Breadline Europe: The Measurement of Poverty* (pp. 1–22). Policy Press: Bristol.

UNDP. (1999). *Human Development Report 1999: Globalization with a Human Face*. Oxford: OUP. Retrieved from http://hdr.undp.org/reports/global/1999/en/

van Kersbergen, K. (1995). *Social Capitalism: A Study of Christian Democracy and the Welfare State*. New York: Routledge.

van Kersbergen, K. & Becker, U. (2002). Comparative politics and the welfare state. In H. Keman (ed.), *Comparative Democratic Politics*. London: Sage.

Veit-Wilson, J. (2000). States of welfare: a conceptual challenge. *Social Policy & Administration*, *34*, 1–25.

Watkins, K. & Fowler, P. (2002). *Rigged Rules and Double Standards: Trade, Globalisation, and the Fight against Poverty*. Oxford: Oxfam.

Wedderburn, D. (1965). Facts and theories of the welfare state. In R. Miliband & J. Saville (eds), *The Socialist Register 196* (pp. 127–146). London: Merlin Press.

CHAPTER 12

A Relational Analysis of Social Exclusion

Dominic Abrams

University of Kent, United Kingdom

and

Julie Christian

University of Birmingham, United Kingdom

ABSTRACT

This chapter advances a framework for conceptualising multiple aspects of social exclusion, and discusses the application and utility of a relational framework for meeting the challenges of managing inclusion interventions. The framework is illustrated using a variety of empirical evidence including findings from two major studies: the National Survey of Prejudice for the Equalities Review, and Age Concern England's national benchmarking survey of Ageism. The outcomes from these and other studies are used to demonstrate that the causes and solutions to social exclusion can be found in the "dynamics" within various relationships. The chapter concludes with a discussion of the role of exclusion and inclusion as forms of social control, and implications of the relational approach for designing interventions.

INTRODUCTION

This book demonstrates that many disciplines have researched social exclusion. However, there is still a lack of clarity and consensus over what is meant by "exclusion" (see, Millar, Chapter 1 and Gordon, Chapter 11). This is not entirely bad news; different approaches to conceptualising social exclusion may be suited to different purposes and contexts, so it may not be desirable to force a single definition. It might also be appropriate to consider a multidimensional framework for exploring social exclusion, because the evidence suggests it is possible to be socially excluded on more than one dimension at any one point in time, so the process of exclusion might be more protracted and complex than previously thought.

Multidisciplinary Handbook of Social Exclusion Research. Edited by D. Abrams, J. Christian and D. Gordon.
© 2007 John Wiley & Sons, Ltd.

To illustrate this perspective, we draw on evidence from one of the first national-level surveys to capture multiple sources of exclusion (Abrams & Houston, 2006). This survey of prejudice for the Equalities Review, focused on six key "equality strands"—age, disability, ethnicity, race, gender and sexuality, and is to our knowledge the first to do so in a single study using common measurement methods. A nationally representative sample of nearly 3,000 adults was asked about their attitudes as well as their experiences of prejudice and discrimination relating to substantial minority groups represented within each of these six equality strands. These were people under 30 and over 70, people with disabilities, Muslims, black people, women, and gay men and lesbians, as well as several other social groups (e.g. different nationalities, asylum seekers, different faiths). We also draw on national surveys of ageism conducted by Age Concern England (ACE, 2005; Ray, Sharp & Abrams, 2006).

In addition to tapping perceptions of equality as a means for understanding exclusion, these surveys also explored personal values. Schwartz (e.g. Bardi & Schwartz, 2003; Schwartz, 2007) has identified 10 basic value orientations that reflect people's needs, temperaments and social experience. According to Schwartz, comparison of the value priorities of groups, individuals or nations can vary depending on the impacts of distinctive experiences and major social changes. His values inventory is a widely accepted measure that forms a routine part of the European Social Survey (ESS) (Schwartz, 2007). Broadly, the 10 values reflect two orthogonal dimensions (self-enhancement vs self-transcendence, and openness to change vs conservation). Within this framework the values of benevolence and universalism (specific elements of self-transcendence) underpin egalitarianism. For example, Schwartz's (2007) analysis of the ESS revealed that acceptance of immigrants into one's country was predicted more strongly by egalitarian values than by other variables including the Human Development Index and a host of demographic factors.

In the Equalities Review survey among the 10 value dimensions in Schwartz's framework, the largest number of people (85%) endorsed equality—more than any other value. However, on other attitudinal measures 92% also agreed that people should all be treated as individuals, suggesting a clear tension between self-transcendence on the one hand and self-enhancement on the other. More striking is that people often regarded equality as a commodity that should not be distributed equally. Whereas fewer than 5% believed it was unimportant to meet the needs of women, people over 70, or people with disabilities, over 20% felt it was unimportant to meet the needs of gay men and lesbians, and asylum seekers. Thus, while equality and social justice are important to people, other values also come into play and may be used to justify inequality and injustice.

Evidence of this sort suggests that it is necessary for researchers and policy makers to consider explicitly the moral and political questions of whether and when social exclusion is necessarily "bad". In much of the writing on both exclusion and equality, it is taken as axiomatic that we need to reduce or eradicate social exclusion. For example, the Equalities Review (2007) sets out a moral economic and social cohesion case for equality. Likewise, Giddens (2007) argues that greater equality of outcome is good for the economy because improving the lot of the poorest will have the largest beneficial impact on society.

Despite this utopian view, we argue that it is important to be aware that social exclusion also works in many people's interests. In the larger scheme of things, some forms of exclusion may reflect what people regard to be an acceptable trade-off. Thus, a comprehensive approach to social exclusion demands not just an ambition to reduce social exclusion but also consideration of questions such as why exclusion is happening, what level of exclusion is acceptable, what forms of exclusion are acceptable, and which for groups or individuals exclusion should be considered legitimate? These questions raise further problems such as the balance of exclusion between different groups. Is the answer to exclusion of elderly people ("prisoners in their own homes" through fear of crime) really to alleviate their anxiety by excluding young people (e.g. incarceration of delinquent juveniles)?

If we imagine exclusion to be like a social form of pollution, its amelioration is unlikely to be achieved by removing the visibility of its undesirable effects. For example, within the context of homelessness, banning street sleeping is not going to make the issue of "rough sleeping" go away. Instead, interventions are needed at many different stages of the process, and most of all by tackling the underlying causes. So, for example, health exclusion may be tackled at a surface level by reducing all hospital waiting lists to a fixed maximum time limit, or by increasing the availability of therapeutic drugs, but a more effective approach to healthcare exclusion is likely to depend on finding ways to distribute preventative healthcare more effectively and at the earliest opportunity. More than drug-based intervention these may well be provision of social support, care and monitoring, facilities for exercise and sustaining social relationships or access to information technology, as well as by facilitating access (e.g. free transportation) to diagnostic healthcare in the first place (see Mason-Whitehead & Mason, Chapter 4).

A RELATIONAL ANALYSIS OF SOCIAL EXCLUSION

We use as a starting point the recent analysis provided by Burchardt and Vizard (2007) for the Equalities Review (2007), extending their prior work on social exclusion (see also Millar, Chapter 1; Houston, Chapter 2; Clapham, Chapter 5; Peattie, Chapter 10). Drawing extensively on Sen's (1985, 2005) analysis, Burchardt and colleagues developed a list of key "capabilities" that are required for greater social equality which, for the purposes of this chapter is likened to social exclusion. This "capabilities list" was based on both the European Convention on Human Rights (EU), and a deliberative polling exercise, thereby combining a philosophically defensible top-down with a socially responsive bottom-up methodology. The approach proposes that capabilities represent the extent to which society provides "substantive freedom" for people rather than necessarily deficiencies in people themselves. It focuses on opportunities, agency and, to some extent, process.

The idea is that there are a number of "key freedoms and activities" that can be used as contra-indices of being socially included. It is a short step to think of these as indices of social exclusion. The Equalities Review (2007) adopted the idea of an Equalities Score-card based on 10 of the features: longevity; physical security; health; education; standard of living; productive and valued activities; individual, family and social life; participation, influence and voice; identity expression and self-respect; and legal security. Underlying these 10 factors is a further set of 73 examples (pp. 127–129). In fact, the primary elements of this list are not so far from previous ideas of basic human needs such as Maslow's (1954) seminal hierarchy (see also Doyal & Gough, 1991) or indeed the 10 basic values for human behaviour identified by Schwartz (2007).

The list approach is useful for highlighting outcomes and measurable elements of equality, but it also has limitations. It operates in a single dimension, thereby limiting its flexibility and potential for development. It has an "irreducible core" that sounds uncomfortably like a set of fundamental principles in the tradition of religious, political and moral absolutists through the ages. But most problematic is that, after defining this irreducible core (the right to life, etc.), it invokes as a principle people's right to the capacity to do "normal" things. In other words, it has as its reference point the majority's status quo. These normal things are then defined, or decided upon, post hoc by asking deliberative panels to come up with them.

There is a risk that the list will tend to focus mainly on outcomes or statuses that happen to be attention grabbing (e.g. acute needs following disasters, the right to a fair trial, self-respect, be creative), not processes (e.g. being stopped from having a fair trial, things that deny self-respect, or stifle creativity). Lists lead us to attend to the features of a society (e.g. the type of school system) and a person's situation (e.g. area of residence) that give them the capability to achieve various outcomes (qualifications) rather than the nature of the relationships and social processes that *change* these capabilities (e.g. the demands of a selective higher education system, the content of a national curriculum, the way teachers are trained to value particular outcomes). Thus, although the approach advocated by the Centre for the Analysis of Social Exclusion and adopted by the Equalities Review (2007) has much to be commended, and proposes practical short cuts such as a spotlight list of indicators, it remains conceptually restrictive on the one hand, and potentially unwieldy on the other. The lists are long, detailed and potentially unending.

In keeping with many of the chapters in this book, we advocate a framework that captures the *dynamics* of social exclusion. This focuses attention on the way different elements combine together to generate or reduce exclusion. A preliminary version of this framework (Abrams, Hogg & Marques, 2005) was developed to widen social psychologists' perspectives on social inclusion and exclusion, with the aim of helping to facilitate more cross-disciplinary dialogue. The psychological literature (see also Hutchison, Abrams & Christian, Chapter 3) captures three readily measurable features of social exclusion: psychological effects, motives likely to be invoked, and responses to being in an exclusionary relationship. The effects of exclusion on individuals are almost wholly negative, both in terms of damage to the self-concept and the emotions or defensive reactions that follow. Exclusion taps into some very fundamental motivations whose bases can span from evolutionary survival principles to more specific goals such as the desire to maintain a particular reputation. The overarching conclusion is that exclusion provokes attempts to establish a legitimate place in the social world. That is, people want to be confident that they are part of a relationship or group that gives them meaning, security and positive prospects.

Although being excluded is almost invariably an aversive experience, people can respond in a variety of different ways, all of which are likely to provide some means of identity maintenance. Five types of response can be distinguished. The first three are methods of resisting exclusion or finding ways to be reincluded. Most simply people may fight back— they can demand to be reincluded. People may also try less confrontational methods such as sustaining reinclusion by various means, ranging from ingratiation to reinforcing boundaries that exclude others and reinstate their own inclusion. Third, people may attempt to re-establish control over the relationship. If all of this fails, a fourth type of response is to question the legitimacy of the exclusion, or question the reasons for it. Finally, a fifth response is to withdraw from the relationship and attempt to move into other, more accepting relationships if they are available. Recognising the motivations in play and understanding the options available for people to respond to exclusion provides clues as which types of intervention might be most effective, and which might be counterproductive.

A FRAMEWORK FOR ANALYSING SOCIAL INCLUSION AND EXCLUSION

By considering the actions and roles of different parties and other factors in processes of social exclusion, it is possible to identify multiple avenues for intervention. Abrams, Hogg and Marques (2005) set out four different elements that must be considered in order to characterise any particular instance of exclusion. These are (a) the actors, (b) the structural level of the exclusion relationship, (c) the forms and modes of exclusion, and (d) the dynamics of exclusion. These four elements correspond to the questions: who, where, how and why/when exclusion happens (see Table 12.1). In the next section we flesh out these elements with specific examples and evidence. We highlight the idea of "exclusion potential" as a control system. We propose that for policy initiatives to be effective, they must be preceded by a careful analysis, using a framework such as this, to locate the most effective nodes for intervention.

Actors in Social Exclusion

Research on social exclusion tends to focus unremittingly on the people who are excluded. But this victim focus is potentially restricting the way policy makers tackle the problem. Abrams, Hogg and Marques (2005) distinguished between two different sets of actors in the process, *sources* and *targets* of social exclusion. Understanding who these actors are and the *relationship* between sources and targets is important for making sense of any particular instance of social exclusion.

Table 12.1 A relational dynamics framework for analysing social inclusion and exclusion

Actors in exclusion relationship (*who*)						
Sources				Targets		

Relationship Context (*where*)						
Transnational	Societal	Institutional	Intergroup	Intragroup	Interpersonal	Intrapersonal

Modes/Forms of exclusion (*how*)				
Ideological/Moral	Representational	Categorical	Physical	Communicative

Dynamics of exclusion/inclusion relationship (*why/when*)			
Independent vs interdependent relationship	Resource inequality	Time frame	Motivational orientation

The sources and targets may be selected for a variety of reasons. Unconventional individuals are highly likely to be the targets of exclusion, particularly if they have a poor fit with an otherwise coherent group. Moreover, individuals may potentially be excluded not just because they look or behave differently from others, but also because their distinctiveness marks them as belonging to an excluded group (e.g. because observers use skin colour as an index of ethnicity). The potency of being excluded as an individual is magnified considerably when the consequence is denial of access to an important social network, effectively reducing the person's social capital. For a comprehensive analysis of over 100 forms in which interpersonal exclusion occurs, see Levine and Kerr (2007) and Kerr and Levine (in press).

Social categories and groups are clearly important targets of exclusion, particularly if they are minorities, are unfamiliar (e.g. foreign) or pose any kind of threat. But categories can be excluded even when they are not the target of overt hostility. As Houston argues (Chapter 2) women are socially excluded because their social category as a whole is largely constrained within particular roles. Other groups, such as Muslims may be excluded because of cultural differences or mistrust and suspicion, as well as because they may be in geographically segregated places (see Percival, Chapter 9).

As well as being targets of exclusion, social categories, and more often groups, are also powerful sources or perpetrators of exclusion. By their very nature, they have the capacity to include and exclude people, and may well do so as a part of their raison d'être. In general, making sense of why a person or group is excluded requires an analysis of their relationship with the person or group that is doing the excluding.

To illustrate this point, consider evidence from Abrams and Houston (2006). Overt prejudice against different social groups differed markedly. For example, whereas only 1 % of respondents expressed negative feelings about women, and fewer than 8 % against younger and older people, 10 % did so against black people, 22 % did against gay men and lesbians, and 38 % did against asylum seekers. These data show that exclusion is not a personality trait of the excluder, but is also something to do with wider perceptions of the excluded targets. But even this is too simplistic as an index of exclusion. For example, people viewed media coverage of Muslims to be more negative than coverage of any other social group. In contrast, when people's own experiences as targets of prejudice and discrimination were assessed, the most frequent bases were age (37 %) and gender (34 %). So the exclusion varies in terms of people's awareness of it, its statistical prevalence and its degree of venom.

The picture changes again when we look at subsets of sources of exclusion. For example, black or Asian respondents were more prejudiced against women than were White respondents. Men were more prejudiced against gay men and lesbians than were women. People with disabilities were more prejudiced against black people than were people without disabilities. These statistics illustrate plainly that our understanding of social exclusion is unlikely to be complete unless we take into account the multiple actors and relationships between them in a particular social context.

The Structural Level of the Exclusion Relationship

A further consideration is the level of social structures that define the actors and provide the medium or vehicle for exclusion to take place. Abrams, Hogg and Marques (2005) identified seven structural levels at which exclusion can arise. Each level provides a context for the one beneath it (cf. Doise, 1986; also Abrams & Hogg, 2004; Hogg & Abrams, 1988; Tajfel & Turner, 1979 for a social identity perspective and Mason-Whitehead & Mason, Chapter 4 for further discussion of "identity"). These levels are the transnational, societal, institutional, intergroup, intragroup, interpersonal and intrapersonal.

At the most general level is *transnational* exclusion based on large-scale geographical, religious or ethnic differences—-where the humanity or rights of entire sections of the global community are diminished or ignored. Examples include national, cultural and economic divides such as the exploitation or trade barriers placed on less developed economic blocks, exclusion based on religious intolerance that is promoted on a global scale (e.g. Islam vs Christianity), and geopolitical classifications that are used to justify the use of force (e.g. the "axis of evil"), moral positions and so on.

The next level is *societal*; the consensual exclusion of particular sets of people within a particular society (e.g. stigmatisation of people who have mental health problems or who smoke). In this type of exclusion there is no strong principle at work, but rather a consensual norm or expectation that enables people to feel it is legitimate to ignore or to constrain others. For example, the characteristics that people feel make it easier for a foreigner to be accepted as "British" appear to involve a tacit combination of skin colour, language and culture, but are not easily reduced to any one of these criteria alone (Abrams & Houston, 2006).

At the *institutional* level, different institutions within society may sanction and legislate for the selective treatment of different groups or individuals, and define their own criteria for inclusion and exclusion. Sometimes these are active (e.g. setting of quotas) and sometimes they appear more passive (e.g. "neutral" selection criteria for admission to universities which still result in a disproportionate number of privately educated children attending Oxford and Cambridge). Likewise, national criteria for the allocation of health services have to be mediated through specific institutions and their representatives (such as NHS trusts, or medical practices). A good example of the mapping of institutional and attitudinal levels is the social exclusion of "illegal immigrants", a category that has been a prime target of political campaigning and legislation for many years. In Abrams and Houston's (2006) survey, the majority of respondents (61 %) felt no compunction about expressing negative attitudes towards this group and almost half (47 %) viewed their equality rights to be unimportant.

Within and beneath both the societal and institutional levels is *intergroup* exclusion whereby particular groups sustain boundaries that establish their differences from other groups. Intergroup exclusion is likely to be more manifest and explicit than other forms because it often involves direct competition or conflict between groups—this type of exclusion takes the form of defining people as "with us or against us". Intergroup exclusion can fluctuate and shift quite quickly as a function of changes in the comparative context (for example, different "enemies" arise each week if one supports a particular soccer club). But this very fluidity also offers multiple routes for intervention (see Abrams, Hogg & Marques, 2005; and Hutchison, Abrams & Christian, Chapter 3).

At the *intragroup* level, exclusion occurs when groups set the criteria by which their members are allowed to define themselves and be treated as legitimate members. These are powerful processes and affect, for example, whether ministers are allowed to remain in a government's cabinet, whether people can be members of sects and cults, whether they are allowed to join organisations, and whether they become enmeshed in criminal subcultures and gangs. More subtly these exclusion mechanisms are relied upon by organisations to ensure members comply with corporate goals and standards (see also Levine & Kerr, 2007).

The final two levels are the interpersonal and intrapersonal. *Interpersonal* exclusion refers to denial of access to a relationship such that one person excludes another. Interpersonal exclusion can provoke major emotional responses, including intense anger, jealousy, depression and even instances of suicide or homicide by jilted partness. It has been proposed that people are highly predisposed to be sensitive to interpersonal exclusion because of its significance both socially and even evolutionarily (Kerr & Levine, in press; Kurzban & Leary, 2001).

Intrapersonal exclusion refers to a cognitive and emotional frame that enables or prevents a person from considering opportunities for inclusion in the first place (e.g. a white person could not easily conceive of becoming black). This is, in a sense, the relationship with oneself, which defines the scope or possibilities for one's inclusion in other relationships. It is strongly constrained by personal and social identity (Abrams & Hogg, 2001; Hogg & Abrams, 1988; Tajfel, 1981). This level is largely overlooked in the research, and certainly the policy, literature. Yet arguably the intrapersonal level is very central to the question of who seems able to rise above an ostensibly impossible set of circumstances. As shown in Jackson's chapter (Chapter 7), one route away from exclusion opens as a function of specific experiences that can change a person's image of themselves and their possible future.

Certain manifestations of social exclusion and inclusion are unique to particular relationship contexts but others permeate across levels. For example, social exclusion of women is embedded at a societal level, it is entrenched but not deliberately advocated institutionally. There is rarely if ever any direct intergroup conflict between men and women, but the dynamics at the intragroup, interpersonal and intrapersonal levels probably sustain the widespread levels of sex inequality. In contrast, social exclusion of Muslims in Britain is located firmly at the institutional level through prevention of terrorism legislation, strongly mistrustful media imagery and so on. This is also manifested at the intergroup level as overt public prejudice and discrimination as well as through racially/religiously motivated physical attacks. It is also probably sustained at the intrapersonal level as the majority of people consider their identity to be non-Muslim. In contrast, there are relatively low levels of inter-religious interpersonal relationships, so the interpersonal level is less directly involved. Indeed, inter-ethnic marriages accounted for just 2% of all marriages occurring in England and Wales in 2001 (ONS, 2001).

Overall, one can conclude that there is an asymmetry in control over exclusion processes. For example, despite individuals' power to exclude other individuals (such as rejection of friends) they do not have the same power as groups or institutions to orchestrate wholesale exclusion of others. Thus, in general, excluders at higher structural levels have more power over those at lower levels than the lower levels do over one another or over higher levels.

Forms and Modes of Exclusion and Inclusion

Abrams, Hogg and Marques (2005) proposed that there is likely to be a strong link between the structural level of the relationship and the mode of exclusion and inclusion that operates within the relationship. We outline these key factors below. At higher structural levels of relationship exclusion is likely to be *ideological* in the sense that it is justified with reference to supposedly universal moral conventions and principles. For example, in many countries the execution of criminals is justified by a consensus within that society that certain acts place individuals irredeemably beyond moral boundaries (cf. Reed & Aquino, 2003). However, in part because such forms of exclusion are so extreme, these same societies do not permit them to be enacted by individuals (e.g. for them to take personal revenge). Consequently, extreme forms of exclusion are often mediated by complex legislative and institutional systems.

A more specific form of exclusion is through shared *social representations* and imagery. To the extent that groups and individuals can be characterised in simple, perhaps dehumanised stereotypes, it is much easier to exclude the entire set. When particular groups and individuals are perceived to be coherent entities (Hamilton, Sherman & Rogers, 2004), there is greater scope for them to be excluded because it is easier to define criteria for doing so. For example, when the Bluewater Shopping Centre in Kent England was concerned about theft and security, it announced a ban on "hoodies"—young people wearing tops with hoods on. The irony is that several of the shops in the Centre were actually selling these types of clothes and of course the age range and characteristics of the purchasers were quite diverse (see also Hale & FitzGerald, Chapter 8). This form of exclusion based on simple cues and stereotypes does not require an explicit ideological framework. Instead it is targeted at a simply defined threat.

An example of the different social representations that can underpin exclusion is the way Muslims, compared with gay men and lesbians, are viewed in British society (Abrams & Houston, 2006). Whereas Muslims are viewed as relatively unfriendly and as competing for resources, gay men and lesbians are viewed as relatively friendly and less competitive. Both groups are the targets of prejudice but for quite different reasons. Muslims are regarded more with fear and anger than any other social group. Gay men and lesbians are viewed with disgust more than any other social group.

A related form of exclusion, which may range from relatively abstract to relatively specific, is the process of *categorisation*. The simple act of partitioning people into different social categories necessarily involves over inclusion and exclusion of members in terms of the assumed sharedness of their characteristics with others of the same category. Notice, however, that as exclusion takes more concrete forms, there is also potential for greater flexibility and likelihood of flux or change. Ideology, law and morality are hard to change, and social imagery may be well established and pervasive. However, psychologically, social categories can often be reassigned, or their meanings or relevance can change relatively quickly depending on the context (Crisp & Hewstone, 2006; Turner *et al.*, 1987).

Age presents a clear example of these categorisation processes. There are fixed age boundaries for certain events in life, such as marriage, driving, leaving school and usually retirement. However, definitions of what age represents "young" and "old" can be extremely flexible. Indeed in one survey (ACE, 2005) people under the age of 25 typically viewed youth as ending by 38 and old age as starting by 55. In contrast, people over the age of 65 viewed youth as not ending until after 56 and old age as not starting until after 67. Consequently, while age is certainly a powerful axis of social exclusion (Ray, Sharp & Abrams, 2006), the application of age for that purpose can vary dramatically. Indeed, while older people may be excluded economically by objective impoverishment, it is younger people who bear the brunt of prejudice and direct discrimination, not just in terms of their age but also their ethnicity, gender, sexuality and religion (Abrams & Houston, 2006; Ray, Sharp & Abrams, 2006).

As well as the broader ideological, representational and categorical components of exclusion, there are more tangible and manifest forms. Thus the application of a "zero tolerance" principle in the case of crime, health or education has to be implemented by people on the ground, and these principles become operationalised in quite explicit and observable ways.

The most obvious manifestation of acts of social exclusion is *physical segregation*, which may vary in the extent to which it is institutionalised and enforced. Physical segregation can range from societal, such as Apartheid or the Berlin Wall, to the interpersonal such as presence of a garden fence, or the distance apart that two people sit in a room (e.g. Macrae *et al.*, 1994), and may be both active (eviction or aggression) and passive (ostracism, denial of access). It is used routinely as a control technique in schools, prisons, housing provision and so on. There are also examples of design that is used to prevent access by certain people, such as installation of sloped narrow bench seating in public areas to prevent people using it for shelter and sleeping. Control (and hence sustained exclusion) over the social underclasses and dispossessed is aided by pervasive CCTV monitoring in many UK cities and towns.

While segregation is not always problematic (as we discuss later), it is well established that segregation is likely to be a significant barrier to building or repairing relationships (Pettigrew, 1998). It is surprising therefore how easily overlooked this can be in areas of policy and practice. Moreover, physical segregation can be created socially even in the absence of walls. Perceptions of such barriers can influence the uptake of housing services offered to help socially include people (Christian *et al.*, 2005). More widely, the most recent Age Concern England national survey of ageism (*n* = 2,000; Abrams, 2006), revealed substantial age segregation both in terms of intergenerational friendships and the age structure of the work place. As shown in Figure 12.1, fewer than 10% of people under 35 have friends aged over 70 while fewer than 25% of those aged over 65 have friends younger than 30. Similarly, in the work place people aged under 35 are much more likely to have co-workers in their own age range (73%) than in the 35–55 (58%) or 55+ (17%) bracket. Whereas ethnic segregation is often viewed as an index of social schism, much less attention is paid to age (or gender) segregation, and yet it is arguable that these have equally profound implications for social exclusion and cohesion.

Even without physical segregation, exclusion and inclusion are powerfully manifested through particular communicative practices, the most obvious being a simple instruction to "go away" or signs "no ball games" and simple ostracism (see Williams, Forgas & von Hippel, 2005). More subtle forms of *communicative exclusion* are speech accommodation or divergence (in which accents or speech patterns shift to show greater or lesser affiliation). For example, people sometimes use patronising "elder talk"—akin to baby talk—when communicating with elderly people (Giles & Reid, 2005; Ryan, Bourhis & Knops, 1991). In other contexts, people are known to use more abstract and hence generalisable descriptions to depict negative acts by members of out-groups but more concrete non-generalisable descriptions for similar acts by members of in-groups (known as evaluative linguistic bias, Maass *et al.*, 1989). Such instances may often be the concrete manifestations of exclusion that is sanctioned or sustained by exclusion at higher levels of generality. Unless exclusion of a particular set of people is tackled at all the levels on which it

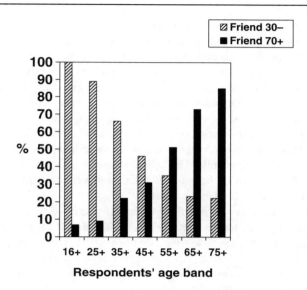

Figure 12.1 Percentage of British people in 2006 who have a friend aged under 30 and who have a friend aged over 70

operates, interventions are likely to have only limited success. This brings us to the issue of the dynamics of social exclusion.

Exclusion Dynamics

The process of exclusion (as distinct from the state of being excluded) is dynamic. It involves a relationship in which at least two parties have uneven potential to gain influence, power or resources. Several features of the relationship will affect the nature of exclusion. Abrams, Hogg and Marques (2005) proposed that these include (a) the level of interdependence, (b) the nature of the valued resource, (c) the time frame and (d) the motivational orientation that is in play.

Independence vs interdependence

Resistance and reaction to social exclusion is unlikely to be strong or coherent unless people are aware of the relevant interdependencies involved. One form of exclusion occurs in "independent" relationships. That is, the excluders have no particular interest in the excluded, and vice versa. Nonetheless the excluders make choices that cause exclusion, perhaps underpinned by "system justifying" accounts (Jost, Banaji & Nosek, 2004). One example is residential segregation such as "white flight", in which economically advantaged majority group members move to live in areas that "have the best schools". This, by default, leaves the "worst schools" in areas populated by economically disadvantaged minorities (cf. Bobo, 1988). In these types of exclusion it may be very difficult for targets of social exclusion to recognise what is happening or to pinpoint any particular sources of exclusion, and thus it may be difficult to counteract. Turning again to the example of age prejudice, both the Abrams and Houston (2006) and ACE (Ray, Sharp & Abrams, 2006) research show that older people are not regarded as a competitive or threatening group in society. In fact the stereotypes of older people are that they are "doddery but dear". This is a classic manifestation of so-called "benevolent prejudice". As shown in Figure 12.2, which is based on data from the 2006 survey (Abrams, 2006) approximately 28 % of people in all age bands view people over 70 as friendlier than people under 30. However, people under the age of 55 regard younger people as more competent and capable by a margin of between 32 % and 22 %. Thus, a substantial degree of discrimination against older people may not be because of direct antipathy towards them but because they are assumed to be incapable.

Other types of relationship are manifestly interdependent—the outcomes of one party are directly affected by the outcomes of the others. It is useful to recognise that in some interdependent relationships, exclusion may be consensual. For example, boys and girls in primary school seem quite happy to self-segregate for purposes of play and social activities (Leaper, 1994). Doctors and nurses may be quite happy to dine in different work place canteens or common rooms. Men and women seem reasonably content with the idea that they should use different restrooms in public buildings. Segregated settings are common in education, health and other public service areas, and there are communities of common interest that are explicitly separate (pensioners' groups, youth clubs, etc.).

Even when segregation appears to be completely consensual, the balance between separation and distinctiveness on the one hand, and inclusion/cohesion on the other should not be assumed to be unproblematic, either conceptually or practically. There is a direct link between the extent to which people apply discriminatory stereotypes and their degree of segregation. For example, Ray, Sharp and Abrams (2006) analysed how low capability stereotypes about older people were associated with intergenerational segregation among respondents who were aged under 35. Those who had no friend over 70 agreed more often (30 %) with a statement that competence declines with age than did those who had a friend over 70 (22 %). This finding is highly congruent with the overall pattern of evidence for effects of intergroup contact across multiple domains (Pettigrew & Tropp, 2006).

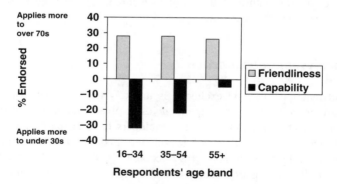

Figure 12.2 Stereotyping on the dimensions of friendliness and capability. Positive numbers are the percentage who rated the trait as more stereotypical of people over the age of 70. Negative numbers are the percentage that rated the trait as more stereotypical of people under the age of 30

Resource inequality

Economic exclusion is potentially devastating for those affected. Early social disadvantages in terms of education, health and housing are well-established predictors of future exclusion. Resource inequality also goes beyond being able to participate for economic goods. It also conveys symbolic value. In situations that involve personal conflict or threat to one's identity, exclusion is likely to be contested and the dynamics are likely to involve a struggle over who is excluded and on what basis. Parenthetically, this is why tokenism is such a powerful mechanism for neutralising such struggles (cf. Kanter, 1977) In these situations, the different parties are likely to focus on their access to valued resources. These resources may be material, economic, health or educational, but it is useful to recognise that resources are also social and psychological. They include and can convey symbolic goods such as prestige, esteem and respect, independence, self-determination and other qualities (cf. Tajfel & Turner, 1979).

Distributive or procedural issues, or both, are likely to be relevant to the distribution of resources in social exclusion. We assume that most individuals and groups generally seek to optimise or maximise their resources, and it is hardly surprising that they do so, in part, by denying resources to others (cf. Sherif, 1966) and protesting when the distribution seems unjustly to work against their own interests (cf. Klandermans, 1997). The difficulty is that distributing resources equally at one level (e.g. between regions) does not guarantee that the resources will be allocated equally at lower levels (e.g. different regions may prioritise elements of health provision differently). A current example is the so-called IVF "postcode lottery", where the levels of IVF treatment offered on the NHS vary depending on the postcode of a person's GP (see Mason-Whitehead & Mason, Chapter 4). Each Primary Care Trust is responsible for deciding the number of IVF cycles offered and inequalities are evident within the UK with some areas providing no IVF treatment on the NHS while other areas offering three IVF treatments and levels of treatment varying depending on where people live.

Unequal access to power also makes it possible that people may be excluded when others rule their behaviour to be "illegal". Justice-based exclusion is potentially explosive because it depends on consensus about the legitimacy of the system and rules that are imposed. When that consensus breaks down, the formerly excluded party is likely to react with anger, and the former excluders to become defensive and even more exclusive, as can be witnessed in the conflicts in Palestine, and more generally between Western and Islamic cultures.

Owing to the politicisation of much of the exclusion research, work concentrates on only a limited subset of the relevant resources, and thereby risks missing some of the other elements that matter to people who are excluded. This is a critical point, because different resources may be focal at different structural levels of social exclusion for different groups. It seems likely that at more abstract (transnational, societal) levels, there may be emphasis on symbolic resources and processes, whereas the dynamics at lower structural levels of relationship (e.g. intergroup, interpersonal) are likely to surround more tangible material outcomes such as specific territory or facilities. For example, governments are likely to justify tax breaks to the wealthy using procedural principles and system-justifying values such as equality of opportunity and performance incentives, whereas individuals in a work group are likely to apply a distributive rule that everyone pays the same amount into the pool for lottery tickets, regardless of their status or income (cf. Tyler & Blader, 2000).

At an institutional level exclusion may be designed to ensure power and control, so the relevant resources are the access to the rule-making and reward mechanisms. At an inter-group level exclusion may be designed to ensure the group is "better" than its competitor, and so the relevant resources could be money, space, or even just "points" and symbolic credits. The UK School league tables are just one instance in which there is greater emphasis on the relative standing of the groups than the absolute performance. Yet, labelling a school as bottom of the table is likely to be read as a very strong message of social exclusion to the members of the school. Classification is a powerful tool of resource-based exclusion. For example, a hidden message of "concessionary" travel passes for people over a particular age is that that these people will not (and perhaps should not) be in full-time employment.

Allocation of resources is also used as a powerful social signal of social inclusion and exclusion. For example, in the Equalities Review survey (Abrams & Houston, 2006), respondents were given an opportunity to donate three lots of five pounds to a number of "charities". The charities were actually fictitious but of greatest interest was how people would decide to allocate these resources depending on the target of the charity. The survey options included four innocuous charities (the Ancient Building Preservation Society, The Equality Forum, the Homelessness Provision Service, the Society for the Constitutional Reform of the Houses of Parliament) together with different pairs of other charities, the latter being of focal interest. Figure 12.3 shows the overall results. First, people were far more willing to donate to "dependent" charities (older people, disabled people, homeless people) than charities that represented competitive social categories. Second, fewer than 8% of people chose to donate to black people, Muslims, or gay men and lesbian communities.

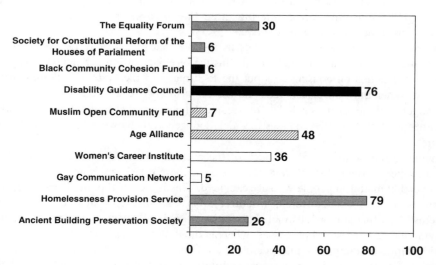

Figure 12.3 Preferences for which two charities should receive £5 donation (percent nominated)
Note: Grey = presented in all versions; other shades = presented only in one of three subsets of the survey.

Behind these statistics, there is further evidence of the principle of unequally distributed equality. For example, in the context of potentially donating to women or gay men and lesbians, support for the Equality Forum rose to 39%. However when the alternative was to donate to the Disability Guidance Council and Black Community Cohesion Fund, donations to the Equality Forum dropped to 21% (with 76% donating to the Disability Guidance Council). Such donations also tended to be self-serving. For example, 85% of Asians donated to the Disability Guidance Council whereas none donated to the Black Community Cohesion Fund. In contrast, 54% of black respondents donated to the Disability Guidance Council and 44% to the Black Community Cohesion Fund. In the same vein, given the choice of the Age Alliance and Muslim Open Community Fund, 54% of Christians and 18% of Asians gave to the former, whereas 2% of Christians and 69% of Muslims gave to the latter. These findings show that exclusion is sometimes exemplified not by negative actions towards the excluded party (harming or withholding) but often by actively favouring the included party. Because these actions feel subjectively positive, people do not necessarily see them as excluders. It is only in the context of relative outcomes within a relationship that the exclusion becomes clearly apparent (see also Mummendey & Otten, 1998).

These types of resource inequality are also likely to relate to the concept of "social capital". As well as the idea that social capital somehow compensates for inequality, it is plausible that greater equality reinforces social capital. Based on trends in North America, one might pessimistically conclude that as globalisation progresses society will be come increasingly atomised and the social capital will ebb away with the older generations (Portes, 1988; Putnam, 2000). On the other hand, trends in Europe indicate that countries with more substantial welfare systems and stronger legal structures, which are generally also the more advanced countries economically, appear to have greater social capital and higher rates of social and political participation and with no or reversed age differentials (Newton & Montero, 2007; Norris & Davis, 2007).

In the case of many groups and individuals, it seems likely that greater social connectedness can help them evade extreme social exclusion. For example, research into stereotype threat (Steele, 1997) has demonstrated that people perform substantially less well on ability tests if they are aware of a negative comparison with another group. A stereotype threat effect has been observed for many such situations, including when black students are informed that their test performance will be compared with whites', or when women who are told their maths performance will be compared with men's. There are a number of reasons why this effect occurs but it seems likely that it depends partly on whether people psychologically buy in to being categorised as a member of the lower status group. This process itself can be changed. For example, Abrams, Eller and Bryant (2006) asked older people to take a cognitive test. Half the participants were told their performance would be compared with that of younger people. As expected, this group performed significantly worse on the test. Based on intergroup contact theory, as well as prior evidence from ACE (Ray, Sharp & Abrams, 2006), Abrams, Eller and Bryant (2006) hypothesised that people who had more positive relationships with younger people would not view younger and older people as members of different social categories. This should protect older people from stereotype threat. As shown in Figure 12.4, consistent with this idea the effect of the "threat" (comparison) instruction was eliminated among older people who had more positive intergenerational relationships.

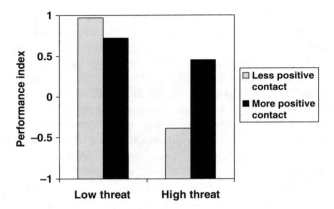

Figure 12.4 Effects of positive intergenerational relationships on older people's performance in the context of low and high stereotype threat (Abrams, Eller & Bryant, 2006)

Time frame

Interpersonal and intergroup exclusion are likely to be capable of substantial ebbs and flows, and changes of focus. It is also likely that relationships that have been exclusive for extended periods become embedded in custom, practice. Such exclusion is gradually more likely to become defined culturally in terms of the natural essence of the included and excluded parties (e.g. the establishment of apartheid in South Africa). Thus, over time and in the absence of countervailing forces, there is likely to be a tendency for social exclusion to become consolidated at increasingly higher structural levels. Taken to extreme levels, the path extends from segregation to governmentally sanctioned genocide. Social exclusion at higher structural levels is likely, generally, to persist over a longer time course. Consequently, change at these levels takes more time. On the other hand, legislation can alter or reverse these trends, as the various new equality duties and flexible working, health and safety, and other initiatives seem to show.

Time also provides an important element in change, however, because of the individual and collective memories (see Pennebaker, Pàez & Rimé, 1997) and expectations that may surround social exclusion. The reframing of past wrongdoings can provide an impetus for establishing more inclusive principles at higher levels. One consequence of the Holocaust and other genocides is the increased concern to establish a common multinational framework for protecting human rights. These developments then pervade other contexts at lower structural levels. For example, as issues of equality and diversity become more strongly framed by an overarching human rights agenda, principles of freedom and equality that govern treatment of different ethnic or religious groups within society may also have an impact on the perceived legitimacy of differential treatment of men and women within those groups. Likewise, the success of one minority group in gaining rights may spur on others to act in similar ways. This crossover phenomenon is illustrated by the establishment of the Commission for Equality and Human Rights in the UK. Consultative work prior to the commission's formation demonstrated clearly that despite very different experiences and expressions of inequality and discrimination, there are common sets of principles that can improve the opportunities for and inclusion of all groups (Abrams & Houston, 2006; Equalities Review, 2007).

Motivational orientation

A further element that helps to describe the dynamics of exclusion is the motivational orientation that characterises participants in exclusionary relationships. In psychology a simple but useful distinction is between an assertive vs defensive orientation, variously labelled, "approach/avoidance", "promotion/prevention" and "challenge/threat" (Blascovich & Mendes, 2000; Mackie & Smith, 2002; Shah & Higgins, 2001). To apply these to social exclusion, it is necessary to consider these assertive and aversive orientations from the perspective of more than one actor and also how different levels of exclusion interact. One way to tackle exclusion is to put into place opportunities or costs at one level that can outweigh those at another. For example, a country may impose severe restrictions on immigration because of ideological and nationalistic sentiment but it may be that within a particular field (e.g. medicine) a chronic shortage of qualified candidates can only be met using immigrant workers. Thus a manager may have to actively recruit members from that group. The threat that encourages exclusion at a higher structural level is outweighed by the opportunities that encourage inclusion at the lower level.

EXCLUSION AND INCLUSION POTENTIAL AS CONTROL SYSTEMS

The use of exclusion as a form of control is apparent at various levels of intensity, ranging from apparently innocuous forms such as denominational schooling through to draconian immigration policies, highly punitive criminal justice systems, dictatorships and genocide. Indeed, exclusion is the preferred and formally sanctioned method of behavioural control in the education system (see Hick, Visser & MacNab, Chapter 6). In reality its effectiveness is wholly dependent on the fact that most people, including children, strongly desire to be included. The real social power is not actual exclusion (this surely represents failure of the system) but the *potential* for exclusion (see also Kerr & Levine, in press). This suggests that in fact inclusion is probably the more effective means of control. Inclusion probably risks backfiring only when it is either forced (e.g. conscription to fight an unjust war) or when apparently open borders turn out to be heavily policed by the more powerful agents (e.g. "choices" that turn out to be obligations to family, church or organisations).

Inclusion based more on consensus and choice seems to offer good prospects. For example, the emphasis on citizenship, national identity and so on, is a useful tool for reminding groups and individuals that have their own agendas that there is an expectation, and sometimes a requirement that they follow the rules, procedures and priorities of the majority in society. The multiculturalism model is not necessarily at odds with this more integrationist emphasis. Echoing the exclusion example above, it may be that the potential for inclusion—demonstrably permeable boundaries between minority and majority groups—could well be sufficient to support stable and enduring social cohesion even when groups remain, for various reasons, quite segregated from one another. Moreover, promoting the potential for inclusion is likely to create more positive motivational effects. Investment in resources that allow people to build strong relationships and extended networks sustained by shared forms of interdependence is likely to establish greater potential for inclusion and to create a net that has both a finer and a more elastic mesh. When people fall, this should be a net that enables them to bounce back, not one that just leaves them languishing a few inches from the ground.

The underlying point is that whereas forced exclusion and inclusion both have significant advantages in terms of the predictability of the outcomes (e.g. society is governed by a rigid and uniform set of codes and clear social boundaries), creating the tangible potential for social exclusion and the potential for social inclusion might both provide more effective and constructive means of social control. This control, albeit in a diffuse form, would support a less unequal society in which exclusion occurs generally in functional rather than dysfunctional ways.

An illustration of this perspective is that after the July 7 bombings in London there was no downshift in people's valuing of equality (Equalities Review, 2007). Indeed the follow-up survey (Abrams & Houston, 2007) revealed that those who were most affected—people more strongly connected to London—were more likely to see Britain as one nation (45 % vs 36 %), more likely to believe Muslims themselves could effectively prevent further acts of terrorism (57 % vs 46 %), and less likely to believe that other Muslims in Britain would support terrorism (43 % vs 49 %). It seems likely that the social framing of the event as one that included all Londoners (rather than one that just affected non-Muslims) may have been responsible for these differences. For example, across the sample, people who perceived Muslims and non-Muslims as one common group or as diverse individuals rather than as two separate groups, were significantly less likely to hold prejudiced attitudes towards Muslims.

DESIGNING INTERVENTIONS

The framework proposed here may seem rather abstract and potentially complex. However, it is intended to help researchers and policy makers evaluate and plan interventions. Specifically, by identifying clearly the relationship context, the modes of exclusion and the dynamics in the exclusion relationship it should be possible to map and evaluate such interventions fairly precisely. Many combinations are possible so it is important to define the goals of intervention clearly. For example, if one's goal was to tackle the exclusion of older people from participation in paid work in a particular organisation, one should first decide at which level to intervene (e.g. institutional), secondly which modes of exclusion to change (e.g. communicative), third which dynamics to work on (e.g. opportunity/promotion for increased productivity). The interventions and measures of their effects should then correspond to these specific elements.

An intervention at the level of society (e.g. changing statutory retirement ages) is unlikely to yield manifest changes measured at the level of interpersonal exclusion (e.g. a specific interviewer's preference for a younger person over an equally qualified older person for a particular job). But it is likely to yield manifest effects in terms of generational differences and cross-national differences (e.g. in income, productivity, etc.). Conversely, unless a very large time frame is used, interventions at the level of interpersonal exclusion (e.g. guidance and rules for interviewers to avoid ageism in selection interviews) are likely to be undetectable if the measures are at the societal level (e.g. age profiles of the working population) because of the numerous other factors that could be influential.

A similar approach is advocated by Fishbein and Ajzen (1975) in their theory of attitude–behaviour relationships, a model advanced as a means to further understanding attitudes and exclusion (see also Sutton, 2003). The methodological lessons of that approach are very valuable. By providing a clear framework (not specific items or lists) ensuring correspondence in the level of specificity of an intervention programme and the measurements of impact, it is possible to get a much firmer handle on what to change and how to go about implementing the programme. Measuring these softer variables alongside more traditional sociodemographics has proven useful in understanding a spectrum of "social inclusion services", ranging from housing uptake (Christian & Abrams, 2003, 2004; Christian & Armitage, 2002) through to participation behaviours of young mothers in training and employment programmes (Christian *et al.*, 2005), thereby demonstrating that the combination of interpersonal, intragroup and institutional levels can all underpin exclusion simultaneously.

CONCLUSION

This book provides an extensive and broad analysis of social exclusion research and policy. Regardless of the particular aspect of exclusion that readers are interested in, we hope that they will gain something from the book as a whole. Work in this area is moving towards a broader and more consensual understanding of what social exclusion is and how it occurs. The challenge now is to generate creative policies and techniques for intervention to build on this knowledge. As we stated at the outset of this chapter, this challenge requires a careful look at what levels and types of exclusion are acceptable within society as well as a clearer focus on tackling what is unacceptable.

A recent report concluded that "the net effect of eight years of Labour government has been to leave inequality effectively unchanged" (Brewer *et al.*, 2006, p. 7). However, it is reasonable to be optimistic that headway is being made. Current efforts to pursue these integrative agendas, such as the launch of the Commission for Equality and Human Rights, suggest that there is awareness of the need to confront these issues in a more holistic and coherent way than previously. Integrative top-down approaches do, however, run the risk of concentrating entirely at particular levels of analysis or on only a limited subset of groups and individuals who are adversely affected by social exclusion. A central message from this book as well as this chapter, is that exclusion is a process not just an outcome and not just a state. It cannot be reduced easily to a list and it will require multiple lines of intervention if we are to deal with it effectively. It is a process that is fundamentally relational. Relationships are both the causes of, and hold the solutions to, social exclusion. By understanding the nature of the relationships and the flow of influences within them, there is hope that we can design policies and interventions that will improve a whole host of other important outcomes.

Acknowledgements

We wish to acknowledge the support of ESRC for funding a seminar series on Social Inclusion, and related experimental research (RES-000-23-0401), the Department of Trade and Industry, Age Concern England and the Commission on Equality and Human Rights for supporting the national survey research and Solihull Council/Learning Skills Council for their sponsorship.

REFERENCES

Abrams, D. (2006). Age and social identity: the subtle and brutal nature of age discrimination. Paper presented at the National Institute of Economic and Social Research Conference on 'Tackling Age Discrimination in Britain: The Employment (Age) Equality Regulations and Beyond", The British Academy, London, 29 September.

Abrams, D., Eller, A. & Bryant, J. (2006). An age apart: the effects of intergenerational contact and stereotype threat on performance and intergroup bias. *Psychology and Aging*, *21*, 691–702.

Abrams, D. & Hogg, M.A. (2001). Collective identity: group membership and self-conception. In M.A. Hogg & S. Tindale (eds), *Blackwell Handbook of Social Psychology* (Vol. 3: Group Processes, pp. 425–461). Oxford: Blackwell.

Abrams, D. & Hogg, M.A. (2004). Metatheory: lessons from social identity research. *Personality and Social Psychology Review*, *8*, 97–105.

Abrams, D., Hogg, M.A. & Marques, J.M. (2005). A social psychological framework for understanding inclusion and exclusion. In D. Abrams, M.A. Hogg & J.M. Marques (eds), *The Social Psychology of Exclusion and Inclusion* (pp. 1–24). New York: Psychology Press.

Abrams, D. & Houston, D.M. (2006). Equality, diversity and prejudice in Britain. Equalities Review. Cabinet Office. Retrieved from http://archive.cabinetoffice.gov.uk/theequalitiesreview// upload/assets/theequalitiesreview/kentequality.pdf

Abrams, D. & Houston, D.M. (2007). Findings from the 2005 National Surveys. Presentation to the Equalities Review Seminar on Tackling Discrimination. Admiralty Arches, London, 12 January.

ACE. (2005). How ageist is Britain? London: Age Concern England. Retrieved from http://www. ageconcern.org.uk/AgeConcern/Documents/how_ageist_is_britain.pdf

Bardi, A. & Schwartz, S.H. (2003). Values and behavior: strength and structure of relations. *Personality and Social Psychology Bulletin*, *29*, 1207–1220.

Blascovich, J. & Mendes, W.B. (2000). Challenge and threat appraisals: the role of affective cues. In J. Forgas (ed.), *Feeling and Thinking: The Role of Affect in Social Cognition* (pp. 59–82). Cambridge: Cambridge University Press.

Bobo, L. (1988). Group conflict, prejudice and the paradox of contemporary racial attitudes (pp. 85–116). In P. A. Katz & D. M. Taylor (eds.), *Eliminating racism: Profiles in controversy*. New York: Plenum.

Brewer, M., Goodman, A., Shaw, J. & Sibieta, L. (2006). Poverty and inequality in Britain: 2006. The Institute for Fiscal Studies, London. Retrieved from http://www.ifs.org.uk/comms/comm101. pdf

Burchardt, T. & Vizard, P. (2007). Definition of equality and framework for measurement: final recommendations to the equalities review steering group on measurement. Equalities Review: Cabinet Office. Retrieved from http://archive.cabinetoffice.gov.uk/theequalitiesreview//upload/ assets/theequalitiesreview/paper1equality.pdf

Christian, J. & Abrams, D. (2003). The effects of social identification, norms and attitudes on the use of outreach services by homeless people. *Journal of Community Applied Social Psychology*, *13*, 138–157.

Christian, J. & Abrams, D. (2004). A tale of two cities: predicting homeless people's uptake of outreach programs in London and New York. *Basic and Applied Social Psychology*, *26*(2/3), 169–182.

Christian, J. & Armitage, C.J. (2002). Attitudes and intentions of homeless people towards service provision in South Wales. *British Journal of Social Psychology*, *41*, 219–231.

Christian, J., Thomas, S., Collyer, M., *et al.* (2005). *Profiling Teenage Mothers Further Education, Training and General Support Needs in Solihull*. Birmingham: Learning Skills Council.

Crisp, R.C. & Hewstone, M. (2006). *Multiple Social Categorization: Processes, Models and Applications*. New York: Psychology Press.

Doise, W. (1986). *Levels of Explanation in Social Psychology*. Cambridge: Cambridge University Press.

Doyal, L. & Gough, I. (1991). *A Theory of Human Need*. London: Macmillan.

Equalities Review. (2007). *Fairness and Freedom: The Final Report of the Equalities Review*. London: HMSO.

Fishbein, M. & Ajzen, I. (1975). *Belief, Attitude, Intention, and Behavior: An Introduction to Theory and Research*. Reading, MA: Addison-Wesley.

Giddens, A. (2007). *Over to You, Mr Brown: How Labour Can Win Again*. London: Polity Press.

Giles, H. & Reid, S.A. (2005). Ageism across the lifespan: towards a self-categorization model of ageing. *Journal of Social Issues, 61*, 389–404.

Hamilton, D.L., Sherman, S.J. & Rodgers, J.S. (2004). Perceiving the groupness of groups: entitativity, homogeneity, essentialism and stereotypes. In Y. Yzerbyt, C.M. Judd & O. Corneille (eds), *The Psychology of Group Perception: Perceived Variability, Entitativity and Essentialism* (pp. 39–60). New York: Psychology Press.

Hogg, M.A. & Abrams, D. (1988). *Social Identifications: A Social Psychology of Intergroup Relations and Group Processes*. London: Routledge.

Jost, J.T., Banaji, M.R. & Nosek, B.A. (2004). A decade of system justification theory: accumulated evidence of conscious and unconscious bolstering of the status quo. *Political Psychology, 25*, 881–919.

Kanter, R.M. (1977). Some effects of proportions on group life: skewed sex ratios and responses to token women. *American Journal of Sociology, 82*, 965–990.

Kerr, N. & Levine, J.M. (in press). The detection of social exclusion. Evolution and beyond. *Group Dynamics*.

Klandermans, B. (1997). *The Social Psychology of Protest*. Oxford: Blackwell.

Kurzban, R. & Leary, M.R. (2001). Evolutionary origins of stigmatization: the functions of social exclusion. *Psychological Bulletin, 12*, 187–208.

Leaper, C. (ed.) (1994). Childhood gender segregation: causes and consequences. San Francisco, CA: Jossey-Bass Publishers.

Levine, J.M & Kerr, N.L. (2007). Inclusion and exclusion: implications for group processes. In A.E. Kruglanski & E.T. Higgins (eds), *Social Psychology: Handbook of Basic Principles* (2nd edn). New York: Guilford.

Maass, A., Salvi, D., Arcuri, L. & Semin, G. (1989). Language use in intergroup contexts: the linguistic intergroup bias. *Journal of Personality and Social Psychology, 57*, 981–993.

Mackie, D.M. & Smith, E.R. (2002). Intergroup emotions and the social self: prejudice reconceptualized as differentiated reactions to out-groups. In J.P. Forgas & K.D. Williams (eds), *The Social Self: Cognitive, Interpersonal, and Intergroup Perspectives* (pp. 309–326). Philadelphia, PA: Psychology Press.

Macrae, C.N., Bodenhausen, G.V., Milne, A.B. & Jetten, J. (1994). Out of mind but back in sight: stereotypes on the rebound. *Journal of Personality and Social Psychology, 67*, 808–817.

Maslow, A.H. (1954). *Motivation and Personality*. New York: Harper.

Mummendey, A. & Otten, S. (1998). Positive-negative asymmetry in social discrimination. *European Review of Social Psychology, 9*, 107–144.

Newton, K. & Montero, J.R. (2007). Patterns of political and social participation in Europe. In R. Jowell, C. Roberts, R. Fitzgerald & G. Eva (eds), *Measuring Attitudes Cross-nationally: Lessons from the European Social Survey* (pp. 205–238). London: Sage Publications.

Norris, P. & Davis, J. (2007). A continental divide? Social capital in the US and Europe. In R. Jowell, C. Roberts, R. Fitzgerald & G. Eva (eds), *Measuring Attitudes Cross-nationally: Lessons from the European Social Survey* (pp. 239–264). London: Sage Publications.

ONS. (2001). Inter-ethnic marriage: data from April 2001 Census. Retrieved from http://www.statistics.gov.uk/CCI/nugget.asp?

Pennebaker, J.W., Pàez, D. & Rimé, B. (eds) (1997). *Collective Memory of Political Events: Social Psychological Perspectives*. Mahwah, NJ: Lawrence Erlbaum Associates.

Pettigrew, T.F. (1998). Intergroup contact: theory, research and new perspectives. *Annual Review of Psychology, 49*, 65–85.

Pettigrew, T.F. & Tropp, L.R. (2006). A meta-analytic test of intergroup contact theory. *Journal of Personality and Social Psychology, 90*, 751–783.

Portes, A. (1988). Social capital: its origins and applications in modern sociology. *Annual Review of Sociology, 24*, 1024–1047.

Putnam, R.D. (2000). *Bowling Alone: The Collapse and Revival of American Community.* New York: Simon & Schuster.

Ray, S., Sharp, E. & Abrams, D. (2006). Ageism: a benchmark of public attitudes in Britain. London: Age Concern England. Retrieved from http://www.ageconcern.org.uk/AgeConcern/Documents/Ageism_Report.pdf

Reed, A. & Aquino, K.F. (2003). Moral identity and the expanding circule of moral regard toward outgroups. *Journal of Personality and Social Psychology, 84*, 1270–1286.

Ryan, E.B., Bourhis, R.Y. & Knops, U. (1991). Evaluative perceptions of patronizing speech addressed to elders. *Psychology and Aging, 6*, 442–450.

Schwartz, S.H. (2007). Value orientations: measurement, antecedents and consequences. In R. Jowell, C. Roberts, R. Fitzgerald & G. Eva (eds), *Measuring Attitudes Cross-nationally: Lessons from the European Social Survey* (pp. 169–204). London: Sage Publications.

Sen, A.K. (1985). *Commodities and Capabilities.* Oxford: North-Holland.

Sen, A. (2005). Human rights and capabilities. *Journal of Human Development, 6*, 151–166.

Shah, J. & Higgins, E.T. (2001). Regulatory concerns and appraisal efficiency: the general impact of promotion and prevention. *Journal of Personality and Social Psychology, 80*, 693–705.

Sherif, M. (1966). *In Common Predicament: Social Psychology of Intergroup Conflict and Cooperation.* Boston: Houghton-Mifflin.

Steele, C.M. (1997). A threat in the air: how stereotypes shape intellectual identity and performance. *American Psychologist, 52*, 613–629.

Sutton, S. (2003). Testing attitude-behaviour theories using non-experimental data: an examination of some hidden assumptions. *European Review of Social Psychology, 13*, 293–323.

Tajfel, H. (1981). *Human Groups and Social Categories.* Cambridge: Cambridge University Press.

Tajfel, H. & Turner, J.C. (1979). An integrative theory of intergroup conflict. In W.G. Austin & S. Worchel (eds), *The Social Psychology of Intergroup Relations* (pp. 33–47). Monterey, CA: Brooks/Cole.

Turner, J.C., Hogg, M.A., Oakes, P.J., *et al.* (1987). *Rediscovering the Social Group: A Self-categorization Theory.* Oxford: Blackwell.

Tyler, T.R. & Blader, S.L. (2000). *Cooperation in Groups: Procedural Justice, Social Identity, and Behavioral Engagement.* New York: Psychology Press.

Williams, K.D., Forgas, J.P. & von Hippel, W. (eds) (2005). *The Social Outcast: Ostracism, Social Exclusion, Rejection, and Bullying.* New York: The Psychology Press.

Author Index

Multidisciplinary Handbook of Social Exclusion Research. Edited by D. Abrams, J. Christian and D. Gordon.
© 2007 John Wiley & Sons, Ltd.

Parker, H. 69
Parker, R. 118–20
Paugam, S. 195
Peattie, K. xvii, 160–1, 176, 213
Pennebaker, J.W. 226
Percival, G. xvii, 164, 216
Peres, Y. 36
Petrie, P. 129–30
Pettigrew, T. 44–5, 222
Phillimore, J. 162
Phillips, T. 163
Piachaud, D. xiv–xvii, 3–4, 6–7, 17–24, 88
Pickett, C.L. 36
Pleace, N. 85
Pope, L. 65
Portes, A. 225
Power, A. 182
Prahaladad, C.K. 176
Putnam, R.D. 225
Pyle 145

Quigley, M. xvii

Ray, S. 212, 219–20, 222, 225
Reder, P. 117
Reed, A. 219
Reicher, S.D. 37
Rhodes, R. 171
Rocard, M. 195
Rodgers, G. 205
Room, G. 2, 6, 10, 13, 69, 79, 88, 172–3
Rothgerber, H. 37
Rousseau, J-J. 194
Ruberry, G. 23
Rutland, A. 41
Rutter, M. 102
Ryan, E.B. 220

Scambler, G. 74
Schachter, S. 40–1
Schmitt, M.T. 33, 36, 38–9
Schwartz, S.H. xiii, 212–3
Selwyn, N. 172, 185
Sen, A. 213
Seyfang, G. 187
Shah, J. 227
Shanks, M. 196
Sherif, M. 223
Silver, H. 194
Simmel, G. 61, 176
Simon, A. 116, 120
Simon, B. 37–8
Sinclair, K. 67, 122
Skuse, T. 120
Smale, M. 68
Smith, J. 149

Sommerville, P. 82, 182
Sontag, S. 60
Sparkes, J. 100
Speak, S. 180, 183
Spears, R. 37, 42
Spicker, P. 196, 206
St Claire, L. 121
Stainton-Rogers, R. 61
Steele, C.M. 31, 35, 225
Stein, M. 122
Steinert, H. 3, 7
Stephens, J. 116
Stiglitz, J. 206
Sumner, C. 75
Sutton, S. 228
Swim, J. 33

Tabberer, S. 65
Tajfel, H. 37, 40, 43, 72, 217–18, 223
Taylor, D.M. 88
Temple, W. 194
Thévenet, A. 195
Thomas, N. 129
Titmuss, R. 194
Tomlinson, A. 171, 181
Tonry, M. 154
Townsend, P. 141, 199, 204, 206
Trickett, A. 143
Triggs, S. 145
Tropp, L. 44–5, 222
Tsakloglou, P. 3, 5–6
Tulloch, D. 87
Turner, J.C. 36–7, 40, 217–18, 223
Turner, R. 45
Twenge, J.M. 34

Utting, W. 122

Vachanis, S. 181
Van Kersberger, K. 195
Veit-Wilson, J. 144, 194, 196–7
Villiamy, G. 96, 100–2
Visser, J. xvi, 99, 101, 103–4, 109, 225

Wakefield, A. 139, 149–50
Walker, A. 170
Warburton, W.A. 34
Ward, H. 120
Watkins, K. 206
Watts, J. 175
Waulmsely 20, 26
Wedderburn, D. 195
Weimann, C.M. 65
Whiteford, L. 67
Whitehead, E. xv, 64
Wigfall, V. 129

Subject Index

ability xiii
abortion 65, 66
Acheson Report 63–4
activism gap 21; *and see* political engagement
adjustment, psychological 30
affect 30, 31, 38
  affective psychology 74
affirmative action xiii
age xiii, 217–19, 220
ageism xviii, 211–2, 220
agency xiv, xvi, 3–4, 7
aggression 29–31, 34
alcohol, and stigma 173; *and see* substance
  abuse
alienation 164
anger 29, 31, 33, 64, 74
Annual Survey of Hours and Earnings 19
Anti-Social Behaviour Orders (ASBOs) xvii,
  138; *and see* crime; criminal justice
  system; youth offending
anxiety 29, 31, 33, 38, 45
Area-based Initiatives 162, 165
Assessment and Action Records 119
assumptive world 88
asylum seekers 212, 216
attachment 30
attitudes 3, 212, 228
Australia 146
Autumn Performance Reports 120

behaviour xv, 228
  anti-social 30, 34, 149
  consumer 175
  deviant 71
  moral 70–1
  passive 34–5
  prosocial 35–6
  self-defeating 29, 34–5
beliefs, belief systems 3, 36
belonging xv, 31–2, 175
biomedical model 62

blame 64
Breaking the Cycle 10
breastfeeding 67–8
British Household Panel Survey 6, 17
British Security Industry Association 149
bullying 104, 123, 130, 149
Burnel Report 205
business xvii, 169ff
  ownership 186
  role in social exclusion 172–82
  sustainability 170
  and see micro-businesses; entrepreneurship;
    small and medium businesses
Business in the Community 181
By Degrees study xvi, 125–9

care, individualised 63
caring work 19; and see childcare; disabled,
  care of; elderly, care of
categorisation 219
Centre for Analysis of Social Exclusion 96,
  212
Centre for the Wider Benefits of Learning 124
Change for Children programme 117
charitable action xvii, 171
Chicago School 71
Child Tax Credit 148
childcare 25, 26
childlessness 66–7
Children (Leaving Care) Act 2000 119, 124,
  125, 128; *and see* children, looked after
Children Act 1948 117
Children Act 1989 118
Children Act 2004 108, 119, 130
children
  abuse and neglect 116
  challenging 100
  and mental health xvi, 109
  obesity among 11
  poverty 10, 64, 96, 145, 147
  rejected 34

Multidisciplinary Handbook of Social Exclusion Research. Edited by D. Abrams, J. Christian and D. Gordon.
© 2007 John Wiley & Sons, Ltd.